GITA

FOR

DAILY ENRICHMENT

365 Reflections On Bhagvad-Gita

Chaitanya Charan

VOICE
Rekindling Wisdom, Reviving Love

Vedic Oasis for Inspiration, Culture & Education (VOICE)

Head Office: Sr. No-50, Katraj Kondhwa Bypass Road,
Opp to Shatrunjay Temple, Kondhwa Budruk,
Pune-411048. Tel: +91-86050-36000

Branch Office: 4, Tarapore Road, Next to Dastur Boys' School,
Camp, Pune 411001.

Email: voicebooks@voicepune.com

VOICE invites readers interested in this book to correspond at the following address:

Sales Manager:
Krishnakishore das
A-102, Bharati Vihar, Katraj, Pune – 411 046
Phone: +91-98224-51260
Email: krishnakishoredas@gmail.com

First Printing: Mar 2016, 2000 Copies

Reviews

"Wisdom texts like the Bhagavad-gita become especially useful when they are brought into modernity by mature and articulate scholar-practitioners. Chaitanya Charan Das is one such person. Through his *Gita-daily* articles, he unlocks many of the mysteries of the text, allowing contemporary readers access to an otherwise often impenetrable scripture."

- Steven J. Rosen (Satyaraja Dasa),
Author of over 30 books on spiritual topics;
Editor, *Journal of Vaishnava Studies* and *Back to Godhead*.

"The Gita-daily series provides readers with succinct, thoughtful meditations based on verses from the Gita. It connects the transcendent scripture to daily life's questions, struggles, and triumphs. Each daily meditation can be read in a few moments, or savored longer while referencing the verse and purport of that day's focus. Either way, the spiritual connection offered by these meditations will help to remind the reader throughout the day of the Gita's wisdom and insight, and bring us to a higher dimension of life."

- Dr Edith Best (Urmila Devi Dasi),
Author of several acclaimed books for children;
Member of ISKCON's Shastric Advisory Council;
Editor of *Back to Godhead*

"Chaitanya Charan is a genuine Bhagavad-gita scholar, in that he approaches this Indian classic in a reverential and meditational mood. His Gita-daily series offers that which may be called "Humanistic Hinduism", i.e. a view which shows the relevance and vibrancy of Hinduism as a living tradition. It addresses a wide variety of topics such as divinity, desire, human psychology, religion and dharma. I very warmly recommend not only reading but immersing oneself in this book."

- Dr. Ithamar Theodor,
Author of award-winning book on the Gita, Exploring the Bhagavad gita;
Philosophy, Structure and Meaning

"These meditations are simply brilliant – crisp, simple-to-understand and yet very profound. I'm deeply impressed. Fortunate readers will identify with and benefit from the practical aspects of these observations and realizations of a very sincere seeker of the truth."

- Hrishikesh A Mafatlal,
Chairman, Arvind Mafatlal Group.

Dedicated to

HDG A C Bhaktivedanta Swami Prabhupada,

the founder-acharya of ISKCON,

Whose masterly commentary
Bhagavad Gita As It Is
underscores the transformative power of spiritual love
that is the Gita's essence

&

To my many Gita-friends, teachers and readers,
who have enriched my appreciation of the Gita

Quick Note for Using This Book

Every article in this book is based on one verse from the Bhagavad gita. The translation of that verse, taken from Srila Prabhupada's *Bhagavad Gita As It Is*, is given in italics at the end of the article. That verse's number is given in the Contents as well as in the header of each page (as each article is one page long). To preserve visual symmetry, two digits are used for both the chapter number and the verse number. Thus, for example, the page header 02.08 means that the article on that page is based on the eighth verse of the second chapter of the Gita.

ୠ୫ଡ଼   ୠ୫ଡ଼   ୠ୫ଡ଼

CONTENTS

Seeing the world through the Gita's eyes

x

Understanding Gita concepts

Choosing intelligent happiness

xvii

Leading a principle-centered life

Learning to love Krishna

Foreword

How many times every day are we faced with questions for which we do not have answers? How often are we compelled to make decisions without clear direction? At one time or another, we all get confused about what to think and what to do and wonder where to turn for perfect knowledge.

On the battlefield of Kuruksetra, even Arjuna, the greatest warrior and devotee of his time, was confused about what to do. Lord Krishna, the Supreme Personality of Godhead, was by his side, but Arjuna, in his illusion, did not turn to Him for answers—not at first. But then Arjuna's transcendental intelligence awakened, and he submitted himself to Lord Krishna to be enlightened. And Krishna reciprocated and answered all his questions.

What if God were available to answer all our questions, just as He was for Arjuna? What a relief—what an incomparable boon—that would be. Well, He is: the answers to the basic questions of life that Krishna gave to Arjuna are available to us all in the *Bhagavad-gita*.

In the *Gita* Krishna advises that one should receive the knowledge from a realized soul coming in the succession of teachers (*guru-parampara*) from Krishna Himself. One of the most important of these teachers was Srila A.C. Bhaktivedanta Swami Prabhupada, who presented the *Bhagavad-gita* as it is in English for all people in the world. And that knowledge has now been made available to us in short engaging, enlightening pieces by Chaitanya Charan Das, a student of a direct student of Srila Prabhupada.

In *Gita for Daily Enrichment*, Chaitanya Charan gives us 365 reflections on the deep meaning and practical relevance of the *Gita*—as many reflections as there are days in the year. Although each reflection is only a page long and can be read in a matter of minutes, one can contemplate its deep significance and practical application throughout the day—indeed, throughout one's life—and our lives can be immeasurably enriched by these meditations.

Chaitanya Charan is both a scholar of the *Gita* and a practitioner of *bhakti-yoga*, which the Gita recommends, so his insights are based on personal experience and realization. He is also knowledgeable in science, psychology, sociology, politics, economics, philosophy, and many other fields, and he expertly applies the wisdom of the *Gita* with reference to these perspectives.

He is also witty and adept with words, as seen in his pithy, provocative titles, such as "Expecting the default to change by default is a dangerous fault," "Resting on our laurels? No resting! Not our laurels!" and the enigmatic "Cry, Vie, Lie, Die, Fie—Tie."

In "The *Gita* calls not for blind obedience but for visionary obedience," Chaitanya Charan suggests how we can properly pursue the *Gita's* wisdom, not blindly but with clear vision and personal responsibility. As another title declares, "The *Gita* lives through those who live the *Gita*," and because Chaitanya Charan lives the *Gita*, the *Gita* comes alive in his book. By taking advantage of its wisdom, presented in his book, we will learn to "Let Krishna permeate, pervade, and possess our heart."

When Srila Prabhupada laid the cornerstone for his Juhu, Mumbai, temple, he said, "Our present movement is based on *Bhagavad-gita—Bhagavad-gita* as it is. . . . If actually we want to take advantage of this *Bhagavad-gita*, then we must take *Bhagavad-gita* as it is—just like Arjuna took. Arjuna, after hearing *Bhagavad-gita*, said, *sarvam etad rtam manye Bg* 10.14]: 'I accept all Your words, my dear Kesava [Krishna], whatever You have said. I accept them in toto.' Just like Bhagavan Krishna says, *sva-karmana tam abhyarcya siddhim vindati manavah* [*Bg* 18.46]. You remain in your business. You remain in your occupation. There is no need of changing. And still, you can become Krishna conscious and make your life successful. This is the message of *Bhagavad-gita*. *Bhagavad-gita* is not going to make any topsy-turvy of the social order or spiritual order. No. It should be standardized according to the authority. And the best authority is Krishna."

Gita for Daily Enrichment: 365 reflections on the Bhagavad-gita is an invaluable aid for properly understanding and applying the *Bhagavad-gita* as it is and making our lives successful. We are indebted to Chaitanya Charan for living the *Gita* and bringing it to life in the pages of this extraordinary book.

Hare Krishna.

Giriraj Swami
February 20, 2016
Sri Nityananda-trayodasi
New Dvaraka, Los Angeles

Introduction

Gita for Daily Enrichment provides condensed nuggets of insight gleaned from the Vedic wisdom-tradition and re-presented in an idiom and style that resonates with contemporary needs, interests and concerns.

The Vedic (Indian) wisdom-tradition has provided some of the loftiest philosophical insights in the world, yet most contemporary people – both Indians and non-Indians – find it difficult to see the relevance of those insights to their daily lives and contexts. This difficulty is caused not by the irrelevance of those insights, but by their inaccessibility: they are generally written in Sanskrit, often using words that have multiple meanings embedded in them. Moreover, they frequently presume familiarity with the subtle nuances of the thought systems within which they developed. Making the totality of Vedic thought accessible to the modern mind requires comprehensive research and exhaustive writing, a massive task upon which many scholars worldwide are working vigorously. Even if this thought becomes accessible, not many people have the time – or, more importantly, the interest – to access this giant body of wisdom. Gita-Daily makes the humble attempt to stimulate interest in Vedic thought by mining and bringing forth small nuggets of wisdom that the contemporary mind can find accessible, relevant and illuminating.

Gita-daily is also a humble attempt to fulfill on a daily basis the standing instruction of Srila Prabhupada to all his followers to write at every opportunity: "Realization means you should write, every one of you, what is your realization. What for this Back to Godhead is? You write your realization, what you have realized about Krishna. That is required. It is not passive. Always you should be active. Whenever you find time, you write. Never mind, two lines, four lines, but you write your realization. *Shravanam kirtanam*, writing or offering prayers, glories. This is one of the functions of the Vaishnava."

Gita-daily is a metamorphosed version of a personal journal of an individual spiritual journey. Over the years, while studying the sacred Vedic scriptures, whenever I would get an insight of how a particular verse or narrative or analysis addressed my concerns, I would phrase that insight in my own words in my personal journal. During my various talks, I would often share some of these insights, gleaned from scriptures but re-presented with linguistic sophistication. Many of those who attended these talks would tell me that they found these re-presentations illuminating, offering them a new light with which to see the latent wisdom in scriptural truths they already knew. Those giving such feedbacks often encouraged, even urged, me to put these insights into writing.

Within the Vedic tradition, I have chosen to focus on the Bhagavad-gita because it is simultaneously profoundly philosophical, unendingly inspirational and eminently practical. Over the last 15 years I have studied the Gita dozens of times and have spoken on it hundreds of times. I have also taught the full Gita as a systematic course several times and have written scores of articles on it. Despite this repeated contact with the Gita, I am even now amazed by its unfading freshness: contemplation on its verses brings rejuvenation, illumination and determination. I feel deeply indebted to the Bhagavad-gita for the sanity, clarity, gravity, tenacity and velocity that it has brought to my life. As an expression of my gratitude to the Gita, I feel impelled to do whatever I can to make its inspiration available as much as possible. But I also realize that most people in today's culture will not have the time or the facility to carry out an intensive or extensive study of the Gita. So the Gita-daily is my humble attempt to repay my debt to the Gita by making its wisdom comprehensible and accessible through daily nuggets of contemplation on one or more of its verses. As I am focussing on the inspirational potency of the Gita and not on its semantic intricacies, I generally don't quote either the Sanskrit verse or its English translation verbatim, but present the relevant import of the verse, rendered according to the theme under discussion. Nonetheless, I have provided the translation of these verses at the bottom of each article. To ensure that these articles don't become too technical or academic, I also don't quote too frequently from the various Gita commentaries by erudite and saintly teachers.

I hope that you find *Gita-Daily* helpful in your spiritual journey in coming closer to the Gita and to its speaker, Lord Krishna, who is forever waiting for us in our own hearts.

Yours in the service of Lord Krishna,

- Chaitanya Charan

GROWING THROUGH LIFE'S REVERSALS

Stop serving God as an advisor

Everyone wants to serve God, but as an advisor. This is true even, and especially, for atheists; their normally non-existent god pops into existence whenever they feel like advising him, and vanishes into non-existence after gratefully accepting their counsel. However, as Arjuna discovered at the start of the second chapter of the Gita (02.06), giving advice to God only frustrates and confuses us: frustrates us because we can't change the inevitable will of providence, and confuses us because our mind keeps coming up with new and self-contradictory advices.

When things go wrong, they are meant to remind us that we are not the controllers. However, we neglect the reminders and, to hold on to our cherished role as controllers, we take on the additional role of advisors to God. The irony is that only when we stop advising God and start hearing from him do we let him do what we actually want him to do: help us.

Hearing the Gita from Krishna enabled Arjuna to redefine his own role in relation with Krishna. Before hearing the Gita, he thought of himself as the controller and Krishna as the cooperator. After hearing the Gita, he understood Krishna to be the controller and himself to be the cooperator. His corrected understanding paved the way for Krishna to guide him to a glorious victory.

When things apparently go wrong, we need to submissively and prayerfully hear from Krishna through his representatives and through the inner voice. Then we gradually realize that Krishna already has the most perfect plan. The only thing wrong in it is that we have taken on the self-appointed role as Krishna's advisor. When we take up the right role of Krishna's assistant, he uses us to do glorious things that far excel our best advises.

❦

Nor do we know which is better—conquering them or being conquered by them. The sons of Dhritarashtra, whom if we killed we should not care to live, are now standing before us on this battlefield.

See beyond life's apparent nonsense to Krishna's benevolent sense

"Why is Krishna doing this?" We may sometimes get this question when things go wrong and life doesn't make sense.

To help us make sense of such situations, Gita wisdom broadens our perspective of life.

Suppose we start watching a drama when the hero is being beaten. We may feel that the drama director has made a senseless plot. But, if we just wait and watch, we may well see how the drama is developing towards a fitting finale.

Gita wisdom helps us understand how this principle applies to our life: we are not perishable material bodies, but are imperishable spiritual souls. The present crisis, no matter how devastating, is just one act in a multi-act drama. In fact, our whole lifetime is just one small part in a multi-lifetime plot that extends to eternity.

No doubt, there are substantial differences between a drama and our real life. Firstly, in our life, we are not spectators but actors. Secondly, and more importantly, the script of our life is not a frozen story; it is an evolving story that is shaped by our choices.

This story can climax, the Bhagavad-gita (02.15) indicates, with our attainment of immortality if we don't let life's ups and downs violate our spiritual focus. Preserving our spiritual focus means not letting life's upheavals cause us to abandon our position as servants of Krishna and assume the position of becoming judges of Krishna. Instead of asking, "Why is Krishna doing this?" we ask, "How can I serve Krishna now?" When we ask this question sincerely and seek its answer internally through prayer and externally through guidance, then we will gradually comprehend the benevolent sense underlying the apparent nonsense happening in our lives.

.

☙❧

O best among men [Arjuna], the person who is not disturbed by happiness and distress and is steady in both is certainly eligible for liberation.

Don't eternalize the present; contextualize it

*W*hen we face problems, they sometimes overwhelm us so much that we can't think of anything else. We feel as if the problem will never be solved. The dread of living with it for all time to come cripples our ability to deal with it constructively. At such times, we succumb to the error of eternalizing the present.

To correct or prevent the error, we can meditate on the Bhagavad-gita (2.16): *nasato vidyate bhavo* "Of the non-existent, there is no endurance." The word asat reminds us that the present is fleeting; it exists now, but will soon be over. To appreciate this, let's think about our past overwhelming problems: a major exam, a critical job interview, a vital public speech. Hindsight shows us that they were not worth getting overwhelmed. They came and they went. So will the present problem. This reflection enables us to contextualize the problem as temporary.

What if the problem seems likely to stay lifelong with us? Gita wisdom reassures us that our life is much bigger than this lifetime, for we are eternal souls. The same Gita verse continues: *nabhavo vidyate satah* "Of the eternal there is no cessation." In the eternal lies our ultimate legacy that is available to us at every moment, even the present moment. That supreme treasure is our all-attractive beloved Krishna. Once we connect with him through devotion and relish the sweetness of his love, the present, no matter how imposing, will no longer seem crushing.

What if the present sometimes makes specific forms of devotional service difficult or impossible? Thankfully, Krishna is an understanding God. He accepts whatever service we render sincerely according to our capacities and circumstances and gives us his grace. That grace will inspire, guide and empower us to integrate the present into our growth path to a glorious future: eternal life with Krishna.

❀

Those who are seers of the truth have concluded that of the nonexistent [the material body] there is no endurance and of the eternal [the soul] there is no change. This they have concluded by studying the nature of both.

Be concerned by change, but not disturbed by it

*T*he world around us is subject to constant change, change that is often unstoppable, uncontrollable and unpredictable. The Bhagavad-gita (02.16) indicates that the best way to cope with change is to focus on the unchangeable: our spiritual nature and our spiritual connection with Krishna.

This focus energizes us with the confidence that no external change can:

1. Harm our essence, our indestructible souls

2. Stop Krishna from loving us

3. Stop us from remembering him and experiencing his loving shelter.

When we meditate on these unchangeable realities of life, we feel reassured us that the external changes are not the end of the world. When we render devotional service sincerely and prayerfully, we realize the tangibility of Krishna's presence, shelter and love. This realization takes us beyond conceptual awareness to experiential confirmation of reality's changeless dimension. Knowing that external change can't affect our core identity, we don't become disturbed by it and so don't get broken down or blown away by it. At the same time, knowing that external change does affect our circumstantial activity, we don't deny or neglect the change; with due concern, we act intelligently to deal with it.

Thus, by showing us how to be concerned without becoming disturbed, Gita wisdom enables us to tackle change calmly and resourcefully.

ॐ

Those who are seers of the truth have concluded that of the nonexistent [the material body] there is no endurance and of the eternal [the soul] there is no change. This they have concluded by studying the nature of both.

Be intense, not tense

The pace and pressure of our contemporary lifestyle often makes us stressed. This tension is a nag that lurks constantly in the background of our consciousness. The nag comes to the foreground as a piercing jab when the sheer unpredictability and uncontrollability of life's changes overwhelm us. If not checked and countered, the jab can cause a nervous breakdown.

Gita wisdom broadens our perspective of life. The Bhagavad-gita (02.16) helps us understand that there are two realms to life: the material realm that is characterized by constant change and the spiritual realm that is beyond the effects of material change. The spiritual realm is much greater, far more stable and infinitely more meaningful than the material realm. We as spiritual beings belong to that indestructible realm and so are beyond being harmed by any material change, no matter how threatening it seems. This knowledge of our indestructible spiritual identity defuses our tension.

Gita wisdom further illumines us that Krishna, our supreme benefactor, monitors and maneuvers the changes of the material realm for the express purpose of elevating us spiritually. This illumination enables us to see change not as a threat to be countered or neglected but as an opportunity to be comprehended and capitalized.

To capitalize this opportunity, we need to be philosophically acute and practically astute to see Krishna's message and motivation in everything. That requires us to replace our default feeling of being tense with the consciously cultivated feeling of being intense, concentrated in our focus on Krishna. When we thus become intense in our devotional consciousness, we see every change as an opportunity to serve Krishna and move closer to him through every situation.

CR&O

Those who are seers of the truth have concluded that of the nonexistent [the material body] there is no endurance and of the eternal [the soul] there is no change. This they have concluded by studying the nature of both.

Be rooted in the unchanging, not the changing

The Bhagavad-gita (02.16) encourages us to meditate on the difference between the unchanging, the spiritual realm within, and the changing, the material realm without. Gita wisdom further urges us to grow our roots in the world within: in realization of our own spiritual identity and our loving relationship with Krishna.

What exactly are our roots? They are our strongest desires, our foremost priorities and, most of all, our defining notions of reality.

We are normally rooted in matter: in possessions and positions, and in pleasures and treasures. Consequently, we find ourselves repeatedly buffeted by the stormy changes that characterize the realm of matter. When we start getting buffeted, our default response is to strive and pray for the end of the storm. If this remains our only response, then we overlook the precious nugget of wisdom that the storm has blown our way. That nugget is: the more external change shakes us, the graver is the reminder that our internal roots are weak and under-developed.

If we take note of the reminder, we will strive to deepen our internal roots and practice devotional service to Krishna regularly and rigorously. Subsequently, when the storms come again, they won't overwhelm us as our inner spiritual roots will have made us emotionally secure and strong. We will not only be less negatively affected by the circumstances, but will also be able to more positively affect those circumstances. We will intelligently and prayerfully find our way through them.

And, most importantly, when the final storm of death blows everything material away, our deep spiritual roots will ensure that it doesn't devastate us, but transports us closer to Krishna or even back to him.

⟨⟩⟨⟩

Those who are seers of the truth have concluded that of the nonexistent [the material body] there is no endurance and of the eternal [the soul] there is no change. This they have concluded by studying the nature of both.

Can't set things right? See things right

*W*henever things go wrong in life, we can generally do something to set them right. But when death strikes, there's nothing that we can do to set it right; the finality of death is unappealable. All that we try, cry, lie and die for is taken away from us in one merciless moment.

By taking away the option to set things right, death thrusts a blessing on us; it prods us to see things right. Gita wisdom enables us to complete the shift of vision that death forcefully prompts.

The Bhagavad-gita (02.23) indicates that our core identity has a sanctity that even death can't violate; we are souls who can't be destroyed even by the most fearsome weapons. We are destined for immortality by our intrinsic nature, but are sentenced to mortality by our inconsiderate choice. Our material bodies are unavoidably time-bound; when we choose to let our sense of self-identity be tied down to our bodies, we suffer the horror of death.

But all of us can, by practicing devotional service regularly, realize our true identity to be beyond our mortal body. Thereby we see death not as an unwelcome termination of our being, but as a welcome transition to a higher realm of being.

Thus, death is ultimately intended to compel us to reclaim our right to immortality, thereby offering us a blessing far greater than a prolonged and prosperous life. However, if we postpone accepting that blessing till death comes upon us, it may well be too late. Far better to accept that blessing nowby meditating on how death is taking its toll around us. The resulting gravity in our spiritual practices can help us not just at death, but also in life – by enabling us to relish spiritual happiness.

ॐ

The soul can never be cut to pieces by any weapon, nor burned by fire, nor moistened by water, nor withered by the wind.

Ask not "Why this?" Ask "How now?"

When we encounter sudden adversities, we usually get the question, "Why is Krishna doing this to me?"

Gita wisdom explains that when we hold Krishna responsible for adversities, we become like farmers who hold the rains responsible for the bad quality yield. The bad yield is caused not by the rains but by the farmers through their sowing of bad seeds. Similarly, adversities are caused not by Krishna but by us through the kind of karmic seeds that we sowed in the past, either in this or previous lives.

Taxing our brain to find the specific karmic seed that caused the present reversal is futile. The Bhagavad-gita (04.17) emphasizes that the intricate workings of karma are too complex for the human mind to comprehend. This incomprehensibility can arise from several reasons such as:

1. Different karmic seeds fructify after different time durations

2. Several karmic seeds may fructify as one event

3. One karmic seed may fructify as a series of events

4. Our memory is volatile and fallible.

The same principle of incomprehensibility obscures the precise extent to which our practice of devotional service burns our karmic seeds.

That's why it's far more fruitful to focus on determining the best seeds to sow now and thereby get the best future yield. Accepting this principle inspires us to revise our question: not "Why this?" but "How now? How can I serve Krishna in this situation?"

Putting aside the "why" question frees us from the resentment that makes a bad situation worse by distorting our perceptions and prompting knee-jerk reactions. Focusing on the "how" question and prayerfully seeking Krishna's guidance activates our devotional creativity. This helps us to not only make the best of a bad situation but to also discover the spiritual good in the materially bad situation.

ॐ

The intricacies of action are very hard to understand. Therefore one should know properly what action is, what forbidden action is, and what inaction is.

Rise from touch-me-not to touched-me-not

*W*e all need a sense of security in our lives. Often, we seek that security by trying to build a cocoon around us, by trying to control our lives with an ironclad set of plans, patterns and routines.

Unfortunately, life frequently cracks and occasionally crushes the cocoon. People don't behave the way we expected them to. Events don't turn out the way we anticipated they would. Our own body and mind don't cooperate the way we presumed they would. These three hope-dashers are known in Vedic parlance as *adhibhautika-klesha, adhidaivika-klesha and adhyatmika-klesha respectively.*

When our hopes get thus dashed, we sometimes go into an hyper-defensive mode, resenting whatever goes wrong and lashing out at whoever we feel is to be blamed. We become somewhat like human touch-me-nots – two-legged versions of the plant which hyper-reacts to any threatening stimulus. We find ourselves exploding at small provocations. Nothing seems to help.

Gita wisdom can help where all else fails. It helps us understand that the problem lies not in the outer situation, but in our inner expectation. We are expecting security where it just doesn't exist: at the material level where change is inevitable and inescapable.

We need to seek security in the right place: at the unchanging spiritual level in our eternal identity and our everlasting relationship with Krishna. Once we find that inner security, material upheavals lose their sting. We function at the material level without being affected by it, like a lotus leaf untouched by water, as the Bhagavad-gita (05.10) indicates. This doesn't mean that we become stone-like; it means that we become motivated by a spiritual vision and a devotional purpose that dwarfs material upheavals.

Then adversities enter into and depart from our lives, but our core remains untouched.

ॐ

One who performs his duty without attachment, surrendering the results unto the Supreme Lord, is unaffected by sinful action, as the lotus leaf is untouched by water.

Don't let inner burdens add to your outer burdens

We often feel strained by the pressure of having so many things to do. Even if we have a heavy workload, our strain frequently comes not from our outer burden but from our inner burden.

What is our inner burden? Our hankerings and frustrations.

We are bombarded by continuous media images that sometimes whisper and sometimes scream to us how we should be: what we should wear, what gadgets we should have and so forth. We hanker and struggle to obey the dictates of the media, but over time practical considerations force us to recognize grudgingly that we can't acquire most of these media ideals. Our inability frustrates us. This combined weight of hankerings and frustrations is our inner burden; it strains us much more than the outer burden of our workload.

Among these two, decreasing the outer burden may not be in our hands, but decreasing the inner burden is. We just have to restrain ourselves by resolving internally to not be seduced by the media images. For this, the Bhagavad-gita (05.23) recommends that we tolerate the urges of hankering and frustration.

To tolerate, do we have to practice dry joyless abstinence, as when a diabetic person gives up sugar?

Not at all. The same Gita verse states that tolerance makes us happy (sukhi).

Gita wisdom helps us replace the outer happiness that we have renounced with a higher, inner happiness that we can attain by connecting devotionally with Krishna, who is the source of all happiness. When we cultivate his remembrance regularly and lovingly, our inner life becomes profoundly enriched. This enrichment propels us on the path to eternal happiness with Krishna. Additionally, as a byproduct it enables us to restrain ourselves. By this restraint, we tap hitherto dissipated mental energy and thereby manage life's unavoidable strains better.

೮೪೦

Before giving up this present body, if one is able to tolerate the urges of the material senses and check the force of desire and anger, he is well situated and is happy in this world.

Krishna's ways may not always be pleasant, but they are always benevolent

When things go wrong and disrupt our lives, a doubt may trouble us: is Krishna really my well-wisher?

While dealing with such doubts, we need to carefully grasp the difference between the pleasant, that which feels good, and the benevolent, that which yields good. A surgery, even when necessary and even when done by a competent doctor, doesn't feel good. Yet it definitely yields good. Similarly, Krishna being the supreme surgeon may act in ways that are not always pleasant, but are always benevolent. He does surgeries only when they are absolutely essential, and he is the most competent of all surgeons, so we can be assured that we are in the safest hands.

To maintain this faith in Krishna when we are being surgically operated through worldly upheavals, we need to use our precious assets of intelligence and patience.

Intelligence: It helps us remember that, as we are not our bodies but are souls, what seems unpleasant at the bodily level may actually be beneficial at the spiritual level. This opens our mind to the possibility that what may be unpalatable today may well be necessary for a palatable tomorrow. After all, we don't know our various attachments, leave alone how to free ourselves from them. So it is only common sense to leave to Krishna matters that he knows far better than us.

Patience: It inspires us to tolerate the unpleasant phase of the surgery and anticipate the benevolent phase, thereby nourishing our devotional optimism. Patience enables us to wait till the benevolence of all that happened eventually becomes manifest, thereby vindicating and strengthening our faith.

When we thus meditate on Krishna as our greatest well-wisher, then, as the Bhagavad-gita (05.29) indicates, no worldly disturbance will be able to steal away our peace.

❀

A person in full consciousness of Me, knowing Me to be the ultimate beneficiary of all sacrifices and austerities, the Supreme Lord of all planets and demigods, and the benefactor and well-wisher of all living entities, attains peace from the pangs of material miseries.

Live beyond life's tornadoes and torpedoes

Life confronts us with challenges both externally and internally. External upheavals – financial and political, for example – are like tornadoes that twist and topple the familiar landscape of our settled daily routines. Internal upheavals – emotional and intellectual, for example – are like torpedoes that puncture and rupture our enthusiasm and faith. Even one of these challenges is difficult enough to endure. But when both confront us simultaneously, enduring this double assault may seem almost impossible. Our very survival externally and our sanity internally may seem to be in jeopardy.

Times like these offer us precious opportunities to gain personal realization of the inestimable value of Gita wisdom. Though the Bhagavad-gita can offer us solace and strength at all times, we don't feel the need when things seem normal in our lives. So, we neither seek its help seriously, nor experience it tangibly.

When life tornadoes and torpedoes us, Gita wisdom escorts us on a journey to the innermost core of our being: our spiritual essence and our relationship with Krishna. There we discover a level of living that is beyond life's worst tornadoes and torpedoes. We recognize that Krishna is ever-available for us in the innermost core of our hearts; no tornado or torpedo can make him leave us even when everyone else and everything else leaves us. Our divine relationship with him is the platform of our real life, our supreme joy and our ultimate love. Once we attain this platform, the Bhagavad-gita (06.22) indicates that we never depart from it, for we understand it is life's greatest gain. When we experience the tornado- and torpedo-proof reality of Krishna's love, no loss can ever shake us.

Then we realize that life's tornadoes and torpedoes were indirect invitations to make this secure level of living as our own.

03∞80

Upon gaining this he thinks there is no greater gain. Being situated in such a position, one is never shaken, even in the midst of greatest difficulty.

Retreat within to treat without

*W*hen external problems trouble us, we may feel that they need to be solved first, and so we can't afford time for our inner life. Paradoxically, Gita wisdom suggests that we need our inner life the most during such troubling times. Let's see why.

The sixth chapter of the Bhagavad-gita states that the greatest yogis retreat deep within the innermost recesses of their hearts. There, they experience the highest happiness that comes by, firstly, re-establishing their personal devotional connection with Krishna, the supreme reservoir of all happiness and, secondly, by realizing the equal spiritual potential of all living beings as integral parts of the supreme (06.32). Such experiences convince them that everyone has the capacity and deserves the opportunity to relish the sublime joy that they have relished. Not only that, they recognize that this inner fulfilment is the greatest necessity of those facing outer turbulence.

Why?

Because they have understood through their personal experience that external stability is difficult to attain or sustain without internal serenity.

That's why they urge us to retreat within to treat without. They recommend that we first stabilize and strengthen ourselves internally by relishing our personal connection with Krishna. Then we won't let our mind blow external problems out of proportion. When we thus regain our sense of perspective, we will acquire the vision and the vigor to intelligently deal with external volatility. By this peaceful and thoughtful approach, we will be able to act effectively for restoring outer stability; otherwise, our feverish and frantic responses will end making bad things worse.

More importantly, this experience of inner rejuvenation and outer restoration will help us realize a principle that will enable us to tackle similar future problems with much greater composure and grace: the principle that we can improve the outer material situation sustainably only by first improving our inner spiritual connection.

ॐ

He is a perfect yogi who, by comparison to his own self, sees the true equality of all beings, in both their happiness and their distress, O Arjuna!

Trust not just Krishna's omnipotence – trust also his omniscience

When faced with a problem, we may pray to Krishna to solve it. On finding that the solution is not forthcoming, we may start doubting: "Why is Krishna not responding to my prayer?"

Gita wisdom assures us that Krishna responds to every single prayer of every single soul.

The problem is that we expect, even demand, him to solve the problem in the specific way that we want. This attitude symptomizes our half-trust in Krishna: our trust in his omnipotence, but not in his omniscience. Put bluntly, we believe that Krishna is strong enough to solve our problem but not intelligent enough. So, we tell him the specific solution and expect him to use his omnipotence to implement it for us. And when it isn't implemented, we start doubting him.

Isn't it better to doubt our assumption that Krishna needs our intelligence?

A fundamental spiritual fact is that Krishna is far more intelligent than us; he is the most intelligent of all living beings. In fact, the Bhagavad-gita (07.10) states that he is the source of everyone's intelligence – including ours. He is not just omnipotent – he is also omniscient.

We all can choose to trust Krishna fully instead of partially. When we trust him fully, we won't impose our intelligence on him by demanding a specific solution. Instead, we will ask him for strength and wisdom: strength to continue serving him even amidst the problem, and wisdom to understand and cooperate with his solution, whatever it may be and whenever it appears.

Trusting Krishna fully will give us two huge returns. Firstly, no matter what problems come, we will be able to stay secure by focusing on how to serve him best in that situation. Secondly, we will be amazed periodically at how he deals with those problems in ways far better than what we could have ever thought.

❀

O son of Prtha, know that I am the original seed of all existences, the intelligence of the intelligent, and the prowess of all powerful men..

Don't give up – grow up

Life's inevitable reversals sometimes fill us with defeatist thoughts: "I have failed yet again. Maybe I should just give up".

At such times, Gita wisdom can free us by pointing out that we are labouring under unnecessarily narrow definitions of success and failure. When things work according to our plans, we consider that to be success; when things don't work according to our plans, we consider that to be failure. When our plans fail repeatedly, we often get frustrated and dejected, and start thinking of giving up.

Gita wisdom broadens our definitions of success and failure by underscoring that we are spiritual beings and that our ultimate success is to attain eternal life by growing up spiritually. Spiritual growth essentially means growth in our faith that Krishna is our greatest well-wisher and that he is, as the Bhagavad-gita (09.10) asserts, overseeing the world.

Faith grows by both human choice and divine grace. When we are about to give up due to material failures, we have a special opportunity to grow in faith by exerting our human choice and thereby attracting divine grace. Let's see how.

Amidst reversals, all of us can make the choice of putting faith in Krishna by not getting disheartened and by continuing to serve him as much as our capacities and circumstances allow. When we thus persevere with faith, we will in due course of time discover that he has arranged things for our ultimate good in a way far better than our best plans. This inconceivable arrangement and our realization of that arrangement comprise the divine grace that further boosts our faith and accelerates our spiritual growth.

Thus, when we utilize the power of faith, reversals will no longer remain causes to give up, but will become opportunities to grow up.

CR80

This material nature, which is one of My energies, is working under My direction, O son of Kunti, producing all moving and nonmoving beings. Under its rule this manifestation is created and annihilated again and again.

Utilize impoverishment as an opportunity for enrichment

When faced with financial challenges, we often worry, "What do I live with?" This worry is, no doubt, valid and important. At the same time, such situations are also invaluable impetuses for asking a more fundamental question: "What do I live for?"

The eleventh canto of the Srimad Bhagavatam describes the story of such a priority reformation, wherein a wealthy super-miser lost everything due to a series of disasters. While trying to make sense of the loss of the ultimate means for living, he discovered the ultimate purpose for living: developing an eternal relationship with Krishna. Being enriched with this sense of purpose, he cast away the feeling of being impoverished and went on to attain life's ultimate success.

To experience similar enrichment, we don't have to go through such traumatic experiences; we just need to study scripture sincerely and apply it diligently.

The Bhagavad-gita (09.22) offers a resounding assurance: when we take care of the whys of life, Krishna takes care of the hows of life. This verse's first part talks about fixing the mind on Krishna undeviatingly and worshiping him wholeheartedly, or in other words, living to love him. That is the why of life. The verse's second part promises that Krishna takes care of all our necessities: he protects what we have and provides what we lack. That is the how of life.

Additionally, the Gita's penetrating philosophical analysis enables us to see how obsession with money doesn't bring happiness; rather, it causes distraction spiritually and agitation materially. On the other hand, focus on Krishna brings profound fulfillment spiritually, and balanced endeavor and sustainable success materially.

These comparative realizations inspire us to replace money with Krishna on the altar of our heart. Thus, material impoverishment gives way to spiritual enrichment.

CᴚᴇᴏⱮ

But those who always worship Me with exclusive devotion, meditating on My transcendental form—to them I carry what they lack, and I preserve what they have

Discover the democracy of misery

*W*hen problems assault us unexpectedly, we often feel indignant that life has handed us a raw deal. We also become haunted by the fear that people may see the reversal – be it financial or familial or whatever else – as evidence that we are inferior to others. These dual feelings of injustice and inferiority generate an overwhelming emotional momentum. We find ourselves propelled into the doleful imagination that we alone are suffering, while others are having a good time.

Gita wisdom freezes our gloomily hyperactive imagination by one sweeping stroke of insight: misery is democratic or equal to all. The Bhagavad-gita (09.33) declares that misery is an inherent, inescapable feature of the material world. So everybody living here has to suffer; the difference between us and others is only a matter of when and how, of the time and the form of the onslaught of misery.

Can we realize this democracy of misery for ourselves? Surely; we just need to use our experience and intelligence to look beyond the surface. Careful contemplation will show us that those people who we imagined were happy – our beloved movie star who makes millions swoon or our dreaded competitor who gets all the right hunches at the right time or whoever else – are all, in their own ways, suffering.

The moment when we discover this democratic nature of suffering is liberating. The gnawing feelings of injustice and inferiority disappear; we experience an empowering inner freedom. The resulting energy enables us to deal with life's reversals in the best possible way materially. More importantly, we gain the conviction to redirect our energy from the fruitless quest for a better place in this world to the fruitful quest for the best place beyond this world: the eternal abode of Krishna.

ॐ

Having come to this temporary, miserable world, engage in loving service unto Me..

Contemplation on Krishna brings illumination

Some people question the spiritual recommendation to think about Krishna at all times and especially in times of distress: "What is its benefit? How is it going to remove my distress?"

Thinking about Krishna connects us with a higher spiritual reality that enables us to see life in a fresh light. Thereby, we detect order and coherence where we earlier saw only disorder and incoherence.

Why does this light come by thinking about Krishna? Because he is the Supreme Person, the Absolute Truth, the source and sustainer of everything, as the Bhagavad-gita (10.08) proclaims. So when we think about Krishna, we connect with a living, loving person who is also omniscient and omnipotent. Our contemplation on him becomes the channel through which he beams down the light of his supreme wisdom in our heart.

This illuminating beam shows us the way to rise to higher, more spiritual levels of consciousness. As we ascend, we get a clearer sense of Krishna's presence and purpose. We understand that he is always in control and is always present with us, to bless, guide and empower us. We also become confident that, even amidst life's distresses, he has his benevolent purpose; if we just keep serving him diligently, we will gradually realize that purpose. Thus, thinking about Krishna helps us become conscious of his presence and purpose, and enables us to do our part in it. By his grace, external situations, even if distressing, stimulate our inner learning and spiritual growth.

More importantly, our elevated consciousness gives us a clearer understanding of Krishna's all-attractive personality and his irresistible beauty. This understanding deepens and strengthens our devotion to him, thereby preparing us to eventually return to him for a blissful life of endless love.

Thus, thinking about Krishna offers us significant this-worldly and unparalleled other-worldly rewards

ఇళ్ళ

I am the source of all spiritual and material worlds. Everything emanates from Me. The wise who perfectly know this engage in My devotional service and worship Me with all their hearts.

Transform disappointment into his-appointment

When life confronts us with disappointments, we can transform them into his-appointments, into opportunities to connect with Krishna at a deeper level and thereby enrich ourselves. The Bhagavad-gita (10.10) proclaims that whenever we strive to serve him with a devotional attitude, he gives us the intelligence to come closer to him through all situations.

Let's see how this can happen during disappointments.

Gita wisdom sets the conceptual foundation by educating us that among all our external and internal assets, devotion alone will stay eternally with us. Moreover, among all our assets, devotion alone will propel us to the eternal destination: the realm of sublime spiritual love, Krishna's personal abode. That's why the Gita urges us to recognize cultivating devotion as life's foremost goal.

Our worldly goals are valuable to the extent they aid us and others in cultivating devotion. Otherwise, from the perspective of eternity, they are distractions that devour our precious time. When we attain material successes, they frequently infatuate us with hopes of similar future successes. Consequently, we no longer feel the necessity or at least the urgency to cultivate devotion. Thus, temporary material pleasures start jeopardizing our eternal spiritual prospects.

To protect us from this colossal loss, worldly disappointments often serve us as essential priority reminders. They freeze our worldly infatuations and force us to re-gather our spiritual bearings.

At such times, if we seek solace and guidance from Krishna, we will get extraordinary inner experiences of his love and grace. These realizations will convince us to stay devotionally focused amidst both success and failure. By becoming thus focused, we will ensure that our future material successes won't be at the cost of our ultimate spiritual success. We will live as happily as is possible in the material world and finally return to Krishna.

ॐ

To those who are constantly devoted to serving Me with love, I give the understanding by which they can come to Me.

Transform pains and strains into gains

𝒟uring our journey through life, we sometimes feel disheartened by the pains of yesterday and the strains of today. The pains of yesterday are all the past reversals that had punctured our morale. The strains of today are all the present obstacles that are deflating our morale. How can we maintain our spirits in such situations?

Gita wisdom encourages us by expanding our definition of gains in life's journey. We are souls meant to rejoice eternally in a loving relationship with Krishna. So from the perspective of our eternal identity, anything that brings us closer to him is a gain, even if it is a total loss at the material level. By this broadened understanding, we see that all our past pains were gains because they contributed to the experiences that brought us to him. And even the present strains can be gains if we use them as spurs to go closer to him.

Gita wisdom offers us this profoundly positive outlook towards life not just at a conceptual level but also at a practical level. When we serve Krishna lovingly, he gifts us the dynamic intelligence by which we can integrate and utilize yesterday's pains and today's strains into our devotional growth pathway so that they become tomorrow's gains. This special Krishna-bestowed intelligence, which the Bhagavad-gita (10.10) calls as buddhi-yoga, enables us to act in ways that the burdensome situations go materially, while we grow spiritually.

When we thus see that we can succeed and are in fact succeeding at the spiritual level, then the sense of burden caused by the dreary material situation dissipates from our heart. Thus energized, we act to the best of our capacity even at the material level and thereby increase the possibility of succeeding at that level too.

ॐ

To those who are constantly devoted to serving Me with love, I give the understanding by which they can come to Me.

Spirituality provides us our own inner sanctuary

We all need encouragement. The regular obstacles and occasional reversals that life brings our way tend to be discouraging.

To regain our spirits, we need our own inner sanctuary where we can withdraw for philosophical reflection and emotional rejuvenation.

Philosophically, we need to make sense of what is happening in our life. With our own intelligence, we may be able to see some of the patterns. But to glimpse the complete picture, we absolutely need divine revelation. The Gita offers us the calming insight that life is intrinsically an undulation of temporary pleasures and pains; we are indestructible souls who can remain unaffected if we just intelligently tolerate.

Emotionally, we need more than just the mandate to tolerate; we need to feel loved. If we get that from affectionate and like-minded devotee-friends, we are fortunate. But if we don't – and even if we do – we need our own inner devotional connection with Krishna. This connection takes us to our inner sanctuary where we feel the warmth of his presence and the reassurance of his benevolent controllership of the world. To establish our connection to the sanctuary, we need to practice devotional meditation regularly, attentively and prayerfully.

The Bhagavad-gita (12.19: *aniketah sthira-matir*) indicates that seasoned devotees don't depend on any external home because they have found their inner sanctuary with Krishna. We can avail of a similar sanctuary ourselves by assimilating philosophical wisdom and cultivating devotional remembrance of Krishna. Initially, we may seek this inner sanctuary as a retreat center for recouping from life's discouragements. But over time we will realize that it is much more; it is an accessible pathway that will take us out of the material world and reunite us with Krishna in the spiritual world.

ॐ

One who is equal to … fame and infamy, who is always free from contaminating association, always silent and satisfied with anything, who doesn't care for any residence, who is fixed in knowledge and who is engaged in devotional service—such a person is very dear to Me.

Inner resonance leads to outer coherence

*W*hy do things keep going wrong?" Life often vexes us thus due to its unpredictable upheavals.

Gita wisdom suggests that we might be asking the wrong question: "After having so much repeated and resounding experience of things going wrong, why are we so naïve as to expect things to go right?"

We might protest, "How can I not expect things to go right? Am I meant to just sit passively and watch glumly as things go on a disastrous downslide?"

Gita wisdom doesn't at all recommend passivity; the Gita was spoken to inspire its original student, Arjuna, to rise from passivity to activity. What Gita wisdom recommends is that we forgo labeling situations as "going right" and "going wrong" and instead focus on our responses so that we are "doing right" instead of "doing wrong."

The Bhagavad-gita indicates that we can suspend mental labeling of situations (13.10: *nityam ca sama-cittatvam ishtanishtopapattishu*) when we fix ourselves in undistracted devotional remembrance of Krishna (13.11: *mayi cananya-yogena bhaktir avyabhicarini*). By this prayerful connection, we experience an inner resonance with Krishna that brings outer coherence to our vision.

What does inner resonance with Krishna mean? It means the realization that he is the supreme controller and the ultimate benefactor. When we are thus reassured that he is in charge and is acting for our benefit, we experience a strong spiritual solace that shelters us from the mind's default tendency to label situations. The absence of negative labels ensures that we are no longer paralyzed or agonized by label-triggered feelings of resentment. With our mental energy thus conserved, we can prayerfully seek Krishna's guidance and act constructively to solve the problem.

Problems thus become opportunities when we realize deeply the certainty of Krishna's shelter and the infallibility of his guidance.

గఙ౮

… Evenmindedness amid pleasant and unpleasant events…—all these I declare to be knowledge, and besides this whatever there may be is ignorance.

Make your memory your treasury

*W*hen the present presents us with difficulties, we often turn to our memories of past emotionally fulfilling moments for inspiration.

As our culture bombards us with a media blitz, our strongest emotions usually come from such media images. For example, our most joyous recent memories may have been when our favorite sports team won a championship or when our favorite hero bashed up a villain in a movie climax.

However, such memories are largely disconnected from our actual lives. So, they provide us feelings without meanings. They may emotionally transport us away from our present difficulties, but when we return to the present, they don't help us much to make sense of what is happening. If we try to draw upon such memories in demanding times, we soon find ourselves internally bankrupt; we get titillation, but no illumination.

Gita wisdom offers us a much better alternative. The Bhagavad-gita (13.10-11) recommends that we cultivate undistracted devotional remembrance of Krishna and thereby steady ourselves amidst life's dualities. To be able to remember him, we need to regularly fill our memory with devotionally surcharging images and experiences of his enchanting deities, soothing holy names, electrifying kirtans, magnetizing pastimes, loving devotees and absorbing service.

When we draw on such a devotional memory bank in difficult times, these memories quickly draw us into them. They enable us to re-experience the warmth of Krishna's love and the reality of his grace, as we had experienced in the past. Thereafter, when we return to the present, we are emotionally enlivened and intellectually empowered to discover, by Krishna's grace, the growth opportunity hidden within the present difficulty.

Thus, when we make our memory a devotional treasury, it offers both emotional relief for our troubled hearts and intellectual direction for our perplexed heads.

೧೪೮೦

...Unalloyed devotion to Me...—all these I declare to be knowledge, and besides this whatever there may be is ignorance

Krishna is not an active imposer or a passive spectator – he is a proactive selector

To Life sometimes slaps us with pointless problems and senseless sufferings. To aid us in responding positively, Gita wisdom offers us an encouraging insight: the world is a school, and the events of our life are integral parts of the curriculum.

The Gita shares this insight not as a nebulous sentiment, but as the key element of a coherent worldview that helps us understand systematically how life's educational process works and what we need to do to learn.

The first thing to learn is the futility of resentment. When we resent what is happening, we just cannot learn from it. We can free ourselves from such resentment by understanding Krishna's benevolent role amidst life's apparently malevolent events.

The Gita (13.23) states that Krishna as the Supersoul in our hearts oversees and permits whatever happens to us. That whatever happens to us is caused by our own past karma is preliminary spiritual knowledge. Gita wisdom builds upon this knowledge by outlining Krishna's specific role in the unfolding of our karmic reactions. He is neither the active imposer nor the passive spectator, but is the proactive selector who ensures that those reactions come upon us in ways that educate and elevate us.

To accelerate our education, Krishna aids us both externally and internally. Externally through the Vedic scriptures, he informs us about the overall direction and destination of the recommended learning trajectory. And internally as the Supersoul, he helps us get realizations through specific life-events. To benefit optimally from his guidance and progress swiftly along the learning trajectory, we need to cultivate a loving attitude by practicing devotional service.

When we thus take Krishna's guidance in facing life, every moment transforms into an illuminating experience as we learn and grow towards life's ultimate fulfilment: eternal love.

∞

Yet in this body there is another, a transcendental enjoyer, who is the Lord, the supreme proprietor, who exists as the overseer and permitter, and who is known as the Supersoul.

Krishna is not just out there; he is also in here

*W*hen life hands out difficulties to us, we may feel forlorn because of the thought that Krishna is far away, somewhere out there in the vast emptiness of space. Gita wisdom informs us that nothing could be further from the truth. Though Krishna is in the spiritual world, he is not there alone – being omnipresent he is also close by, right here in our own hearts.

The Bhagavad-gita (15.15) confirms this when it declares that Krishna personally resides in the hearts of all living beings. The revelation of Krishna's indwelling presence comes at the end of a series of verses (15.12-14) that demonstrate his love for all of us. By giving examples that range from the external cosmological realm to the internal physiological realm, these verses indicate that Krishna, out of love for us, maintains the entire material realm to facilitate our existence. His love for us is so great that he is not satisfied just by arranging for our material existence; he also arranges for our spiritual welfare by making himself available to us in our own hearts as a friend and guide.

Why is Krishna personally present in our heart?

Because he wants to do all that he can to help us. He is not satisfied with imparting through the Vedic literature the generic philosophical understanding that our present sufferings are the just results of our own past misdeeds. He wants to always be by our side, giving us solace and strength in our times of trial. As our bosom partner, he actively and lovingly helps us to tolerate and transcend life's miseries. If we just take his guidance, he will expertly help us to grow and go towards the spiritual realm that is beyond all suffering.

ॐ

I am seated in everyone's heart, and from Me come remembrance, knowledge and forgetfulness. By all the Vedas, I am to be known. Indeed, I am the compiler of Vedanta, and I am the knower of the Vedas.

Searching for the villain can't help us in finding the hero

*W*hen things start going wrong in our life, our false ego goes into a default defensive, scheming to find a villain on whom to lay the blame for spoiling the dream plot of our life. However, this search for a villain puts us in a negative frame of mind, wherein we just can't see the positive reality – and certainly not the ultimate positive reality, Krishna's supreme heroism and his unflinching love for us

The Bhagavad-gita (16.03) states that the unwillingness to find faults in others (*apaishunam*) characterizes the virtuous. Does this unwillingness imply that we passively accept the status quo? Not at all. Gita wisdom guides us to actively search for the villain within instead of without. It reveals how the sinister persuasions of our false ego have misled us into accepting the role of a villain who seeks to unscrupulously usurp the position of the ultimate hero, Krishna.

The plot of the world is moving for Krishna's pleasure, not ours. But this doesn't mean that we count for nothing, as our false ego often darkly mutters in its bid to stop us from joining Krishna's plot. When we play our part in the plot for Krishna's pleasure, we too have our moments of glory, as did Hanuman in service to Lord Rama in the Ramayana.

When we accept this bittersweet truth, then we realize that our life's mission is not to discover and blame a villain without, but to discover and love the hero within our own hearts. To fulfill this mission, we need to locate and execute the villain within: our own false ego. When we succeed in this mission, then no external villain can ever spoil the plot of our eternal love-story with Krishna.

◌੪੪◌

…Nonviolence; truthfulness; freedom from anger; renunciation; tranquility; aversion to faultfinding; compassion for all living entities; freedom from covetousness; gentleness; modesty; steady determination…—these transcendental qualities, O son of Bharata, belong to godly men endowed with divine nature.

"Got big problems?" Krishna is bigger

When life's problems overwhelm us, our vision becomes distorted. We start feeling that the problems are ultra-big, bigger than even Krishna. Consequently, we become so preoccupied in coping with them that our spiritual practices like chanting become distracted. We may even feel that the distraction is justified: "Krishna, you understand how big this problem is. I need to deal with it first before I can resume proper devotional meditation on you."

Gita wisdom helps us understand that resuming proper contemplation on Krishna is the first way to deal with any problem. The Bhagavad-gita (18.58) reminds us that if we become conscious of him, he will, by his grace, help us to cross over all problems. His grace often expresses itself as a perspective-restoring insight: He is far bigger than any problem. For him, solving our biggest problem is no big deal; he can empower us to tackle or transcend it by one moment of illumination.

Thus Gita wisdom enables us to beat the problem– and the mind that is fretting over it – down to size by proclaiming to it how big Krishna is: "Let me not tell Krishna how big my problems are; let me tell my problems how big Krishna is." Such an inner proclamation corrects our vision distortion; we no longer see the problem as overwhelming. We realize that, just as Krishna's grace has enabled us to weather many problems in the past, so it will enable us to weather this problem too. That realization loosens the problem's anxiety-inducing grip on us. Reserves of hitherto choked mental energy break free and soon solutions emerge.

Over time, we start seeing the bigness of worldly problems as opportunities to deepen our awareness of the bigness of Krishna. Then problems no longer agitate us, but instead stimulate us.

☙❦❧

If you become conscious of Me, you will pass over all the obstacles of conditioned life by My grace. If, however, you do not work in such consciousness but act through false ego, not hearing Me, you will be lost.

Stop the hurry, worry, sorrystory – seek Hari

In youth, we are mostly in a state of hurry, having so many things to do and imagining that we can bend the world to our will.

In middle age, we are mostly in a state of worry, having learnt through life's hard lessons that so many things may go wrong and fearing that we may not be able to control things when they go wrong.

In old age, we are mostly in a state of feeling sorry for ourselves, lamenting all the things that we did wrong or all the things that went wrong despite our best efforts.

The Bhagavad-gita outlines this unfortunate life-trajectory when it declares (18.58) that those who refuse to connect with Krishna will suffer and perish. The same verse offers a far better alternative life-trajectory when it states that those who connect with Krishna will pass over all obstacles by his grace.

Let's see how this may happen in our "hurry, worry, sorry" life.

When we bring Hari (Lord Krishna) in our lives, then his wisdom frees us from:

1. Hurry by clarifying our priorities so that we focus on life's most important things without trying to do everything that everyone around us feels we should be doing,

2. Worry by giving us the conviction that Krishna is always in control and will guide us to safety even when things appear to be going disastrously wrong.

3. Sorry feelings by showing us how even if we have irrecoverably lost material opportunities, they would have at best alleviated our problems only temporarily, whereas spiritual opportunities that can solve our problems permanently are still available inalienably.

ༀ

If you become conscious of Me, you will pass over all the obstacles of conditioned life by My grace. If, however, you do not work in such consciousness but act through false ego, not hearing Me, you will be lost.

The blend of encouragement and enlightenment brings empowerment

Life's reversals can often be demoralizing. To regain our morale, we need both enlightenment (knowing what to do) and encouragement (feeling confident that we can do it). Those who encourage without enlightening often end up delivering shallow, cosmetic or insubstantial platitudes. Those who enlighten without encouraging often end up delivering holier-than-thou, impractical or unappealing sermons.

Lord Krishna blends enlightenment and encouragement endearingly in his message of love, the Bhagavad-gita. Therein, he first gives encouraging reassurances of the indestructibility and invincibility of the self (2.11-30), then proceeds with enlightening analyses that illuminate for Arjuna the best course of action among the bewildering multiplicity of options open for him (2.31-18.63) and concludes with encouraging promises of his all-round loving help when Arjuna takes up the best course of action (18.64-72).

Thus the Gita harmonizes enlightenment and encouragement in a majestic message that fills us with hope not by denying the harshness of reality, as does much new age spirituality, but by revealing to us a higher, sweeter reality. This reality is the reality of love, Krishna's love for us and our dormant love for him. This love reigns supreme eternally in the ecstatic world of Krishna to which we belong and which we can attain by harmonizing our life with devotional principles.

Gita wisdom offers us hope not just in the future but also in the present. It introduces us to a living, loving God who helps us even in the here-and-now by offering guidance from within and by orchestrating events from without so as to facilitate and accelerate our return to him.

So next time we feel demoralized – or better still, even before we feel demoralized – we can empower ourselves with morale-boosting doses of Gita wisdom.

ॐ

Because you are My very dear friend, I am speaking to you My supreme instruction, the most confidential knowledge of all. Hear this from Me, for it is for your benefit.

SEEING THE WORLD THROUGH THE GITA'S EYES

The great blunder of the great materialist dream is neglect of the greatest being

The great materialist dream is that happiness is found in material things: money, sex, TV, video games, 4G net connections. But today this dream finds itself punctured psychologically, sociologically and ecologically.

Psychologically, more people than ever before are succumbing to stress, depression, hypertension, addiction and even suicide.

Sociologically, corruption, sexual abuses and violent conflicts over trivial issues are on a rapid upward spiral.

Ecologically, super-disasters are no longer a doomsday prophecy; they are an imminent reality.

What went wrong with the materialist dream?

Gita wisdom informs us that its lethal error was to leave out the most important factor: Krishna.

This was precisely the blunder of the prototype of all godless materialists, Duryodhana, as is evident in his statement in the Bhagavad-gita (01.10). He assessed the strengths of his forces, who were mostly godless materialists like him, and those of his opponents, who were devotees. He dreamt of victory based on the material superiority of his forces. But he neglected the Krishna-factor – with fatal consequences.

At the dawn of modernity, godless materialists made a Duryodhana-like assessment of the world situation. They dreamt of victory over nature based on calculations of their material strengths, primarily the knowledge-acquiring power of science and change-effecting power of technology. But they neglected the God-factor.

Humanity became enamored by this great materialist dream and abandoned its connection with God. Consequently, people lost their self-mastery and suffered psychologically; lost their moral compass and suffered sociologically; and lost their environmental reverence and suffered ecologically.

Fortunately, each of us individually has the power to correct the errors of the past. If we rebuild our own inner connection with Krishna, we will become increasingly satisfied, stabilized and strengthened. Our examples and words will inspire many others to re-establish their own divine connection, thus contributing towards an auspicious God-centered global destiny.

೧೩೮೦

Our strength is immeasurable, and we are perfectly protected by Grandfather Bhishma, whereas the strength of the Pandavas, carefully protected by Bhima, is limited.

Did nothing in life prepare you for life?

From middle age onwards, the human body usually starts undergoing a miracle of the wrong kind. Unfortunately, many such miracle-afflicted people go into a denial mode and frantically conceal the signs of bodily decline by hair-dyes and face-lifts. They can hide these symptoms of aging from the world, but not from their own hearts. They can scarcely face the silent terror that creeps into their hearts whenever they think of how their dear body – their only vehicle to pleasure – is on an irreversible, terminal downslide.

Gita wisdom can help and heal such people by posing a surgically probing question: "Did nothing in life prepare you for life?"

This question applies to all of us, whatever our age.

The Bhagavad-gita (02.27) indicates that the decline and demise of the human body is a universal, undeniable truth of life. Preparing for life, Gita wisdom informs us, means preparing for this inescapable downslide of life.

Our materialistic culture makes us believe that preparing for life means preparing to make it big in life: earning money, pleasure and prestige. Material success has its place in life, but allowing it a monopoly on our life-preparation is suicidally shortsighted.

Gita wisdom compensates for our shortsightedness. It guides us to realize our spiritual identity and to redirect our search for happiness from the material level to the spiritual level. This redirection empowers us to tolerate and transcend the body's inevitable decline; for we know that time can never decimate our spiritual identity or deplete our devotional happiness in remembrance of Krishna.

Thus, Gita wisdom helps us to not only learn from life the futility of material existence, but also to learn of a destination beyond this futility: a life of eternal love with Krishna.

ॐ

One who has taken his birth is sure to die, and after death one is sure to take birth again. Therefore, in the unavoidable discharge of your duty, you should not lament.

Today's medals will be tomorrow's baubles

One of our innermost drives is the drive to show the world that we are someone significant. This drive impels us to win medals, which we hope will serve as visible evidences of our glory. Medals are most popular in sports. But they also have their avatars in other fields as trophies, certificates, awards, badges, dress-stripes. Such medals often generate intense emotions, which are self-evident in sporting arenas as laughs and cries, roars and grunts, cheers and jeers.

Far less evident than the intensity of these emotions is their ephemerality. The emotional value of a medal peaks if and when we finally attain it – and people appreciate us. But soon after that peak, the medal-value starts slipping down a steady southbound curve as the world moves on, and our life returns to its dreary and draining routine. No doubt, there are occasional spikes when others see the medal and praise us, or when we see it and relive sweet memories. Nonetheless, these spikes can't arrest the overall pattern of irreversible devaluation.

The inexorable passage of time causes our cherished medals to fall from grace, being reduced to mere baubles. And to the extent we have wedded our self-worth to the medals, to that extent our heart sinks with them into the ignominy of oblivion.

Gita wisdom urges us to wed our self-worth to something much more enduring: our relationship with Krishna. The Bhagavad-gita (02.40) indicates that our spiritual advancement – our attraction to Krishna – is never destroyed, not even devalued. The world may or may not recognize its value, but Krishna consciousness provides an inner enrichment that frees us from dependence on the world's evaluation.

Getting that enrichment is life's ultimate medal, indeed, existence's ultimate trophy.

ॐ

In this endeavor there is no loss or diminution, and a little advancement on this path can protect one from the most dangerous type of fear.

41

To be true to oneself, go beyond the fashionable and the conventional to the spiritual

We live at the receiving end of a massive propaganda blitz from our materialistic culture. Consequently, the likings of so many people change obediently in tune with the fashions.

In such a cultural scenario, a few people stick to their own ways of living, saying that they want to be true to themselves.

This sentiment is good, but Gita wisdom emphasizes, we need to first, know what the true self is: the soul. We are presently covered both internally and externally: internally by our mind's conditionings and externally by our culture's conceptions. To be true to our self means to act according to our nature as souls and thereby delight in loving Krishna. For that, we need to do two things: Counter the outer cultural influences by placing ourselves in a spiritually conducive environment. And counter the inner mental influences by cultivating a devotionally receptive attitude.

Otherwise, in the name of being true to oneself, we may well be holding on to outdated conventions that are as untrue to our true self as are the current fashions. The conventions that we follow in the name of being true to ourselves may well be nothing more than the external influences that had affected our ancestors.

The real criterion for deciding what is true to oneself is not what is conventional, but what is spiritual, that is, conducive for our realization of our true self. Using this criterion, spiritually realized people, the Bhagavad-gita (02.52) indicates, stay uninfluenced by what they are hearing now, what they have heard in the past and what they will hear in the future. They are fixed in their inner connection with Krishna and in all those things which sustain that connection.

Such steady focus on the self is the true standard of being true to oneself.

৩৪৪০

When your intelligence has passed out of the dense forest of delusion, you shall become indifferent to all that has been heard and all that is to be heard.

Our eyes are meant for something far better than winning the misery championship?

Most of us have entered the misery championship. Here's how.

The qualifying rounds: Our contemporary culture assaults our eyes with visually alluring images of sensuous objects. When we undergo the misery of the tormenting desire to get those objects, we win the qualifying rounds of the misery championship.

The initial rounds: The images are doctored professionally to look much better than the real objects. So, when we visually consume those objects by possessing and enjoying them, our experience never lives up to the hype. By experiencing the misery of frustrated expectations, we win the initial rounds.

The later rounds: The sheer number of visually alluring worldly objects is so great that we can never consume all of them. That's why no matter how many objects we consume, many more keep tormenting us. When we experience the misery of perpetual torment, we win the rounds that lead to the finals.

The final: The pleasure from visual consumption of worldly forms is fleeting but intoxicating. Becoming addicted to that intoxicating pleasure, we see as sources of pleasure the very objects that are sources of our misery. When we dedicate our life to courting and embracing misery as if it were pleasure, we win the misery championship and get the privilege of drinking from the cup of visual misery for the rest of our life.

Gita wisdom liberates us from this miserable game by revealing misery-free ways of visual enjoyment. As souls, we can feast visually on the transcendentally enchanting form of Krishna and thereby get ever-increasing spiritual happiness. By thus fixing our consciousness on Krishna, as the Bhagavad-gita (02.61) indicates, we can steady our intelligence and opt out of the misery championship.

೫೪೫೦

One who restrains his senses, keeping them under full control, and fixes his consciousness upon Me, is known as a man of steady intelligence.

What we hold mentally holds us mentally

Our media continuously offers us high-octane sensory stimulation, especially for our eyes. As compared to the rapidly changing and colorfully overdressed images that are dished out to us on TV serials, movies and commercials, the sensory fare provided by daily real life appears poverty-stricken. Consequently, our mind plays truant from real life at every possible opportunity, preferring to dwell on the titillating images on display in our mental gallery.

This mental truancy may initially seem to be just a pleasant and harmless distraction. But Gita wisdom alerts us about the dangerous consequences of such distractions. The Bhagavad-gita (02.62-63) outlines step-by-step the process by which our thoughts gain an unstoppable momentum that steamrolls our moral and intellectual safeguards, and propels us to self-destruction. When we hold on to an image mentally, we give it a foothold in our mind. And before we realize it, the foothold becomes a full-hold. The dream of enjoyment conjured by the image makes us oblivious to all other considerations and propels us toward its fulfillment, be it moral or immoral, prudent or imprudent. Often, this short-sightedness ends in tragic self-destruction.

To protect us from such a fate, Gita wisdom offers an alternative trajectory for our mind: the process of bhakti-yoga. The yoga of devotion offers our senses rich devotional stimulants like enlivening holy names, enchanting Deities, enlightening scriptural verses and energizing sacred songs. By practice we can learn to hold these devotional stimulants mentally. When we hold Krishna-thoughts mentally, the same psychological process that had dragged us down materially raises us up spiritually. Those divine thoughts hold us mentally, and we gradually find ourselves absorbed in Krishna and enriched by his encouraging, loving presence. That absorption and enrichment is life's supreme security and ultimate fulfillment.

છ8૦

While contemplating the objects of the senses, a person develops attachment for them, and from such attachment lust develops, and from lust anger arises.

Whatever catches the eye catches the I

*O*ur eyes are often like voracious heat-seekers scanning the horizon for sensually hot objects.

Our materialistic culture fully exploits our visual hunger. By planting seductive billboards often at every conceivable (and sometimes even inconceivable) corner, it corners us into ceaseless visual stimulation and thoughtless mental agitation. Once our mind is agitated by material desires, we almost instantaneously forget or neglect our spiritual identity and our devotional destiny. We become possessed by an illusory sense of I-ness. We think of ourselves as males or females, as our bodies, as capable of enjoyment independent of Krishna. Due to this misconception, we become disconnected from him. Our pleasure-seeking propensity loses its spiritual avenue. Soon it gravitates down a materialistic free fall toward the object that invaded us through the eyes. Thus, once temptations catch the eye, they soon catch the I – the bewildered soul overcome by materialistic misconceptions

The Bhagavad-gita empowers us to fight off such visual captivity when it:

1. Cautions us that mental distraction by even one of the roaming senses is lethal enough to blow away our intelligence (02.67) and

2. Urges us to zealously guard each one of our senses from misdirection (02.68).

We can police our eyes more easily when we let them drink sumptuously the beauty of Krishna as manifest in his Deities, because then our visual hunger is not repressed but redirected and satisfied. As we steadily habituate our eyes to feasting on Krishna's beauty, he catches our eye and snatches our real "I" – the soul – out of the clutches of illusion back into his eternal embrace.

ॐ

An intelligent person does not take part in the sources of misery, which are due to contact with the material senses. O son of Kunti, such pleasures have a beginning and an end, and so the wise man does not delight in them.

Use not the social mirror – use the scriptural mirror

The social mirror refers to society's opinion that lets us know how we look in its eyes. This mirror often perverts the reality, especially in materialistic cultures like ours.

An egregious example of perversion by the social mirror is the 'torches of freedom' campaign used to induce women to smoke that started in the 1920s. This campaign exploits the sentiments of the women's liberation movement to market custom-made female cigars as 'torches of freedom.' Using many popular female icons, the media propaganda propelled thousands of women into smoking. It was all done in the name of freedom, but practically no one asked how smoking the cigarette was going to bring freedom. Pressurized by this campaign, many women smoked just so that they wouldn't look old-fashioned. Such is the deluding power of the social mirror!

Most media propaganda may not be so blatant, but its effects can be just as harmful. It glamorizes the trendiest gadgets, dresses and cars. This impels many people to go on purchasing sprees that are generally unnecessary and frequently unaffordable. They purchase and parade the latest wares of the fashion circus in the hope of seeing an approving reflection of themselves in the social mirror. But the social mirror is mortifyingly unstable; it shows a thing as shiny today and as rusty tomorrow. Thus, the social mirror ends fleecing people of their hard-earned money and making a fool out of them.

The Bhagavad-gita (02.69) indicates that spiritualists perceive and value things differently from the materialists. Instead of the social mirror, they use the scriptural mirror. This time-honored mirror shows them their real identity as souls with the potential for lasting devotional happiness. By using the scriptural mirror, they change themselves in ways that are not fleetingly titillating but are eternally fulfilling.

ॐ

What is night for all beings is the time of awakening for the self-controlled; and the time of awakening for all beings is night for the introspective sage.

Uni-dimensional technological progress is like hitting the bull's eye of the wrong target

Cellphones, internet, robots – the technological advances in our society are impressive. Yet they haven't made people happier, as the rising statistics of stress and depression demonstrate.

What might have gone wrong?

Might our exclusive focus on material progress be like hitting the bull's eye of the wrong target?

The Bhagavad-gita (02.69) intimates metaphorically that the targets for materialists and spiritualists differ drastically. Materialists strive to control the outer world; spiritualists, the inner world.

Materialists develop technology to control the outer world because they presume that the outer world is the source of happiness. However, happiness is essentially an inner state. That state is often disrupted by outer disturbance but is not necessarily created by gaining outer control. For example, not getting food on time troubles us, but getting food on time doesn't make us happy; it just removes the negative feeling of hunger temporarily.

This principle applies to all forms of outer control, no matter how sophisticated the technology. A dysfunctional internet connection troubles us, but a functional connection – even a superfast connection – doesn't make us happy.

In general, the effort to control the outer world can at best avoid misery temporarily, but can never bestow lasting happiness. The more we seek happiness through outer control, the more we become frustrated when we can't control, leading thereby to stress and depression.

Gita wisdom informs us that we are souls who can experience positive happiness from only one source: an inner connection with Krishna, who is the source of all happiness. When we learn to discipline all the emotions which disrupt that connection, we become happy – steadily, positively, unflappably happy – irrespective of the presence or absence of outer control.

If we don't develop our inner Krishna-connection, all our technological advances will remain accurate hits at the wrong target.

ॐ

What is night for all beings is the time of awakening for the self-controlled; and the time of awakening for all beings is night for the introspective sage.

Be not slick about sin – be sick about sin

A tragic trend of our times is the glamorization of immoral sexual indulgences as fashionable, as slick, as cool. This is especially evident in soap operas that portray sexual immorality as bold and adventurous. The intoxication generated by such illicit sexual fantasies often blinds people to its real-life consequences that are evident in the increasing statistics of sexual abuses like rape, incest and pedophilia. Most civilized people feel sickened when they hear of such abuses, yet these same people rarely feel sickened by their causes: the ubiquitous sexual images that are displayed on billboards, fashion ramps and celluloid screens.

Gita wisdom makes explicit the cause-effect connection between sexual images and sexual abuses. The Bhagavad-gita (03.39) unmasks lust by declaring it to be an eternal enemy (*nitya vairi*) that acting like an insatiable fire (*dushpurenaanalena*)devours our intelligence. Sexual images that offer visual indulgence serve as a readily combustible fuel for the fire of lust. When this fuel is fed constantly, the fire of lust becomes a conflagration that devours people's intelligence, conscience, common sense, even humanity. It is pertinent to remember that the people who perpetrate horrendous sexual abuses are not some two-horned demons from another planet; they are humans like us, but humans whom lust has perverted into monsters.

If we wish to stop such abuses, improved police regulation is not enough; that will check the circumstantial cause, but not the root cause. That root cause is the inordinate aggravation of lust through the misleading glamorization and popularization of sexual images as slick. We need to end the double standards of being sickened by the effects of lust – sexual abuses – and allured by the causes of lust: sexual images.

We can no longer be slick about sin; we need to become sick about sin.

ॐ

Thus the wise living entity's pure consciousness becomes covered by his eternal enemy in the form of lust, which is never satisfied and which burns like fire.

48

Harmonize the sword with the word

We often dread communal violence. So, we frequently fear theocracies due to their likely intolerance towards people who don't abide by their sectarian beliefs. Naturally then, we may feel apprehensive when we read the Bhagavad-gita's glorification of saintly kings who live and lead according to scriptural wisdom (04.02).

However, the Gita destroys our sectarian categories right at the start of its message. It declares that we are not our bodies, but are eternal souls who have no intrinsic connection with the bodies that we presently inhabit. Bodily misidentification is the basis of all sects, including even sects with religious nomenclature like Christians, Muslims and Hindus.

Gita wisdom takes us beyond all our sectarian notions of identity to our universal essence as souls. It recommends that we act on that spiritual level for the holistic welfare of everyone. To fulfill that universal purpose, it urges us to harmonize the word, our intellectual resources, and the sword, our administrative resources.

The Gita illustrates this harmony through the example of Krishna, who is actually God himself descended to the earth. In the context of the Mahabharata, Krishna plays the role of a prince, an administrator who uses the sword when necessary to check sectarian materialism. But in the context of the Gita, he accepts the role of a spiritual intellectual who empowers the warrior-prince, Arjuna, with the word for rising individually and socially beyond sectarianism to the spiritual level. The Gita recommends the word as the preferred way for raising consciousness. However, for those who have not only buried themselves in sectarian materialism but are bent on similarly burying the whole society, it sanctions the sword only as a last resort.

Thus, through this harmony of the word and the sword, Gita wisdom takes us beyond sectarianism.

ॐ

This supreme science was thus received through the chain of disciplic succession, and the saintly kings understood it in that way. But in course of time the succession was broken, and therefore the science as it is appears to be lost.

Don't romanticize or demonize; utilize and realize

*M*any people romanticize the world, picturing it to be the arena where they will fulfill their fantasies. When the world dashes and smashes their dreams, they sometimes oscillate to the other extreme and demonize it, painting it as an intrinsically evil place meant to be shunned at all costs.

The Gita advocates a balanced middle approach between these two poles of romanticization and demonization. The Bhagavad-gita (05.29) declares that the world belongs to God, Krishna. So, it should be utilized for his service. When we lovingly offer the resources of the world to the Lord of the world, this devotional contact with the all-pure Lord purifies us. This purification peels away the layers of ignorance and forgetfulness that have obscured our spiritual identity for eons.

As we realize our spiritual identity, we understand that rendering devotional service to Krishna is our natural, eternal activity as his beloved children. This understanding inspires us to continue serving Krishna with conviction and devotion. Then, as we rise from self-realization to God-realization, we discover that all the peace and joy we were constantly searching for externally was available all along in our own hearts in our devotional connection with Krishna, the source of all peace and joy. Facilitating us to get that realization is the world's ultimate purpose.

Thus, Gita wisdom helps us steer clear of the extremes of romanticization and demonization in dealing with the world. By showing us the middle path of utilization, it leads us to life's ultimate perfection: realization of Krishna.

രു൭ൟ

A person in full consciousness of Me, knowing Me to be the ultimate beneficiary of all sacrifices and austerities, the Supreme Lord of all planets and demigods, and the benefactor and well-wisher of all living entities, attains peace from the pangs of material miseries.

We need a break – from the mind

Our mind harasses us constantly with internal proposals for material enjoyment. The current culture does externally what the mind does internally: bombard us relentlessly with promises of material enjoyment.

This seconding of the mind by the culture is not surprising because every culture is a product of the prevalent collective mind. What people think and believe and desire expresses itself in their external actions and environments, which combine to form their culture. Most people nowadays have no knowledge about their spiritual identity and destiny. So they unsuspectingly embrace their mind's proposals for material enjoyment and thereby create the fabric of today's aggressively materialistic culture. Thus, our spiritual integrity comes under a formidable two-pronged attack: internal and external.

To protect ourselves, we absolutely need to take a break from the mind. Placing ourselves physically in the devotional culture based on Gita wisdom provides us a break from the mind's external attack. Placing ourselves intellectually and devotionally in Gita wisdom provides us a break from the mind's internal attack. The combination of culture and wisdom provides us devotional experiences, and nourishes our conviction that real happiness is found not in materialism but in devotion. When we become deeply convinced of this truth, the effect will be miraculous: we will be able to not only counter, but also convert the mind. The Bhagavad-gita (06.27) describes how diligent spiritual practice rids the mind of passion, makes it peaceful and reorients its inclinations. The day our mind becomes spiritually inclined, from that day our inner life becomes joyful – forever.

Thus, absorption in Krishna helps us break free from the onslaughts of the mind, initially temporarily by silencing it and eventually permanently by converting it.

☙❧

The yogi whose mind is fixed on Me verily attains the highest perfection of transcendental happiness. He is beyond the mode of passion, he realizes his qualitative identity with the Supreme, and thus he is freed from all reactions to past deeds.

51

Focus not on the reality of nature; focus on the nature of reality

The reality of nature: Most mainstream science today begins with the assumption of the reality of nature. In trying to understand nature, science equates the natural with the material. All the great theories of science are essentially attempts to understand what nature really is. These theories have led to enormous technological advancement, but a coherent conceptual framework about nature has remained elusive. For example, quantum physics and relativity are violently contradictory in their conceptions of the reality of nature: the first says waves; the second, particles. And no reconciliation seems anywhere near the horizon; in fact, even the location of the horizon appears unknown.

The nature of reality: Gita wisdom accepts the reality of nature, but focuses on the nature of reality. Reality, the Bhagavad-gita (07.06) indicates, is an integral whole centered on the Supreme Absolute Truth, Krishna. Nature is Krishna's energy, emanating from his wisdom and working under his will. Gita wisdom deems the current scientific approach misdirected, for it agonizes over the reality of nature without apprehending the nature of reality. Studying nature as if it were an independent reality without considering its connection with the whole is an intrinsically fragmented approach. Such an approach can yield at best disjointed islands of comprehension amidst an ocean of incomprehension. More consequentially, it can't show us the end of the ocean because the ocean alone is the object of study. The exclusivist study of matter can't illuminate the principles or purposes for living because both these are non-material concepts. The resulting darkness sentences millions to meaningless existence.

Gita wisdom releases us from this sentence by informing us that life's purpose is loving harmonization with Krishna. It offers the key principle of devotionally utilizing everything, including nature, for that purpose. By, using nature as a tool for transforming our hearts from disharmony to harmony, each one of us can realize the nature of reality.

৩৮০

All created beings have their source in these two natures. Of all that is material and all that is spiritual in this world, know for certain that I am both the origin and the dissolution.

Don't rumble, grumble and tumble –be humble

Our media periodically presents us with celebrities who are self-obsessed egotists. Three words sum their life-trajectory: rumble, grumble, tumble.

Rumble: These people are so self-obsessed that they don't find any subject except themselves worth talking about. As soon as they get a chance, they start rumbling about all the Mount Everests they have scaled, though most people can't see any mount nearby, leave alone the Everest.

Grumble: When life doesn't make way for their dreams, they start grumbling as if the combined weights of multiple Mount Everest were crushing them. As reality grinds into their dreams and leaves little room for self-praise, their self-obsession vents itself in self-pity.

Tumble: Gradually but inevitably, time diminishes and decimates their vaunted abilities, leaving them with nothing to brag about. As much as they had raised themselves high in the sky by their self-obsessed imagination, that much is their tumble as reality fells and flattens their fanciful Everests.

This life trajectory might be a bit exaggerated, but we will probably find in our own heart a miniature version of such an egotist, downsized according to our abilities, waiting to propel us on a similar tragic trajectory.

Humble: Gita wisdom opens a better trajectory for us. The Bhagavad-gita (07.08) indicates that our abilities are not our own; all abilities belong to Krishna. The abilities that we presently have are borrowed from him for the duration that our past good karma warrants. As soon as our good karma runs out – and none of us know when it will – our abilities will return to their actual owner, leaving us only with the consequences of our use, underuse or abuse of those abilities. This insight grounds us in humility.

Gita wisdom reveals a further dynamic, devotional dimension of humility: replacing self-obsession with Krishna-glorification. When we use our abilities to glorify Krishna, we relish the supreme fulfillment.

ॐ

I am the ability in man.

The more sex is glamorized, the more it gets devalued?

*O*ur contemporary culture constantly glamorizes sex through gaudy images permeated with sexual undertones and overtones. Due to this incessant glamorization of sex, most people live perpetually in a state of artificial sexual stimulation; sex tends to be a perennial top-ranker in their wish list.

Paradoxically, the more people glamorize sex in their imagination, the more they devalue it in real life. This devaluation takes two forms:

1.An increasingly utilitarian approach to sex: Many people, often unmarried, indulge in sex casually just for getting a short-lived high or, more frequently, just for temporarily getting rid of a tormenting urge.

2.An increasing feeling of emptiness in the experience of sex: Many people find the actual sexual experience disappointing and even boring because the experienced pleasure always turns out to be pale and stale when contrasted with the fantasized pleasure.

Gita wisdom offers a fascinating insight on sex. The Bhagavad-gita (07.11) states that sex, when performed in harmony with natural spiritual principles, is an opportunity to experience the divine. Sex offers humans the divine pleasure of assisting God in bringing new life into the world.

However, humanity is the only species in nature that unnaturally divorces copulation from procreation by artificial means like contraception. This unnatural divorce divests sex of its divine aspect, thereby reducing it to a primarily physical activity. The pleasure in it usually gets reduced to the secretion, ejection and reception of chemicals. This, according to Gita wisdom, is a disastrous devaluation of sex that distracts us from the purpose of sex and the purpose of life itself.

To help us restore sex to its proper dignified place in our life, Gita wisdom gently urges us to redirect our quest for happiness to the spiritual level and harmonize sex with that quest.

CREO

I am the strength of the strong, devoid of passion and desire. I am sex life which is not contrary to religious principles, O lord of the Bharatas [Arjuna].

Dig the grave of materialism, functional and fanatical

Materialism comes in two main brands: fanatical materialism which claims that matter is all that exists; and functional materialism which claims that matter is all that matters.

Fanatical materialists have no empirical or logical proof that nothing exists beyond matter. They reject the time-honored warning that materialism strips life of meaning, purpose and fulfillment. They neglect the sociological findings that materialism inevitably breeds immorality and perversity. For them, matter is their one and only god, unquestionable and non-negotiable, no matter what the cost.

Functional materialists are far more numerous than their fanatical cousins. These milder materialists don't deny the non-material or spiritual level of reality; they just delay thinking about it because they are too enamored by material pleasures.

Material life's inbuilt upheavals like bereavements, accidents and diseases expose the hollowness of faith in materialism. Such exposes impel functional materialists to inquire seriously about what lies beyond matter. If they have had some devotionally congenial impressions (sukriti), they seek relief by approaching Krishna, as the Bhagavad-gita (7.16) confirms.

Fanatical materialists rarely wake up even after undergoing life's upheavals. They need far stronger shock treatments that may span several lifetimes in sub-human bodies and subterranean places. To save them from such unnecessary suffering, devotees offer them spirituality in an appealing form like sanctified food. If fanatical materialists somehow appreciate Krishna, at least in his easily appreciable form as prasad, then this appreciation tills the ground of their hearts for the sowing of the seeds of pious credits.

Due to these pious credits, both brands of materialists, on being betrayed by materialism, feel inspired to repose faith in Krishna. Over time, they experience that Krishna never lets them down, although they had let him down for so long. Energized by this experience, they dig a grave for their materialism and bury it forever.

ॐ

O best among the Bharatas, four kinds of pious men begin to render devotional service unto Me—the distressed, the desirer of wealth, the inquisitive, and he who is searching for knowledge of the Absolute.

We can't create paradise, nor were we created in paradise – but we can go to paradise

*M*any technologists feel that hi-tech appliances will gradually provide necessities and luxuries for more and more people. Thus, they posit that we humans will create a technological paradise on earth.

In radical contrast, many environmentalists feel that nature provides for the needs of all its inhabitants through its delicate and intricate harmony. We were created into paradise, they aver, but we are ruining it by our reckless technological interferences into nature's workings.

Who is right: the technologists or the environmentalists?

"Neither," answers Gita wisdom.

The Bhagavad-gita (08.15) indicates that our world is intrinsically miserable and temporary. Even at its pristine best, it is no paradise – it is filled with disease, old age and death.

Of course, environmentalists are right about the counterproductive effects of the indiscriminate adoption of technology. When we try to make things better using technology, we might seem to succeed temporarily. But over time we frequently end up making things worse, not better. This is evident in the imminent specters of pollution, deforestation, desertification, climate change and exhaustion of fossil fuels – most of which originated in our techno-driven attempts to transform this world into paradise. So, technologists often get it much more wrong than do environmentalists.

Taking this discussion to a deeper philosophical level, Gita wisdom indicates that existence has three essential principles (*tattva-traya*): the living beings, material nature and Krishna. Technologists ascribe the power of creating paradise to living beings; environmentalists ascribe it to material nature. But that power rests with Krishna alone. And he informs us that eternal paradise awaits us if we learn to love him and thereby return to his abode. On our devotional journey back to Krishna a natural, eco-friendly lifestyle presents far lesser distractions than an artificial techno-centric lifestyle. Nonetheless, the devotional journey is possible through both. That's why devotees focus neither on technology nor on ecology, but on Krishna.

☙❧

After attaining Me, the great souls, who are yogis in devotion, never return to this temporary world, which is full of miseries, because they have attained the highest perfection.

Material nature is characterized by cyclic process, not linear progress

Our mainstream culture makes us believe that life at the material level is linearly progressive; so, our efforts can make things better materially. This belief is so deeply ingrained in our culture that we hardly ever scrutinize or even notice it.

However, this belief is not reflected in the course of nature. Widespread in nature are demonstrations of not linear progress, but cyclic process. Within each generation, trees grow and shed leaves in cycles. From one generation to another, life forms repeat the same cycles: creation, growth, maintenance, reproduction, deterioration and destruction. Overhead, the planets move about in cycles. The phases of the moon are cyclic, as are the alteration of seasons. Even our units of time are cyclic. The Bhagavad-gita (08.19) underscores that such cyclic changes of repeated creation, maintenance and destruction are an inherent, invariable feature of material existence.

Of course, we humans have more free will than other species. So we can, if we so desire, try to militate against this cyclic nature. We can temporarily bend nature through human-made technology and temporarily coax history to support our pet notion of linear progress through selective rewriting.

But we just can't change the cyclic nature of our own lives: we begin with childhood and end in the second childhood, old age, where we often become helpless like children. Further, we can't change the cyclic nature of the repetition of birth and death.

Therefore, Gita wisdom urges us to use our free will not to futilely bend nature from cyclic to linear, but to transcend material existence by progressing in spiritual life. When we connect lovingly with Krishna through devotional service, then and then alone do our hopes for linear progress actualize; by his mercy, we are raised straight upwards to his eternal abode.

ॐ

Again and again, when Brahma's day arrives, all living entities come into being, and with the arrival of Brahma's night they are helplessly annihilated.

Attraction to the supernatural is natural

Supernatural stunts in cartoons and sci-fi movies attract not only common people, but also diehard skeptics who usually denounce anything supernatural. They happily suspend their skepticism and enjoy watching stunts that are naturally impossible.

Despite their commitment to naturalism, what makes them enjoy the supernatural? It's the heart.

Naturalism helps us see in the world the orderliness that our head demands. This orderliness gives the head a sense of control, of knowing what to expect and how to respond.

But this orderliness also brings in its wake ordinariness.

The naturalist worldview with its predictable law-governed landscape banishes mystery out of the world. Yet our heart longs for the exciting and extraordinary, the magical and the marvelous. This longing finds a gateway to fulfillment in fiction. No wonder the heart pushes the head aside to enjoy fiction.

Gita wisdom informs us that we can enjoy more than just a few such moments, as offered by fiction; we can enjoy an eternity of them. Moreover, we don't have to squeeze that enjoyment out of fantasy; we can savor it in a reality that exceeds fantasy.

We are souls who can relish an eternal loving relationship with the supreme stunt star, Krishna. As he is the controller of material nature (Bhagavad-gita 09.10), he isn't bound by its laws. The only law that binds him is the law of love; to reciprocate love with his devotees, he sometimes acts inside natural laws and sometimes outside them.

The result? Krishna-lila: Adventures with the most fantastic fabric of magic within the most touching tapestry of love.

Our attraction to the supernatural is natural. And it's naturally fulfilled in Krishna-lila. Fiction is a distant and distorted reflection of this original.

Why settle for anything less than the original?

ॐ

This material nature, which is one of My energies, is working under My direction, O son of Kunti, producing all moving and nonmoving beings. Under its rule this manifestation is created and annihilated again and again.

Go beyond captivity to futility and utility

As practicing spiritualists, we may face the question, "What should be my attitude towards the material world?"

Let's first look at the three broad attitudes that we can have towards the world:

1. **Captivity:** When we live primarily for material pleasures, we try to bring the material world under our captivity. We hope to bend the world to our will so as to extract our desired pleasures from it. Paradoxically though, as long as we try to bring the world under our captivity, we stay under its captivity; we remain captivated by its seductive promises of pleasure. We can't strive for any pleasures beyond the worldly.

2. **Futility:** When we chase after worldly pleasures, we realize that they are elusive to get; even if we get them, they turn out to be shallow and unsatisfactory; even if we settle for them, time drags them away. When we thus realize their elusiveness, shallowness and temporariness, we reject them as futile.

3. **Utility:** Gita wisdom informs us that we are souls and children of Krishna. We can relish spiritual happiness if we become pure by rendering devotional service. To that end, we can use all the worldly resources that are helpful in serving him. The Bhagavad-gita points to this principle of utility when it (09.27) urges us to offer all our activities and resources to Krishna.

Thus, our attitude towards the material world needs to go beyond captivity to futility and utility: rejecting as futile the material pleasures that make us forget Krishna, and accepting as useful the material resources that help us serve him.

ॐ

Whatever you do, whatever you eat, whatever you offer or give away, and whatever austerities you perform—do that, O son of Kunti, as an offering to Me.

The world is in a mess – as usual

The daily news of natural disasters like hurricanes and human-made distresses like corruption show that the world is in a terrible mess. Seeing this, we may feel: Can I, one small human being, make any significant difference?

Gita wisdom informs that we surely can – provided we first see things differently. We need to see that the messy state of the world is its usual nature, as the Bhagavad-gita (09.33) indicates.

Does this mean that we become callous towards the sufferings of people?

Not at all; it just means that we don't let sentimentality prevent us from acknowledging reality. The world is like a hospital; suffering is to be expected here. The earlier the people in a hospital unsentimentally accept the inevitability of suffering there, that much earlier they can get on with the treatment – either take it themselves or administer it to others or do both.

The most potent treatment in this hospital-like world is devotional service to Krishna, as the same Gita verse states. Just as basic medical education explains how an oral medicine can counter a back-pain, basic philosophical education explains how devotional service can counter the world's pressing problems. Let's understand this briefly.

Human-made distresses are caused by people excessively infected by the modes of passion and ignorance. Natural disasters are the mass karmic reactions to disharmonious actions done by societies afflicted by the lower modes. In both cases, the cause is infection by materialism.

Devotional service cures this infection by providing us experiences of higher spiritual happiness. The more we practice and share devotional service, the more we contribute not only to minimizing the mess here but also to helping people become successfully discharged from this hospital and return to eternal joyful life with Krishna.

That is the significant difference each of us can – and should – make.

⚮

Therefore, having come to this temporary, miserable world, engage in loving service unto Me.

The Gita shows the route to the root

"*Let's* go back to our roots." This passion consumes many people. Some of them take the route of genealogical investigation for discovering unsung ancestors. Others take the route of historical research for discovering unknown national glories.

At a deep, often subconscious level, we are frequently motivated by the feeling that we may have lost something precious due to having forgotten our roots. By going back to our roots, we hope to reclaim that lost treasure.

Gita wisdom agrees with our hope: we do indeed have a priceless legacy to regain by going back to our roots – our spiritual roots. The Gita asserts that we are at our core souls, and our present birth in particular clans and countries is circumstantial, temporal and peripheral to our real identity. So, if we wish to search for our actual roots, we need to search for our spiritual roots, lest our quest go off on a tangent.

The Bhagavad-gita (10.08) reveals Krishna to be the ultimate root of everything in existence – including our clans and our countries. When we retrace our roots back to him, there we discover our ultimate legacy awaiting us: eternal love. We realize that the root of all our roots, Krishna, is the supreme object for our love. He is all-attractive, he already loves us and he is longing for our love. Loving him makes us everlastingly happy.

Gita wisdom further offers us the route to enter into that life of endless love: the simple yet sublime practice of bhakti-yoga. When we thus take the route of devotion to the root of Krishna, we attain the ultimate love that transcends death and flourishes for all of eternity.

☙❧

I am the source of all spiritual and material worlds. Everything emanates from Me. The wise who perfectly know this engage in My devotional service and worship Me with all their hearts.

"Live for the moment?" But the moment doesn't live for you

"*Live* for the moment." So chimes the materialist credo. It is a curious slogan, assuming as it does that a moment is itself an entity worth living for. But within the materialist belief system, the moment is just a unit of time that has no sentience; it doesn't live for us. In fact, it doesn't live at all.

Therefore, no one can live for the moment; everyone lives the moment for something.

What is the something that materialism wants us to live for?

Ultimately, it is just material pleasure. And material pleasure is never available at every moment. It is limited because both the external objects of enjoyment and the bodily tools for enjoyment are temporary. That's why material pleasure never lives for more than a few moments. So living for material pleasure means living for those few moments – and hankering and lamenting for all the remaining moments.

Isn't there a better something to live for?

Gita wisdom offers the best something to live the moment for: Krishna. He is a loving, endearing person, who lives every moment for us if we choose to live our moment for him. Krishna is the supreme reservoir of unending happiness. When we connect with him through devotional remembrance, we start relishing a sublime happiness that is far superior to the most glamorized material pleasure. Whereas worldly objects of enjoyment are temporary, Krishna is eternal. Whereas our bodily tools for enjoyment are temporary, our spiritual connection with Krishna is eternal because we as souls are eternal. All we need to do is revive that ability by practicing devotional service.

The Bhagavad-gita (10.09) indicates that those who have revived that ability live every moment joyfully for Krishna – for all moments to come, eternally.

ॐ

The thoughts of My pure devotees dwell in Me, their lives are fully devoted to My service, and they derive great satisfaction and bliss from always enlightening one another and conversing about Me.

Devotion protects us from destruction by distraction

Just as weapons of mass destruction can destroy thousands of bodies, weapons of mass distraction – the mass media – can destroy thousands of minds. Let's see how.

All of us are innately pleasure-seeking. Usually, our search for pleasure is primarily driven by the mind, which searches almost exclusively at the material level. Our mind gets attracted to anything new that promises material pleasure, be it an event, object, person, concept or experience. However, the charm of newness surrounding that object soon fades, and the mind loses interest in it. It gets attracted to some other new thing, and when disappointed there, to yet another new thing. Thus, the mind stays in a default distraction mode. Our mass media with its multiple TV channels and innumerable internet sites increases manifold the avenues of distraction for the mind, thereby keeping us distracted aimlessly and endlessly. The mass media act as weapons of mass distraction that destroy our mental capacity for deep thought.

How can we protect ourselves from such distraction?

By absorption in Krishna.

The Bhagavad-Gita (10.41) points out that whatever attracts us in this world is a spark of Krishna's splendor. As the things of this world are just sparks, their potential to hold our attraction is short-lived, and so we keep getting distracted from one thing to the next. As Krishna is the whole, his potential to hold our attention is infinite, and so our attraction to him can be ever-lasting.

Tragically however, even when we come in contact with Krishna, the mind stays in its default distraction mode and doesn't let us become absorbed in him. We can end this distraction by using Gita wisdom to strengthen our intellectual conviction that absorption in him will deliver us internally far greater pleasure than all the pleasure that is alluring us externally.

ॐ

Know that all opulent, beautiful and glorious creations spring from but a spark of My splendor.

Grasp the sense, the nonsense and the trans-sense of worldly mania

*O*ur world is beset by various manias: filmstar-mania, sportstar-mania, musician-mania, to name a few. Some of us may have wondered: why do people spend so much of their hard-earned money, their precious time and especially their emotional energy on these ephemeral and fallible icons? Why can't they see the irrationality and the profligacy of their mania?

Gita wisdom offers fascinating insights on this issue. The Bhagavad-gita (10.41) indicates that whatever we find attractive in the world derives its potency to attract from the all-attractive Supreme Lord, Krishna. This insight reveals the sense, the nonsense and the trans-sense of worldly mania:

The Sense: We recognize that the cause of maniac attraction is not the particular person, but the spark of Krishna that is manifesting through that person.

The Nonsense: We understand the futility and the tragedy of all worldly mania. A spark of fire can allure but never deliver the warmth available from the whole fire. Similarly, the temporary feats of worldly heroes can allure but never deliver the fulfillment of heart and upliftment of spirit available from the eternal and unlimited qualities of the supreme hero, Krishna.

The Trans-sense (The Transcendental Sense): We can become encouraged in our attempts to enhance our attraction for Krishna by contemplating thus: "If a tiny spark of Krishna has so much attractive potency, how much more attractive potency must Krishna have? If I just persevere in my devotional service and beseech Krishna's mercy, soon he will remove all of my heart's misdirected attractions which are like the rusts on iron that are preventing me from being drawn in by his magnetic all-attractiveness. When I become purified, I will be overpoweringly, irresistibly attracted to Krishna, and thereby attain life's ultimate perfection."

☙❧

Know that all opulent, beautiful and glorious creations spring from but a spark of My splendor.

Take a sage look at time management

"*Time* management" is a trendy word. The trend, though, is to focus on management, not on time. People value time for its utilitarian worth, as a resource to be managed so as to get things done. Viewing time as a resource naturally elicits its comparison with money. Time is more precious than money, say people with a sage look.

A sage looks at time, informs Gita wisdom, with a far deeper appreciation, valuing it not just for its utilitarian worth, but also for its intrinsic worth – for what it is, in and of itself. The Bhagavad-gita (11.32) emphasizes that time is a manifestation of Krishna.

Gita wisdom dramatically spiritualizes our vision of time management. It helps us understand that our time is not ours; it is Krishna's. In fact, it is not just Krishna's; it is Krishna. This means that we are not managing time, we are managing Krishna. As Krishna is the supreme manager, managing him essentially means letting ourselves be managed by him. So from a spiritual perspective, time management actually means managing our life according to Krishna's plan, orienting it to revive our love for him.

Time management with this vision can be called spiritual time management, as contrasted with material time management that sees time merely as a resource. Spiritual time management is supremely rewarding – both in the present and in the future. In the present, material time management often makes us feel pressured, strained, and tense due to all that needs to be done, whereas spiritual time management makes us feel enlivened due to the contact with Krishna as time that each moment offers. In the future, material time management can't award us even one thing that will last beyond death, whereas spiritual time management can award us divine love that will last forever and ever.

രുജ്ഞ

The Supreme Personality of Godhead said: Time I am.

History is His-story

*H*istory, if seen from a purely materialistic perspective, seems to be nothing more than a list of names of dead successful people. Decade after decade, century after century, millennia after millennia, people come, people live, people die. What is the point of it all?

Gita wisdom offers us an alternative perspective of history that doesn't deny the futility of the material reality, but reveals an additional divine dimension that can help us find meaning amidst the madness and direction amidst the destruction.

The Bhagavad-gita (11.32) describes that time is a manifestation of Krishna. Overall, the eleventh chapter of the Gita demonstrates the dynamic connectedness of Krishna with the material world: he is not just a passive cosmic presence, but also an active universal agent who is shaping history according to his benevolent will for the gradual purification and eventual redemption of all.

This enlightened vision of Krishna as the ultimate historical agent enables us to see history in a new light as His-story. Krishna is orchestrating the chaotic and even destructive events on the world-stage as the unavoidable storm necessary to raise human consciousness to the divine level. There and there alone can the human heart relish an unbreakable calm in a life of eternal loving service to Krishna.

This insight provides us, as it did to Arjuna, with the double empowerment of relief and confidence:

1. **Relief** because we realize that we don't have to worry about how everything and everyone will shape up; there is a far greater intelligence taking care of that.

2. **Confidence** because we recognize that if we just do our part, a higher agent will come to our aid, in fact, use us in his aid, and bring about a beneficent result for one and all.

ॐ

Time I am, the great destroyer of the worlds.

We don't have to stay suspended between the unknowable and the unavoidable

*A*s we rush about on our daily routines, we periodically check the clock to see if we are on time. Yet we rarely check where we are in time, where we are headed as time rushes us unerringly forward.

If we checked, we would find ourselves suspended between two mighty destinies: the unknowable and the unavoidable.

1. **The unknowable:** The future extends ahead of us, like an opaque looking glass, through which we can see very little. And whatever little we see can change by one rap on the glass, one upheaval in the tiny something that we call the present.

2. **The unavoidable:** What doesn't change within the looking glass is what we are least inclined to look at: the unavoidable miseries of old age, disease and death. These are the disagreeable invariables among the unknowable variables that otherwise comprise our future.

We try fervently to wish away this unavoidable while wishing even more fervently that the unknowable turns out to be palatable. Life renders both wishes futile.

Yet, Gita wisdom assures us, life is not doomed to futility. The Bhagavad-gita (13.09) indicates that the miseries of old age, disease and death, when observed unblinkingly and unflinchingly, compel us to seek an alternative trajectory for our future.

And an alternative does exist.

Gita wisdom reminds us that we are indestructible souls, who can reclaim eternal life by redirecting our love towards Krishna. This redirection brings a reassuring, knowable fixture in the unknowable variables of life: Krishna's omni-benevolence that orchestrates everything for our ultimate good. This redirection gradually makes the entire material level avoidable, transcended by absorption in immortal spiritual love.

Realizing that we are not suspended in the uncertainty of uncaring chance, but are enveloped in the certainty of unfailing love is life's greatest discovery.

ॐ

….The perception of the evil of birth, death, old age and disease; detachment;…—all these I declare to be knowledge, and besides this whatever there may be is ignorance.

Don't let lifestyle get in the way of living

"*You* are your watch!" So says a billboard. It implies that our watch makes a statement about who we are, what our status is and what our economic bracket is.

Such infatuation with externals characterizes our culture, which almost compels us to equate lifestyle with living. By constantly bombarding us with ads, billboards and commercials, our culture sucks much of our mental energy into dreaming about improving our lifestyle. Indeed, lifestyle becomes the purpose and essence of our living. This obsession with lifestyle deprives us of the simple and real joys of living at even the material level, what to speak of the spiritual level. It doesn't leave us the time, the peace or the patience to form meaningful relationships with the persons around us – leave alone the person within us, Krishna.

Gita wisdom frees our living from being so lifestyle-driven. The Bhagavad-gita (13.12) indicates that understanding the eternality of spiritual knowledge (*adhyatma-jnana nityatvam*) characterizes those in knowledge. With Gita wisdom, we understand that the difference between lifestyle and living largely parallels the difference between the material and the spiritual.

Most of what today's culture calls lifestyle keeps us riveted to the material level. There, we get at best a tiny bit of unfulfilling pleasure and at worst a lot of unbearable misery. Real living, on the other hand, happens only at the spiritual level. The soul alone is alive and is the source of all the activity associated with living. At the spiritual level alone can we form meaningful relationships with Krishna and with all living beings as his children – and thereby relish lasting and fulfilling happiness.

When we give the spiritual its due priority in our lives, then lifestyle can no longer come in the way of living.

ॐ

Accepting the importance of self-realization; and philosophical search for the Absolute Truth—all these I declare to be knowledge, and besides this whatever there may be is ignorance.

Be not human silkworms – be humans

Nature is rich with demonstrations of spiritual truths. One central truth is that our misery is often self-inflicted, as nature demonstrates through the silkworm. It makes a cocoon around itself for the sake of protection, but that very cocoon usually ends becoming the cause of its destruction.

Gita wisdom indicates that we are, in a way, human silkworms. We are essentially spiritual beings, but are currently encaged by material desires that propel us to seek protection and pleasure in material objects.

However, everything material is by its very nature temporary. That's why, as time takes its toll, the same material things that promise to be sources of protection become the causes of devastation. Whatever gives us pleasure when we possess it gives us pain when time dispossesses us. The Bhagavad-gita (13.22) indicates that our own desire to enjoy the material (*bhunkte prakrti jaan gunaan*) creates a cocoon of material attachments that end in misery. Thus do we become human silkworms.

The silkworm, by its death, provides valuable silk to humans. In pitiful contrast, we, by our death, don't provide anything valuable to anyone. This dissimilarity indicates that we are no good at imitating silkworms; it's best that we start acting as humans.

Gita wisdom underscores that humans have the potential to ascend to a spiritual arena that is beyond destruction. Unleashing that potential involves redirecting our need for protection and pleasure towards Krishna. When we make Krishna the center of our hearts and lives, then everything we do, far from increasing our entanglement, accelerates our journey towards the spiritual level of consciousness. There, our longing for protection and pleasure is never frustrated, but ever fulfilled – and fulfilled beyond the greatest promises at the material level.

ॐ

The living entity in material nature thus follows the ways of life, enjoying the three modes of nature. This is due to his association with that material nature. Thus he meets with good and evil amongst various species.

Spiritual enforcement reaches where legal enforcement doesn't

Corruption, crime, cruelty – these are increasing by the day. Faced with this spiral, the law enforcement agencies are often not only overworked, but also under-staffed. After all, the law enforcers will always be outnumbered by the citizens. Worse still, many times the law-enforcers themselves become law-breakers. Supervisors may be appointed to watch the law-enforcers, but who will oversee those supervisors? When everybody is corruptible, where will the hierarchical ladder of supervisors rest?

Nowhere, if people restrict themselves to a materialist view of life.

But this restrictive view is not mandatory. Gita wisdom explains that if we free ourselves from materialism, the rest for this ladder will become self-evident: Krishna, the supreme supervisor of all supervisors. The Bhagavad-gita (13.23) indicates that Krishna resides in the heart of all of us as the overseer and permitter (upadrashta anumanta ca).

When we become aware of the presence of Krishna in our own hearts, that awareness reinforces our conscience and checks us from our own immoral impulses. The check comes in two primary ways. Initially it comes as fear, when we wish to avoid the negative karmic consequences resulting from immoral actions. Eventually it comes as love, when we wish to attain eternal love for Krishna, an attainment that preliminarily requires moral conduct. Thus, our awareness of Krishna makes us our own policepersons protecting us from ourselves.

Undoubtedly, some people will not care for morality and will perpetrate crimes. So law enforcers are indispensable in human society. But their work becomes unmanageable when most people have no inner moral checks and tend to break the law at the smallest opportunity. Their work becomes much easier when most people have access to spiritual wisdom that reaches where law enforcers can't – into the hearts of people – and turns on the moral compass there.

ॐ

Yet in this body there is another, a transcendental enjoyer, who is the Lord, the supreme proprietor, who exists as the overseer and permitter, and who is known as the Supersoul.

How the world sees us is not as important as how we see the world

We often worry about how the world sees us: "Do people notice me? Which way do heads turn when I arrive?"

This outside-in approach seems natural for us because the outside world seems much easier to know than the inside self. The school, the media and the culture tell us about the world. But who tells us about the self? Practically no one. As the inside is a disconcertingly dark area, we focus on an area that seems better lit: the outside.

Such an outside-in approach makes us feel that we are nobodies if we can't evoke the world's nod, smile or pat. Unfortunately, what the world approves is often both fickle and superficial: fickle because it changes constantly with the fashions, and superficial because it doesn't address our innermost needs. Consequently, we feel distressingly insecure, ever-dependent on the world's unsteady and unsatisfactory judgment.

If we want to be internally secure, we need to adopt an inside-out approach. Gita wisdom aids us in this by systematically informing us about what lies inside: the soul, the real me. The Bhagavad-gita (13.32) indicates that as souls we have nothing to do with the world; our real life is in loving service to Krishna in the eternal spiritual world. This knowledge profoundly alters our perception of the world around us. We see it as a passing station on our journey to his abode. Instead of agonizing about how the world sees us, we focus instead on how we see it, how we can use it to develop our loving relationship with him. We learn to see in every worldly situation an opportunity to serve him and move closer to him.

Once we develop this vision, we can experience security and serenity even amidst the world's uncertainty.

CRED

Those with the vision of eternity can see that the imperishable soul is transcendental, eternal, and beyond the modes of nature. Despite contact with the material body, O Arjuna, the soul neither does anything nor is entangled.

Mind the medium through which you experience the world

In our culture, we mostly experience the real world second-hand: not by directly interacting with it using our senses, but by receiving it as depicted by the media, especially television.

When television reports events from the real world, as in the daily news, it reports not transparently but selectively, focusing on those real life events that are entertaining. Even its reports of non-entertaining tragic events like natural calamities are conveyed in an atmosphere that says: "don't take this seriously." This is evident in the concluding call of the daily news: "do join us tomorrow." Why join again after having heard enough news of death and deceit and destruction to cause several sleepless nights? Only a miniscule fraction of the news affects us directly, and an even lesser fraction of those events can be affected by us. Then why join again? To be entertained. The unspoken message is: "All this is meant to entertain. Join us tomorrow for another session of entertainment."

The point is not that we stay ignorant of worldly events but that we rise beyond being merely entertained by them to becoming illumined through them about the true nature of the world. For such illumination, we need to make scriptural knowledge the medium for our experience of the world. The Bhagavad-gita (13.35) recommends that we use jnana-chakshu (eyes of knowledge) to analyze our experience of the world. Such a vision will enable us to see philosophical truths demonstrated through worldly events. The more we see the Gita's message vindicated in real life, the more we will feel inspired to apply it in our own lives. Only then will our experience of the world become meaningful and fruitful by preparing us to seek eternal blissful life beyond this world of mortality and misery.

ॐ

Those who see with eyes of knowledge the difference between the body and the knower of the body, and can also understand the process of liberation from bondage in material nature, attain to the supreme goal.

Self-help can't help without divine help

The Bhagavad-gita (14.10) indicates how the subtle forces of nature known as the modes exert competing psychological influences on us. Their contrary influences cause our feelings to change rapidly, unpredictably and inexplicably, for example, from introspection (induced by the mode of goodness) to agitation (induced by the mode of passion) to frustration (induced by the mode of ignorance)

Some of us may experience this downward spiral when we try to apply sensible principles from self-help books, principles that often align with the mode of goodness. However, the horse race pace of our lifestyle catapults us into the mode of passion which creates priorities at variance with our principles. Further, passion eventually – and often inevitably – degenerates into ignorance; our unbalanced priorities create relentless stress that makes us seek relief in self-defeating practices, indulgences that offer fleeting pleasures and lasting troubles.

Principles in goodness, priorities in passion, practices in ignorance – this aptly describes the fate of self-help.

The Gita (14.26) points the way to real self-help: seek divine help. Devotional service connects us with a power greater than the power of the modes: the power of Krishna. That divine connection empowers us to resist and reject the self-sabotaging influences of the modes. Only then can we harmonize our principles, priorities and practices, and gradually experience fulfillment internally and achievement externally.

CR&O

Sometimes the mode of goodness becomes prominent, defeating the modes of passion and ignorance, O son of Bharata. Sometimes the mode of passion defeats goodness and ignorance, and at other times ignorance defeats goodness and passion. In this way there is always competition for supremacy.

Go beyond rapidity and vapidity to clarity and serenity

*O*ur current materialistic culture impels us to lead lives characterized by rapidity and vapidity:

- **Rapidity:** In the rapid mode, we are in a tearing hurry to get things done, to somehow cope with the pressure of the many items that jump out at us from our to-do list.

- **Vapidity:** In the vapid mode, we are in a passive frenzy to get things forgotten, to somehow get away from the tiresome pressure by burying ourselves in mindless entertainment.

These two modes broadly correspond to the Bhagavad-gita's descriptions of the modes of passion and ignorance respectively. Gita wisdom points out that our life will be more meaningful spiritually and more fruitful materially if we switch to functioning at the higher levels of goodness and transcendence.

- **Clarity:** Functioning in goodness, the Gita (14.11) explains, brings clarity. This clarity enables us to practically implement the time-management tips recommended by many contemporary management teachers like classifying and prioritizing our work according to urgent and non-urgent, important and non-important etc. But more significantly, this clarity empowers us to choose not just our actions, but also our desires. We realize that many of the desires induced by the consumer culture are irrelevant to us as spiritual beings. Further, we recognize our core need for a loving relationship with the Supreme. So, while taking care of our material requirements, we reorganize our life lives so as to satisfy that spiritual need.

- **Serenity:** When we use this clear perspective of life to streamline our desires, we transcend the material and connect with the divine, thereby relishing an unshakeable serenity. Thanks to this inner serenity, we become guided to contribute effectively as channels of divine change in the outer world.

⚛

The manifestations of the mode of goodness can be experienced when all the gates of the body are illuminated by knowledge.

Be not dulled and lulled by TV

Few consumer products shape the contemporary home as much as a television. Few images represent a contemporary family better than a group of people, physically cloistered and emotionally distanced, huddled around a TV, staring, cheering, glaring and leering at the alluring images that whiz in and out of existence on the screen. For most people who watch TV, there is neither meaningful contemplation nor purposeful action; there is just mindless consumption of the sound-and-sight fare being dished out.

This effect that TV often has on us is, from the perspective of the Bhagavad-gita (14.13), typical of the mode of ignorance. This mode reduces us to a kind of paralysis by divesting us of our capacities of both contemplation and action. The effect of the mode of ignorance can perhaps best be described as the dulling and lulling effect:

- **Dulling effect:** Our intellectual faculties get atrophied by disuse so that we find it difficult to use them even when we need and want to.

- **Lulling effect:** Our physical capacities get weakened by continuous inactivity so that we become prone to many of the diseases typical to a sedentary lifestyle.

Gita wisdom describes that, if we wish to break free from this paralyzing effect of the mode of ignorance, then we need to annul our desire for lazy illusory pleasure and kindle our desire for dynamic spiritual happiness. We can do both by rendering devotional service to Krishna. And the more we practice devotional service, the more we get tuned to a spiritual TV that keeps beaming to us the presence and guidance of Krishna constantly, thereby inspiring us toward joyful contemplation and fruitful action.

ॐ

When there is an increase in the mode of ignorance, O son of Kuru, darkness, inertia, madness and illusion are manifested.

Insanity is not compulsory

We have probably witnessed normal sane people suddenly behaving abnormally, even insanely. We may have seen this happening to ourselves. For some people, this abnormal self-defeating behavior becomes so habitual that, though it threatens their career, relationships, finances, health and even life, they passively rationalize it by saying, "That's just the way I am; that's my nature."

Is it really? Is insanity compulsory?

No, declares Gita wisdom. All of us are souls who are originally characterized by not just sanity, but also serenity and even felicity. The Bhagavad-gita (14.13) indicates that insane behavior (*pramada*) results from the predomination of the mode of ignorance in our mind. This accumulated mode of ignorance first sabotages our normal intelligence (*aprakasha*), then distorts our normal behavioral pattern (*apravrtti*), and finally impels us to self-destructive actions.

Among the three modes, the mode of ignorance is the lowest and the basest. That's why it perverts our original nature the most. Thankfully, this perversion, no matter how detrimental, is never irreversible. All of us have the power to reclaim our original pure nature. For this return to purity, we need to consciously expose ourselves to places (e.g. temples), people (e.g. devotees), actions (e.g. chanting) and emotions (e.g. ecstasy in kirtans) that are surcharged with spirituality. These transcendental stimuli revoke the influences of ignorance and invoke our dormant spiritual tendencies. The more we practice the art of exposing ourselves to transcendental influences, the more we become situated in our spiritual nature.

The ultimate transcendental influence – in fact, the source of all transcendental influences – is Krishna himself. When we expose ourselves to him internally by constantly thinking of him, then his presence in our consciousness protects us from all possible negative influences. Constant thought of Krishna is our best inner security and is eventually the source of the supreme everlasting ecstasy.

೧೪೪

When there is an increase in the mode of ignorance, O son of Kuru, darkness, inertia, madness and illusion are manifested.

Change not just the state of mind – change also the state of being

*M*any popular self-help books claim that we will become happy if we just change our state of mind from negative to positive. Is this true?

Certainly, changing a habitually pessimistic attitude to a consciously optimistic attitude can help us feel better. But will it change the reality that all of us have to grow old, get diseased and die? Will it change the miserable nature of material existence where we frequently don't get what we want and regularly get what we don't want? Will it change the fact that all material pleasures are too short-lived to satisfy our longing for constant happiness?

An honest answer to these questions has to be in the negative, as even a little contemplation on our own experience of material life will confirm.

The Bhagavad-gita (15.07) indicates that both the sensual and the mental levels are sources of suffering for the soul, whose original existence is beyond both these levels. At that trans-sensual, trans-mental spiritual level of being, the soul delights in an eternal loving relationship with Krishna, the source of supreme happiness.

We cannot return to the spiritual level of being merely by seeing the positive side of life while continuing to live materialistically. Instead, we need to follow the twofold path outlined by the Gita (13.10-11):

1. Leave the material level of being by becoming equipoised towards both the materially positive and the materially negative,

2. Transfer ourselves to the spiritual level of being by making Krishna the goal of our life and cultivating a lifestyle and social circle that furthers this goal.

Only when we spiritualize our values and purposes for living and thus change our state of being to spiritual will our longing for lasting happiness be factually and eternally fulfilled.

ॐ

The living entities in this conditioned world are My eternal fragmental parts. Due to conditioned life, they are struggling very hard with the six senses, which include the mind.

We are aliens on earth

*T*he possibility of aliens coming to the earth fascinates the contemporary imagination: "Can we encounter life-forms from other parts of the cosmos?" Science fiction regularly glamorizes this possibility, whereas science normally dismisses it.

Gita wisdom offers us an unexpected third perspective. It acknowledges the existence of extra-terrestrial life forms, but then reverses our alien-finder scope by raising the question: "Might we ourselves be the aliens here?" This question might seem outlandish because we are accustomed to think of ourselves as our material bodies whose entire existence is wedded to the earth. We tend to presume, "We belong to the earth, or, more precisely, the earth belongs to us."

However, is this presumption really justified? Life on earth is the only life that most of us remember or conceive. Nonetheless, isn't life on earth radically at odds with life as we would like it to be? We want to live forever, yet life on earth doesn't allow us to live forever. We want to be constantly happy, yet life on earth makes us only occasionally happy and instead makes us frequently miserable.

The drastic difference between our lofty expectation of life and its shoddy materialization on earth is undeniable. When we stop denying the undeniable, then we see the truth of the Gita assertion that the earth is alien to us and we are aliens on the earth. The Bhagavad-gita (15.07) indicates that we are souls, spiritual parts of Krishna. We belong originally to his eternal ecstatic abode, but are presently struggling under the shackles of the mind and the senses.

Once we recognize the alien-ness of earth, we can become one-pointed in expediting our stay here and striving to return where we belong – and thereby reclaim the life for which we long.

Ɑఙ৪ঞ

The living entities in this conditioned world are My eternal fragmental parts. Due to conditioned life, they are struggling very hard with the six senses, which include the mind.

Guard against the last-ditch attack of the false ego

The notion that we are ourselves God is the false ego's ultimate weapon. The false ego is the subtlest of all the subtle material elements. Its foundational weapon is the illusion that makes us, spirit souls, misidentify with our material bodies.

Releasing us from the deceptive grip of the false ego and restoring us to the dignity of our true ego as the beloved children of Krishna – this is the essential purpose of spirituality. All our philosophical analysis and all our devotional practices are meant to conquer the false ego and enthrone Krishna as the Lord of our heart.

That's why, if we start seeking authentic spirituality, the false ego makes a last-ditch effort to maintain its grip on us by putting on a spiritual masquerade. It tempts us with the ultimate hallucination, the supreme megalomania: "You yourself are God." Many intellectual seekers succumb to this ruse, and soon they become converted into mouthpieces of the false ego. These misguided spiritualists use all their intellectual brilliance to misinterpret scripture and misuse logic for marketing the anti-scriptural and illogical claim that we are God. The Bhagavad-gita (15.07) declares unequivocally that we are eternally the parts of God, never God – as is the overall scriptural conclusion. Further, logic exposes the patent absurdity of this god-claim: "How can God come under illusion? That would make illusion greater than God – and that contradicts the very definition of God as the Supreme Being."

When we encounter this absurd claim, we need to be penetrating enough to see through its spiritual masquerade and vigorous enough to expose it for what it is: the ultimate egocentric hallucination.

ॐ

The living entities in this conditioned world are My eternal fragmental parts. Due to conditioned life, they are struggling very hard with the six senses, which include the mind.

"Seeing is believing" reflects trust in the untrustworthy

The Bhagavad-gita (15.10) warns us against unwittingly subscribing to the childish idea of "seeing is believing." This idea, known in philosophical parlance as naïve realism, is the primitive belief system in which one imagines that reality is the way it appears to be. This belief system is based on an unquestioning trust in our senses as conveyors of reality. However, such trust is highly questionable because the senses provide us a link to reality that is ontologically inadequate and operationally unreliable. Let's see how:

1. **Ontologically inadequate:** The senses being material can never give us access to the nonmaterial dimensions of reality: God, the soul, the spiritual world.

2. **Operationally unreliable:** The senses subject us to a variety of misperceptions by making us see what doesn't exist, as in the case of mirages.

No wonder then that Gita wisdom deplores as misled those who unthinkingly trust their senses, believing that what looks good is actually good. Such people self-righteously sentence themselves to the sufferings of material existence. Worse still, they deprive themselves of the life of meaning and fulfilment that awaits them at the invisible spiritual level in loving service to Krishna.

Instead of trusting the untrustworthy senses that are inadequate and unreliable guides to reality, Gita wisdom urges us to trust scriptural vision for gaining a fuller and safer picture of reality. This vision of reality integrates our longing for immortality and our longing for love in a magnificently coherent Krishna-centered worldview. And the practice of devotional service transforms this intellectual vision into an experienced reality.

Thus it is that Gita wisdom urges us to see beyond what looks good to what is actually good: our personal, spiritual and eternal relationship with Krishna.

༺ཨ༻

The foolish cannot understand how a living entity can quit his body, nor can they understand what sort of body he enjoys under the spell of the modes of nature. But one whose eyes are trained in knowledge can see all this.

Matter points to matters that matter more than matter

*M*ost of us usually remain preoccupied with our material needs and desires, and consequently with the material world where we hope to fulfill them. When matter is all that matters to us, why should Krishna, who resides far beyond the world of matter, matter to us?

Because, Gita wisdom answers, even the material world is dependent on Krishna for its sustenance.

The Bhagavad-gita (15.14) states that Krishna is the shelter of the body that we have taken shelter of – he arranges for the digestive mechanism that enables the body to function. This verse comes at the end of a three-verse sequence (15.12-14) that analyzes how our existence and enjoyment in the world of matter depend on something – rather someone – beyond matter. We may enjoy the good-looking face or the sweet-sounding voice of a person we love, but neither we nor our beloved arranged for the beauty of that face or the melody of that voice. And certainly the face muscles or the voice cords didn't arrange themselves because they being made of nonliving matter don't have adequate self-organizing or self-sustaining capacities.

This section of the Gita speaks directly to those of us who think that matter is all that matters; it prompts us to recognize that even the matter that matters to us depends on something beyond matter. By directing our thoughts to the non-material organizing person who underlies matter, Gita wisdom gradually raises our consciousness. It subtly prods us to realize that the creator must be much more beautiful than the creation, so we would be better off by loving the eternal creator than the temporal creation. When this realization enters deep into our heart, developing our relationship with that source of all beauty becomes for us the matter that matters the most.

੨੪੪

I am the fire of digestion in the bodies of all living entities, and I join with the air of life, outgoing and incoming, to digest the four kinds of foodstuff.

Materialism is wrong – and wrongheaded

Materialism, the idea that matter is all that exists, is on a mass seduction campaign nowadays, especially through the media. To see through its seduction, let's analyze how it is wrong intellectually and wrongheaded practically.

Materialism is wrong intellectually because it cannot withstand logical scrutiny that starts with an objective study of the world. If matter were all that existed originally, as materialism assumes, why and how did conscious beings come into existence in a world of unconscious matter? Materialism asks us to believe that it somehow happened without offering any supportive evidence.

Materialism is wrongheaded because it sticks obstinately to wrong notions even in the face of decisive contrary evidence. Many people adopt materialism because it promises happiness in the here-and-now, primarily through sex and money. However, increasing sociological evidence is proving irrefutably that materialism is a liar. Its promise of erotic delights has given way to a nightmare of divorces, heartbreaks, abortions and sexually transmitted diseases. Its promise of wealth has given way to the nightmare of constant financial insecurity for most people and an unending tormenting craving for more money among everyone, even the super-wealthy.

This analysis can help us see the truth of the declaration of the Bhagavad-gita (16.09) that materialism is detrimental at best (ahitah) and disastrous at worst (kshayaaya).

As an alternative to materialism, Gita wisdom offers us a dualist and personalist vision of reality. It integrates the two dimensions of reality – material and spiritual – by revealing that they both are energies of the all-attractive supreme person, Krishna. This holistic worldview is intellectually appealing and practically endearing. Intellectually, it explains coherently how a conscious supreme being activates his spiritual and material energies to manifest the world. Practically, it enables us to lead a balanced life of devotional service that yields fulfillment in this world and endless ecstasy in the next.

ॐ

Following such conclusions, the demoniac, who are lost to themselves and who have no intelligence, engage in unbeneficial, horrible works meant to destroy the world

The immaterial is not immaterial

The word "immaterial" can refer to "that which is not made of matter" and "that which doesn't matter." The immaterial (the non-material) is immaterial (unimportant) – so believe the ungodly who consider the material to be everything.

The Bhagavad-gita (16.09) outlines the consequences of their unidimensional worldview: it impels them to a live-for-the-moment materialistic lifestyle that not only keeps them spiritually bankrupt but also removes all safety valves from their materialism. Consequently, it is only a matter of time before their materialism assumes unhealthy proportions. This disproportionate materialism can lead to two major devastating consequences. Firstly, it misfires to harm the very earth that is its indispensable arena. Secondly, it backfires to wreck the very materialists who triggered it. We see these consequences unfolding on the global scene today as specters like climate change jeopardize our planet and weapons of mass destruction jeopardize humanity.

Gita wisdom explains that even if we consider our material lives to be of primary importance, still we cannot dismiss the immaterial (the non-material or spiritual) as immaterial (unimportant). Only when we nourish ourselves spiritually will we have the inner strength to restrain our material side from going out of control.

No doubt, some materialists may be regulated. But they are the exceptions, not the norm. Their regulated living is usually a carry-over from their past regulated habits. It is not due to their materialism but in spite of it. There is very little in materialism to make anyone regulated and a lot to make everyone unregulated.

That's why most people need spiritual nourishment to become and stay materially regulated, especially amidst today's wildly materialistic culture. Of course, regulation of materialism is just a side-benefit of spiritual nourishment. Its main benefit is an abiding love for Krishna that ultimately catapults us back to his eternal blissful abode.

ॐ

Following such conclusions, the demoniac, who are lost to themselves and who have no intelligence, engage in unbeneficial, horrible works meant to destroy the world.

Ignorance with intellectual wings is the worst ignorance

The Bhagavad-gita (16.09) indicates that the atheistic, being possessed by their meager intelligence, flourish in self-destructive and world-destructive activities. In these people, ignorance not only resides, but also flies with the wings of the misdirected intellect.

To be in ignorance is bad; these are the wingless atheists.

To be in ignorance and to imagine oneself to be in knowledge is worse; these are the budding wing atheists.

To be in ignorance, to imagine oneself to be in knowledge, and to imagine one in knowledge to be in ignorance is worst; these are the flying atheists, who aggressively proselytize for their religion of disbelief.

This third category is where fanatical atheists belong. These intolerant devotees of atheism baptize themselves as the saints of reason and strut with a holier-than-thou attitude of condescension towards anyone who doesn't agree with their belief in disbelief. Gita wisdom informs us that they are born with ungodly qualities and they aggravate those negative traits by their lifestyle choices and especially their intellectual rationalizations.

When spiritual seekers face such confirmed and convinced atheists, the best way – and often the only way – to serve them is to pray for them from a distance. The sixteenth chapter of the Gita describes the inauspicious destinations to which they are headed due to their foolhardy intellectual self-righteousness. Spiritual seekers pray that such atheists save themselves from their unfortunate fate by using the wings of their intelligence to fly not away from God but towards him.

ॐ

Following such conclusions, the demoniac, who are lost to themselves and who have no intelligence, engage in unbeneficial, horrible works meant to destroy the world.

The earthbound are dearth-bound

*M*any people are earthbound in their conception of life; they think of the earth as the only arena for their existence. They generally acquire this limiting picture of life because of an underlying materialist notion of the self: the idea that there is nothing more to their identity than their material body.

The Bhagavad-gita (16.09) points out that such a materialist worldview is deficient in conception (alpa-buddhayah) and detrimental in consequence (kshayaaya jagato 'hitah). The next verse (16.10) indicates this toxic consequence by stating that those subscribing to this view come under the control of desires that are insatiable (kamam ashritya dushpuram). Let's see how this happens and why it is damaging.

Because of their adherence to the materialistic worldview, the arena of their quest for happiness gets restricted to the material realm. Having cut themselves off from access to spiritual happiness, material pleasures become their only sources of happiness – and these they seek with a feverish frenzy.

However, all earthly objects being finite and mortal can offer them pleasures that are at best finite and mortal. But as the heart longs for unlimited and unending happiness, they discover to their dismay that, even if they get the best worldly pleasures, those pleasures are just not good enough – rarely good enough in quality and never good enough in quantity. Consequently, the craving for more gnaws and consumes them from within, thereby making them perpetually dissatisfied or dearth-bound.

Gita wisdom frees us from being earth-bound in conception and dearth-bound in consequence. The Gita's teachings about our spiritual identity and devotional destiny in Krishna's eternal abode free us from being earth-bound in our worldview. And the Gita's guidelines for rendering loving service to Krishna free us from being dearth-bound in our quest for happiness.

ॐ

Following such conclusions, the demoniac, who are lost to themselves and who have no intelligence, engage in unbeneficial, horrible works meant to destroy the world. Taking shelter of insatiable lust and absorbed in the conceit of pride and false prestige, the demoniac, thus illusioned, are always sworn to unclean work, attracted by the impermanent.

When style violates sense, style deserves to be violated

few things obsess the contemporary mind as much as the latest styles. Most people today are possessed by the craze to parade themselves with the trendiest dresses, hairstyles and gadgets. As they are exposed relentlessly to hi-tech, high-octane ads, billboards and commercials, they become victims of the methodical and sometimes diabolical media propaganda by the peddlers of these products. This propaganda beguiles them into believing that stylishness is a pre-requisite for prestige, which in turn is a pre-condition for happiness. People being social creatures feel a strong need to be validated by their social circle. The media propaganda exploits their need for validation and manipulates them into aping the fashions glamorized in the social mirror.

Gita wisdom equips us to counter this sinister manipulation. The Bhagavad-gita (16.10) indicates that the ungodly embrace the temporary (mohad grhitvasad grahan) because they are bewitched by the craving for prestige (dambhamana madanvitah). When we understand that we are not our physical bodies, but are spiritual beings, we seek our self-worth in our loving relationship with Krishna. This inner connection and fulfillment enables us to evaluate styles rationally based on their functionality – and not just their fashionability. If a style doesn't serve a useful function, then investing our time, thought and emotion to acquire it doesn't make sense. When style violates sense, then our inner security empowers us to choose the sensible over the stylish. No doubt, our violating a senseless style may raise a few eyebrows in the social circle that has sold itself to that style. But those raised eyebrows are a small price to pay for being bold models and living spokesperson of basic sanity and authentic spirituality.

Why should we be timid when we can be bold?

०३८०

Taking shelter of insatiable lust and absorbed in the conceit of pride and false prestige, the demoniac, thus illusioned, are always sworn to unclean work, attracted by the impermanent.

You are meant for more than a weary, dreary and scary reality

*W*eary, dreary, scary: these three words convey broadly the reality of modern materialistic life. Let's see how:

Weary: The huge workloads, the overbearing deadlines, the breakneck pace – all these typical characteristics of our working lives drain us physically and especially mentally. Perhaps the best evidence of this weariness is our eagerness for the weekend break, and the dismay and resentment that sweeps over us when our work encroaches on our weekend.

Dreary: To get relief from our weariness, we usually bury ourselves in entertainment. But most entertainment today is centered on extravagant displays of lust, anger and greed, displays that become the stuff of our dreams. However, most of these reel-life displays are unrealizable in real-life. Over time, our inability to actualize these fantasies makes us dejected and dreary.

Scary: The economic, familial and medical uncertainties that dog us are scary enough. All the more scary is the thought of the inevitable doom that awaits us at the time of death. We may try to avoid thinking about death, but we can't get rid of death and its scariness.

Thus, the reality of materialistic life is unpalatable, even brutal. However, we don't realize it because the glitz and glamor of our culture expertly masks it. The Bhagavad-gita in its sixteenth chapter unmasks crass materialism and helps us see (16.11) how it leads to immeasurable anxiety till the moment of death.

Gita wisdom informs us that we can have a better life. As spiritual beings, we have the right to delight eternally in a loving relationship with Krishna. If we just stop being taken in by material allurements and learn to love him, we can reclaim our lost right to ever-lasting happiness.

സ്ഥ

They believe that to gratify the senses is the prime necessity of human civilization. Thus until the end of life their anxiety is immeasurable.

Your desire is your power – don't waste it

*G*reen consciousness has made us increasingly aware that natural resources are limited and so need to be used carefully.

Yet there is one natural resource that we keep squandering indiscriminately. That grossly overspent resource is not a collective, global resource, but an individual, local resource: our power to desire.

This power to desire is actually the only resource that we can call truly our own; all other resources come temporarily under our partial control and then soon go out of control. But the power of desire is something that is always ours as long as we live.

Unfortunately for most of us, this power is dissipated fruitlessly; we consciously or subconsciously expend it on any good-looking object that passes our vision or imagination. This thoughtless exertion of the power to desire frequently results in our own exhaustion. Additionally, the Bhagavad-gita (16.12) indicates that the power of these desires, once triggered unrestrainedly, overpowers our moral sense and drags us into self-destructive actions. One spinoff of such self-defeating actions is the rampant eco-destruction that has assumed alarming proportions in recent times.

If we wish to manage our desires more productively, the Bhagavad-gita stands ready to educate and train us in desire management.

Education: The Gita educates us about our true nature as souls and about the true nature of the material world as a place that can provide us happiness only when we utilize it in serving the source of the world, Krishna.

Training: The Gita trains us in focusing our desires on Krishna, the source of all happiness. It further equips us to desire worldly objects only to the extent that they can be used in Krishna's service.

By using Gita wisdom to conserve and utilize our desires, we can uproot mental exhaustion, self-destructive action and ecological destruction.

৫৪৩০

Bound by a network of hundreds of thousands of desires and absorbed in lust and anger, they secure money by illegal means for sense gratification.

Cry, Vie, Lie, Die, Fie – Tie

The Bhagavad-gita (16.7-20) describes the mentality of the godless materialists who ruin themselves and those around them by their inordinate infatuation with temporary things. Their tragic life-story can be summarized as cry, vie, lie, die, fie.

Cry: Being enslaved by their innumerable and insatiable self-centered desires, they live perpetually dissatisfied, forever craving, worrying and crying for more (16.11-12).

Lie: Their uncontrollable and irresistible desires drag them into ignoble and immoral actions (16.12).

Vie: Their moral blindness makes them ruthlessly competitive towards whoever comes in their way, and they delight in making schemes to destroy their opponents (16.13-15).

Die: All their materialistic scheming is abruptly terminated when they run full speed into the dead end of death (16.11).

Fie: Having let their untrammeled materialism torpedo their spiritual consciousness and devotional opportunity, they find themselves after death in arenas with little if any spiritual or even material prospects (16.19-20).

Tie: The Gita (16.24) concludes the chapter by urging us to tie our intelligence to scriptural directions and use the strength of that upward connection to protect ourselves from being dragged down by our self-defeating materialistic obsessions.

◌৩৪৪০

Bound by a network of hundreds of thousands of desires and absorbed in lust and anger, they secure money by illegal means for sense gratification

We can do better than join the society of materialistic fanatics

*R*ampant corruption and blatant inequity characterize our current socioeconomic system. What is their cause?

They are symptoms of the materialistic fanaticism afflicting humanity. Just as religious fanatics care for nothing and no one except their twisted religious beliefs, materialistic fanatics care for nothing and no one except their materialistic agendas for self-aggrandizement.

The Bhagavad-gita outlines (16.13-15) the psychology of such materialistic zealots: they don't feel any hesitation in slaughtering their own morality and even the lives of other people on the altar of their materialism. This description in the Gita is chillingly reminiscent of the cold-blooded manipulation, exploitation and destruction of enemies that is routine for many of today's economic barons who collude with underworld dons.

The Gita prefaces this description by stating the fundamental misconception that underlies their heartless and horrendous materialism. It describes (16.08-09) their non-spiritual, even anti-spiritual, worldview that rejects the existence of God and the soul. Because they conveniently dismiss out of existence the spiritual dimension of life, no control valve is left to check their untrammeled materialism. The Gita notes (16.17) that their religious pretensions, if any, are just a utilitarian mask.

Thankfully, Gita wisdom doesn't leave us feeling helpless about this all-devouring materialism. Its sixteenth chapter concludes (16.24) with a call for return to scripture-based balance of material and spiritual values. We can respond to this direction-providing call for balance individually and collectively.

Individually, each one of us has the power to attain and sustain that balance, thereby protecting ourselves from becoming victims-cum-participants in the materialistic mess around us. And collectively all of us can set the example and share the word that can inspire many others to free humanity from the stranglehold of materialism.

ॐ

The demoniac person thinks: "He is my enemy, and I have killed him, and my other enemies will also be killed. I am the lord of everything. I am the enjoyer."

.

We cannot get pure devotion by mere donation

"This person gives liberal donations for charitable causes." Statements like these are becoming increasingly common in the public profiles of well-to-do individuals. This trend may inspire more people to become charitable, but potentially for all the wrong reasons.

The Bhagavad-gita (16.15) outlines such a messed up motivation for charity: as a public relations tool to proclaim one's economic status. Such charity is unenlightened and unfruitful (ity ajnana vimohitah): unenlightened because it ignores the reality that everything that we have belongs to Krishna; and unfruitful because it doesn't increase our devotion for him, which alone brings life's greatest happiness.

Of course, what the Gita discourages is not charity per se, but the self-centered, egoistic motivation underlying it. Genuine motivation is critical for external donation to kindle internal devotion. If we want to offer our heart to Krishna, but can't because it is occupied by wealth, then offering wealth to him is the most real, practical and essential way ahead for us. By such devotionally-inspired donation, we offer a part of our heart to him and thereby offer him a place in our heart.

However, if we let the desire to broadcast our financial stature dominate us, then our donation is an offering not so much to Krishna as to our own ego. By such charity, we simply offer one more part of our heart to our ego. Of course, giving donation to Krishna will always benefit us, but the burden of the inflated ego will make our progress towards him slow and labored.

Gita wisdom empowers us with insights and practices to clarify and purify our motivation. Sincere motivation bridges the gap between mere donation and pure devotion, thereby making our progress towards Krishna swift and sweet.

⚜

"I am the richest man, surrounded by aristocratic relatives. There is none so powerful and happy as I am. I shall perform sacrifices, I shall give some charity, and thus I shall rejoice." In this way, such persons are deluded by ignorance.

Don't let inconsequential possibilities paralyze you

Our culture offers us so many possibilities for life's trivialities that choosing among them often swallows much of our energy and emotion. For example, TV offers so many channels that just surfing channels to find the best often becomes a fussy issue. The same consuming spectrum of choice confronts us for almost everything from tooth-pastes to clothes.

Despite this fuss over possibilities, even the best possibility usually turns out to be anticlimactic. The possibilities allure far more than they deliver; that's why channel-surfing often excites more than channel-watching.

Moreover, this fuss over possibilities misdirects our energy and emotion from the consequential to the inconsequential. The decision about which channel we watch will most likely be inconsequential after a month – or even a week. On the other hand, the decision to invest that same time in gaining spiritual insight and relishing devotional joy will be consequential for all of eternity. But when we are hyper-stimulated materially, we become paralyzed spiritually. When our energy and emotion are consumed with multiple material possibilities, a scenario that the Bhagavad-gita (16.16) describes as aneka citta-vibhranta, then we have practically no energy and emotion left for connecting with Krishna. When our connection with Krishna is thus disrupted, we soon find Krishna consciousness tasteless.

Thus our infatuation with material possibilities extracts a double toll: material dissatisfaction and spiritual disaffection. Sober contemplation on this dual loss will help us realize that material possibilities are not worth so much of our time and thought. This will inspire us to muster the willpower to disentangle our energy and emotion from material infatuation. When we invest our thus-freed energy and emotion in enhancing our Krishna consciousness, then we will experience as reality the fulfillment that always remained just a possibility in material life.

CR80

Thus perplexed by various anxieties and bound by a network of illusions, they become too strongly attached to sense enjoyment and fall down into hell.

All bluff, no stuff – that's enough

The Bhagavad-gita (16.17) describes the godless to be self-complacent and impudent (atma-sambhavitah stabdah). They throw morality and spirituality to the winds for the sake of pursuing self-centered pleasures. To further their egocentric ends, they create a façade of being know-all and do-all; of knowing all that matters and being able to do all that matters. Their external self-assuredness may impress us; we may even feel tempted to become like them.

Gita wisdom helps us see through the façade by showing how the godless, despite their aggressive posturing, are doing nothing new. They are playing the oldest game that there is to play: playing god. And they will meet, sooner or later, the same old result that all such imitator gods have met: frustration, devastation and destruction. They will be frustrated on being outclassed by others; devastated on being defeated repeatedly; and destroyed when death ends their egomania permanently. The sixteenth chapter of the Gita explains that even at present while they flaunt their glory externally they are internally tortured by the innumerable and insatiable desires that burn within their mind and senses.

Thus, when we look at such people with the eyes of the Gita, we will see that behind all their bluff, there is no stuff. Naturally, we will feel, "That's enough." Far from being impressed by them, we will feel concerned for them. Instead of becoming tempted to join the game of playing god, we will become more determined to return to our original position as eternal servants of Krishna and relish the security, serenity and ecstasy thereof. And we will pray that they too quit their doomed game and return to his merciful shelter.

ॐ

Self-complacent and always impudent, deluded by wealth and false prestige, they sometimes proudly perform sacrifices in name only, without following any rules or regulations

Don't let parasites suck your mental energy

Sometimes we feel mentally tired even when we are not physically tired. What causes this mental tiredness? Among its various causes, a common, major, and avoidable cause is the indiscriminate over-exertion of our power to desire. This over-exertion results from our unwittingly welcoming too many superfluous desires in our minds. The Bhagavad-gita (16.21) indicates that these distracting desires that prevent us from acting in our best interests fall into three broad categories: lust, anger, and greed.

Lust and greed often fuel our desires for the many worldly objects that enter our vision and imagination, be they glitzy forms or gaudy products. These desires are innumerable and most of them are practically unfulfillable in real life. Consequently, a conscious or subconscious irritation builds up within us. When this irritation becomes intolerable, we succumb to anger, which vents itself mentally as sulkiness, verbally as snappiness and physically as beastliness. In this way, lust, greed, and anger cumulatively divert our mental focus away from the main goals of our life, both material and spiritual. The resulting inattentiveness makes us falter and blunder while pursuing those goals. As our plans misfire and backfire, and nothing seems to be working in our lives, we get mentally exhausted and exasperated.

Thus, our mental exhaustion originates not so much in the external difficulties that life puts in our path as in the internal diversions that prevent us from treading that path effectively. The diversions of lust, greed, and anger are therefore like mental parasites that live off our mind's energies. That's why Gita wisdom urges us to immunize ourselves against these debilitating parasites by diligently serving Krishna externally and remembering him internally.

☙❧

There are three gates leading to this hell—lust, anger and greed. Every sane man should give these up, for they lead to the degradation of the soul

The obnoxious is obnoxious because it is noxious

A prevailing intellectual fad sees all value-judgments as subjective: "If you think something is obnoxious, it is obnoxious for you – but not necessarily for me or anyone else."

This subjectivity may be true for arbitrary value-judgments, but not for the Bhagavad-gita's value-judgments because these are connected with real-life consequences.

Here's an example to understand this. Alcoholics judge a bottle of alcohol as desirable; non-alcoholics, as undesirable. Are these judgments subjective? Not if we consider the real-life health consequences that beset alcoholics and bypass non-alcoholics.

Just as value-judgments are non-subjective in the area of physical health, Gita wisdom asserts that they are non-subjective in the area of spiritual health. We are all eternal blissful souls who are afflicted with the disease of misidentifying ourselves with material bodies that subject us to mortality and misery. By regaining our spiritual health, we end this misidentification and thereby the associated bodily suffering.

Gita wisdom deems obnoxious certain materialistic activities because of their noxious effect on our spiritual health; they aggravate both the sensual desires and the karmic bonds that exacerbate our bodily misidentification. The Bhagavad-gita (16.23) cautions that such unfortunate consequences befall those who neglect scriptural judgments. Their increased bodily misidentification worsens their misery as disease and old age torment them on their way to death, the ultimate tribulation.

Fortunately, we can transcend this fate. By recognizing the objectivity of the Gita's value-judgments, we can distance ourselves from spiritually noxious activities. Gita wisdom also helps us see all bodily sufferings as impetuses for accelerating our spiritual health recovery program, a program that minimizes our misery in this life and eliminates all misery in the next.

To those out to compromise moral objectivity, Gita wisdom offers a gentle yet grave reminder: the consequences don't compromise.

ॐ

He who discards scriptural injunctions and acts according to his own whims attains neither perfection, nor happiness, nor the supreme destination

Look towards the fixed lighthouse, not the moving lighthouses

Navigating life's journey amidst the unpredictable worldly ups and downs is like navigating a boat in dark, turbulent waters. Just as the boat would be lost without a lighthouse, we would be lost without a reliable basis for our decision-making.

We usually make our decisions using one or more of these four main lighthouses:

1. Culture: Everyone does it.

2. Tradition: We have always done it.

3. Mood: It feels good.

4. Reason: It seems logical.

However, these are fallible, movable lighthouses that at times point to the safe ground of time-tested truths and at times point to the dangerous rocks of short-sighted trends. Guided by them, we may sometimes land and sometimes sink.

That's why, before using these lighthouses, we need to ascertain where they stand by comparing them with the one lighthouse that always stands on the firm ground of perennial truth. That immovable, infallible lighthouse is the word of God, the Bhagavad-gita, which is ever pointing to our highest interests. This indeed is the reason why Krishna urges us in the Gita (16.24) to always make scripture the first and the last basis of our decision-making.

☙❧

One should therefore understand what is duty and what is not duty by the regulations of the scriptures. Knowing such rules and regulations, one should act so that he may gradually be elevated.

Don't let materialist monomania mess your life

*O*ur life is becoming increasingly dominated by machines, mechanistic thinking and mechanical behavior.

Machines: As technology pervades our life, we spend more time with machines than with people. Even when we spend time with people, machines encroach frequently; the thoughts of the ringing of the cellphone or the beeping of a message are rarely far away from our minds. At home, the TV often receives our attention more than our family members.

Mechanistic thinking: The more we interact with machines, the more that interaction tends to make our thinking mechanistic. We extrapolate subconsciously from our experience with machines and expect conscious people to function like mechanical entities that respond predictably to standard inputs. When people fail to behave according to these expectations, we turn off from them. Over time, our relationships become at best superficial and unfulfilling, or at worst disrupted and wrecked.

Mechanical behavior: Our mechanistic thinking also makes us mechanical in our own behavior. We act like robots run by stimulus-response programs: allured by seeing a new gadget, tempted by seeing a sexually appealing form and so forth. We feel frequently titillated, rarely satisfied. Our brain cells fire continuously, but our heart remains dead to deep fulfilling emotions.

Such a materialist monomania, the Bhagavad-gita (18.22) indicates, is representative of knowledge in the mode of ignorance. Those with such knowledge mistake one fragment of reality – the material level in our case – with the full reality. Beyond the material level lies the spiritual level. Awaiting us there is a real life of authentic emotions and genuine reciprocations with Krishna and through him with everyone.

If we wish to stop materialist monomania from messing our life, Gita wisdom stands ready to guide us along the journey from ignorance to transcendence.

℘℘

And that knowledge by which one is attached to one kind of work as the all in all, without knowledge of the truth, and which is very meager, is said to be in the mode of darkness.

A moment of indulgence can cause a lifetime of repentance – beware

The news periodically features stories of talented individuals who ruin their promising prospects by succumbing to immorality and greed. For the sake of quick gains, they throw away their integrity and end up disgraced. A moment of indulgence leads them to a lifetime of repentance.

What impels them to such tragic short-sightedness?

The Bhagavad-gita (18.25) describes that short-sighted action unmindful of the consequences is typical of the mode of ignorance, which is the subtle force of nature that impels our mind toward self-destruction.

This destructive psychological force is strengthened and facilitated by our culture with its glamorization of live-for-the-moment lifestyle. Due to this prevailing culture, even people who are not normally immersed in the mode of ignorance get carried away by spells of short-sighted impulsiveness. That's how intelligent people act unintelligently.

Understanding the cultural setting that breeds self-defeating behavior can be sobering and empowering. It can be sobering if it makes us aware that we ourselves are vulnerable to such behavior. It can be empowering if it stimulates us to search for ways to protect ourselves from the culture's influences. If we are fortunate, this search brings us to Gita wisdom. The Gita's recommendations to assimilate spiritual wisdom and adopt temperate habits help us plug in to the mode of goodness. This mode expands our inner vision and thereby enables us to make prudent, far-sighted choices.

In addition to cultivating the mode of goodness, Gita wisdom emphatically urges us to practice devotional service and go beyond the modes to transcendence. By connecting us with Krishna who is the supremely stable shelter existing beyond the three modes, devotional service empowers us to quickly counter the destabilizing influences of the modes, gradually attain self-mastery and finally regain our lost love for Krishna.

~

That action performed in illusion, in disregard of scriptural injunctions, and without concern for future bondage or for violence or distress caused to others is said to be in the mode of ignorance.

Lewdness is not boldness

"This movie is filled with bold scenes." Sentences like these are common in movie reviews. It is now standard to use "boldness" as a rationalization of lewdness, of blatant obscenity and strident sexuality.

The Bhagavad-gita (18.32) indicates that people captivated by ignorance get things backward: they mistake the virtuous to be vicious and the vicious to be virtuous. As if that were not bad enough, they also strive to intellectually rationalize their miscalculations. Their rationalizations ruin them far more than their miscalculations.

Let's see how "boldness" is ruining society today.

A cursory look at the daily news shows the heavy social costs of rationalizing obscenity: images of explicit sexuality are often seen next to reports of horrible sexual violence. One doesn't have to be a Sherlock Holmes to figure out that the first is a major cause of the second.

The Gita (03.41) states that the road to self-mastery begins with regulation of sensual expressions of lust. This regulation implies strictures against public depictions of overt sexuality. Such strictures are not hangovers of an outdated puritanical culture; they are essential safety nets to prevent human culture from degenerating to a bestial level.

Just as bacterial culture refers to an environment that facilitates the growth of bacteria, human culture refers to an environment that facilitates the growth of the humane side of human beings. Obscenity in the public media sabotages this basic purpose of human culture. How? By systematically provoking the immoral carnal drives among humans, thereby bringing out their bestial side and burying their humane side.

Gita wisdom offers us devotional enrichment that enables us to first regulate and then eliminate immoral carnal desires. Seeking, savoring and sharing that spiritual enrichment in today's materialistic culture is real boldness.

꧁꧂

That understanding which considers irreligion to be religion and religion to be irreligion, under the spell of illusion and darkness, and strives always in the wrong direction, O Partha, is in the mode of ignorance.

Protect the conscience from being dumbed and numbed and dumped

A security provider who has protected us for millennia from ourselves has now been branded as outdated and unneeded; its very right to existence is being questioned.

That beleaguered battler is, of course, our conscience, the voice within who cautions us when we do wrong and commends us when we do right.

When we blatantly displayed sexual obscenity on TV, our conscience protested. We hit it on the mouth with a rock on which was emblazoned "the right to enjoy beauty." The impact made the conscience dumb. That our "right" started erasing the difference between human society and animal society didn't matter; the right was what mattered.

When we piled up tons of explicit content on the internet, our mute conscience expressed shock with its eyes. Not tolerating its audacity, we gave it an injection on which was embedded "the right to sexual freedom." The jab left it numb. That our "right" led to the skyrocketing of horrendous sexual abuses like rape, incest and pedophilia didn't matter; the right was what mattered.

When we legalized the murder of the infant by the mother, our conscience, though dumb and numb, still shuddered. Not wanting to see even its face, we threw it out of the door using a bouncer whose T-shirt roared "the right to moral relativism." That our "right" to choose which morality, if any, to follow bred psychopaths whose "morality" told them that nothing was wrong in massacring innocent people didn't matter; the right was what mattered.

The Bhagavad-gita indirectly predicts our getting the rights wrong when it states (18.32) that intelligence in the mode of ignorance perceives everything topsy-turvy (*sarvarthan viparitams ca*).

Does our dumbed, numbed and dumped conscience have any chance of survival?

Only if we dare to ask ourselves a hard question: without it, do we have any chance of survival?

⚮

That understanding which considers irreligion to be religion and religion to be irreligion, under the spell of illusion and darkness, and strives always in the wrong direction, O Partha, is in the mode of ignorance.

Seek the true tool to your self before you seek to be true to yourself

The Bhagavad-gita (18.58) indicates that all of us have essentially two choices in making our life's decisions: to act according to the voice of Krishna and be eternally liberated, or to act according to the voice of the ego and be endlessly entangled.

Often, people say that while making decisions one should follow the voice within so that one can be true to oneself. But Gita wisdom prompts us to introspect: how can one be true to oneself when one doesn't know one's true self?

As long as our internal vision is hazy, our inner voices are likely to be mazy; the many voices that clamor within us are likely to lead us into maze-like complications. True, there is the voice of our pure conscience, the voice of Krishna as our indwelling friend and guide, speaking within us, but that voice is generally obscured by many other voices that have become embedded inside due to outside influences of materialism. Principal among these many pseudo-inner voices is the voice of the ego, which, while masquerading as our true self, takes us further and further away from understanding that self.

That's why this Gita verse urges us to base our decisions on the voice of God as it is externally manifest to us through scripture. This scriptural voice is the tool to our true self, because it guides and empowers us to make attitudinal and behavioral choices that minimize and mute the many unauthentic inner voices. Then does the voice of our pure conscience become clear and self-evident – and guide us to be constantly true to our self.

ॐ

If you become conscious of Me, you will pass over all the obstacles of conditioned life by My grace. If, however, you do not work in such consciousness but act through false ego, not hearing Me, you will be lost.

UNDERSTANDING GITA CONCEPTS

Cultivate the intelligence to ask questions – and the courage to question those questions

Sometimes we ask intelligent questions about spirituality and demand immediate answers. But frequently our questions stem from dubious assumptions and downright misconceptions that need to be amended before we can understand the answers.

The Bhagavad-gita illustrates this process of questioning one's questions. In its first chapter (01.35) Arjuna asks several rhetorical questions that are meant primarily to justify his views and choices. Krishna responds to Arjuna by questioning those questions. He challenges and counters the presumption that gave birth to those questions. That presumption is Arjuna's misidentification with his material body. When Arjuna shows the courage to let his questions be questioned, he then understands how his materialistic paradigm was fundamentally, fatally flawed. Thereafter, he gets a new vision of life: its spiritual nature, its divine essence and its devotional purpose. With this vision, Arjuna finds his questions automatically answered, his course of action indubitably clarified and his determination unshakably restored.

The Gita thus illustrates the pre-requisites for acquiring spiritual wisdom: not only the intelligence to ask questions, but also the courage to question those questions.

Without this courage, we will simply attempt to fit the Gita's spiritual wisdom into a convenient corner in the cupboard of our materialistic preconceptions. We may feel satisfied at having understood the Gita, but we will stay deprived of much of its empowering wisdom.

With this courage, we will gradually recognize that Gita wisdom offers an entirely new conceptual cupboard. When we revise our preconceptions according to the Gita's worldview, then we too will experience the dramatic transformation and dynamic empowerment experienced by Arjuna. We will progressively realize our core identity as indestructible spiritual beings and our ultimate destiny as blissful participants in a life of endless love with Krishna.

❧

O maintainer of all living entities, I am not prepared to fight with them even in exchange for the three worlds, let alone this earth. What pleasure will we derive from killing the sons of Dhritarashtra?

The Gita's message is not just specific and historical, but also generic and universal

*T*he Bhagavad-gita takes a specific real-life situation, examines it philosophically and offers a universal pragmatic solution.

The Gita begins with Arjuna's weak-hearted capitulation: at the end of the first chapter (01.46) he puts aside his bow. His action expresses his intention: "I will not fight." The message of the Gita infuses Arjuna with clarity of vision and firmness of resolution, as evidenced in his concluding declaration: "I will do your will." (18.73)

Why does Arjuna not conclude with the specific resolution: "I will fight"? Because after hearing the profound wisdom of the Gita, his vision has been lifted far beyond the specific battlefield dilemma: "Should I fight or not?" That's why, though the Gita in its initial chapters repeatedly exhorts Arjuna to fight, such exhortations become increasingly infrequent as its discussion becomes deeper and broader.

The Gita's battlefield setting is historical, not mythological. Still, it is the setting, not the substance. The substance of the Gita is its majestic analysis of the universal existential perplexity that confronts all of us: "What should I live for?" The conclusion of the analysis is a call for love: "Live for love: love of Krishna and all his children." This philosophy, when understood holistically, reveals divinity's love for humanity and inspires reciprocal human love for the divine.

Like Arjuna, we can choose to respond to our specific dilemmas with the universal panacea of loving surrender: "O Lord, I will do your will." Reciprocating with our surrender, Krishna will provide us from within our heart the clarity of vision to resolve the dilemma. More importantly, we will also discover through the dilemma a pathway to Krishna's supreme abode, the world of eternal love that is free from all material dilemmas.

ॐ

Sanjaya said: Arjuna, having thus spoken on the battlefield, cast aside his bow and arrows and sat down on the chariot, his mind overwhelmed with grief

Spirituality expands our conception of life dramatically and majestically

Is life a doomed journey from a station called birth to a station called death with a bit of pleasure and a lot of pain sprinkled between?

We may have never thought of our own lives in such stark terms. But this is the unvarnished reality of life at the material level, isn't it? Then why don't we realize it? Because today's materialistic culture specializes in covering reality with countless varnishes through television, movies, amusement parks and gaudy gadgets that infatuate us with fantasies about worldly enjoyment.

However, these varnishes can't change the reality that all our struggles to lay our hands on worldly enjoyment will be rendered futile when death lays its hands on us. When reminded of our inevitable mortality, we feel overwhelmed by a haunting sense of existential despair: "Am I meant for casual destruction by a bug or a bang?"

Gita wisdom liberates us from this despair. Right at the start of its profound message, the Bhagavad-gita (02.11-02.30) logically and philosophically establishes that we are souls, eternal and indestructible. This message expands our conception of life dramatically and majestically:

Dramatically because we understand that the bodily pleasures and pains that excite or agitate us so much are inconsequential in the light of the reality that we have had many such bodies; that we as souls are forever secure, beyond all bodily upheavals.

Majestically because we understand that we can reorient our desires from matter to Krishna and thereby attain a majestic destination: eternal life of love with Krishna in his supreme abode.

This vision reveals that death is not the end of our existence; it is not an inescapable defeat; and it is not worth lamenting over, as the Bhagavad-gita (02.11) indicates.

ႜ႒

The Supreme Personality of Godhead said: While speaking learned words, you are mourning for what is not worthy of grief. Those who are wise lament neither for the living nor for the dead.

Krishna is realer than reality

In our times of trouble, we may doubt, "Does Krishna really exist?" Gita wisdom turns this doubt on the head by prompting the doubt: "Does the world around me with all its troubles really exist?"

We may answer, "The world obviously exists because it tugs and pulls at me, making real demands and bringing real consequences." Gita wisdom responds: "Is this level of reality much higher than the reality of dreams? While we dream, doesn't the dreaming reality also make demands and bring consequences? Just as the worries of the dream disappear when we wake up physically, the worries of the world disappear when we wake up spiritually."

No doubt, the waking reality is higher than the dreaming reality because we return to the same waking reality each day when we wake up, unlike the dreaming reality, which is different and disconnected each night. Still, the waking reality is not the highest reality. Why? Because it doesn't last forever – we won't return to it when we go to our final sleep at the time of death.

The highest reality is the spiritual reality, wherein we as souls reciprocate eternal love with Krishna. The purpose of life is to reach that reality by purifying and raising our consciousness. To keep us focused on this purpose, the Bhagavad-gita (02.16) urges us to see the realm of matter as unreal due to its temporality and the realm of spirit as real due to its eternality.

When amidst our real troubles we take shelter of Krishna through prayer and mantra meditation, the experience of his love will solace, encourage and invigorate us. Then we will realize for ourselves that Krishna is realer than what we normally call as reality – even when the whole world falls apart, he is always there with us and for us.

ॐ

Those who are seers of the truth have concluded that of the nonexistent [the material body] there is no endurance and of the eternal [the soul] there is no change. This they have concluded by studying the nature of both

Give Krishna his due to prevent death from taking more than its due

Death has a right on our physical body. We can't stop it from consuming its due, but we don't have to give it more than that. Let's understand what this means.

We exist at three levels: physical, mental and spiritual. Among these levels, death has no right over our spiritual existence. For the soul death is an inconsequential event, like the discarding of old clothes. When we don't know our spiritual identity, we assume that we are our bodies. So death seems like the destruction of our entire self, a feeling that, the Gita (02.19) indicates, arises from ignorance.

Does death have a right over our mental existence? No, but we often give it that right unnecessarily. The mind being constituted of subtle matter is not destroyed when the physical body is destroyed by death. But practically because we let ourselves be infatuated by fantasies of physical pleasures, our mind gets attached to and entangled in the physical body. Due to this attachment, we are mentally devastated by death; we feel as if we are losing all that we have lived for. As long as we give physical pleasures more than their due, we will be forced to give death more than its due.

Fortunately, we don't have to give physical pleasures more than their due. We can satisfy our thirst for happiness by remembering Krishna internally and by serving him externally. If we practice such devotional engagement daily and diligently, our mind will gradually become free from infatuation with physical pleasures. It will become situated more and more on the spiritual platform and so will be less and less affected by events at the physical level like death.

Thus, by diligently giving Krishna our due daily devotional service, we can prevent death from taking more than its due.

ॐ

Neither he who thinks the living entity is the slayer nor he who thinks it slain is in knowledge, for the self slays not nor is slain.

We are dressed by and for our desires

Our desires determine and define us; we are, Gita wisdom indicates, dressed by and for our desires. Let's see how:

Dressed by our desires: The Bhagavad-gita (02.22) compares the body to a dress and transmigration to replacing one dress with another. Just as our desires play a key role in determining our cloth dress, so they play a key role in determining our bodily dress. The Bhagavad-gita (08.06) indicates that our desire at the moment of death determines our next bodily dress. Thus, we become dressed by our desires.

Dressed for our desires: Our bodily dress is not only a product of our desires, but is also a vehicle for them. For example, if we have a dominant desire to eat indiscriminately, nature facilitates our desire by giving us the body of a hog that can gorge on stool. Thus the soul in a hog's body is dressed for its desire to eat undiscriminatingly. Though all bodies may not seem as unpalatable as a hog's, still every material body is a bad deal for us. Why? Because it subjects us, eternal blissful souls, to the inevitable miseries of material existence.

Fortunately, we can use the power of our desires to our advantage by judiciously choosing the best desire: the desire to love Krishna. If we subordinate all our other desires to this central desire, then we will be able to think of Krishna in life and death, and thereby return back to him. There we will regain our original form, our eternal dress, our svarupa, which is non-different from ourselves and is best suited for serving him. Thus we will be dressed by and for our desire to serve Krishna – eternally and ecstatically.

ॐ

As a person puts on new garments, giving up old ones, the soul similarly accepts new material bodies, giving up the old and useless ones.

The soul is life's amazing and empowering secret

*W*hen we come to know a pleasant secret, we feel amazed. Naturally therefore, we feel immensely amazed when we come to know life's great secret. That secret is disarmingly simple: what we were looking for was always with us – we didn't find it because we searched in the wrong places.

The Bhagavad-gita (02.29) indicates that when we come to know about the soul, we look upon it as amazing. We recognize that much of what we were seeking at the level of the body was always our own at the level of the soul.

We wanted to look beautiful at the level of the body. We were frustrated by the looks we were born with if those looks were not good enough. Or we were frustrated by the setting in of age which took away whatever good looks we had. Yet all along as souls, we had always been beautiful.

We wanted to attract the love of others at the level of the body. We were frustrated due to rejection by some, neglect by others and the demise of the few who had fulfilled that desire temporarily. Yet all along as souls, we had always attracted the love of the most loving and lovable person, Krishna.

We normally feel that others have caused our frustration. So, when we realize that we ourselves had caused our frustration by looking for beauty and love in the wrong places, we cannot but be amazed. With positive guidance from Gita wisdom, this amazement gives way to empowerment. We tap our dormant power to redirect our search from matter to spirit. By seeking happiness in our spiritual relationship with Krishna, we begin a fresh, glorious chapter in our life. Thereafter, life becomes a constant adventure of relishing and sharing the simplicity and the profundity of the amazing secret that Gita wisdom has revealed to us.

CRED

Some look on the soul as amazing, some describe him as amazing, and some hear of him as amazing, while others, even after hearing about him, cannot understand him at all.

The world is a station, not a destination

Some people ask: "Isn't it natural to feel happy when we succeed and feel unhappy when we fail? Why does the Gita ask us to suppress such natural emotions and stay equipoised amidst success and failure?"

What the Gita discourages is not the natural expression of emotions but the unnatural escalation of transient emotions. It reminds us that we are on a multi-lifetime journey that will take us through numerous stations which correspond with our various life-experiences. Some stations will be clean and pleasant; others, unclean and unpleasant. Similarly, some of our life-experiences will be joyful and relishable; others, painful and intolerable.

Our life-journey is meant for a glorious eternal destination: the supremely blissful abode of Krishna. For our train to reach that destination, we need to move emotionally closer to him through all our life-experiences. We can do this by focusing on cultivating his devotional remembrance internally and harmonizing our response to external situations with that focus. The level of harmonization can range from at best utilizing those situations as impetuses for remembering him to at least navigating through them without getting emotionally entangled.

However, we often stay on emotionally at a departed station even after the train of life has moved on. This prevents us from experiencing the present fully, learning the wisdom it contains and capitalizing on the devotional growth opportunities it brings. Worse still, by living on emotionally in the past, we sometimes sentence ourselves to unnecessary misery, as, for example, in the tragic incidents of sports fans committing suicide just because their favorite team lost a match.

To save us from such avoidable miseries caused by obsessive fixation on the past and to help us progressively relish eternal spiritual emotions, the Gita (02.38) urges us to not get carried away by transient worldly emotions.

☙❧

Do thou fight for the sake of fighting, without considering happiness or distress, loss or gain, victory or defeat—and by so doing you shall never incur sin.

Materialism in a religious costume is still materialism

The Bhagavad-gita (02.42-43) deems as undiscriminating (*avipashcitah*) and shortsighted those people who think that religion has no purpose other than to provide material gains. These people see praying as nothing more than as a method of free or cheap shopping. By holding fast to such a materialistic and utilitarian view of religion, they close the doors that could have led to the development of their spiritual potential. They are largely materialists in a pious garb who neglect the spiritual essence and purpose of religion: reviving love for God.

Gita wisdom prods us to realize that lasting happiness can never come by trying to fulfill specific material desires, as religious materialism tries to do. Why? Because such desires are insatiable and innumerable. Rather, lasting happiness can come only when we repose our love in the eternal and reciprocal object of love, Krishna.

Religious materialism may at times work in terms of satisfying some of our desires, but it never works in terms of satisfying our heart. Why? Because such materialism keeps our vision locked within the material gifts that temporarily satisfy our desires, blinding us to Krishna, whose love alone can satisfy our heart completely and eternally.

That's why the Gita cautions us to not be allured by materialism when it tempts us by donning a religious costume.

CR80

Men of small knowledge are very much attached to the flowery words of the Vedas, which recommend various fruitive activities for elevation to heavenly planets, resultant good birth, power, and so forth. Being desirous of sense gratification and opulent life, they say that there is nothing more than this.

Chemical highs cheat us of spiritual highs

All material pleasures are essentially chemical highs. Whenever we perceive any attractive object with our senses, the corresponding sensory mechanisms secrete certain chemicals. This chemical secretion gives us a temporary titillation that we call enjoyment. As our bodily capacity to secrete any chemical is limited, the enjoyment that we can ever get from any chemical high is also limited.

On the other hand, spiritual happiness exists in a realm far beyond chemical secretions; it depends on the connection of love between the soul and Krishna. This connection, being spiritual and eternal, floods us with a happiness that is free from the limits of matter and time.

We may wonder: "Are spiritual joys too not chemical phenomena?"

No, because their locus is in the soul. Of course, as long as we are embodied, all our emotions will generally correspond with a chemical expression in the body. However, spiritual emotions, unlike material emotions, are not limited by the secretory capacity of the body and can continue even when that capacity is exhausted. This is evident in the fact that we can remember Krishna and thereby relish spiritual happiness in the most adverse of material circumstances, such as severe bodily pain or the last stages of terminal disease, when chemical secretion or material enjoyment is no longer possible.

The Bhagavad-gita (02.44) indicates that attachment to material pleasures takes away the freedom of consciousness necessary to achieve and relish spiritual absorption. That's why, the more we delight in chemical highs, the more our consciousness gets riveted to our material body which secretes these chemicals and the more it becomes desensitized to spiritual emotions.

When we understand this mutual exclusivity of material enjoyment and spiritual fulfillment, then we can forego fleeting chemical highs for everlasting spiritual highs.

ॐ

In the minds of those who are too attached to sense enjoyment and material opulence, and who are bewildered by such things, the resolute determination for devotional service to the Supreme Lord does not take place.

Put the world out of the equation by the strength of devotion

Work without attachment for success or failure." This message of the Bhagavad-gita (02.48) begs the question: what are we to work for if not for success?

Love, answers Gita wisdom.

Love is our innermost need. We seek success as a means to love; we hope that, if we become successful, the world – especially the people in it whose love we thirst – will love us more.

Unfortunately, the world frustrates our hope in one of four ways:

1. We don't succeed or
2. Even if we succeed, it doesn't attract the love that we had expected or
3. Even if we are loved, people love us for our success and not for who we are. This makes us perpetually insecure because we become internally dependent on external success, attaining and preserving which is never entirely in our hands. or
4. Even if we experience authentic love, it ends agonizingly at the time of death.

To avoid such frustration, Gita wisdom urges us to put the world out of the equation by seeking a love beyond the world – the love of Krishna. He is forever waiting in our heart to reciprocate love with us. We can start loving him by practicing bhakti-yoga which guides us to perform our worldly activities as offerings of love for him. This devotional motivation inspires us to do those activities to the best of our capacity, thereby ensuring that we frequently get success. But the focus on Krishna provides an inner security and satisfaction, replacing the insecurity and frustration that had troubled us earlier.

Thus, the sweet paradox of the Gita's message is that, by putting the world out of the equation, we lay the best foundation for attaining love and also success not just in the next world but also in this world.

ॐ

Perform your duty equipoised, O Arjuna, abandoning all attachment to success or failure. Such equanimity is called yoga.

Whatever catches our attention catches us

The advertising industry offers us visual confirmation of an important teaching of the Bhagavad-gita.

The Gita (02.62-63) describes how giving our attention to any object stimulates irrational desires that impel us to self-defeating behavior. These verses outline a universal psychological principle that can be summed in the phrase "whatever catches our attention catches us." This principle is exploited to the hilt by the advertising industry through its ubiquitous billboards and commercials. These depict sense objects in provocative poses to catch our attention, captivate us with sensual desires and incite us to impoverishing splurges and injurious indulgences.

But this same principle can also free us if we intelligently redirect our attention towards Krishna, who makes himself available and attractive to us by appearing in various ways: his enchanting deities, his soothing holy names, his electrifying kirtans, his magnetizing pastimes, his loving devotees or his fulfilling service. These are, in a sense, Krishna's commercials and billboards.

When we use these manifestations of Krishna to engage our minds in the service of remembering him, then spiritual happiness doesn't remain an abstract conception or a utopian aspiration; it becomes a concrete reality and a living experience. If we strive to consciously give our attention to the aspect of Krishna that attracts our heart, we soon pleasantly discover that he has caught our attention and thereby caught us. And his catching us is supremely auspicious. When our heart becomes filled with memories of him and love for him, material desires get crowded out of there – and we become free to delight forever in divine love.

ॐ

While contemplating the objects of the senses, a person develops attachment for them, and from such attachment lust develops, and from lust anger arises.

Ask first "Who am I?" not "What is my?"

*O*ur life-story is essentially the story of our quest for happiness. This quest is directed by a driving question. For spiritualists, the question frequently is, "Who am I?" For materialists, the question usually is, "What is my?"

These questions reflect two radically different conceptions of life. The Bhagavad-gita (02.69) points to these two antipodal worldviews metaphorically: "What is night for the materialists is day for the spiritualists, and what is day for the materialists is night for spiritualists." Here day refers to the sphere of activity and night to the sphere of inactivity. For materialists, the sphere of activity is material enjoyment; for spiritualists, the sphere of activity is spiritual realization. Let's look at their underlying worldviews.

Materialists are governed by the unexamined assumption that they will become happy by acquiring and consuming material objects. As they stay preoccupied with questions like "What is my?" or "What can be my?" they scarcely have the mental space to consider the question, "Who am I?" They often buy unthinkingly into the notion that they are their bodies.

Spiritualists refuse to let themselves be governed by unexamined assumptions, no matter how popular. They recognize that the two assumptions – material things bring happiness and the self is material – involve piling one assumption on another, thereby building a fragile glass palace of assumptions.

Moreover, they also realize that the sequence of these assumptions reverses the natural flow of reasoning. To put first things first implies asking the question "Who am I?" before pursuing a stereotyped way to happiness. When they complement their critical introspection with Gita wisdom, they discover that their essential self is spiritual. This discovery opens the door for them to relish spiritual happiness in loving relationship with Krishna. That, they gradually realize, is life's best happiness.

അ഼ഽ

What is night for all beings is the time of awakening for the self-controlled; and the time of awakening for all beings is night for the introspective sage.
..

The Gita lives through those who live the Gita

Some people ask, "The Bhagavad-gita was spoken thousands of years ago. How can its guidelines be practical today?"

This question originates in a fundamental misunderstanding about the nature of the Gita wisdom-tradition. A living scriptural tradition can never exist in an airtight-sealed vacuum of scriptural guidelines. If any tradition tries to do so, it will soon find itself in the trashcan of history.

What keeps a tradition living is its model practitioners, those seasoned spiritualists who have deeply internalized the scriptural guidelines and have gained an innate sense of the essence and purpose of the guidelines – the principles underlying those guidelines. Being constantly oriented by this sense, they demonstrate through their words and actions how those principles are applicable and beneficial in contemporary scenarios.

The Bhagavad-gita demonstrates a keen awareness of this critical, even indispensable, role played by model practitioners when it states (03.21) that a society's values and purposes are determined by its role models. The Gita wisdom-tradition lives through those who live according to its values and goals.

When we have the opportunity to associate with such practitioners, rich spiritual dividends await us if we grab that opportunity wholeheartedly. To grab that opportunity means that we don't restrict ourselves to memorizing the words that they speak. Their words are important, no doubt, but they may not apply verbatim when circumstances change in our lives, as will inevitably happen. To grab that opportunity means to observe, contemplate and assimilate the principles that they demonstrate, and seek inspiration therein. When we shape our spiritual practices according to such inspiration, then our resulting spiritual sense will show us how the Gita's principles are applicable in various situations. And our life-experiences will bear out for us their practicality and, indeed, their vitality.

ॐ

Whatever action a great man performs, common men follow. And whatever standards he sets by exemplary acts, all the world pursues.

Spiritual advancement comes not by defining but by refining

Spiritual advancement is essentially a journey of our heart's affection towards Krishna, a journey that can get sidetracked by many detours. One tempting detour is over-intellectualism, wherein we get preoccupied with ratiocination instead of transformation. At such times, doubts and questions about logical, informational and theological technicalities engulf us, leaving us with little desire or energy for self-reformation.

This unidimensional intellectuality is often triggered by the modern scientific approach, which glamorizes expertise in reasoning while neglecting character as subjective and irrelevant. The scientific approach deems understanding of a subject to be the result of analyzing, reducing and defining.

This defining approach that is central in the study of matter becomes peripheral in the study of spirit. No doubt, defining has its place in spiritual life; it helps us to gain basic intellectual conviction and to discern authentic spirituality from shallow- or pseudo-spirituality. However, the spiritual realm essentially lies beyond the reach of the intellect. We may glimpse it partially using intellectual conceptualization, but can grasp it properly only by spiritual purification.

The Bhagavad-gita (03.32) indicates how all knowledge – even knowledge about spiritual subjects – is rendered futile (*sarva-jnana vimudhams*) for those whose consciousness is misdirected away from the spiritual level (*acetasah*) to the material level. Correcting this misdirection of consciousness is primarily a process of refining, not defining. Just as refining of gold frees it from impurities, refining of consciousness frees it from the impurities of anti-devotional or immoral desires that keep it trapped at the material level.

When we refine our consciousness by practicing devotional service, spiritual wisdom arises within our hearts, bringing thereby clear and deep understanding that supersedes the most rigorous defining.

ॐ

But those who, out of envy, do not regularly follow these teachings are to be considered bereft of all knowledge, befooled, and ruined in their endeavors for perfection.

We are products, but not prisoners, of our past

"*Is* this just the way I am? Am I a prisoner of my past?" Gloomy thoughts like these may haunt us when we fail in our resolutions to give up our past bad habits.

Gita wisdom offers us the empowering insight that we are products but not prisoners of our past. The Bhagavad-gita (03.34) indicates that, though our past actions have embedded themselves as our present attachments and aversions, we are not slaves of these mental inclinations. Our default likes and dislikes can only push us; they can't force us. We can prevent a push from becoming a compulsion by activating our internal power to counter-push.

To activate this counter-pushing power, we need to align ourselves with scriptural guidelines that give us access to higher powers. The most empowering scriptural guideline is to cultivate constant remembrance of Krishna. By remembering Krishna, we relish a sublime happiness that protects us from being lured by external pleasures.

Our past habits act on us primarily by alluring us towards the pleasures that we had indulged in the past, but had subsequently given up. When we develop the habit of seeking and finding happiness in remembrance of Krishna, then our past habits gradually lose their power over us. Our devotional satisfaction acts initially as an effective counter and eventually as a decisive crusher of all anti-devotional impulses. Then we become completely free from our past, free to rejoice eternally in reciprocating love with Krishna.

Thus, when we align with Krishna through devotional service, that divine alignment frees us from our past and helps us chart a future of ever-increasing freedom.

છ૭૮૦

There are principles to regulate attachment and aversion pertaining to the senses and their objects. One should not come under the control of such attachment and aversion, because they are stumbling blocks on the path of self-realization.

Illusion makes us oblivious to the obvious

Nothing is as amazing as our obliviousness to the reality whose obviousness is evident all around us: death. This was king Yudhishthira's insightful observation in the Mahabharata; he uses the word "amazing" as a euphemism for "amazingly dumb."

Why are we so oblivious? The Bhagavad-gita (03.39) indicates that our knowledge is covered by the illusion spread by lust. This illusion first makes us believe that we can and will enjoy life through our senses. Then it protects this belief by blinding us to the facts that play spoilsport, especially the fact of death that acts as the greatest spoilsport.

Let's see how this fanciful blinding plays out in our times. Death is obvious in the daily news headlines as well as in popular movies. Yet, because these media portray death primarily as an information item or an entertainment commodity respectively, we stay oblivious to the grimness of death. In a typical action movie, the bullets whiz all around the hero, but somehow never kill him. Likewise, we subconsciously believe that, though the bullets of death whiz all around us, they will somehow never down us. This belief survives, even flourishes, despite having no supporting evidence and having universal opposing evidence. The pervasiveness of this blind belief is scary testimony to the power of illusion.

Gita wisdom informs us that the more we free ourselves from lust, the more the grip of illusion on us decreases, and the more we realize as obvious the reality to which we were earlier oblivious. This reality includes the fact of death, but also extends beyond it to the fact of our eternal life of love with Krishna in the arena beyond death.

Put as an equation, our journey from "oblivious" to "obvious" reflects the difference between the spellings of these two words:

Oblivious – LI (Lust-induced Illusion) = Obvious

৵৹

Thus the wise living entity's pure consciousness becomes covered by his eternal enemy in the form of lust, which is never satisfied and which burns like fire.

Enrich yourself with the supreme legacy of immortal love

The Bhagavad-gita (04.01) indicates how Krishna shares spiritual offers the ultimate legacy to all of us, his children. That legacy is knowledge about the best path to transcendence, the path of unending love: bhakti-yoga. By practicing bhakti-yoga, we can easily, quickly and happily redirect our love from the temporary to the eternal. This redirection elevates us to the immortal realm, where we delight in eternal love with him. Thus, Krishna's legacy for us forms a bridge between the realm of mortality, the material world where we presently reside, and the realm of immortality, the spiritual world where we eternally belong.

Even if we receive the best possible legacy from our parents, it will be stripped away from us by the irresistible pull of time. But Krishna as the supreme parent offers us a legacy that time has no power to touch, leave alone steal.

Krishna not only offers this unique legacy, but also sets up a system of disciplic succession to keep it available generation after generation. He even personally descends to our world again and again to remind us of what is waiting for us. Thus he demonstrates how much he loves us and how much he wants us to receive and relish the legacy.

Normally, children are eager to receive their parent's legacy, but unfortunately we are lethargic to receive Krishna's immortal legacy. Why? Because we are infatuated with mortal pleasures and treasures. To free us from such infatuations, Krishna provides in the Gita penetrating analysis about the futility of everything material that is disconnected from him.

By contemplating this sobering reality and, more importantly, contemplating the inspiring reality of Krishna's love, we can motivate ourselves to turn our heart from the world to him. When we offer him our love, immortal enrichment will soon be ours.

℘℘

The Personality of Godhead, Lord Shri Krishna, said: I instructed this imperishable science of yoga to the sun-god, Vivasvan, and Vivasvan instructed it to Manu, the father of mankind, and Manu in turn instructed it to Ikshvaku.

Cherish the power of love, not the love of power

*P*ower. That's what motivates most politicians today. Because they usually have worldly values and goals, they imagine that worldly power is their gateway to happiness. They may talk love of people, but they mostly walk love of power.

Gita wisdom unveils before us political leaders of an entirely different genre: leaders who are philosophically illuminated and devotionally motivated. The Bhagavad-gita (04.02) calls them rajarshis, which is translatable as saintly kings or royal sages. Either way, the designation indicates that they embody an intriguing harmony of worldliness (conveyed by the word raja, king) and other-worldliness (conveyed by the word rishi, sage).

The Gita indicates that these saintly kings are connected to a disciplic succession that traces back to the source of all wisdom and love, Krishna. Through this disciplic connection, they become educated, trained and realized in the spiritual purpose of the world. They understand that the world is ultimately an expression of Krishna's love – he has provided it as an arena for us to redirect our love to him and thereby attain eternal life and happiness.

Such devotional vision enriches the worldly administration of these saintly kings with an otherworldly aspiration: the power of love. They recognize that their own – and their citizens' – well-being lies in channeling the power of love from the human heart to the divine heart. So they don't labor under the illusion that worldly power brings happiness. Consequently, their talents and energies become free to be utilized for implementing sound, scripture-based policies that herald the all-round good of everyone.

We are all in our own way leaders, big or small. If we start embodying the power of love instead of the love of power, then we can set off small but significant ripples of influence that will contribute to restoring our polity to moral integrity and spiritual sanctity.

ॐ

This supreme science was thus received through the chain of disciplic succession, and the saintly kings understood it in that way. But in course of time the succession was broken, and therefore the science as it is appears to be lost.

Living the Gita is not about turning back the clock, but about turning on the compass

*S*ome people ask, "To practice the Gita, do we need to turn back the clock to the time thousands of years ago when it was spoken?"

Not necessary, answers Gita wisdom, because its message is not merely historical, dating back to thousands of years ago. Essentially its message is transcendental – so it is relevant at all times.

The Bhagavad-gita (04.02) outlines how its essential message was passed down generation after generation through learned and realized spiritual teachers. The message is passed down not by verbatim parroting of the original text, but by authentic assimilation and faithful transmission of its essence.

Gita wisdom is not as much a static, frozen information that exists in some primeval manuscript as it is a dynamic, living wisdom that exists in the hearts of those who have aligned their lives according to its compass. That's why the Gita says that its wisdom is passed down not through the careful preservation of its manuscript, but through the living examples of its learned and realized spiritual teachers. Those who love and live the Gita, by their presence, experience and guidance, demonstrates how its wisdom is not abstract but concrete; not outdated, but cutting edge; not theoretical but practical; not a matter of the head, but an affair of the heart.

The Gita's core message is not as much about turning back the clock to some pristine time in remote prehistory as it is about turning on the compass to align ourselves with time-independent universal principles of living and loving that our ancestors were better aligned with. By harmonizing ourselves with those principles, we can apply the Gita even today and relish the same supreme enrichment of wisdom and devotion that its followers throughout history have relished.

C3§O

This supreme science was thus received through the chain of disciplic succession, and the saintly kings understood it in that way. But in course of time the succession was broken, and therefore the science as it is appears to be lost

To comprehend the Gita, focus on its original originality

*M*any people interested in the Bhagavad-gita often wonder, "It has so many interpretations. How do I understand which is the best?"

The Gita itself points to the answer, outlining (04.02) how its wisdom was traditionally received in spiritual lineages of teachers that extend back to its original speaker. It further points (04.03) to the need for reviving such lineages, thereby conveying that they are the best sources for understanding its wisdom.

Why are they the best sources?

Because they preserve the original originality of the Gita.

Our contemporary thought enthrones a particular brand of originality: the finding of some insight that no one has ever found before, an insight that one can then claim as one's original insight. This cult of originality has spawned numerous interpretations of the Gita that are at times as much in keeping with its original spirit as promiscuity is in keeping with chastity.

The currently fashionable connotation of the word "originality" is only one of its meanings – and a recent one at that. Foundationally, originality pointed the other way, to that which was as close to the origin as possible. This connotation is still evident in the usage "original water", referring to water close to its pristine condition.

The Gita is essentially a map for navigating the journey of life, as are road-signs for navigating an expressway. Once we recognize the map-like role of the Gita, we can easily understand that its best interpretation will not be the one that discovers new, hitherto unthought-of meanings of the road-signs, but the one that finds the intended meaning of those who originally put those signs on the road.

It is this original originality of the Gita that the spiritual lineages preserve and make accessible, enabling us to get the maximum benefits of Gita study.

ॐ

This supreme science was thus received through the chain of disciplic succession, and the saintly kings understood it in that way. But in course of time the succession was broken, and therefore the science as it is appears to be lost.

Krishna is a trans-cosmic enjoyer; don't reduce him to a cosmic constable

Some people think that the purpose of God's existence is to protect them while they enjoy life.

Krishna as God in his highest manifestation is much grander than a mere cosmic constable. He is a trans-cosmic enjoyer, delighting in eternal pastimes with his devotees in the spiritual world. He descends for inviting us to join him, as the Bhagavad-gita (04.09) indicates.

During his descent, he also restores order in this world, but that order is not intended to create an arena for us to enjoy this world. Life here is fraught with danger, frequented with distress and finished with death. Our fervent craving to enjoy in such a world indicates the massive disorder within our heart. Krishna comes to correct that inner disorder.

How does he do that? By love. He reveals his splendid love-filled pastimes to attract our heart back to him. As we become attracted to him, we start seeing this world as an arena not for enjoyment but for redirecting our love back to him. This vision inspires us to exile disruptive material desires from our heart, thereby restoring inner order.

In earlier ages, Krishna also established external order as an aid for restoring inner order. But the present age of Kali is a time-slot meant primarily for those souls who want to defy him. That's why in this age he focuses more on restoring internal order for those who want it than on establishing external order for everyone. If we want inner order, he makes it extraordinarily easy through his ever-accessible incarnation as the holy name.

When we take shelter of the holy names, we realize that even amidst this disorderly age Krishna is very much with us, ready to restore order within, and help us join his transcendental life of love.

ॐ

To deliver the pious and to annihilate the miscreants, as well as to reestablish the principles of religion , I Myself appear, millennium after millennium .

Those who let reason usurp Krishna in their heart end up worshiping a false god

"*Isn't* that mythology?" This doubt may trouble us whenever we hear about Krishna's super-human pastimes such as lifting Govardhan hill that seem too unreasonable to believe.

Reason has helped us to make sense of much of the natural world. It has helped us discover the laws of nature that are foundational to technology. Naturally, therefore, we value reason.

Gita wisdom acknowledges the potency of reason. At the same time, it cautions us against ascribing omnipotence to reason by using it to judge the omnipotent God. Why? Because thereby we commit the logical blunder of denying God his defining attribute of omnipotence. If God cannot do anything beyond what nature allows, he is subordinate to nature. If he cannot do anything beyond what reason fathoms, he is subordinate to reason. Either way, he is no longer supreme, no longer omnipotent. A non-omnipotent god is a meaningless god – not God, but a cartoon of God.

By transferring omnipotence from God to reason, we install reason as a surrogate god.

But reason is a false god.

Reason cannot satisfy our heart's hankering for love. Reason cannot provide the emotional warmth necessary to face life's adversities with dignity. Reason cannot replicate the rich fulfillment that a life of reciprocated feelings begets.

Only Krishna – and a life devoted to him – can.

What this analysis implies is not that we abandon reason altogether, but that we adopt a different kind of reason, a proper philosophical reasoning (tattvatah) as indicated in the Bhagavad-gita (04.09). This reasoning is not extrapolated unwarrantedly from our finite experience with nature, but is derived warrantedly from recognition of Krishna's omnipotence. When seen in this light, the seemingly mythological pastimes become revealed as confirmations of Krishna's divinity: "Because he is God, naturally he can do such things."

ༀ

One who knows the transcendental nature of My appearance and activities does not, upon leaving the body, take his birth again in this material world, but attains My eternal abode, O Arjuna.

Unravel the mystery of the Infinite's descent into the finite through love

"*How* can the Supreme who is beyond all limits of space and time appear within those limits?" This is one of existence's greatest mysteries.

Gita wisdom indicates that love alone can resolve this mystery, because love alone creates the mystery in the first place. It is Krishna's love for all of us that motivates him to descend to the material world. Witnessing us undergoing the nightmare of material existence – suffering the traumas of old age, disease, death and re-birth, life after life – Krishna cannot stop himself from intervening to rescue us. He intervenes by personally entering into our nightmare; he descends into the world of matter, empowering with his inconceivable potency the finite to host the infinite. His unfathomable love for all of us inspires him to suspend the normal laws of nature and transcend the usual limits of logic. Though he appears and acts in the limited realm of matter, he remains unlimited and non-material. Though he seems to be another mortal to those whose thinking is bound to matter and materialist conceptions, he reveals himself to be the ultimate immortal to those who activate their devotion and thereby free their thinking from the fetter of matter.

When we engage in devotional service, we realize that Krishna's love, even if inconceivable to our analysis, is undeniable to our experience. This inspires us to not let our head block his entry into our heart. Once he enters our heart, the warmth of his loving presence there wakes us from our materialist slumber. Then we regain our spiritual wisdom and thereby unravel the mystery of his descent. When we thus conceive the inconceivable through love, the Bhagavad-gita (04.09) indicates that we also achieve life's supreme success: fall fully in love with Krishna and return to him for a life of eternal love.

ॐ

One who knows the transcendental nature of My appearance and activities does not, upon leaving the body, take his birth again in this material world, but attains My eternal abode, O Arjuna.

Devotion raises our knowledge of Krishna from superficial familiarity to substantial understanding

The Bhagavad-gita (04.09) states that those who know in truth the divine birth and activities of Krishna become liberated and return to his eternal abode.

On reading this extraordinary promise, we may naturally get the question: "Millions of people such as me already know Krishna. Will all of us be liberated?"

Yes, answers Gita wisdom, provided we know him in truth. The verse indicates that we need to not just know but also understand Krishna, as is conveyed through its use of a significant phrase *vetti tattvatah* (know in truth). The principle of knowing in truth highlights the all-important difference between superficial familiarity and substantial understanding.

We may know Krishna superficially, having heard about him from grandparents or TV or comics. At this level, we often see him as a mythological or historical character, as a colorful figure in our cultural landscape.

Gita wisdom explains that we need to take this knowledge to the next level of understanding by permeating it with devotion. When we render devotional service to Krishna, we understand him to be a living, loving God whose ever-new glory and ever-fresh beauty makes us feel that we have never really known him. We discover his ever-available mercy in the flood of love that inundates our heart in reciprocation for every drop of love that we offer him.

When we are thus charmed by Krishna, we relish a sublime fulfillment that gradually frees us from the worldly desires that bind us to material existence. On being thus freed, we attain, as promised in this Gita verse, the ultimate result of understanding Krishna: return to his abode for a life of eternal love.

༚༁༂

One who knows the transcendental nature of My appearance and activities does not, upon leaving the body, take his birth again in this material world, but attains My eternal abode, O Arjuna

The Gita offers not just another worldview, but also another world to view

"That's just another worldview to add to the confusing plethora of worldviews." Thus do skeptics dismiss Gita wisdom. They argue that as we can't know which worldview, if any, is true, we had best forget metaphysics.

This argument betrays a dangerous frivolousness towards life's most serious questions. Would we be so frivolous about any serious field like, say, medicine? Would we argue that the many systems of medicine are such a confusing mess that we had best forget medicine? Certainly not. Because we know that medicine is a serious matter, a matter of life and death. Metaphysics is an even more serious matter, a matter of perennial liberation or perpetual entanglement.

Surely such a serious matter deserves more than just skeptical dismissal. The Bhagavad-gita indicates (04.10) that if we wish to attain eternal life, we need to break free from the shackles of hotheaded, frustrated skepticism (*krodha*).

How would we find our way among the various systems of medicine?

We would explore and accept as valid a system that satisfies an objective criterion: "Does it work? Does it cure diseases?"

Gita wisdom urges us to similarly explore and accept as valid that metaphysical system which works, which answers life's questions satisfactorily. If we study the Gita diligently, we will find that its worldview answers those questions with an irresistible intellectual flair.

More importantly, the Gita also offers another world to view. Its teachings on yoga, culminating in bhakti-yoga, comprise a systematic, progressive method for awakening our dormant spiritual perception. With this inner vision, we perceive a whole new world of life and love that comprises eternal exchanges of affection between Krishna and his devotees. This world beckons us as our ultimate destination.

An intellectually satisfying worldview and an emotionally appealing world to view – these rewards are more than enough incentive to sacrifice skepticism on the altar of spiritual ambition.

ॐ

Being freed from attachment, fear and anger, being fully absorbed in Me and taking refuge in Me, many, many persons in the past became purified by knowledge of Me—and thus they all attained transcendental love for Me

Tap HIS grace by Humbleness, Inquisitiveness and Service-mindedness

The coach is often the most important shaper of an athlete's success; the systematic and sympathetic guidance of a coach is critical for an aspiring athlete.

When we start practicing spiritual life, we become spiritual athletes. Like material athletes, we too need a coach. The spiritual coach, known usually as the guru, is all the more essential on the spiritual path because the journey is mostly internal and the terrain, not easily perceivable. The guru, the Bhagavad-gita (04.34) states, is the seer of truth (tattva-darshi). Having made the journey and linked with Krishna's supreme vision, the guru can clearly show us that which we can barely see.

To ensure that the guru becomes an effective channel of Krishna's vision, we need to center our relationship with him on this Gita verse's three-point guideline. This guideline can be represented by the acronym HIS (Humbleness, Inquisitiveness, Service-mindedness):

1. **Humbleness (*pranipatena*):** As we can't discern the internal landscape, we need indispensably an attitude of humbleness: "I don't know the way; you do. Please be my guide".

2. **Inquisitiveness (*pariprashnena*):** This injunction of the Gita indicates that it calls not for blind faith in the name of humbleness, but for a development of our capacity for spiritual perception. By this perception, we start seeing for ourselves what the guru is seeing.

3. **Service-mindedness (*sevaya*):** The destination of our spiritual journey is the realization that loving service to Krishna is the only source of lasting fulfillment. We progress towards that realization by serving Krishna as per the guru's instructions.

Thus, HIS grace works in three progressive steps: humbleness enables the guru to show us the way; inquisitiveness enables us to start seeing the way ourselves; and service-mindedness enables us to move along the way.

☙❧

Just try to learn the truth by approaching a spiritual master. Inquire from him submissively and render service unto him. The self-realized souls can impart knowledge unto you because they have seen the truth

Faith bridges the gap between personal realization and scriptural revelation

We may get the question: "What is the role of faith in understanding the Bhagavad-gita?"

Faith helps us persevere in our spiritual journey till our personal realization catches up with scriptural revelation.

We begin our spiritual journey by intelligently examining the Gita's basic philosophical teachings: the temporality and misery of life in the arena of matter, and the eternality and the ecstasy of life in the arena of spirit. By open-minded experimentation based on these teachings, we gradually realize their truth. Let's see how.

The Gita is not just a book of analysis but of action; all its analysis is meant to gear to action its original student, Arjuna – and its subsequent students, all of us. When we act to apply the Gita's basic principles in our own lives, we experience a dual inner transformation. Firstly, the fuzziness around matter clears, helping us to see material indulgences as sources of misery. Secondly, the vagueness around spirit lifts, helping us to perceive spiritual reality centered on Krishna as rich and relishable. By such dual reformulation of our vision, we realize the veracity of the Gita's basic teachings.

Subsequently, when some Gita teachings don't seem real or sensible, we can bank on our past experiential confirmation of its teachings. This track record helps us repose faith in those scriptural revelations that our personal realizations have not yet reached. The Bhagavad-gita (04.39) points to this role of faith (sraddhaval) in paving the way to the attainment of realized knowledge (labhate jnanam). This realized knowledge deepens our faith, which then bridges the gap between our present realization and presently unrealized scriptural knowledge.

Over time, this symbiosis of reposed faith and realized knowledge engenders a living and deepening devotional experience of the supreme reality – Krishna himself.

ॐ

A faithful man who is dedicated to transcendental knowledge and who subdues his senses is eligible to achieve such knowledge, and having achieved it he quickly attains the supreme spiritual peace

.

Delight in the devotional chain reaction of faith and knowledge

Faith is the most precious asset on the spiritual path. It enables us to pursue diligently that which we cannot perceive directly: the treasure of love for Krishna. This faith when coupled with spiritual knowledge leads to a devotional chain reaction. Let's see how:

Faith as the root of knowledge: The Bhagavad-gita (04.39) asserts that the faithful attain spiritual knowledge. Without some initial faith at least in the form of a sympathetic curiosity, we won't enquire sincerely about the spiritual dimension. And, when some scriptural teachings don't make sense immediately, the common-sense faith that Krishna's intelligence is greater than ours will keep us going.

Faith as the fruit of knowledge: We can increase our faith by deepening our spiritual knowledge. For this, we need to scrutinizingly study scriptures like the Gita and appreciate their import by associating with Gita-lovers and Gita-livers. As our knowledge increases, our doubts diminish and disappear. And as we apply that knowledge, magic happens within our heart. Our emotions and values reform; we become more selfless and pure. This amazing transformation naturally increases our faith.

The Devotional Chain Reaction: Our initial faith may be tender, but acquiring spiritual knowledge strengthens our faith. And this enhanced faith inspires us to study scripture more and thereby deepen our spiritual knowledge, which further boosts our faith. Thus faith and knowledge interact in a devotional chain reaction that culminates in life's supreme attainment: eternal love for Krishna.

☙❧

A faithful man who is dedicated to transcendental knowledge and who subdues his senses is eligible to achieve such knowledge, and having achieved it he quickly attains the supreme spiritual peace.

Renunciation is super-ambitious, not un-ambitious

*M*any people assume that renunciation symptomizes a lack of the ambition to struggle for material pleasures. Such people deride as unambitious those who renounce worldly pleasures – be it entirely by embracing monkhood or partially by regulating material enjoyment.

Gita wisdom acknowledges the existence of such kneejerk renunciates who renounce the world because of their inabilities and frustrations. But it also underscores that such superficial renunciates are at best shadows and at worst caricatures of authentic renunciates, who are among the world's most ambitious individuals. Authentic renunciates turn away from the world not because they lack the ambition to seek its pleasures, but because they possess the acumen to see through those pleasures. They understand that all worldly pleasures are intrinsically and unavoidably temporary. Be it winning a video game or climbing Mount Everest, be it eating one's favorite pizza or flirting with Miss or Mr. Universe, no material achievement offers happiness that lasts. Thus, the thought that motivates them to turn them away from material pleasures is not "that's too tough," but "that's too tiny."

Authentic renunciates are convinced that there is more to life than fleeting material pleasures. Their logic is sound: as all of us long for happiness round-the-clock, there must exist a happiness that satisfies round-the-clock. They complement this logical introspection with scriptural information: the Bhagavad-gita (05.21) declares that the spiritual happiness accessible by connecting internally with the divine is imperishable. This scriptural knowledge sparks within them the ambition to achieve that inexhaustible happiness of devotion, no matter what the price. The price is high: disconnecting oneself from anti-spiritual material pleasures through renunciation, and reconnecting oneself constantly with Krishna through loving remembrance.

The willpower to pay such a high price defines not the unambitious, but the super-ambitious.

ॐ

Such a liberated person is not attracted to material sense pleasure but is always in trance, enjoying the pleasure within. In this way the self-realized person enjoys unlimited happiness, for he concentrates on the Supreme.

Be not allured by the pleasure that is pregnant with suffering

*W*hy does the Bhagavad-gita ask us to regulate indulgence in sensual pleasures? To protect us from unnecessary suffering.

The Gita (05.22) states that such pleasures are the wombs of suffering. The graphic analogy of a womb (yoni) conveys how we may mistakenly equating invisibility with non-existence. Just as the infant within the womb is not visible in the early stages of pregnancy, the suffering within sensual indulgence is not visible in the early stages of enjoyment.

But just as the infant will be born in due course of time, so will the suffering materialize. When we see hedonistic lifestyles glamorized on billboards and in commercials, we don't see the distressing and disastrous consequences of such living. However, such invisibility of those consequences doesn't imply their non-existence; we just need to look hard in the right places. A look at sociological surveys reveals alarming statistics of sexually transmitted diseases, divorces, rapes, and lust-induced psychological problems that range from depression and addiction to suicide and murder. These problems may have varying specific causes, but they frequently have an underlying generic cause: uncontrolled sexuality. In terms of the womb analogy, these sufferings comprise the delivery of the suffering pregnant in sense pleasure.

Abortion can prevent the delivery in ordinary pregnancy, but there is no abortion to prevent the delivery of the suffering pregnant in sense indulgence. That's why the next verse of the Gita (05.23) states that, if we wish to live happily, we need to tolerate the desires for sensual enjoyment and not indulge in them. Tolerance becomes easier if we cultivate remembrance of Krishna and experience a higher happiness thereof, thus making the lower pleasures of sense indulgence initially resistible and eventually undesirable.

༺ॐ༻

An intelligent person does not take part in the sources of misery, which are due to contact with the material senses. O son of Kunti, such pleasures have a beginning and an end, and so the wise man does not delight in them

.

View the world as an object for reciprocation, not recreation or rejection

Many prospective spiritualists have the question: "To become spiritual, do we have to turn our back to the world?"

Gita wisdom offers an unequivocal answer: "No; we just have to raise our eyes beyond the world to Krishna."

The Bhagavad-gita (05.29) informs us that the world belongs to Krishna and is meant for his service. To grasp the significance of this information, let's look at the three broad attitudes that people can have towards the world:

1. **Recreation:** Those with this attitude treat the world as a good place made for their enjoyment. They presume that Krishna exists primarily to provide and protect their worldly enjoyment. Their attitude represents the path of karma.

2. **Rejection:** Those with this attitude see the world as an evil place made to give them suffering. They see its apparent pleasures as baits that entice and entrap. Those with this attitude focus more on going away from the world than on going towards God. Their attitude represents the path of jnana.

3. **Reciprocation:** Those with this attitude view Krishna as the central reality of existence, and see the world as a subordinate reality meant for his service. They see the world as an arena for reciprocating love with him, for making loving offerings to him through service and for witnessing enlightening demonstrations of his teachings. To them, worldly pleasures are distorted reflections of the spiritual joys available through loving service to Krishna. Their attitude represents the path of bhakti.

The Gita indicates that the third attitude reflects the most evolved understanding of the world.

When we cultivate this attitude, our eyes become fixed on Krishna, and so the world can no longer lock our eyes with its pleasures. By this devotional vision, we can stay spiritual even while being in the material world.

૱ઈ૰

A person in full consciousness of Me, knowing Me to be the ultimate beneficiary of all sacrifices and austerities, the Supreme Lord of all planets and demigods, and the benefactor and well-wisher of all living entities, attains peace from the pangs of material miseries.

To save you from you, couple the real self with the Supreme Self

"Why did I do that?" This question often troubles us whenever we look back at an unworthy action that we did on the spur of the moment. Seeking an honest answer leads us to an unpleasant conclusion: my greatest enemy is me.

The question, then, begs itself: who will save me from me?

The Bhagavad-gita (06.05) answers, "Me." The literal translation of this enigmatic verse reads: "Elevate the self with the self; do not degrade the self with the self. The self is the friend of the self and the self is also the enemy of the self."

To make sense of this verse, we need to understand the dual sense of the word "self." This dual sense arises from the fact that we are spiritual beings trapped in material bodies. Our spiritual side –our real self – prompts us to seek devotional fulfillment, whereas our material side, our illusory self, pushes us to seek worldly enjoyment. For all practical purposes, the illusory self can be equated with the mind, as the translations by most prominent Gita commentators substantiate.

With either translation, the essential question remains: how can we save ourselves? To understand the answer, let's consider a metaphor.

Our situation is like that of a boat on an ocean. For the boat to stay steady amidst the wavy and stormy ocean, it needs to be coupled to something steadier than itself: an anchor. Similarly, if we wish to stay steady amidst the materialistic storms that shake us through provocative situations and passions, we need to couple with something steadier than ourselves: the ultimate spiritual anchor, Krishna, who is the soul of the soul, the Supreme Self.

Therefore, the complete answer to the question, "Who can save me from me?" is: "Me, by coupling with Krishna."

⚬⚬

One must deliver himself with the help of his mind, and not degrade himself. The mind is the friend of the conditioned soul, and his enemy as well.

Take the mind's promises with a bucketful of salt

Whenever we see an ad promising a huge gain for a tiny price, we tend to become skeptical. Such skepticism is the understandable and desirable effect of living for years in a commercialized society out to get our money.

Yet when similar over-hyped promises of enjoyment come internally from our mind instead of externally from ads, we often cast aside our customary skepticism and get carried away.

Why do we believe our mind so uncritically? Because we think that the mind is me. So, we feel that the mind's ideas are my ideas. Once we take ownership of an idea, we become ready to do anything to implement it. Only later when the consequences show the counter-productivity, even the stupidity, of the idea do we wonder exasperatedly why we acted so irrationally. Such moments can help us see the wisdom in the Bhagavad-gita (06.06) recommendation that as long as the mind controls us, we should treat it like our worst enemy.

The first step in breaking free from the mind's control is to become skeptical about its promises. When we are skeptical about a person, we take that person's promises with a pinch of salt. However, given the track record of the mind in misleading us millions of times, we need to take its promises with not just a pinch but a bucketful of salt.

When we consistently feed the mind large doses of skepticism, then gradually it gives up its fanciful ideas for material enjoyment. When we also give ourselves repeated experiences of the refined pleasures of devotional service to Krishna, the mind slowly starts taking a liking for spiritual joys. Only when the mind has fully transferred its affection from matter to Krishna can we safely put aside our salt-bucket.

❀

For him who has conquered the mind, the mind is the best of friends; but for one who has failed to do so, his mind will remain the greatest enemy.

Go beyond the stocking of information to the flowing of service

As we live in an information-centered age, we are often stimulated by new information. When we encounter the Bhagavad-gita, we tend to seek stimulation in new spiritual information. If we let this search for new information become an obsession, we will end up knowing much spiritual information, but experiencing little spiritual fulfillment.

Why?

Because spiritual fulfillment comes from love, not knowledge.

Gita wisdom explains that we are all conscious spiritual beings whose deepest need is love. To relish real and eternal happiness, we need to love the all-attractive, all-loving Lord of our heart, Krishna. To love him, we need to know him. So, Gita wisdom provides abundant spiritual information about him.

Nonetheless, the goal of the spiritual path is not information but devotion. Information is useful to the extent it serves as a means to the end of devotion. If information alone becomes our end, we will not connect devotionally with Krishna and so won't experience deep spiritual happiness. As we are innately pleasure-seeking, desires for material pleasures will continue to torment us. At best, we will stay stuck at the intellectual platform where we may delight in showing off our spiritual knowledge to others. At worst, our thirst for pleasure will drag us down to the sensual level or even the sinful level.

To rise from the intellectual level to the spiritual level, we need to let scriptural information spur us into transcendental action, into practical service to Krishna. Service expresses our devotion if we have it, and our desire for devotion if we don't have it. When we thus go beyond stocking information to immersing ourselves in the flow of service, our information will, by Krishna's mercy, blossom into realization. This integration of information and realization will, as the Gita (06.08) states, grant spiritual satisfaction.

ॐ

A person is said to be established in self-realization and is called a yogi [or mystic] when he is fully satisfied by virtue of acquired knowledge and realization. Such a person is situated in transcendence and is self-controlled. He sees everything—whether it be pebbles, stones or gold—as the same.

To see stone and gold equally, see beyond stone and gold to Krishna

The Bhagavad-gita (06.08) shares a puzzling recommendation: see stone and gold equally.

How is this possible?

To understand, let's analyze the statement at three progressive levels:

Detached material level:

Gita wisdom indicates that the value of material objects is relative. For example, cricket is deemed valuable by Indians, but not Americans; baseball is deemed valuable by Americans, but not Indians. Fashions are another example. If a dress is dubbed fashionable, its value skyrockets. If it is dubbed unfashionable, its value nosedives.

This relativity of value extends to everything material – even paper currency, which many people consider objectively valuable. If economic upheavals cause currency devaluation, the notes remain, but their noteworthiness diminishes or even vanishes.

By dispassionately extending such material analysis to stone and gold, we can see the relativity of the value-tags assigned to them, and thereby see both equally.

Detached spiritual level:

Gita wisdom gives us knowledge of our identity as indestructible non-material souls. This knowledge helps us recognize that we spiritual beings can never get any happiness from anything material, so we can equally disregard everything material, be it stone or gold.

Engaged Devotional level:

Gita wisdom soars higher than the previous detached intellectual (*jnani*) level to the engaged devotional (*bhakti*) level. At this pinnacle, we value material things from Krishna's perspective, based on whether they can be utilized in his service and whether they can bring us closer to him. Consequently, devotees may accept stone as if it were gold if it can be used to construct a temple for him and may reject gold as if it were stone if it allures them away from him.

By this Krishna-centered equality of vision, we can stay spiritually focused amidst materially alluring and repelling circumstances, and steadily march towards Krishna.

ॐ

A person is said to be established in self-realization and is called a yogi [or mystic] when he is fully satisfied by virtue of acquired knowledge and realization. Such a person is situated in transcendence and is self-controlled. He sees everything—whether it be pebbles, stones or gold—as the same.

To access the Absolute Truth, reject the absolute rejection of absolute truths

Due to the spread of postmodernism, many people tend towards metaphysical relativism: the idea that absolute truths are impossible because cultural, historical and intellectual biases distort all truth claims.

Biases are inherent even in systems of knowledge normally considered objective, such as modern science. Many philosophers of science have shown how the preconceptions of scientists, the paradigms of the scientific establishment and the prevailing intellectual trends of society shape the direction and destination of scientific research.

Does the prevalence of biases justify the idea that "There are no absolute truths"?

No. Because that idea is itself a claim to absolute truth. Thus, it falls squarely in the genre of other self-refuting assertions such as "I can't speak a word in English" or "I don't exist."

As the rejection of absolute truths is self-contradictory, absolute truths are possible. But are they accessible? Can we go beyond our biases to access those truths?

Gita wisdom offers a process of purification that takes us beyond all material influences to the universal spiritual essence. The Bhagavad-gita (06.20) indicates that we can perceive spiritual reality when we stop the material mind. Various cultural, historical and intellectual biases misdirect our mind and skew our perception. When we freeze the mind by purification, we gradually access universal spiritual reality.

As stopping the mind is an onerous process, Gita wisdom endorses bhakti-yoga as an easier alternative. Bhakti centers on constant contemplation on Krishna. We are souls, parts of Krishna. So, our bhakti connection with him revives our spiritual nature and re-activates our innate faculty for transcendental perception, which has long been atrophied because of our obsession with material things.

By the activation of this transcendental perception, we go beyond the mind and its inevitable biases to the uncontaminated and unconstricted experience of the absolute truth.

ॐ

In the stage of perfection called trance, or samadhi, one's mind is completely restrained from material mental activities by practice of yoga. This perfection is characterized by one's ability to see the self by the pure mind and to relish and rejoice in the self.

Krishna-thoughts are soothing, satisfying, strengthening, sublimating

*M*aterialists often challenge spiritualists: "Why do you spend so much time thinking about Krishna when all that thinking doesn't give any tangible return?"

The key word here is 'tangible.' As today's materialistic culture evaluates everything in terms of money, it makes us believe that returns are tangible only when they are financially measurable. However, the level of our thoughts determines our happiness as much as, if not far more than, the level of our finances. So, if our thought-level is improved, isn't that improvement also a tangible return?

Yes, definitely.

By this more realistic standard of tangibility, Krishna-thoughts offer four tangible returns:

1. **Soothing:** The uncertainties of life make us anxiety-ridden. Thinking about Krishna – the only ultimate certainty in existence – counters these anxieties and soothes our heart.

2. **Satisfying:** The endless parade of tempting objects that assault our senses makes us chronically discontented. Thinking about Krishna – the reservoir of all pleasure – eradicates this discontent and grants deep satisfaction.

3. **Strengthening:** The continuous battle with our lower desires leaves us internally exhausted. Thinking about Krishna – the source of all vitality – replenishes our inner energy stock and strengthens us.

4. **Sublimating:** The impurity and immorality in our materialistic culture tends to mentally degrade us. Thinking about Krishna – the abode of all purity – cleanses and sublimates our mind.

Once we start relishing such rich returns, we will realize, as the Bhagavad-gita (06.22) indicates, that no gain is greater than this. Then we will turn the culture's challenge on its head: "When contemplation on Krishna offers so many tangible returns, why should I let even one moment pass without thinking about him?"

ॐ

Gaining this he thinks there is no greater gain. Being situated in such a position, one is never shaken, even in the midst of greatest difficulty.

Seek the one achievement that misery cannot reach

All of us want to achieve something glorious in life. Unfortunately, even if we achieve something special materially, whatever we achieve still leaves us prone to the twin miseries of hankering and lamenting. We hanker because, no matter what we gain, the feeling that we need to gain something more keeps dogging us. And we lament because whatever we gain is taken away by the upheavals of life – inevitably.

For an achievement to be truly glorious, it should catapult us beyond the reach of hankering and lamenting. Is there any such achievement? And can it be attained?

Yes, answers Gita wisdom to both questions.

The Bhagavad-gita (06.22) indicates that the achievement of divine trance takes us beyond the range of hankering and lamenting.

Freedom from hankering: When this trance-like state makes us lovingly absorbed in Krishna, that absorption satisfies us so completely that we realize there's nothing more to be gained. He fulfills all our heart's longings for love, beauty and happiness so perfectly that the hankering for anything else can't even touch our heart, leave alone torment it.

Freedom from lamenting: Worldly achievements are extrinsic to us, whereas love for Krishna is intrinsic to us as souls. It is a part of our very being; in fact, it is our original spiritual nature. That's why no material upheaval can ever strip this gain away from us. Even when disasters strike at the material level, they don't affect our core treasure and so can't cause lamentation.

This supreme achievement is not only real, but is also realizable for each one of us. All that we need to do is cultivate remembrance of Krishna regularly. Over time, this remembrance will become habitual, natural and perpetual, and life's supreme achievement will be ours.

ॐ

Upon gaining this he thinks there is no greater gain. Being situated in such a position, one is never shaken, even in the midst of greatest difficulty.

Glue the mind to meditation, not mediation

Many of our problems often seem to have an inbuilt mental glue. They stick to our minds constantly. Especially during our mantra meditation, we frequently find our mind doing mediation about problem-solving. The mind pretends to act as an intermediary between us and the problem. As a mediator, it promises to find a solution, but actually it makes us distracted, distressed and drained.

Gita wisdom helps us understand that the glue is present not in the problem, but in our own mind. When we misconceive that our sense of security depends on worldly conditions, then problems that threaten the worldly status quo appear overwhelming. So, we become mentally preoccupied, even obsessed, with tackling that threat, thereby unwittingly glueing our mind to it. When we try to meditate in such a situation, meditation starts seeming like a waste of time that blocks us from real problem-solving.

To meditate attentively amidst problems, we need to address the root problem: our misplaced sense of security. Putting our sense of security back in its proper place requires intelligence sustained by conviction (*buddhya dhruti-grihataya*), as indicated in the Bhagavad-gita (06.25). This involves two steps:

1. **Intellectual recollection:** Reminding ourselves that the only authentic security is in our spiritual relationship with Krishna – that alone is lasting, everything else is passing.

2. **Mental reorientation:** Redirecting our minds to seek security in Krishna through meditation.

This two-step inner change will help us see meditation in a fresh light: not as a distraction from the real issues of life, but as the most real issue of life that lays the foundation for dealing with all the other issues of life. This reformed vision will not only glue the mind to meditation, but also make it calm and clear so that after the meditation it can mediate and solve the problems more effectively.

☙❧

Gradually, step by step, one should become situated in trance by means of intelligence sustained by full conviction, and thus the mind should be fixed on the self alone and should think of nothing else.

Reality is more fascinating than what we have been allowed to believe

Today's mainstream ideology is materialism, which doesn't allow people to believe in non-material or spiritual truths. In the materialistic conception of life, the only possible enjoyment is material enjoyment, and reality is interesting to the extent it offers material enjoyment. But all materially enjoyable objects are limited and all material pleasures are finite, so the enjoyment available in the materialistic worldview is inescapably temporary. And when no enjoyment is available, reality becomes boring.

In delightful contrast, the Bhagavad-gita (06.30) indicates how an advanced spiritualist sees Krishna everywhere. As Krishna is the reservoir of all happiness, this vision makes reality constantly fascinating. Such a vision is perceived not through one's material senses, but through one's spiritual senses.

Our spiritual senses are presently dormant, but we can awaken them by the process of devotional service centered on mantra meditation. The divine sound of mantras aligns our spiritual sense perception with the vision of advanced spiritualists. This alignment enables us to discover that reality is much more fascinating than what dogmatic materialism has allowed us to believe.

Where the material senses see only the purposeless motions of matter according to impersonal laws and mechanical forces, the spiritual senses see the purposeful actions of a benevolent God. Where the material senses see worldly happenings only as favorable or unfavorable or immaterial for our self-centered enjoyment, we now see worldly happenings as potential forums for learning and growth. We understand that Krishna can use these events as timely demonstrations of the timeless truths he has taught in the Gita, especially the supreme truth of his unfailing love for us. Once we start seeing life as a school for experientially learning spiritual truths, reality becomes endlessly fascinating as a setting for the demonstration of those empowering truths.

CRRO

For one who sees Me everywhere and sees everything in Me, I am never lost, nor is he ever lost to Me.

To know Krishna is to relish a thrilling, fulfilling, unifying awareness of reality

Awareness: that's what differentiates the living from the non-living. Though all living beings are aware, most of them are aware only of material reality.

The capacity to be aware of spiritual reality: that's what differentiates human beings from other living beings. Though all human beings have this capacity, few utilize it.

The awareness of spiritual reality: that's what differentiates spiritualists from other human beings. Not all spiritualists, though, ascend to awareness of the pinnacle of spiritual reality: Krishna.

The active awareness of Krishna as the ultimate spiritual reality: that's what differentiates devotees from other spiritualists.

The Bhagavad-gita points to this progressive enrichment of awareness when it states (07.03) that among thousands, few endeavor to know Krishna, and among those who endeavor, fewer still actually know him in truth.

What does knowing Krishna in truth mean?

It doesn't mean theoretical, informational knowledge of Krishna as a historical personality. Millions already have that, and millions more can acquire that just by reading a relevant book.

It means practical, experiential awareness of Krishna as the acme of truth, the paragon of beauty, the ocean of happiness. To be aware of Krishna is to relish an unending flood of wisdom, beauty and joy. Thanks to Krishna's all-attractiveness, we fall in love with him – completely, eternally, purely.

When we become aware of Krishna, we don't become unaware of other features and levels of reality; rather, we see them from a higher perspective, just as we would see the road traffic from atop a skyscraper.

Awareness of Krishna not only heightens but also unifies our perspective. We see all of reality not as discrete and discordant sets of perspectives, but as coherent and concordant subsets of visions within the superset of the absolute reality, Krishna.

This unifying awareness is thrilling and fulfilling. It is life's supreme attainment.

ॐ

Out of many thousands among men, one may endeavor for perfection, and of those who have achieved perfection, hardly one knows Me in truth.

Anahankara = an + aham + car (I am not my car)

"*You* are your car," claims a billboard displaying a person driving a flashy car. The ad indicates how one's car determines one's image in a status-driven world. Additionally, the ad's equalization of a conscious person with an insentient vehicle illustrates how we misidentify with that which we are not.

The subtle arrangement that brings about such misidentification of the soul with the body is called *ahankara*. Significantly, the Bhagavad-gita (07.04) also mentions *ahankara* as one of the eight material elements. Thus, ahankara is both an object and a concept – the object, a material element, is the tool through which the concept, the misidentification, is manifested and maintained. *Ahankara* as an object, as a material element in our body, will remain as long as we are in material existence. But ahankara as the concept of misidentification will disappear when we become self-realized, as the Gita (13.09 - *anahankara*) alludes to.

To counter the delusion caused by *ahankara*, we can contemplate the car-body analogy from ontological and functional perspectives. Just as the driver is ontologically different from the car and is functionally its activator, the soul is ontologically different from the body and is functionally its activator.

With this exposé of *ahankara*, we can see how our culture aggravates ahankara to absurd levels, as in the ad's equalization of a person with a car. Just as the desire to enjoy a car causes a person to misidentify with it, the desire to enjoy the body causes us to misidentify with it. As an antidote to such desires, we can use a creative, non-historical etymology of the word *ahankara* as aham + car "I am my car" and cultivate *anahankara* by training ourselves to respond: "No, I am not my car. So, I won't be driven by unnecessary bodily desires."

❀

Earth, water, fire, air, ether, mind, intelligence and false ego—all together these eight constitute My separated material energies.

Those who dismiss the invisible as insubstantial dissipate their lives in the insubstantial

We human beings have an intelligence more advanced than our nonhuman fellow beings. This developed intelligence enables us to think beyond the immediate issues that occupy the animals: eating, sleeping, mating and defending. We can ponder the ultimate issues: the meaning of existence, the source of creation and the supreme goal of life.

Unfortunately, some people dismiss ultimate issues as insubstantial: "Why bother about things that you can't see or touch? Just enjoy the here-and-now." Such spiritual shortsightedness sentences them to an insubstantial existence not much different from that of animals. They dissipate their life in the pursuit of animalistic pleasures – an existence that is exposed as meaningless and fruitless in the face of inevitable death.

Among such people, the Bhagavad-gita (07.15) refers to one category as *mayayapaharita jnanah*, those whose knowledge has been stolen by illusion. This designation acknowledges that these people have knowledge, but underscores that illusion has blinded them to the purpose of knowledge: to find a pathway for going from the animal level to the spiritual level. These people use their knowledge for the opposite purpose: to erect intellectual misconceptions and technological distractions that keep them away from the spiritual level.

For those of us who wish to fulfill the purpose of knowledge, Gita wisdom offers a philosophical and experiential pathway to the world beyond. When we use our intelligence to comprehend and apply Gita wisdom, we discover answers to life's ultimate questions. And we find our consciousness rising from the visible to the invisible, from the material to the spiritual, from the mundane to the divine. Gradually, we realize our identity as integral parts of the all-attractive source of everything, Krishna, and progressively achieve life's supreme goal: ecstatic eternal love for him.

ॐ

Those miscreants who are grossly foolish, who are lowest among mankind, whose knowledge is stolen by illusion, and who partake of the atheistic nature of demons do not surrender unto Me.

Those who make donkeys the Gita's role models sentence themselves to the donkey-like roles

"Work is worship is the central teaching of the Bhagavad-gita." So claim many people.

If they were right, then wouldn't it make the creature that works extremely hard, the donkey, the Gita's role model?

But the Gita doesn't consider the donkey as its model. Of course, it (05.12) urges us to cultivate equal vision towards all living beings including animals such as donkeys, to see them all as sparks of spirit, similar in spiritual essence to us. Additionally, it uses the standard metaphor of a donkey (*mudha*) to refer to people who labor pointlessly, without any spiritual insight or interest. The donkey subjects itself to unnecessary torture, carrying huge loads for tiny rewards, lumps of grass that it could have got without becoming a beast of burden.

Similar to the donkey, the Gita (07.15) indicates, are those people who exhaust their human intelligence and energy for gaining the bodily pleasures of eating, sleeping, mating and defending – pleasures available to animals. Humans who labor for these animalistic pleasures labor like donkeys, unnecessarily and unproductively. Thus Gita wisdom indicts the "work is worship" brigade. For the Gita, such sloganeers are models, no doubt – but models to be avoided, not emulated.

Of course, the Gita shows the way to authentically make work into worship (18.46: *sva-karmana tam abhyarca*). But that way is far different from the self-serving notion that work itself is intrinsically, automatically worship. That way begins by recognizing the enormous potential of human life as a launching pad from mortality to immortality. To attain immortal life in Krishna's imperishable abode, we need to devote quality time for exclusively worshiping him. This singular devotion transforms our heart into an altar for the continuous worship of Krishna. With this inner sanctification when we engage in our worldly work, he graciously accepts our work as a form of worship.

By thus cultivating a deep devotional disposition, we can all transform our work into worship.

Those miscreants who are grossly foolish, who are lowest among mankind, whose knowledge is stolen by illusion, and who partake of the atheistic nature of demons do not surrender unto Me.

Devotional spirituality offers breaks that are much more than brakes

The racehorse-pace of life nowadays impels many people to apply brakes, lest they break down. These break-seekers often explore spirituality for utilitarian purposes. Just as one may dive into a swimming pool to get a refreshing break, they dive into popular forms of spirituality such as yoga, meditation or devotional music.

Anticipating such mindsets, the Bhagavad-gita (07.16) states that the hope of relief from distress is one of the primary impetuses for people to explore the spiritual dimension of life. Today when stress is among the most widespread forms of distress troubling everyone – even successful people – the hope for stress relief impels many towards spirituality.

Such stress-relief seekers often see feel-good experience as the essence of spirituality. So, they frequently downplay or discard philosophy as a needless baggage that will weigh them down during the dive. However, if they study the Gita open-mindedly, they will realize that philosophy is not an unnecessary load, but a necessary compass. This compass helps them understand what the dive is about, why it offers relief and how they can dive deeper to gain greater relief. That is, philosophy provides an intellectual framework for comprehending spiritual experience.

Additionally, those who dive deep into the ocean of devotion with the compass of philosophy discover immense experiential treasures. They discern a whole new world hidden underwater, concealed from the vision of those whose eyes are glued to material things. That world is where we all belong as spirit souls meant for a life of everlasting love with Krishna. When they get a taste of the sweetness of devotion, they realize that devotional spirituality offers much more than a brake for slowing down material life. It provides a permanent break from all worldly miseries and an eternal re-union with the Lord of the heart.

ॐ

O best among the Bharatas, four kinds of pious men begin to render devotional service unto Me—the distressed, the desirer of wealth, the inquisitive, and he who is searching for knowledge of the Absolute

Raise the curiosity radar from the how questions to the why questions

Curiosity is one of our defining characteristics – we are shaped by what we seek and find on our curiosity radar. Science, philosophy, literature and all such monuments of human intelligence began in curiosity.

The curiosity radar is present not just in human beings but also in animals. For example, dogs sniff and search wherever they are placed. However, the curiosity radar of animals searches at a much lower level than that of humans. Animals ask practical questions of the *how* type: "How can I continue to exist – how can I get food, sleep, sex and shelter?" We alone can ask philosophical questions of the *why* type: "Why does anything exist at all?" and "Why do I exist?"

Unfortunately, our curiosity radar usually searches at a low animal level due to the inner force of our worldly desires and the outer influence of the materialistic culture. If we use our intelligence to raise our radar and start asking the *why* questions, we are guided by divine will to founts of spiritual wisdom such as the Bhagavad-gita. Thus, through his words, Krishna enters our curiosity radar.

The Bhagavad-gita points to this progression when it (07.16) outlines the four kinds of people who come to Krishna – the distressed, the financially needy, the inquisitive and the knowledgeable. Our initial curiosity that inspires us to know Krishna places us among the inquisitive. Our subsequent curiosity that inspires us to love him, understanding that such love is the purpose and perfection of existence, places us among the knowledgeable.

When we animate our curiosity about Krishna with devotion, he reveals himself as an eternally, ever-increasingly attractive person – delightfully different from all other curiosity objects that lose their charm with the passage of time. Indeed, Krishna's continuous self-revelation transforms life into an exciting adventure in endless love.

℃ℬ℘

O best among the Bharatas, four kinds of pious men begin to render devotional service unto Me—the distressed, the desirer of wealth, the inquisitive, and he who is searching for knowledge of the Absolute.

Cultivate devotion not for its survival value but for the value it brings to survival

*T*he struggle for survival characterizes the existence of all living beings – nonhuman and human. So, while evaluating whether a particular thing is worth doing, we often focus on its survival value: will it help me in my struggle for survival?

This survival-centered criterion frequently determines whether we take up the practice of devotional service. The Bhagavad-gita (07.16) acknowledges that people usually worship Krishna expecting the removal of the miseries they feel are threatening their survival (arto) or the bestowal of the wants they feel are necessary for their survival (artharthi).

Such considerations are largely self-centered and are spiritually under-informed. Still, the Gita (07.18) indicates that Krishna appreciates even this preliminary devotion. Simultaneously, he gently encourages us to rise to a higher level of devotion, as is evident in his special appreciation of those who worship him selflessly. If we reciprocate with his compassionate overtures and strive to render selfless devotional service for his pleasure, then gradually we open ourselves to receive a much greater gift: eternal spiritual love for him. As he encompasses and embodies everything that our heart desires (Gita 07.19: vasudevah sarvam iti), loving him satisfies our heart fully and forever.

Thus, we discover that devotional service has actually brought us a gift far greater than survival value. It has brought value to survival – it has granted the undying love that makes life eminently worth living. Enriched with this love, we recognize that survival is not ultimately valueless, ending helplessly in unavoidable death. Rather, we realize that survival is supremely valuable, serving as a springboard for launching us on a spiritual journey that culminates in Krishna's world of immortal love.

❀

All these devotees are undoubtedly magnanimous souls, but he who is situated in knowledge of Me I consider to be just like My own self. Being engaged in My transcendental service, he is sure to attain Me, the highest and most perfect goal

Krishna is everything, but everything is not Krishna

The Bhagavad-gita (07.19) states that the wise surrender to Krishna, understanding him to be everything (*vasudevah sarvam iti*). Does this verse describe a naïve pantheism that worships everything as God?

The negative answer is evident in the verse itself; the wise surrender to Krishna, not to everything. When the object of their surrender is Krishna – not everything – why do they consider him to be everything? Because they understand the subtle and sublime relationship between him and his creation.

Krishna is not a god who delights in majestic aloofness from his creation, considering contacting it below his divine dignity. He is not only the source of everything, but also its shelter and summit – everything rests in him, and the best of everything manifests a spark of his splendor, as the Gita (10.41) states. Everything that exists is an extension of his grace, an expression of his merciful desire to help us love him. Though the world's beautiful things may distract us from him, they are actually meant to remind us of his supreme beauty. Though the world's dangerous things may cause misery, they are meant to graphically remind us of the futility of loving anything independent of him, thereby spurring us to redirect out love to him. Thus Krishna is everything, in the sense that he has manifested as his energy in everything.

At the same time, everything is not Krishna; he resides separate from everything, as the Gita (09.04: *na caham teshva avasthitah*) indicates. He is the charming Supreme Person, residing in the spiritual world and eternally reciprocating love with his devotees.

Gita wisdom describes the process of devotional service that alone enables us to understand Krishna in truth. When we serve him devotedly, we gradually realize the inconceivable yet relishable relationship between him and everything.

ॐ

After many births and deaths, he who is actually in knowledge surrenders unto Me, knowing Me to be the cause of all causes and all that is. Such a great soul is very rare.

Cultivate the love that goes as far as the head goes – and also goes beyond it

To love anything in this temporary world, we need to suspend our head and close our eyes to the misery that will inevitably result because of the frustration of that love. Sooner or later, time will rupture and shatter our sweet dreams. Even before that, the deluding sheen of worldly things will gradually decline and disappear, leaving us disappointed. Given this gloomy prognosis, worldly love can captivate us only by sidelining our intelligence.

Gita wisdom invites us to a love of a different kind – a love that asks us not to give up our intelligence, but to go beyond our intelligence. The Gita (18.63) invites us to deeply deliberate its message of love and then decide whether to tread its path of love. This bold call for intellectual investigation of its teachings reveals how its message of love differs dramatically from worldly love that flourishes by intellectually paralyzing us.

The trajectory of the Gita's message goes as far as our intelligence goes, meaning that its wisdom answers the sharpest of our intelligence's questions about how and why its love is enduring and fulfilling: as we are eternal souls and Krishna is the eternal all-attractive Supreme Person, our spiritual love for him can triumph over death and continue forever.

After giving us intellectual conviction, the Gita grants us experiential confirmation. In delineating the path of love, bhakti-yoga, the Gita's trajectory supersedes the intellect, going into the realm of transcendence. Therein by bhakti-yoga we experientially realize and relish the supreme sweetness of devotion. Thus, the Gita goes to the heart not by suspending the head but by transcending it. As the Gita (07.19) indicates succinctly, when we ascend the highest summit of knowledge, we realize that Krishna is everything. Love for him fulfills our heart's longing forever.

ॐ

After many births and deaths, he who is actually in knowledge surrenders unto Me, knowing Me to be the cause of all causes and all that is. Such a great soul is very rare

Be not fanatical – be fanatically focused

*S*ome people ask Krishna devotees, "When the Vedic culture includes the worship of so many gods, why are you a Krishna fanatic?"

Because Krishna devotees simply follow the Gita, which, it is important to note, teaches not fanaticism but fanatical focus.

The Gita (07.23) recognizes the existence of many gods and also acknowledges that their worship produces results. By accepting the reality and the efficacy of various paths, the Gita steers clear of fanaticism. Nonetheless, it concludes (18.66) by unambiguously recommending worship of Krishna alone. Why? Because Gita wisdom explains that Krishna alone is eternal as he is the Supreme Person residing in the imperishable spiritual world. In contrast, the various gods are temporary as they are administrators of various cosmic utilities in the perishable material world. Consequently, worshipping Krishna yields the eternal result of residence in his everlasting abode, whereas worshipping the gods yields temporary material results that cannot free the worshiper from the cycle of birth and death. So, the same Gita verse (07.23) that acknowledges demigod worship deems demigod worshipers as *alpa-medhasah,* deficient in philosophical insight.

Those with adequate philosophical insight recognize that life's supreme success is the conquest of mortality by realizing our innate spiritual nature as souls. To attain this success, one needs to redirect one's love from the temporary to the eternal, from matter to Krishna. Extraordinary success requires singular, even fanatical, focus. That's why those seeking the most extraordinary success of attaining immortality don't let their devotion get distributed over various demigods. Significantly, focused devotion to Krishna enables one to make authentic spiritual advancement thereby seeing all living beings as inter-related family members in Krishna's family. Thus, this fanatical focus, far from breeding intolerance, engenders authentic respect for all living beings, including the demigods and the demigod worshipers.

૦૪૪૦

Men of small intelligence worship the demigods, and their fruits are limited and temporary. Those who worship the demigods go to the planets of the demigods, but My devotees ultimately reach My supreme planet.

Those who desire to be fused are confused

*M*any people think that the ultimate goal of spirituality is to merge into God, whom they conceive as a dazzling all-pervading spiritual light known as Brahman.

Gita wisdom explains that this desire for fusion arises from a fundamental confusion about God's nature, a confusion that originates in unwarranted intellectual overconfidence.

The Bhagavad-gita (07.24) declares as unintelligent (*abuddhayah*) those people who consider the Supreme Person, Krishna, to be a temporary manifestation of the impersonal Brahman effulgence. The Gita's characterization of such impersonalists as "unintelligent" is intriguing. After all, their very desire to seek a spiritual goal beyond worldly pleasures is a sign of intelligence. They astutely perceive that all material persons are imperfect and impermanent, thereby making all worldly relationships disappointing and frustrating. Unfortunately, gaining this insight makes them overconfident, impelling them to extrapolate it beyond its valid jurisdiction. They erroneously assume that all persons per se will be marred by deficiencies and defects. Consequently, they infer incorrectly that going beyond the personal to the impersonal is the only way to freedom from misery. So, they desire to dissolve their existence into that impersonal light, hoping to thereby become forever peaceful.

Gita wisdom underscores that their mistake is to equate their experience of reality with the totality of reality. They are called unintelligent because they lack the intelligence to realize that Krishna being supreme can be what they can't be: personal yet perfect; with form yet without limitation; with relationships yet without frustrations. If they are fortunate enough to associate with learned and advanced devotees, they can understand Krishna's inconceivable omnipotence thereby overcoming their intellectual deficit. If they are bold enough to make Krishna the supreme object of their love, they get the ultimate spiritual returns: not just peace, but also ever-lasting, ever-increasing love.

ॐ

Unintelligent men, who do not know Me perfectly, think that I, the Supreme Personality of Godhead, Krishna, was impersonal before and have now assumed this personality. Due to their small knowledge, they do not know My higher nature, which is imperishable and supreme.

Excess makes a good thing worse than bad

*T*he Bhagavad-gita (7.24) indicates that impersonalists who consider Krishna's form to be a temporary and illusory product of the impersonal Brahman are *abuddhayah*, bankrupt of intelligence.

Impersonalists conceive the Absolute Truth as impersonal, devoid of any personality, quality or activity – they are classic and tragic examples of taking a good thing so far as to make it disastrously bad.

The good thing about them is that they have gained an insight into the futility of all worldly forms. They have recognized that these forms being temporary can never offer lasting pleasure but can instead cause bondage and suffering. Consequently, they conclude that such forms are products of illusion, and seek a reality beyond these forms.

The bad thing about them is that they extrapolate their insight about forms from the material realm, where it holds true, to the spiritual realm, where it doesn't. Gita wisdom informs us that the spiritual realm is characterized by non-decaying, non-temporal forms among which Krishna's form is the supreme reality and manifests the ultimate beauty. Not knowing or taking heed of this information, the impersonalists make their insight about worldly forms into an absolute truth. They go so far as to place it on a pedestal higher than the actual Absolute Truth, Krishna. They infer erroneously and disastrously that Krishna's form is a product of illusion, thereby directly contradicting the revealed wisdom of the Gita and the realized vision of great devotee-sages.

To mistake a counterfeit note to be genuine, as the materialists do by mistaking material forms to be real, is sad. But to mistake the genuine note to be false, as the impersonalists do by mistaking Krishna's form to be illusory, is tragic. No wonder the Gita laments their intellectual bankruptcy.

౨౪౮౦

Unintelligent men, who do not know Me perfectly, think that I, the Supreme Personality of Godhead, Krishna, was impersonal before and have now assumed this personality. Due to their small knowledge, they do not know My higher nature, which is imperishable and supreme.

Respecting Krishna's rights is the right way to receive his revelation

Ours is an age of rights; we recognize that every individual has certain inviolable rights. As our rights consciousness expands, it is befitting that we recognize Krishna's rights. His right that has the most bearing on our relationship with him is his right to conceal or reveal himself according to his will.

We often disrespect this right of Krishna when we make premature demands from him on the devotional path. Soon after we start studying his sacred scriptures, we demand prompt and clear understanding. Soon after we start chanting his holy names, we demand swift and steady taste.

While making these demands, we forget our own disqualifications that the:

- Perceptions of our senses are finite,
- Conceptions of our mind are fallible
- Convictions of our intelligence are fragile
- Commitments of our heart are fickle

When we have all these disqualifications, isn't our demand for insight and taste presumptuous? No wonder our presumptuousness makes Krishna exercise his right to conceal himself, as he indicates in the Bhagavad-gita (07.25).

Meditating on our disqualifications engenders humility. By acknowledging Krishna's rights, we recognize his supremacy – and his personality, that is, his self-existence as a person with his individual preferences.

In this world, we can come close to a person only when we recognize their likes and dislikes, and modify our behavior accordingly. The same principle applies when we approach Krishna.

Of course, Krishna is much more than an ordinary person; he is extraordinarily, supremely merciful. That's why, despite all our disqualifications, he has given us some understanding of his message and some taste in his remembrance. Meditating on his mercy engenders gratitude.

When we approach Krishna with humility and gratitude, he exerts his right to reveal himself, and grants us both penetrating insight and captivating taste.

ॐ

I am never manifest to the foolish and unintelligent. For them I am covered by My internal potency, and therefore they do not know that I am unborn and infallible.

The trans-logical logic of love resolves seeming scriptural contradictions

The Bhagavad-gita (07.26) states initially that no one can know Krishna, but eventually it (18.55) states that he can be known by devotion.

How do we make sense of these contradictory statements?

Gita wisdom indicates that these statements are not contradictory but paradoxical. Paradoxes are statements that seem contradictory at first glance, but convey a deeper reconciling truth that is best expressed through the apparent contradictions.

Scriptural traditions sometimes use paradoxes as conceptual tools to impel, even compel, us to break free from the shackles of logic. Logic is no doubt valuable, even essential, for discerning truth at many levels. But if we insist that only the logical deserves to be called true, we deprive ourselves access to truths that lie beyond the scope of logic. To appreciate how something can be not logical yet true, we need to differentiate between the illogical and the trans-logical. Illogical ideas are so silly that they cannot stand before the scrutiny of logic, whereas trans-logical truths are so lofty that the scrutiny of logic cannot stand before them.

Let's now look at how paradoxical Gita verses point to trans-logical truths.

We as well as our powers of logic are finite, whereas Krishna is infinite. So in a sense, it's only logical to expect that the finite cannot know the infinite. Thus, we logically infer that logic is inadequate for understanding Krishna. This is the trans-logical truth conveyed by the Gita (07.26).

The Gita (18.55) takes us beyond logic to love, or, more precisely, to the trans-logical logic of love. Attracted by our love, Krishna uses his omnipotence to make the impossible possible, to render the unknowable knowable, to grant the finite a vision of the infinite.

Thus, the paradoxical verses forcefully draw our attention to the trans-logical truth of the loving omnipotence of Krishna.

०३८०

O Arjuna, as the Supreme Personality of Godhead, I know everything that has happened in the past, all that is happening in the present, and all things that are yet to come. I also know all living entities; but Me no one knows

.

Balance the here and the hereafter through bhakti-yoga

*G*ita wisdom declares the world we live in, the here, to be a place of ephemerality and misery. So, it deems the spiritual world, the hereafter, the destination that the intelligent aspire for. At the same time, the Bhagavad-gita's central message is a call for connection, not rejection: the connection of the here with the hereafter, not the rejection of the here for the hereafter.

If we care only for the here, we become attached to the here and blinded to the hereafter. If we care only for the hereafter, we become apathetic and irresponsible about the here.

How do we achieve the dynamic balance between the here and the hereafter? Through bhakti-yoga which sees both the here and the hereafter as arenas in Krishna's supreme jurisdication.

The Gita points to this devotional balance when it (08.07) exhorts Arjuna to cultivate remembrance of Krishna and perform his prescribed duty of fighting. Generalizing this exhortation helps us arrive at the universal balancing principle: aspire wholeheartedly for the hereafter and act responsibly in the here.

By keeping in mind the eternality and the beauty of the hereafter, we can avoid infatuation with the fleeting pleasures and the deluding promises of the here. By keeping in mind the role of the here as the arena that shapes us for attaining the hereafter, we can face the challenges of the here with wisdom and determination.

This dynamic balance enables us to make effective contributions in the here and attain the best possible destination in the hereafter.

⚜

Therefore, Arjuna, you should always think of Me in the form of Krishna and at the same time carry out your prescribed duty of fighting. With your activities dedicated to Me and your mind and intelligence fixed on Me, you will attain Me without doubt

Don't shoot the messenger; study the message

In the past, despots would routinely shoot messengers who brought bad news. Today, shooting is replaced by labeling – those who raise discomforting issues are often sidelined or silenced by pejorative labels.

This trend of labeling dubs authentic spiritual teachers as pessimists whenever they report the Gita's message (08.15) that this world is a place of intrinsic and inescapable misery. Might such labeling be a modern form of shooting the truthful messenger? After all, doesn't the daily news confirm that psychophysical, interpersonal, and environmental problems (*adhyatmika, adhibhautika and adhidaivika klesha*) routinely cause misery? Can't we see objectively how disease and old age embarrass, immobilize and oppress people around us? Can we deny that death devastates lives all over the world? Thus, if we think objectively, the so-called pessimistic Gita teachers are just stating facts.

"But as those facts are so negative," we may wonder, "won't we be happier by not dwelling on them?"

No, they reply, because those negative facts are just the beginning of a positive message. The Gita doesn't deny our desire to be happy; in fact, it deems that desire our intrinsic right. It explains that we, as souls who are by nature *sat-cit-anand* (eternal-enlightened-ecstatic), are innately joyful. We can re-experience our joyful nature by reviving our spiritual love for Krishna. When we mistakenly seek joy at the material level that is filled with misery, we unnecessarily frustrate ourselves. Gita teachers point to the misery inbuilt at the material level so that we don't let vain hopes for material enjoyment cheat us of our right to happiness at the spiritual level.

Thus, if we can just stop labeling the messenger and start pondering the full message, we will discover that its essence is not pessimistic, but optimistic – sweetly, sublimely, supremely optimistic.

ॐ

After attaining Me, the great souls, who are yogis in devotion, never return to this temporary world, which is full of miseries, because they have attained the highest perfection

Gain double empowerment for destination eternity

Eternity is a universal longing of all living beings, human and sub-human. This longing can be discerned in all species through the ingenious and indefatigable efforts they make to live for as long as possible. However, because everything material is by its very nature temporary, no species can live forever at the material level.

Does this mean that the longing for eternity is doomed?

No, not at all. We as souls are immortal; we just need to start living at the spiritual level.

The Bhagavad-gita (08.15) indicates that we can attain life eternal if we redirect our love from temporary matter to eternal spirit, specifically the supreme spiritual reality: Krishna.

Gita wisdom explains that this redirection is especially possible in the human form, for this form offers us souls the capacity for metaphysical enquiry. By utilizing this capacity, we can recognize the inescapable temporality of the material level and detach ourselves from it. Further, we can recognize the incorruptible eternality of the spiritual level and attach ourselves to it. Thus, we can love the spiritual and thereby achieve the eternal.

If we wish to activate our love for the spiritual, Gita wisdom stimulates us with a rich revelation of life in the spiritual world. Life there is an everlasting delightful celebration of love with the all-attractive, all-loving Absolute Truth, Krishna. For easily and effectively redirecting our love from matter to him, Gita wisdom provides us the process of bhakti-yoga.

Thus, the Gita's double empowerment for us is the twin revelation of Krishna as the goal in eternity and bhakti as the process to eternity. Thus empowered, we can march confidently on a spiritual journey that culminates in destination eternity.

This is life's supreme success. It beckons all of us. Why miss it?

ॐ

After attaining Me, the great souls, who are yogis in devotion, never return to this temporary world, which is full of miseries, because they have attained the highest perfection

Death is a nightmare we can wake up from

"*I* will die one day." We find such thoughts hard to stomach because our insides recoil at the prospect of our annihilation. We may try to evade the death sentence that hangs on our head by trying to do something that will guarantee us a place in the history books, hoping thereby to live on in the memories of people. However, time destroys relentlessly the memories, the people and even the history books.

Gita wisdom shows us a more realistic way out of our death sentence by revealing an arena beyond death. The Bhagavad-gita (08.20) directs our attention to another realm of existence that is free from the destructibility that mars our material realm.

Gita wisdom explains that death is a nightmare which we suffer only as long as we remain asleep in the materialistic conception of life. As soon as we wake up spiritually, we become aware of our spiritual identity and glory:

1. Our spiritual identity as eternal souls who can't be destroyed by anything, even death.

2. Our spiritual glory as the beloved children of the all-attractive Supreme, Krishna, who is forever inviting us to a life of eternal love with him in his supreme abode.

All of us can wake up to this heart-warming reality by tapping the power of divine sound, especially the supreme power of the holy names of Krishna.

Thus, by informing us about our immortal life at the spiritual level and endowing us with the means to wake up to that reality, Gita wisdom rescues us from the nightmare of death.

ॐ

Yet there is another unmanifest nature, which is eternal and is transcendental to this manifested and unmanifested matter. It is supreme and is never annihilated. When all in this world is annihilated, that part remains as it is.

Bhakti is not just cultural or historical; it is also universal and eternal

The historical dating of spiritually significant events is often an exercise in irrelevance. Consider, for example, the mainstream academic opinion that characterizes bhakti as a cultural Indian movement that became widespread in medieval times.

Such a cultural and historical characterization of bhakti misses its essence. Gita wisdom indicates that bhakti correlates with the innate nature of the soul to love and serve the Supreme. It is thus present in the heart of all living beings at all places – east and west – and at all times: ancient, medieval, modern and post-modern.

Bhakti is the universal principle that underlies and unifies the world's great religious traditions. These traditions are centered on adoring, worshiping and praising some manifestation of God such as Christ, Allah or Buddha – they are essentially expressions of bhakti. They have some differences because the non-sectarian longing of the human heart for God is often expressed according to prevailing cultural norms. Also, this inner divine longing may be expressed less or more at different times depending on the receptivity or hostility of the prevailing sociopolitical circumstances. Yet beyond such variations in the form and frequency of its expression, bhakti remains the universal nature of the heart. This trans-sectarian, trans-historical essence of bhakti is conveyed in the Bhagavad-gita's declaration that bhakti is imperishable (09.02 - avyayam).

Authentic bhakti exponents who understand bhakti's universality focus not on converting people from one religion to another, but on empowering them to discover their own latent devotional nature and to develop it to its full potential. Those thus empowered become joyous exemplars and instruments of universal bhakti in this world, and attain the eternal life of bhakti in the next.

⚬౸

This knowledge is the king of education, the most secret of all secrets. It is the purest knowledge, and because it gives direct perception of the self by realization, it is the perfection of religion. It is everlasting, and it is joyfully performed

Confirmation comes by conformation

We may sometimes wonder: "Are the statements in the Bhagavad-gita about God's existence and benevolence to be accepted on faith alone? Isn't there any way to confirm them?"

There is indeed – confirmation comes by conformation.

The Bhagavad-gita (09.02) states that its message is pratyakshavagamam, directly perceivable by one's own experience. Thus the Gita's approach in presenting its wisdom is bold and beckoning; it invites us to try out its teachings by expanding our consciousness from matter to spirit and thereby experience the higher realities it talks about.

Gita wisdom asserts that there is more to reality than the material realm that we presently perceive and pursue. To access this higher reality, we need to awaken our spiritual faculty, our latent capacity to perceive the spiritual realm. As souls, this faculty is intrinsic to us, but it has been lulled to sleep by protracted disuse. This atrophy has been caused by our prolonged fascination with material pleasures and our resultant fixation in material reality.

Accordingly, to arouse our spiritual faculty, we need to decrease our material fixation by regulating our worldly indulgences and expose ourselves systematically to stimuli that activate our spiritual faculty – stimuli such as Deities, scripture and holy names.

When we thus conform our lifestyle to the model given in the Gita, then we start perceiving spiritual reality with increasing clarity and perspicacity. The more our spiritual faculty awakens, the more we experience the existence, the beauty and the love of Krishna to be life's defining realities.

❀

This knowledge is the king of education, the most secret of all secrets. It is the purest knowledge, and because it gives direct perception of the self by realization, it is the perfection of religion. It is everlasting, and it is joyfully performed

Krishna's pastimes are fantastic, but not fantasy

We may find Krishna's pastimes of magically killing demons fantastic.

Yes, they are fantastic, in the sense that they demonstrate Krishna's capacities to effortlessly accomplish feats that would be impossible for us humans. However, though his deeds may be fantastic, they are not fantasy. They are not concoctions of a mythological imagination on the riot; they are demonstrations of a fundamental philosophical reality: Krishna's omnipotence. If his deeds seem incredible, that's how they are meant to be. After all, he's God; he's the supreme controller and is free to do what he likes.

If we find this simple logic of God's omnipotence questionable, that's because our intellect has been taken hostage by the currently fashionable worldview of naturalism. This worldview grants God only a token existence; its worshipable supreme deity is nature and its laws. Naturalism allows God to exist subject to the inviolable condition that he behave himself properly, meaning that he not violate the laws of nature. If he dares to transgress the sacred laws of nature, he is at once banished to the Siberia of mythology.

Gita wisdom refuses to bow down to this dictatorship of naturalism. It doesn't buy in to the conception of an impotent God imprisoned to the realm of the natural and the predictable. Instead, it unambiguously upholds the truth of God's supremacy – far from being controlled by nature, he is in full control of nature, as the Bhagavad-gita (09.10) indicates. That's why he can bend the laws of nature to his will whenever he wills.

Once we recognize and reject our misconceived devotion to nature, the door swings open for us to devote ourselves to the transcendental supreme. The cynical head can no longer block the charmed heart from falling in love with Krishna and his fantastic deeds.

ॐ

This material nature, which is one of My energies, is working under My direction, O son of Kunti, producing all moving and nonmoving beings. Under its rule this manifestation is created and annihilated again and again.

Avoid a void within

In our introspective moments, we often sense a void within: a feeling of incompleteness, even emptiness. This void in our heart is due to our not having a satisfying object for our love.

We generally offer our love to the people and things of the world, but experience shows that nothing of this world satisfies our heart's longing completely. Nonetheless, this longing for love is indispensable among our core needs. So, hoping to fulfill this need somehow or the other, we keep searching for the right object, shifting our love from one object to another. Unfortunately, nothing fills the void; to the contrary, experience enlarges it as more and more objects turn out to be incapable of filling it.

For some people, this inner void becomes so gigantic that it consumes their entire sense of being – it even dominates their conception of all of existence. They infer mistakenly that the void itself is life's ultimate reality. So they make entering that void their life's supreme goal.

Both these categories of people – the materialists who live with the void as life's unavoidable reality and the voidists who live to attain the void as life's ultimate reality – are victims of a root misconception: the assumption that the only way to fill the heart's void is by a worldly, material object.

The Bhagavad-gita (09.11) points to the cause of this misconception: they are ignorant of the best non-material other-worldly object of love, the transcendentally enchanting Supreme Person, Krishna. When we offer our heart's love to him, he being eternal and perfect reciprocates inconceivably and wonderfully, exceeding our expectations and fulfilling our heart's longing fully and forever.

Learning to love Krishna, therefore, is the best way – indeed the only way – to avoid a void within.

CREO

Fools deride Me when I descend in the human form. They do not know My transcendental nature as the Supreme Lord of all that be.

Devotion to the greatest soul makes the small soul a great soul

We usually long to prove our greatness to the world.

At first sight, Gita wisdom seems to repress this ambition for greatness; it informs us that we as souls are immeasurably small and are eternally servants of Krishna. If we are less than microscopic and are always servitors, how can we ever become great?

Curiously, the same Bhagavad-gita that declares the soul to be tiny also addresses (09.13) some souls as great souls (*mahatma*). As the soul doesn't morph like a size-adjustable computer-generated image, how do small souls become great souls?

The answer is found in the next line: these great souls live sheltered by the divine nature (*daivim prakrtim ashritah*). This divine nature is the grace of Krishna, manifested as Shrimati Radharani, the supreme mediatrix. By bestowing devotion, she enables the small soul to connect with the greatest soul, Krishna, and thereby become great – not in size, but in influence.

Krishna uses the souls devoted to him as his instruments. Through them, his infinite power, wisdom and compassion appears and acts in this world. Being thus divinely empowered, these devoted souls perform great deeds helping everyone attain life's supreme treasure of eternal love and happiness. Thus, they engage in the highest spiritual welfare for all living beings. Due to their great deeds, the Gita rightly acclaims them as great souls.

Significantly though, these great souls never think that they are great. Why? Because they live constantly in the light of the supreme greatness of Krishna and find therein a fulfillment far greater than that obtained by dwelling on their own greatness.

Thus, Gita wisdom doesn't repress our ambition for greatness, but redirects it spiritually. It thereby enables us to ultimately transcend that ambition, while also productively utilizing it for the service of Krishna and all his children.

☙❧

O son of Pritha, those who are not deluded, the great souls, are under the protection of the divine nature. They are fully engaged in devotional service because they know Me as the Supreme Personality of Godhead, original and inexhaustible.

Love is a prize far bigger than the palliative of peace

*S*ome spiritual aspirants ask: "I had thought of spirituality as a state of peaceful withdrawal from the world while seated in a smart yogic posture. But the path of bhakti involves various practical services that don't seem peaceful. Are these actually spiritual?"

Yes declares Gita wisdom. It reminds us that our innermost need is not peace but love. We act in the world because we hope to express and experience love. However, when the world's temporariness and uncertainness thwarts our hopes for love, we seek spirituality to apply the balm of peace to our hurt heart.

Thus love is our heart's cherished prize. When this prize seems out of reach, we try to settle for the consolation prize of peace.

But the cherished prize of love is not beyond us, Gita wisdom assures. It begins by confirming our realization that the quest for love in the world is destined for frustration sooner or later. Next it expands this realization by pointing out that beyond the world is an object that can fully and eternally satisfy our heart: Krishna. We can awaken our love for him not by rejecting the world, but by engaging the world in his service. Worldly events are not irritating distractions but are adventurous opportunities to express our love for him dynamically.

To offer us models for this dynamic spirituality, the Bhagavad-gita (09.14) describes the most evolved spiritualists in not *peaceful* but *love-ful* terms: they constantly glorify Krishna, they strive and struggle to serve him, and they take rigid vows to ensure that their service-offerings to him are tangible and substantial.

When we infuse our spirituality with such devotional dynamism, we become enriched with a love that far exceeds the palliative of peace.

ॐ

Always chanting My glories, endeavoring with great determination, bowing down before Me, these great souls perpetually worship Me with devotion.

The temporary is a means to the eternal – not the eternal a means to the temporary

The power of illusion often makes us mistake the means to be the ends and the ends to be the means.

Even among believers, many get misled by religious materialism. They mistake the things of this world to be the ends and devotion to Krishna to be the means for acquiring those ends. However, our connection with worldly things is temporary, whereas our connection with Krishna is eternal. The Bhagavad-gita (09.21) points out that those who worship Krishna indirectly for material purposes gain only temporary results at best. To reduce the eternal to a means to the temporary is to tragically underuse the eternal.

When Krishna can offer us eternal life, why should we settle for anything less?

To regain the eternal life that is due to us as undying souls, we need to make the temporary the means to the eternal. That is, we need to use the things of this world as the means to render devotional service to Krishna and thus attain the ends of eternal love for him.

To protect ourselves from mixing up our means and our ends, we need to regularly connect with things that focus on the eternal, specifically the supreme eternal reality Krishna. These things include the texts, the spiritualists and the environments that cherish pure love for Krishna. By thus sharpening our focus on the eternal, we can progress towards the supreme eternal destination: Krishna's world of pure spiritual love.

ॐ

When they have thus enjoyed vast heavenly sense pleasure and the results of their pious activities are exhausted, they return to this mortal planet again. Thus those who seek sense enjoyment by adhering to the principles of the three Vedas achieve only repeated birth and death.

Krishna is impartially partial

*T*he Bhagavad-gita (09.29) states two paradoxical features of Krishna's nature:

1. He is equal to all and does not consider anyone to be an object of aversion or affection.

2. For those who worship him with devotion, he offers himself to them, and they offer themselves to him.

These two features suggest that Krishna is both partial and impartial. How can that be?

The key to understanding Krishna's mysterious nature is to remember that he is not an impersonal principle but a sentient person. Being a person, Krishna is neither neutral, nor partial; he is reciprocal. When we try to avoid him, he reciprocates by not interfering in our lives and lets us stay under the supervision of the impartial law of karma. When we try to love him, he reciprocates by showering his love on us and intervening to take special care of us.

If Krishna exhibited stone-like neutrality towards all, there would be hardly any possibility of developing a loving relationship with him. After all, how many people, if any, can love a stone?

If Krishna were not reciprocal, love for him would remain mostly an abstract intellectual conception. It is Krishna's reciprocity that makes his personality emotionally tangible and eminently lovable. It is Krishna's reciprocity that makes love for him *real*.

As Krishna is reciprocal, he is indeed partial to those who try to reciprocate love with him: his devotees. He offers special protection and grace to those who choose to love him. But as he is universally reciprocal, he allows everyone to love him and thereby avail of his partiality. In fact, he publically declares his partiality to attract everyone to benefit from it.

Thus, Krishna is impartially partial: he impartially leaves the doors to partiality open for everyone.

ॐ

I envy no one, nor am I partial to anyone. I am equal to all. But whoever renders service unto Me in devotion is a friend, is in Me, and I am also a friend to him.

Bhakti brings equality and universality on the spiritual path

Ours is an age that idealizes the equality of all human beings. The American Declaration of Rights which enshrines this equality is widely considered a watershed in human history. Significantly, a similar egalitarian declaration was made by the Bhagavad-gita thousands of years earlier.

The Gita (09.32) espouses the path of bhakti-yoga – the path of pure love for God, Krishna – as the best method for the empowerment and elevation of all, including even women, *vaishyas* [merchants] and *shudras* [workers]."

Is the reference to women, vaishyas and shudras a sexist or a casteist putdown? Not at all; rather, it is the opposite. Let's see how.

In orthodox Indian society, there were two major forms of conventional religiosity: ritualistic materialism (*karma-kanda*) and speculative impersonalism (*jnana-kanda*). According to their puritanical standards, those with non-intellectual traditional engagements like home-keeping, agriculture or manual labor didn't have the time or the disposition for ritual purity or metaphysical probing. Consequently, they were deemed under-qualified for spiritual advancement.

The Gita offers a nominal tip of the hat to this conventional notion and then delivers its universalist bhakti message which practically nullifies that notion. Bhakti is a path of the heart – which all of us have – and the path of grace – which all of us can get if we approach Krishna through his devotees. Thus, bhakti opens the doors to spiritual enfranchisement for everyone – even those conventionally considered disenfranchised.

How does this universalism of bhakti apply to our times? It guarantees that when we practice bhakti diligently, our backgrounds, even if non-spiritual or anti-spiritual, don't disqualify us from life's greatest success: pure love for Krishan and attainment of his supreme abode.

⋈

Those who take shelter in me, though they be of lower birth -- women, vaishyas [merchants] and shudras [workers] -- can attain the supreme destination.

Knowledge about Krishna is not for pooling, but for pulling

*O*ur times are characterized by an infatuation for information. Those with the ability to commandeer uncommon bits and bytes of information on the spur of the moment often leave others wide-eyed and open-mouthed.

Such infatuation may grip even us spiritual seekers, enslaving us to the temptation of showing off our knowledge about Krishna. This exhibitionist urge may well become the driving motivation of our scriptural study, thereby making us miss the actual purpose of such study.

Gita wisdom is unambiguous about the purpose of acquiring knowledge about Krishna. The Bhagavad-gita (10.08) declares that those who know him as the ultimate source and sustainer of everything become wholeheartedly devoted to him. This indicates that knowledge about Krishna is meant to pull our heart to him, to inspire us to love him. When we come to know how beautiful and lovable he is – and how eager he is to reciprocate love with us – how can our heart not be moved to love him?

Sadly however, when we approach knowledge about Krishna with an information-hunting agenda, then the information gets pooled in our head, but doesn't exert any pull on our heart. As long as our heart being already filled with the craving to get the world's admiration, it has little, if any, space left for loving Krishna. Consequently, despite our brandishing esoteric information about him, our heart remains unfulfilled, thirsty, lonely – parched of love.

All of us have the power to amend or avert this unfortunate state of affairs. If we cherish the correct purpose while acquiring knowledge about Krishna, then that knowledge will come alive in our heart, pull us towards him and eventually grant us the ultimate fulfillment.

☙❧

I am the source of all spiritual and material worlds. Everything emanates from Me. The wise who perfectly know this engage in My devotional service and worship Me with all their hearts.

Krishna is not just God; he is my God

The belief that God exists is good. But much higher is the recognition that Krishna is God in his highest manifestation. Still higher is Krishna's enthronement in our heart as "my God."

Gita wisdom leads us towards this ultimate spiritual summit. The Bhagavad-gita (10.08) states that those who understand Krishna's supreme position become wise and worship him with all the emotions of their heart. A significant point in this verse is the sequence: the understanding of Krishna's supreme position engenders, facilitates and reinforces devotion to him.

This sequence counters the assumptions that underlie karma-kanda and jnana-kanda. In karma-kanda, people worship different demigods to get some material benefits. Such people may say that this demigod is "my god," but their statement is largely sentimental and is philosophically unfounded. Some such philosophically uninformed people may apply the term "my god" to a god-man, a politician or even a sportstar or a moviestar – anyone who provides material benefits. The sequence of this Gita verse reveals how a devotee's acceptance of Krishna as "my god" is not similarly sentimental or utilitarian; it grows from a thorough philosophical understanding of Krishna's supremacy.

In jnana-kanda, people treat devotion as a tool to knowledge. They assume that merging into the impersonal oneness of Brahman is life's highest goal. To progress towards this goal, they utilize the difference between worshiper and worshiped as a convenient fiction. According to them, when one attains the peak of knowledge, the fictional difference is rejected. The sequence of this Gita verse thoroughly debunks this notion by declaring that at the peak of knowledge devotion is reinforced – not rejected.

Such is the metaphysical depth of this verse! No wonder that it is one of the four verses that are celebrated as the *Chatur-Shloki* Gita (Gita in four nutshell verses).

☙❧

I am the source of all spiritual and material worlds. Everything emanates from Me. The wise who perfectly know this engage in My devotional service and worship Me with all their hearts.

Bhakti offers emotional liquidity that is above, not below, intellectual solidity

We may sometimes wonder how to harmonize the two aspects of our human personality: the head and the heart. A preponderance of the head makes us so intellectually solid that we become impervious to essential human emotions. At the other extreme, a preponderance of the heart makes us so emotionally liquid that we lose the solid ground of essential human rationality.

Gita wisdom puts first things first: understanding self-identity comes before achieving inner harmony. When we, despite being immortal souls, mistakenly identify ourselves with our mortal bodies, our worldview and pleasure-quest both get restricted to the material realm. Within this shrunk vision, excessive emotional liquidity makes us sentimentally crave for material pleasures; we live in denial of the reality that temporary pleasures can never satisfy our longing for permanent happiness. In Vedic parlance, this is the path of karma. Excessive intellectual solidity makes us want to give up all emotions, even our craving for pleasure; we live in denial of the reality that we can't live without pleasure. In Vedic parlance, this is the path of jnana.

Gita wisdom integrates both these paths in a higher-level synthesis that eliminates their unsustainable denials. That synthesis is the path of bhakti, which expands our vision to perceive our spiritual identity. Understanding our identity helps us regain a viable intellectual solidity that launches us into a whole new universe of spiritual emotions. This universe is permeated with flowing and flooding emotions, but that emotional liquidity is above, not below, intellectual solidity. This emotional flow doesn't drag us down into material illusion, but moves us up towards the highest spiritual reality, Krishna, as indicated in the Bhagavad-gita (10.10).

It is in this bhakti universe that our head and heart attain the perfect balance, and we relish the ultimate fulfillment.

❀

To those who are constantly devoted to serving Me with love, I give the understanding by which they can come to Me.

Mirrors make us self-conscious; the Gita makes us conscious of the self

*F*ew things make us as self-conscious as a mirror. The sight of a mirror often makes us involuntarily check and adjust our hair, our dress and our overall looks.

However from the Gita perspective, few things make us as self-*unconscious* as a mirror. Glancing at a mirror usually increases our bodily misidentification, thereby aggravating our forgetfulness of our spiritual identity.

Of course, the path of devotion doesn't require us to give up mirrors; it just asks us to take care that they don't steal our spiritual awareness. More importantly, the devotional path doesn't require us to give up our concern about how we look; it simply urges us to redirect our concern to the real me. The real me refers not just to the soul, but also to the real state of our consciousness beyond our externals.

For this, we need a special mirror: the mirror of Gita wisdom. When we study the Gita, seeking not just information but also introspection, then different Gita verses speak to us at different times, according to the state of our consciousness. This helps us detect and eradicate our hidden material desires, and also arouse and energize our dormant devotional desires.

The more we familiarize ourselves with the Gita's verses, the more they will act as friendly guides on our journey to Krishna. In fact, over time, we will realize that through these verses it is Krishna who is extending his friendly hand to lead us back to him, as he promises in the Gita (10.11). We will start seeing the Gita as a personalized mirror held in front of us by Krishna to stimulate reflection. Thereafter, Gita study will never again be dry and stale; it will become endlessly exciting and enlightening.

◌⃝

To show them special mercy, I, dwelling in their hearts, destroy with the shining lamp of knowledge the darkness born of ignorance.

See eye-to-eye with Krishna to gain an enlightened eye and an enlivened I

*W*hen we are diseased and seek treatment, we need to see eye-to-eye with the doctor. We need to understand and accept the diagnosis and the treatment as the doctor understands it. This acceptance enables us to do our part in the treatment properly and thereby facilitates our recovery.

The same principle applies to our spiritual sickness. When we approach the supremely trustworthy doctor Krishna for spiritual treatment, we need to see eye-to-eye with him. We need to understand and accept the diagnosis and the treatment as he understands it. He diagnoses our sickness to be spiritual amnesia, due to which we have forgotten both our real identity as souls and our real life of love with him in his eternal abode. As treatment he prescribes regular exposure to spiritual stimuli that remind us of him and of our real life with him.

Arjuna, the original student of the Gita, is the paragon of seeing eye-to-eye with Krishna, as is evident in his wholehearted acceptance of Krishna's words (10.14: *sarvam etad ritam manye*). When we follow in Arjuna's footsteps and see eye-to-eye with Krishna, we facilitate our spiritual recovery. This recovery provides us two precious gifts:

1. **An enlightened eye:** We start seeing through the worldly temptations that have previously deceived us. We also start seeing the benevolent plan of Krishna underlying the random-seeming events that happen in our life.

2. **An enlivened I:** When we start remembering and serving Krishna regularly, he reciprocates by awakening divine emotions in our heart. By these emotions and reciprocations, our real I, the soul, becomes enlivened – expansively, ecstatically, eternally enlivened.

Thus, seeing eye-to-eye with Krishna restores our spiritual health and establishes us in an enlightened and enlivened life.

ॐ

O Krishna, I totally accept as truth all that You have told me. Neither the demigods nor the demons, O Lord, can understand Your personality.

To equate the shadow of scripture with its light is to shadow scripture

*S*ome new Gita students get the question, "Why do some Gita teachers disrespect others who interpret the Gita in a different way?"

Because authentic Gita teachers feel morally dutybound to ensure that innocent seekers – like those asking this question – who seek the light of the Gita don't get deviated towards its shadow. Thus, their intent is not to disrespect anyone, but to respect the sanctity of the Gita.

Let's understand what the light and the shadow of the Gita are. The Bhagavad-gita offers the inner light of wisdom for helping us choose the desires that bring the best out of us. The Gita indicates (10.14) that the way to receive its light is to wholeheartedly accept its entire message.

Unfortunately, many people cherry-pick Gita verses that fit into their worldview and lifestyle. By quoting and professing to follow these verses, they seek prestige in circles where the Gita is respected. Such people may be connected with the Gita, but they are living not in its light but its shadow.

Those who live in the Gita's shadow deprive themselves of its supreme gift. What downgrades many of these people from the category of self-deprivers to social misleaders is their insistent claim to be living in the Gita's light. They blatantly quote verses out of context and propagate ideas that differ from, even militate against, the Gita's teachings. And they publically propagate these erroneous ideas, thereby shadowing the Gita's true meaning.

Authentic Gita teachers long for all souls to be blessed by the Gita's light. That's why they assertively point out the difference between its light and its shadow – not out of disrespect for those living in the Gita's shadow, but out of respect for the Gita and concern for those seeking its light.

༺༻

O Krishna, I totally accept as truth all that You have told me. Neither the demigods nor the demons, O Lord, can understand Your personality.

The Bhagavad-gita is infinitely pregnant with wisdom

Good books are a joy to read. Great books are a joy to not just read, but also re-read. During the re-reading of great books we discover many nuggets of wisdom that we had either missed entirely or gathered only fragmentally during our earlier readings. For the greatest books, this process of discovery can be continued for many, many re-readings.

For the Bhagavad-gita, however, this process of joyous re-reading can be continued ad infinitum. That's because the discovery in Gita re-reading is not a one-way process, but a two-way process: it is not just we who find hitherto undiscovered nuggets of wisdom, but it is also Krishna who shares hitherto unrevealed nuggets during our re-readings.

The Gita is special, even unique, because it is spoken directly by God himself in his highest manifestation as Krishna. Because Krishna is Absolute, he is non-different from his word. That's why each time we connect with the Gita by prayerful contemplation, we connect with Krishna himself. And he being pleased by our endeavors to connect with him reveals to us new facets of his enchanting glory. Because his glory is infinite, his revelation and our discovery as mediated through Gita study can continue forever. And the more we make our consciousness receptive by rendering devotional service, the more this process of revelation and discovery becomes increasingly exciting and fulfilling.

Thus, many books may be pregnant with wisdom, but the Gita alone is infinitely pregnant with wisdom. It is to this world of infinite and infinitely increasing wisdom that the Gita (10.18) invites us through the ecstatic exclamation of its original student Arjuna: "The more I hear, the more I want to taste the nectar of your words."

☙❧

O Janardana, again please describe in detail the mystic power of Your opulences. I am never satiated in hearing about You, for the more I hear the more I want to taste the nectar of Your words.

The goal of spiritual knowledge is not just discovery but also recovery

*S*ome of us may get the doubt: "Science is exciting because therein we constantly discover new things. In spirituality, all the knowledge is already given in the scriptures, so there's nothing new to discover. Won't this make spirituality boring?"

No, because the aim of knowledge in the two domains is different. In science, the purpose of knowledge is to acquire new information about things: what they are and how they work. As information doesn't live or love, its potential to excite us rests primarily in its novelty. Once we discover that information, say, a new equation, its freshness and its charm ends; thereafter, its value remains only in its functional utility.

In contrast, the purpose of spiritual knowledge is to revive our relationship with Krishna, the forgotten lord of our heart. As Krishna is a living and loving person, knowledge about him is exciting not just because of its novelty, but also because of the reciprocity of the object of that knowledge. We may get an inkling of this excitement in the thrill we feel on meeting a forgotten childhood friend who still remembers us and is delighted to meet us.

The preceding analysis is not to deny the fact that we do discover a lot of new information in the scriptures. But the essential gift of the scriptures is to help us not in discovering new information, but in recovering an old map that shows the way to a long lost treasure. The map is of our inner landscape and the treasure is the ultimate wealth hidden in our heart: Krishna and our love for him.

The Bhagavad-gita (10.18) indicates that to the extent we seek scriptural knowledge for reviving our relationship with Krishna, to that extent it will remain constantly fresh.

૱

O Janardana, again please describe in detail the mystic power of Your opulences. I am never satiated in hearing about You, for the more I hear the more I want to taste the nectar of Your words.

Time expresses Krishna's tough love

The Bhagavad-gita (10.32) identifies time as a manifestation of Krishna. Time is one of the most forceful teachers about the temporary nature of worldly existence.

All of us can learn about the fragility and the perishability of all things material by everyday observation and common sense inference.

Yet most of us don't. Why? Because of our strong desires to enjoy the world. These desires maintain their hold on us by making us averse to contemplating on the harsh realities of life, for such contemplation would make apparent the futility of worldly desires.

Due to our lack of contemplation, we see sickness and death shoot down people all around us, yet we imagine that we have a suffering-proof armor – or will soon get one.

However, time demonstrates the truths we deny by making the unthinkable unavoidable; time forces us to dry and die. The prospect of being ground into oblivion by the relentless grinding of time can horrify us – till Gita wisdom helps us realize that time is Krishna in disguise.

Time is the guise through which Krishna expresses his tough love, an expression that is necessary for those who don't learn from his gentle love in the Gita. Gita wisdom helps us to connect the "tough" side of time with the "love" side and learn the indispensable lesson: the futility of loving the ephemeral and the urgency of redirecting our love to the eternal.

When we start learning and living this lesson, time reveals itself to be Krishna waiting with open arms to welcome us back home.

ॐ

I am all-devouring death, and I am the generating principle of all that is yet to be. Among women I am fame, fortune, fine speech, memory, intelligence, steadfastness and patience.

Life is a disaster movie in slow motion

*D*isaster movies generally show people caught in a natural disaster trying heroically to save themselves and others from impending doom. However, not many of the people who like to watch disaster movies would like to be caught in an actual disaster themselves; there's no guarantee of a fairy tale ending. Even fewer are the people who realize that all of us are already living in a real-life disaster; hundred percent of the people reading this article will be wiped out hundred years from today.

This carnage is caused by the disastrous feature of the world known as death that, the Bhagavad-gita (10.34) reminds us, devours everyone without exception.

Despite the cent-percent casualty rate, most of us don't feel that life is like a disaster movie. One reason is that the movie of life unfolds in slow motion. So it's possible to forget the direction of its motion if we want to. And we fervently want to.

The reality of death is inconvenient and unpleasant for us. It ruins our hopes for success and glory in this world. So we want to forget it. And forget we do.

But even if we forget it, the disaster movie is for real. And we are not spectators. We are actors who dream of being victors, but end up being victims.

We don't have to be victims, though. We can't stop the disaster, but we can come out of its arena. Analogically speaking, we can stop living in the movie.

Gita wisdom informs us that the jurisdiction of death extends only to the body, not to the soul. So when we realize our spiritual identity by practicing devotional service, death changes from a horrible disaster to a welcome transfer: transfer to the eternal blissful kingdom of Krishna where there are no disasters.

CR80

I am all-devouring death.

The present is all that we have – and all that we will ever have

*W*e frequently lead life as if it were a practice run for next time. All of us want to do valuable, special, big things in life, but the time for them seems to be "sometime in the future." The present appears boring at best and burdensome at worst; it looks like something we have to get over with to reach the exciting future.

Unfortunately, that much-anticipated future never comes. Because when the future comes, it has become the present. And that present – like our present present – becomes devalued and wasted by our lackadaisical, practice-run attitude as we keep longing for the future.

If we wish to actualize our potential, we need to recognize that the present is all that we have – and all that we will ever have. To help us upgrade our estimation of the present, Gita wisdom offers us two pertinent insights:

1. **Time is divine:** The Bhagavad-gita (11.32) declares that time is a manifestation of Krishna. This understanding spiritualizes our vision of time management; we value time not just because it gives us the opportunity to do many things, but because it is Krishna himself offering us that opportunity.

2. **Every moment is precious:** Life at the material level usually reserves importance for certain moments: for example, the moments on the field for cricketers; the moments of exam for students; the moments of the interview for job seekers. Most other moments usually become mere run-ups for those big make-or-break moments. In devotional life, certain moments may be more important for our services externally, but every moment is equally important internally. Each moment is a precious opportunity to remember Krishna and move closer to him in our own hearts.

Thus, bhakti brings to our life a perennial novelty: the moment for action is now.

ॐ

Time I am, the great destroyer of the worlds.

Divine empowerment makes mission impossible mission unstoppable

In the Bhagavad-gita (11.33), Krishna assures Arjuna of success in his battle against formidable ungodly forces, provided he just becomes determined to assist in the divine mission. This assurance is vindicated in the Kurukshetra war wherein Arjuna overcame impossible odds time and again, especially while fulfilling his vow to avenge his son Abhimanyu's death by killing Jayadratha before sunset.

On that day, the Kauravas arrayed all their forces just to thwart Arjuna. Still, he penetrated deep into their ranks and came close to Jayadratha. But by then the sun had come close to the horizon. He was so close and yet so far – reaching Jayadratha seemed impossible. Nonetheless Krishna, who by his counsel during the course of the day had ensured that Arjuna didn't get stymied in lesser fights, now deployed his omnipotence. Summoning his divine disk, he covered the sun, thus lulling the Kauravas into a false sense of complacency. Grabbing that reprieve, Arjuna shot Jayadratha and achieved his goal. Mission impossible had, by Krishna's grace, become mission fulfilled.

Krishna's assurance applies not only to the specific, historical battle that Arjuna fought five thousand years ago, but also to the universal, inner battle that all of us have to fight against the ungodly forces in our own hearts. When our attempts to live virtuously are repeatedly thwarted by the internal ungodly forces, we may become disheartened, and start feeling that combating these forces is a mission impossible. However, if we just maintain our resolve to serve Krishna, he will slowly but surely bless us with sublime happiness and divine power. These blessings will stimulate a strong, spontaneous attraction toward him that will empower us to overcome all obstacles. By such experiences of empowerment, we will become surcharged with the conviction that our spiritual advancement is not a mission impossible, but a mission unstoppable.

ༀ

Therefore get up. Prepare to fight and win glory. Conquer your enemies and enjoy a flourishing kingdom. They are already put to death by My arrangement, and you, O Savyasaci, can be but an instrument in the fight.

Change the stories you tell yourself about yourself

*O*ur mind is rarely satisfied with the world and especially with our present position in it. Consequently, it frequently goes into flights of fantasies of what we will achieve and how the world will praise us. Cricket lovers may fantasize themselves as hitting a match-winning sixer for the national team on the last ball of a world cup final.

Sometimes these fantasies perversely take the form of nightmares. If someone irritates us, we may mentally play and replay a future furious confrontation with that person. Most of our worries are nothing but the mind's perverse fantasies.

These fantasies are the stories we tell ourselves about ourselves. While these stories are mostly unreal and unrealizable, they indicate our mind's present definition of happiness. Though this definition is usually wrong, its level of wrongness reflects our current consciousness and our overall spiritual advancement. Initially in our spiritual life, our imagination may be primarily about grossly immoral anti-devotional indulgences. Gradually our imagination will change to the successes that we can achieve in our devotional service. And again within our devotional dreams, initially our imagination will be more self-centric, focusing on how we will be glorified for doing extraordinary service. Gradually it will become Krishna-centric, gravitating towards how Krishna and his devotees will be pleased by our service.

In addition to observing this gradual spiritualization of our imagination, we can also stimulate such spiritualization by consciously telling devotional stories about ourselves to ourselves. We can train our imagination to leap and fly within the ambit of Krishna consciousness, visualizing, for example, how we will chant attentively, study diligently, serve selflessly and help many others to attain Krishna's mercy. Such spiritualization of our imagination is an emotionally potent way of applying the recommendation of the Bhagavad-gita (12.08) to internally "reside in Krishna."

❦

Just fix your mind upon Me, the Supreme Personality of Godhead, and engage all your intelligence in Me. Thus you will live in Me always, without a doubt.

Devotion harmonizes our emotional and rational faculties

*A*ll of us have an emotional faculty and a rational faculty. But in most of us, these two faculties are not integrated in a healthy balance.

People with a predominant emotional faculty tend to be hotheaded. Their overly strong emotions often rush them into decisions without due evaluation of various factors. They often speak and act in ways that they regret later.

People with a predominant rational faculty tend to be coldhearted. Their over-analytical nature frequently makes them unable or unwilling to express emotions effectively. They usually struggle to develop deep, meaningful relationships.

How can we harmonize both these faculties?

We first need to find a platform higher than both the emotional and the rational. Once we situate ourselves on that stable platform, we can evaluate the promptings of both these faculties calmly and, according to time-place-circumstance, integrate them appropriately. That stable platform is the spiritual platform. The easiest and quickest way to reach the spiritual platform is devotional service.

In the parlance of the Bhagavad-gita, we can roughly equate the emotional faculty with the mind and the rational faculty with the intelligence. When the Gita (12.14) urges us to offer our mind and intelligence to Krishna in devotion, it shows us the way for attaining the elusive balance between our emotional and rational faculties.

Devotional service offers us not just the best way to the spiritual platform but also the best access to the supreme power: the grace of Krishna. When we try to serve him, he helps us overpower the deficiencies that impede our devotional service. By his grace, we learn how to harmonize both our emotional and rational faculties, thereby becoming balanced individuals: sensitive but not impulsive, and calm-headed but not cold-hearted.

☙❧

One who is ... always satisfied, self-controlled, and engaged in devotional service with determination, his mind and intelligence fixed on Me—such a devotee of Mine is very dear to Me.

Gita wisdom is explicitly descriptive and implicitly prescriptive

Good teachers give explanations; great teachers give explanations and examples. Thus a great sports coach doesn't just explain to budding sportspersons what to do, but also gives examples of sports champions who do it. Those examples are not just descriptive but also prescriptive. As the champions are models for the novices, latent in descriptions about them is the prescription: "You too should do like this and become like this."

Krishna being the greatest teacher often uses in the Bhagavad-gita this same strategy of being explicitly descriptive and implicitly prescriptive. Acting as our spiritual coach, Krishna repeatedly describes the champion spiritualists: the pure devotees. Consider, for example, his description (12.17) of the advanced devotee as one who stays equipoised amidst all dualities. This verse is overtly descriptive; it outlines the characteristics of seers. Simultaneously, it is covertly prescriptive; it contains direction and inspiration for what we can and should become. Those who consider the discipline required to apply this prescription as impractical, as asking for too much, as "not for me," are like faint-hearted sports rookies who recoil from the discipline that has made champions champions. They are too chicken-hearted for pure devotion and they won't get it.

Fortunately, all of us can be lion-hearted enough to at least try. If we do so, pleasant surprises and rich returns await us. In sports, those without basic talent can never become champions; they are permanently unqualified. In pleasant contrast, nobody is unqualified in bhakti because it requires only devotion, which even the materially untalented can cultivate. Moreover, sports champions achieve at best some short-lived fame, whereas pure devotees achieve eternal prema – an infinitely richer return. And, most importantly, if we strive sincerely Krishna by his omnipotent mercy empowers us to rise to levels that had earlier seemed impossible

ॐ

One who neither rejoices nor grieves, who neither laments nor desires, and who renounces both auspicious and inauspicious things—such a devotee is very dear to Me.

The Gita calls not for blind obedience, but for visionary obedience

The idea of obeying someone often seems repellant to the contemporary mind: "I can think for myself; why should I obey anyone?" This repulsion to obedience seems all the more justified in the religious field where terrorists, in the name of obeying scripture, attack innocent people. But in fairness to religion, the secular field has also seen fanatics like Hitler's Nazis or Stalin's Communists who, in the name of obeying the ideology of their leaders, have killed innocent people in millions. So the actual problem is not religion or even obedience, but blind obedience – be it of religious or secular dogmas.

Why do some people become blind followers? One reason is that they want to avoid the responsibility of thinking about and choosing their own actions. Some such intellectually irresponsible people seek the easy way out by following faithful-seeming religious zealots who, though swearing by an ancient book, interpret it to suit their own purposes. Other intellectually responsible people obey secular leaders who promise that their godless ideologies will solve all problems.

The Bhagavad-gita doesn't subscribe to such an ethos of intellectual irresponsibility. Its presentation of multiple options for spiritual advancement, its sober and sensitive response to intelligent questions, its carefully reasoned arguments to substantiate its concluding call for devotional activism as the best pathway to individual and global well-being – all these set the scene for obedience that is not blind but visionary.

The basis of this visionary obedience is Krishna's extraordinary example. Despite being not just Arjuna's guru but also God himself, he doesn't demand obedience merely on the authority of his position; he quotes (13.05) scripture (shastra) and past saintly teachers (sadhu) to substantiate his message.

This tripartite foundation (*guru-sadhu-shastra*) for our thinking makes our obedience visionary: "I can think for myself; that's why I choose to obey Krishna."

CRSO

That knowledge of the field of activities and of the knower of activities is described by various sages in various Vedic writings. It is especially presented in Vedanta-sutra with all reasoning as to cause and effect.

Resting on our laurels? No resting! Not our laurels!

In material consciousness, whenever we achieve any success, we tend to parade it and brag about it. We often carry this tendency with us into our devotional life. This becomes evident when we achieve something worthwhile in devotional service – be it external in terms of completing a demanding service assignment or internal in terms of implementing a challenging resolution for self-mastery. At such times, we tend to exhibit our laurels and rest on them, thereby exposing ourselves to two unnecessary dangers.

Resting: The first danger in resting on our laurels is that the rest offers our inner adversaries – our mind and senses – time to recover, regroup and retaliate. When we achieve anything, we usually do so by disciplining and dovetailing our mind and senses. This inner success offers us a precious opportunity to press home our hard-earned advantage and push forward towards greater self-mastery. However, when we complacently rest on our laurels, we not only lose the upper hand, but also unwittingly give our inner adversaries a free hand for counter-attacking.

Our laurels: The second, greater danger in resting on our laurels is that the thought "These are my laurels" may itself give our ego an opportunity to penetrate and pervert our consciousness. It may make us claim credit for successes that have actually been achieved primarily by the grace of Krishna and only secondarily by our endeavors. By claiming credit, we lose our enriching inner connection with Krishna and let our ego tighten its shackles on us.

Cautioning us about such dangers, the Bhagavad-gita (13.08) reminds us that adambhitvam, the absence of the bragging tendency, characterizes those in knowledge.

༺༻

Humility; pridelessness; nonviolence; tolerance; simplicity; approaching a bona fide spiritual master; cleanliness; steadiness; self-control…—all these I declare to be knowledge, and besides this whatever there may be is ignorance

Science and Bhagavad-gita both go from the visible to the invisible

The fall of a fruit. Millions of people had seen this specific event that Newton saw. What made Newton different was that he went beyond this visible specific event to the invisible universal principle: gravity. Most scientific insights emerge from the search for the invisible universals that underlie the visible specifics.

A similar search underlies Gita wisdom. Millions have seen the specific event called death. What makes Gita students different is that they go beyond the specifics by asking the underlying universal questions: "What is death? Why does it exist? Will we end with death or will we live on beyond death?" The Bhagavad-gita (13.09) indicates that such contemplation is the springboard to authentic spiritual knowledge – our thoughts rise from visible matter to invisible spirit.

Thus, both science and Gita wisdom operate on the same intellectually sophisticated principle of going beyond the visible to the invisible. What differentiates them is the scope of the invisible: science usually assumes the invisible to be material, whereas Gita wisdom acknowledges that the invisible includes the material and the spiritual.

Due to their different scopes, science and Gita wisdom require different methods of verification and yield different end-results.

Methods of verification: Scientific postulates being connected primarily with the external world can be verified by physical experiments. The Gita's postulates being connected primarily with the internal world can be verified by spiritual experiments, that is, inner experiences. These experiments involve practicing yoga, specifically bhakti-yoga, and observing how our consciousness transforms as predicted by Gita wisdom.

End-results: As matter is temporary, the end-result of science is temporary: technologically-improved living conditions till death destroys everything. As spirit is eternal, the end-result of Gita wisdom is eternal: devotionally-inspired attainment of the eternal spiritual world.

ଔଷୠ

…The perception of the evil of birth, death, old age and disease…—all these I declare to be knowledge, and besides this whatever there may be is ignorance.

Denying our blindfolds keeps us blind

The Bhagavad-gita (13.09) indicates that the wise contemplate seriously the inevitability of death in our present existence. The Gita integrates this pessimistic-seeming contemplation into an optimistic worldview that explains how all of us, as eternal spiritual beings, have a right to immortality. We have lost that right because of being covered by materialistic passions and pursuits, just as people lose the right to see because of being covered by blindfolds.

Just as blindfolded people find blindness unnatural, we find our vulnerability to death unnatural. This conflict between our aspiration for immortality and our perception of mortality – like the conflict between the blindfolded people's longing to see and awareness of their inability to see – has the potential to spur us into spiritual action for reclaiming our immortality.

Unfortunately, we neglect this conflict by subconsciously denying our mortality; we imagine that we will not die, at least not in the near future. Our lack of concern about our mortality perpetuates our self-imposed death sentence. We are like blindfolded people who deny that they have blindfolds and so do nothing to remove them, despite having the power to do so.

We have the power to remove the blindfolds, that is, rise beyond the death sentence. How? By raising our consciousness to the spiritual level. Death can destroy only our material body, not us as souls. By practicing devotional service, we can go entirely beyond the arena of death. When by sustained devotional practices we develop our love for Krishna, we can attain his eternal abode that death can never reach.

ॐ

...The perception of the evil of birth, death, old age and disease...—all these I declare to be knowledge, and besides this whatever there may be is ignorance.

Don't slip on the philosophical banana peels of scriptural paradoxes

*S*ome of us may be put off by the apparently contradictory statements in the Bhagavad-gita. Several such statements are found in the thirteenth chapter of the Gita wherein, for example, the Absolute Truth is said to have hands everywhere and also to have no hands at all (13.14-13.15).

These statements are like philosophical banana peels; if during our spiritual journey we are not careful while dealing with them, we will stumble, slide and fall.

Dealing with them carefully means not reacting with derision or dismissiveness, but responding with humility and maturity.

1. **Humility:** Humility protects us from succumbing to the temptation of scoffing at such statements. It enables us to pause and consider: "When many of the wisest people in human history have found profound wisdom in the Gita, maybe I am mistaking as absurd that which is abstruse. Maybe I am overestimating my capacity to grasp the Gita's message."

2. **Maturity:** Maturity will empower us with the broad-mindedness to acknowledge that perspectives other than our present ones are possible and even valuable. Gita wisdom aims to elevate our consciousness to higher perspectives. To prod us towards that end, it sometimes drops tantalizing nuggets of wisdom that are intuited from those higher perspectives. What seems from our perspective a blatant contradiction is seen from a higher perspective as a brilliant paradox: a statement involving surface contradictions that forcefully stimulates hearers to seek a deeper unifying truth. The Gita uses paradoxes in its thirteenth chapter to convey the reality that the Absolute Truth has a form, but a form radically different from ours.

Therefore, when we encounter incomprehensible-seeming statements in the Gita, we needn't slip on these philosophical banana peels. Instead, we can see them as pointers to the nourishing bananas of esoteric insights awaiting us ahead on the path.

೧೮೦

14-15 Everywhere are His hands and legs, His eyes, heads and faces, and He has ears eyerywhere. In this way the Supersoul exists, pervading everything. The Supersoul is the original source of all senses, yet He is without senses...

End your divorce from reality

*I*magine a group of people who desire to play a virtual-reality video game. Their desire divorces them from the reality of their identity and propels them into an illusory cyber-world. In that world, they experience virtual emotions by misidentifying with a video game character.

Similarly, when we desire to enjoy material things, the Bhagavad-gita (13.22) indicates that our desire divorces us from the reality of our spiritual identity. Further, it propels us into the illusory material world that we presently inhabit. Here, we experience artificial emotions by misidentifying with our physical bodies.

Usually people's involvement with a video game is casual and enjoyable. In contrast, our involvement with the material world is consuming and distressing. It is so consuming that it often obliterates our awareness of our spiritual identity, making us believe erroneously that the material reality is the totality of reality. And it is largely distressing because it subjects us to the many miseries of material existence – psychophysical, social and environmental – as we limp our way to the terminal sufferings of old age, disease and death.

Gita wisdom shows us how to end our divorce from reality. It enlightens us about our spiritual identity and delineates the process of devotional service that gives us experiences of spiritual fulfillment. Just as video game players must give up the desire to enjoy the game for returning fully to reality, we need to give up the desire to enjoy the illusory material world for returning fully to the spiritual level. The easiest way to give up that self-imprisoning desire is by cultivating the desire to serve Krishna, which quickly connects us with spiritual happiness. When we thus redirect our desires, we return to the joyful spiritual reality where we originally belong.

☙❧

The living entity in material nature thus follows the ways of life, enjoying the three modes of nature. This is due to his association with that material nature. Thus he meets with good and evil amongst various species.

Guard against the vice of the wise

We often think of those with developed intellect as wise. We may even see a developed intellect as an indicator, or at least a facilitator, of spiritual advancement. No doubt, a developed intellect can aid in studying books, memorizing quotes, analyzing ideas, grasping concepts and verbalizing thoughts – all of which can aid deep philosophical understanding. However, this is not enough for spiritual advancement.

Gita wisdom states that the intellectual faculty belongs not to the spiritual level, but to the material level, albeit a subtle material one. Like everything material, the intellect can be a double-edged sword; it can take us towards Krishna or away from him. The Bhagavad-gita indicates that a developed intellect is a symptom of the mode of goodness. It also cautions (14.06) that this mode binds intellectuals by inducing in them a sense of intellectual superiority.

They can often expertly justify their views to others, especially those with a lesser intellect. However, despite their expertise, their views don't necessarily reflect reality because their views arise not from scriptural revelation but from personal speculation. Their developed intellect makes them dependent, even insistent, on such speculation; they dismiss submissive scriptural study as naïve and demeaning. They fail to realize that submissive scriptural study within a faithful tradition can connect them with Krishna, who is the supreme source of all wisdom, including their own. Due to their addiction to speculation and their rejection of tradition, they rarely understand reality holistically.

More detrimentally, by rejecting scriptural traditions, they deny themselves access to the process of devotional service that can liberate them from material attachments. Consequently, despite their lofty speculations, they frequently remain shackled by petty attachments.

Thus, the unwillingness to seek the aid of scripture is the vice of the wise, a vice that prevents their wisdom from leading them to freedom.

ॐ

O sinless one, the mode of goodness, being purer than the others, is illuminating, and it frees one from all sinful reactions. Those situated in that mode become conditioned by a sense of happiness and knowledge.

Go beyond indecision and indiscretion to introspection and inspiration

*W*hat should I do now?" We frequently face this question when life's perplexities disrupt our routines. We usually respond based on not just the external situation, but also our internal mood at the moment. As our mood often changes randomly, its unpredictability often worsens our perplexity.

Gita wisdom helps us understand that our moods derive from the modes, which are subtle forces that shape our interactions with matter. The Bhagavad-gita (14.10) indicates that the three modes are in perpetual conflict within our consciousness. Let's look at the typical mood induced by each of the modes:

1. **Indecision**: Characteristic of the mode of ignorance, indecision prevents us from both thinking clearly and acting decisively. Sometimes, indecision degenerates into self-pity, frustration and even senseless violence.
2. **Indiscretion**: Triggered by the mode of passion, indiscretion goads us towards acting without thinking. Usually, indiscretion aggravates our perplexity.
3. **Introspection**: Stimulated by the mode of goodness, introspection enables us to think carefully for ascertaining the best course of action and then act calmly for implementing it. For our introspection to work soundly, it needs to be guided by scriptural instruction.
4. **Inspiration**: Gifted by the indwelling Lord, the Supersoul, who exists beyond the three modes, inspiration resolves the entire perplexity in one moment of epiphany.

These four moods are not always discrete; they frequently comprise a spectrum with indecision and indiscretion on the negative side, and introspection and inspiration on the positive side. Inspiration is usually not in our hands, but introspection surely is. Even when we feel indecisive or indiscreet, we can make our introspection active and effective by seeking appropriate scriptural instruction.

This, in fact, is what Arjuna did in the Bhagavad-gita: though he was paralyzed by indecision in the beginning, he utilized introspection and instruction to become enlivened by inspiration.

Sometimes the mode of goodness becomes prominent, defeating the modes of passion and ignorance, O son of Bharata. Sometimes the mode of passion defeats goodness and ignorance, and at other times ignorance defeats goodness and passion. In this way there is always competition for supremacy.

Bhakti-yoga trains us in unemotional emotionality

*S*ome readers of the Bhagavad-gita are struck by a paradox: "The Gita asks us to be neutral towards emotions like happiness and distress. But it also recommends bhakti, which is through and through an emotion. How can we be both unemotional and emotional?

By being unemotional materially and emotional spiritually, answers Gita wisdom.

The Bhagavad-gita explains that we are souls who are meant for an emotionally rich life with Krishna at the spiritual level. Presently however, we are misidentifying with our temporary material bodies. This misidentification cuts us off from spiritual emotions and fills us with material emotions.

We are like movie spectators who because of identifying with a movie character become cut off from their real life emotions and get filled with reel-life emotions. To return to normalcy, the spectators need to stop being emotionally involved in the movie and start having emotionally stimulating exchanges with others in real life. The Gita recommends these same two steps by urging us to be unemotional materially and emotional spiritually.

Most of us are too materially entangled to immediately access spiritual emotions. So, we need a path and a process to raise our emotions from the material level to the spiritual level. The Gita paves the path through the analysis in its fourteenth chapter of how the three modes of material nature trigger various material emotions within us. Among such emotions, emotions in the mode of goodness are the most conducive for activating spiritual emotions. So, we need to harmonize our lifestyle with that mode. Then, we can transcend even goodness and unemotionally observe the arrival and departure of various material emotions in our consciousness.

As the most practical process to traverse this path, the Gita (14.26) exhorts us to practice bhakti-yoga undeviatingly. By activating our spiritual emotions, this yoga of spiritual love enables us to tolerate and eventually transcend material emotions.

ॐ৪০

One who engages in full devotional service, unfailing in all circumstances, at once transcends the modes of material nature and thus comes to the level of Brahman.

Be a part – be not apart

*S*ome people equate becoming spiritual with becoming unambitious. However, bhakti spirituality centers on ambitiousness, albeit of a kind different from the individualistic ambitiousness glamorized by our present culture.

Contemporary culture often defines success as an individual's ability to carve an identity distinct from others, to stand apart from the rest of the world. Today, the major identity-defining question is: "How are you different from others?" Few things demonstrate this obsession with distinctiveness better than the patent absurdity of many of the Guinness Book Records. Records like a couple kissing for forty-six hours or a person having nails six feet long may be *distinctive*, but are they contributive to anything worthwhile?

Gita wisdom offers the most contributive trajectory for our ambitiousness. The Bhagavad-gita states (15.07) that all of us are spiritual parts of the supreme whole, Krishna. Parts become largely useless when disconnected from the whole. Similarly, when we seek happiness separate from Krishna, we become frustrated. We come under the foolish fantasies and the draconian dictates of the mind and the senses – struggling to fulfill these is what we frequently call ambitiousness. Such struggle in a life apart from Krishna never satisfies us because everything material is temporary, whereas we long for lasting happiness.

We can choose an alternative, more productive form of ambitiousness: devotional ambitiousness. This essentially means striving to be a part of Krishna, to lovingly play our role in his benevolent plan. Just as parts gain value when connected with the whole, our individual human endeavors gain value when we connect them with him through devotional service. By playing our part in his master plan for the holistic welfare of everyone, we tangibly and constructively contribute to the world. Moreover, because he is eternal and all-attractive, loving him brings eternal fulfillment.

❦

The living entities in this conditioned world are My eternal fragmental parts. Due to conditioned life, they are struggling very hard with the six senses, which include the mind

Go within, beyond the external – and the internal

*M*any self-help books tell us that we can become peaceful by going within. But is the within actually peaceful? In our own experience, we often find it filled with disturbing emotions like tension, stress, resentment, worry, and frustration. These inner disturbances impel many people to seek relief in TV, movies and similar outer distractions. In some people, such disturbances become so acute as to cause them serious mental health problems.

Does this mean that we shouldn't seek peace within? Not exactly. We need to first understand what is truly internal to us before seeking peace in it. We normally define as external the physical world that we talk and walk in, and as internal the mental world that we think and feel in. However, we base this definition on the assumption that we are the body: as the physical world is outside the body, we call it external; as the mental world is inside the body, we call it internal.

Gita wisdom underscores that this underlying assumption about our identity is false; it explains logically and systematically how we are not the body but are the soul. From the viewpoint of the soul – from our actual viewpoint – both the body and the mind are external. The Bhagavad-gita (15.07) indicates that both the body and the mind cause the soul to struggle and suffer (*manah shastanindriyani prakriti sthani karshati*).

The only truly internal world for the soul is the world of its loving relationship with Krishna. That alone is eternal – and is eternally beyond the ups and downs of both the body and the mind.

Krishna resides both in the spiritual world and also within our own hearts. By cultivating his regular remembrance, we can go beyond the physical and the mental worlds to the spiritual world – in consciousness while in this life and in entirety thereafter. By being thus absorbed in him, we can find lasting peace.

ॐ

The living entities in this conditioned world are My eternal fragmental parts. Due to conditioned life, they are struggling very hard with the six senses, which include the mind.

"Seeing is believing" drags humans to the animal level

The Bhagavad-gita (15.10) reproaches as deluded (*vimudha*) those materialists who are blind to the soul due to their overdependence on their undependable senses. "Seeing is believing" is the credo that such people use self-righteously to justify their disbelief in everything invisible. Sadly, their credo drags them down to the bestial level both intellectually and practically.

Intellectually: "Seeing is believing" is a permanent progress stopper. Our advanced human intelligence enables us to infer underlying invisible principles from visible phenomena. Without such inference, we can gain no deep understanding of the world – neither scientific nor philosophical. As "seeing is believing" censors everything invisible, it reduces our human intelligence to nought and condemns us to the same epistemological boat as animals.

Practically: "Seeing is believing" drags humans down to animalistic indulgences. An animal wandering in a desert believes in the mirage that it sees and chases after the non-existent water, thereby condemning itself to perpetual thirst and eventual death. Similarly, dogmatic materialists refuse to believe in the spiritual because of its invisibility, thereby depriving themselves of spiritual happiness. Consequently, they chase after the only pleasures that remain available to them: material pleasures. As we are spiritual beings, material pleasures can never give us real happiness, so Gita wisdom compares such pleasures with mirages. By chasing futilely after those mirage-like pleasures, materialists condemn themselves to insatiable craving and repeated births and deaths in material existence.

The Gita aptly addresses the devotees of "seeing is believing" by the word *vimudha* that invokes the image of a special ass (vi – special; *mudha* – ass) and conveys the misfortune of human beings behaving asininely.

ॐ

The foolish cannot understand how a living entity can quit his body, nor can they understand what sort of body he enjoys under the spell of the modes of nature. But one whose eyes are trained in knowledge can see all this

The Gita provides the eye to see the I

We see not with our eyes but with our knowledge. Where our eyes see a line graph curved sharply downwards, our knowledge of economics helps us see a recession. In general, it is our knowledge that enables us to make sense of the shapes and colors that our eyes show us.

Seeing with knowledge is a principle that we regularly accept and apply in our daily life. Scientists too apply this principle with equal, if not more, frequency in their research. They see the bent trajectory of a light ray and see in the vicinity an invisible object with a super-strong gravity pull: a black hole.

Gita wisdom urges us to apply this principle in our spiritual life too. The Bhagavad-gita (15.10) states that we can see the soul with *jnana-chakshu*, the eye of knowledge. This knowledge is provided by the Gita itself in multiple ways:

1. Objective analysis of the differences between the body and the soul (Chp 2)

2. Methodical delineation of the characteristics of the soul (Chp 13)

3. Penetrating portrayal of the illusions that bind the soul to the world of matter (Chp 16)

4. Illuminating account of the various paths of yoga that facilitate the perception and liberation of the soul (Chps 3-6, 13,18)

5. Endearing elucidation of the supreme path of bhakti-yoga that not only liberates the soul but also situates it in its ultimate life of divine love in the spiritual world (Chps 7-12, Chp 18).

The more we systematically and prayerfully study this profound knowledge given in the Gita, the more we develop and refine our eye of knowledge. Thereby we gain the eye to see the I – the soul – as the essence of our identity.

༅

The foolish cannot understand how a living entity can quit his body, nor can they understand what sort of body he enjoys under the spell of the modes of nature. But one whose eyes are trained in knowledge can see all this

Enlightenment is universal, beneficial and non-imitable

The word "enlightenment" is frequently used in spiritual circles. But what exactly does it mean? It essentially means understanding where to direct our heart's longing for love and directing it accordingly. The Bhagavad-gita (15.19) states that the enlightened offer all their heart's love to Krishna, understanding him to be the supreme person, the highest truth, the ultimate reality.

As compared to popular notions of enlightenment such as seeing a dazzling light or feeling a pulsating current, the Gita's definition is far more universal, beneficial and non-imitable. Let's see how:

Universal: Love is the deepest thirst of all living beings. By explaining how enlightenment fulfills this universal thirst, Gita wisdom makes enlightenment intelligible for everyone, rejecting thereby the idea that it is meant for a select few.

Beneficial: Love, when misdirected, becomes the cause of our greatest suffering. If enlightenment didn't address our need to love and be loved, what would be the benefit of becoming enlightened? By explaining how the enlightened directing of our love towards Krishna will make us eternally, supremely and completely happy, Gita wisdom shows how enlightenment is practically beneficial.

Non-imitable: Gita wisdom explains that the enlightened express their love for Krishna by serving him and fulfilling his mission in this world. Krishna's mission is to make all living beings eternally happy by reviving their dormant love for him. Therefore, the enlightened give up all worldly pleasures that militate against Krishna's mission. So, we can recognize the enlightened by observing their characteristics: the values, purposes and activities of their life. As these cannot be imitated for long, pretenders soon become exposed when subjected to scrutiny. Additionally, these characteristics also provide us parameters for evaluating our own progress towards enlightenment.

Understanding enlightenment thus can inspire us to march confidently and enthusiastically along the Gita's pathway to enlightenment.

☙❧

Whoever knows Me as the Supreme Personality of Godhead, without doubting, is the knower of everything. He therefore engages himself in full devotional service to Me, O son of Bharata

Peel the cosmic onion to discover spiritual diversity in unity

Just as we need to peel off multiple covering layers to reach the essence of an onion, we need to peel of multiple covering layers to reach the essence of the cosmos.

Scientists are among today's most prominent cosmic onion peelers; using their material tools and techniques, they peel the panorama of material phenomena to seek an underlying order. Yet their search, even if successful, is profoundly, permanently incomplete; their particles, forces and laws hardly relate with the experiences and emotions that are the driving realities of our daily lives.

Gita wisdom recommends a more realistic approach to cosmic onion peeling: "Begin the enquiry with that which all of us know really exists: our own consciousness." After all, consciousness is the necessary reality that enables us to do any enquiry at all. Because material science focuses only on matter and neglects consciousness, its peeling fails to reach consciousness.

However, if we start with consciousness, as do spiritual scientists, the Bhagavad-gita (13.31) indicates the reality we will discover: underlying the variety of matter is the uniformity of spirit, the source of all consciousness.

Significantly, the Gita doesn't stop the peeling there; it doesn't assume, as do the impersonlists, that the uniformity of spirit is a barren homogeneity. It peels further and reveals within that uniformity an eternal diversity: the diversity of innumerable individual souls centered on one supreme individual, Krishna. And unifying these diverse individuals is the ultimate reality: love, love so endearing that it attracts even the all-attractive. This, the Gita (15.20) indicates, is the greatest of all secrets.

Thus, when we successfully peel beyond the endpoints of material *jnana* (science) and spiritual *jnana* (impersonalism), we discover to our delight that the very love that is presently life's driving purpose is in its pristine and potent form existence's crowning reality.

CRSO

This is the most confidential part of the Vedic scriptures, O sinless one, and it is disclosed now by Me. Whoever understands this will become wise, and his endeavors will know perfection

Hell is meant not to cause us suffering but to save us from suffering

Some exclusivist religions claim that those who don't accept their dogmatic beliefs will be sent by God to hell forever. In refreshing contrast to such narrow-minded conceptions, Gita wisdom presents a broad-minded, refined understanding of the universe as a university with Krishna as a constant benevolent guide. Those who learn the art of seeking spiritual happiness graduate from the university and regain everlasting joy in Krishna's personal abode.

Unfortunately, some people adamantly refuse to learn this lesson. Instead, as the Bhagavad-gita (16.21) indicates, they imagine that unrestricted indulgence in lust, anger and greed are gateways to pleasure. Such perverse fantasies make them mentally deranged, thereby alienating them from their right to inner spiritual happiness and sentencing them to repeated misery in material existence. To shorten their suffering and to accelerate their learning, nature sends them to a severe transitional classroom named hell. This classroom makes apparent the miserable nature of material existence and the terrible consequence of wanton indulgence – twin lessons that they couldn't grasp in more congenial classrooms. Thus, the primary purpose of hell is not condemnation but education that enables stubborn souls to minimize their self-inflicted suffering.

Additionally, hell is not only a temporary but also a non-mandatory classroom. A far better classroom is our present world. And Krishna goes out of his way to help us learn the art of happiness here itself. The Gita refers passingly to hell, but reveals elaborately a concerned, committed, compassionate God who through his educational message does his best to not only protect us from hell but also pave our way to the eternal world.

To conclude, God doesn't cast anyone to hell forever; instead, he does all that he can to guide everyone for attaining his abode forever.

ॐ

There are three gates leading to this hell—lust, anger and greed. Every sane man should give these up, for they lead to the degradation of the soul

Lack of devotional appetite is natural yet unnatural

As spiritual seekers, we may at times feel apathetic or averse to spiritual practices such as meditation or prayer that connect us with Krishna and nourish us spiritually. This absence of devotional appetite symptomizes that we are afflicted with spiritual anorexia.

Anorexia is a peculiar bodily disorder in which the patients need food, but don't feel any appetite. This lack of bodily appetite is natural yet unnatural; it seems natural as long as the patients are in the grip of anorexia, but is seen to be unnatural as soon as they become healthy.

Similarly, our lack of devotional appetite is natural yet unnatural. It seems natural as long as we are in the grip of the illusory energy that distorts our longing for Krishna into craving for worldly objects. In this diseased condition, because our desires are mostly fixated on worldly objects, we have very little desire left for directing towards Krishna. So lack of interest in him seems to be our habitual and therefore natural state. But when we practice bhakti-yoga and purify ourselves, we start realizing and relishing higher happiness in our devotional relationship with Krishna. And when we taste such bliss and progress on the path towards spiritual recovery, we understand that our lack of eagerness to consistently connect with him is unnatural – it symptomizes our spiritual anorexia.

Just as an anorexic person can be cured by taking a regular and regulated diet, similarly we can be spiritually cured by a regular and regulated diet of devotional practices. Though such a regimen may seem unpleasant initially, the Bhagavad-gita (18.37) reassures us that we will eventually experience it to be pleasant: sublimely, supremely pleasant.

૰

That which in the beginning may be just like poison but at the end is just like nectar and which awakens one to self-realization is said to be happiness in the mode of goodness.

Claiming that the unknown is unknowable is claiming to know the unknown

"God is so great that we tiny creatures can never know him." So claim some people.

At first sight, this position seems reasonable and even humble. However, it neglects the reality that God is so great that he transcends not only affirmation, but also negation. We can neither know what he is nor, what he is not. The statement that he is unknown to us reflects our humility. However, the statement that he is unknowable to us indicates that we are overstepping beyond humility to claim unwarrantedly that we know him in the sense that we know that he is unknowable.

True, we cannot know God by our own efforts. But the claim that we can never know him minimizes his potency; it makes him impotent to reveal himself to us. He is so great that he can enable even us finite beings to know his infinite glories. Of course, we can never know him in full, but we can know him enough to fall completely in love with him.

Gita wisdom furnishes us with knowledge of God in his sweetest manifestation as Krishna. This knowledge is not meant to be merely an anthology of textual statements. Rather, it is a symphony of transformational realizations that begins only when we cultivate devotion for him, as the Bhagavad-gita asserts (18.55: *bhaktya mam abhijananti*). The more we render devotional service to him, the more he progressively reveals his unlimited glory to us. With every passing day, the supreme unknown becomes increasingly, deliciously known. And yet, because he is infinite, he remains tantalizingly, everlastingly unknown.

Krishna's self-revelation as an enchanting blend of known-unknown makes the life of loving him an eternal adventure of exhilarating ecstasy.

❀

One can understand Me as I am, as the Supreme Personality of Godhead, only by devotional service. And when one is in full consciousness of Me by such devotion, he can enter into the kingdom of God

With Krishna, we flourish; without Krishna, we perish

*L*ife presents us with so many alternatives, all with their own complex and unpredictable implications, that the task of choosing among them can become overwhelming.

Gita wisdom rescues us by pointing out that we ultimately have two essential choices that lie with each one of us at every moment. The Bhagavad-gita (18.58) outlines them: move towards Krishna and gradually scale over and beyond all obstacles, or move away from Krishna and get lost in the mesh of worldly delusions and distresses.

When we choose to move away from Krishna, our pleasure-seeking nature causes us to get blown whichever way the wind of worldly desire blows in our hearts. Worldly desires require strenuous work before fulfillment, yield meager pleasure on fulfillment and blow with increased power after fulfillment. Their overall effect is to make us lose our bearings and stay trapped in their spell – lifetime after lifetime.

Fortunately, we have an alternative: we can choose to move towards Krishna by practicing devotional service. When we practice devotional service, we understand his will as it is revealed generically in the scriptures and specifically for us through our devotee-guides. Once we become mindful of his will and act according to it, we become increasingly connected with him and the everlasting pleasure that he is waiting to bestow upon us. Being thus fortified by inner fulfillment and guided by his voice from within, we can resist the stormy winds of desire and stay on track toward attaining eternal happiness.

A simple sutra to remind ourselves of these life-trajectories is: with Krishna, we flourish, without Krishna, we perish. By bearing in mind the contours of these two choices and their concomitant consequences, we can get a defining guideline to navigate life's mazes and make the best choice, now and always.

☙❧

If you become conscious of Me, you will pass over all the obstacles of conditioned life by My grace. If, however, you do not work in such consciousness but act through false ego, not hearing Me, you will be lost.

.

Don't give up the intelligence; go beyond the intelligence

Intellectuals sometimes feel alienated from scriptures due to what they feel are its inconsistent or illogical statements. As their intellect has been their guide and strength throughout their lives, they distrust anything that seems to require them to give up their intellect.

This common apprehension about scriptures is turned on its head by the Bhagavad-gita. The Gita (18.63) calls upon us to use all of our intelligence to deeply deliberate its message – and then to decide for ourselves our course of action. This bold call for intellectual investigation of its teachings is arguably as far as one can go from the conventional stereotype that scriptures require one to give up one's intelligence.

Gita wisdom asks us not to give up the intelligence, but to go beyond the intelligence. Giving up one's intelligence is required for those dogmatic beliefs that can't stand intellectual scrutiny. Going beyond the intelligence is required for those experiential systems of spiritual practice that offer us deep experiences that the intellect can't reach. The trajectory of the Gita's message goes as far as our intellect goes, meaning that its wisdom stands sustained intellectual scrutiny. But then its trajectory surpasses the farthest reach of the intellect – and goes further into the realm of individualized experience.

Analysis is the forte of the head, and experience, the forte of the heart. When we offer our heart to Krishna, our spiritual vision gradually awakens, thereby offering us experiential realization about how any seeming inconsistencies actually point to majestic higher-level truths.

Thus, unlike many belief systems that ask us to give up the head for reaching the heart, Gita wisdom goes through our head to reach our heart.

ॐ

Thus I have explained to you knowledge still more confidential. Deliberate on this fully, and then do what you wish to do.

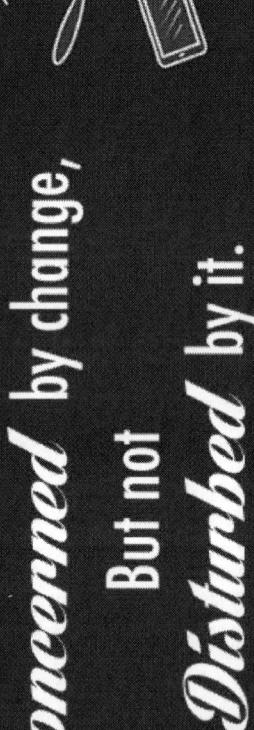

Be *Concerned* by change,

But not *Disturbed* by it.

Don't
GIVE UP
GROW UP.

...... **Transform** ......

Disappointment Into His *Appointment.*

The *World* is a station,
Not a *Destination*

Those who desire to be **Fused**
are **Confused.**

Happiness is always a *byproduct,*

Never a

Product.

Go beyond infinite longings

Long for the infinite.

Study makes us

Steady

and

Sturdy.

Seek
not a problem free Life.
Seeks a
Purpose filled life.

Page 316

Surrender is not about Giving up,

It is about

Going up.

Page 342

The Bhagavad-gita enthrones the path of love

*T*hose familiar with the Gita sometimes raise the question: "When the Gita mentions various spiritual paths like karma-yoga, jnana-yoga and ashtanga-yoga, what is the need to stress only the path of bhakti-yoga?"

Because that is the stress of the Gita itself, as is evident in its unambiguous conclusion (18.66) that we abandon all other paths and adopt the path of love, bhakti-yoga. Of course, the Gita analyzes other spiritual paths too. But all that analysis is meant to prepare the ground for the enthronement of bhakti-yoga as the most recommended path. Let's understand the rationale for this enthronement.

A beautiful painting can be appreciated only through refined aesthetic emotions – not through emotion-less scrutiny. Similarly, the Bhagavad-gita reveals a beautiful conception of God as Krishna, a conception that can be appreciated only through refined devotional emotions – not through emotion-less physical gymnastics or intellectual polemics (11.53-54). To develop these refined emotions, the Gita recognizes that we need to first unglue our mind from worldly objects whose temporary beauty distracts us perpetually from the eternal beauty of Krishna. For this intermediate purpose of curbing distracting material emotions, it discusses multiple paths like the path of detached dutifulness (karma-yoga), the path of analysis (jnana-yoga) and the path of austerity (ashtanga-yoga).

However, the Gita encourages us to associate with those who are relishing the beauty of God (10.09) and by their inspiration supplant our material emotions with refined devotional emotions. This refining of emotions helps us to develop our devotional-aesthetic sensibility and thereby relish the beauty of Krishna. Once we fall in love with him, we can easily and swiftly return back to his eternal abode, which is the Gita's ultimate destination and life's supreme perfection.

That's why authentic Gita teachers stress bhakti-yoga.

ॐ

Abandon all varieties of religion and just surrender unto Me. I shall deliver you from all sinful reactions. Do not fear

The Gita centers on neither rituals nor doctrines but on a love affair

The Bhagavad-gita (18.66) concludes with the radical call to abandon all dharmas and just surrender to Krishna alone. What is the rationale for this call?

To grasp the rationale, let's first understand what the word dharmas may refer to in this context. The Vedic tradition outlines three broad paths: the path of ritual religiosity (karma-kanda), the path of doctrinal speculation (jnana-kanda), and the path of worship (upasana-kanda). All these paths comprise various dharmas.

The Gita asks us to abandon all other paths for the sake of the path of devotional worship. Thus, it implies that we reject rituals and doctrines, and make our life into a love affair with Krishna.

We may wonder: "But the path of devotion also has its rituals and doctrines. Are they to be abandoned?" No, because those rituals and doctrines are not alternative paths; they are assistants on the path of devotion.

At the same time, they may become obstacles on the devotional path if we get caught in their technical details and forget their essential purpose. This verse sharply reminds us that the ultimate purpose of all the doctrines and all the rituals is to help us love Krishna. The doctrines can tell us why to love Krishna and the rituals can tell us how to love him, but we alone have to choose to love him. The Srimad Bhagavatam (1.2.8) echoes this theme when it asserts that we gain nothing but labor if we merely proclaim the doctrines or enact the rituals but don't learn to love Krishna. Only when we consciously desire to love Krishna will the doctrines and rituals assist us on our devotional journey.

Thus, the radical conclusion of the Gita inspires us to make love for Krishna our exclusive aspiration.

ॐ

Abandon all varieties of religion and just surrender unto Me. I shall deliver you from all sinful reactions. Do not fear

The Gita is categorical and rhetorical

*M*any people say, "The Bhagavad-gita is all things to all people; it recommends different paths for different people."

Does it? Reading the Gita shows that it does indeed address many paths including the paths of religious materialism, detached action, intellectual reflection, introspective meditation and selfless devotion.

Careful reading of the Gita, however, shows that it doesn't endorse all of these paths equally. This becomes most clear in its climax (18.66) where its message becomes categorical and rhetorical:

1. **Categorical** because this verse unambiguously rejects all other paths to proclaim the path of selfless devotion.

2. **Rhetorical** because it proleptically removes apprehensions that those who accept the path of devotion may face problems because of rejecting other paths by unequivocally proclaiming Krishna's personal protection for them.

Here's a rough metaphor to help us grasp the Gita's strategy. A champion boxer starts a match by throwing light punches in the air that are intended to draw the opponent close enough so that a single knockout punch can finish the match. Similarly, the Gita outlines various paths so as to draw closer individuals who are infatuated with those paths. When they become drawn into the Gita's flow of thought, its masterly analysis knocks out their infatuations about the superiority of their pet paths, thereby facilitating their acceptance of the path of selfless devotion.

If we subordinate our preconceived reasoning to the Gita's reasoning, we can discover how the path of devotion fulfills our deepest needs and aspirations. But if we superimpose our reasoning on the Gita's reasoning, we gain nothing except the self-serving and misleading satisfaction that it supports our path.

The choice is ours.

ॐ

Abandon all varieties of religion and just surrender unto Me. I shall deliver you from all sinful reactions. Do not fear.

Four stages in Gita study: Veneration, Comprehension, Application, Transformation

*T*he Bhagavad-gita is a profoundly empowering book. To tap its power, we need to develop our relationship with it through four progressive stages:

1. **Veneration**: Some of us may have been brought up in a culture that venerates the Gita. We may have placed our copy of the Gita on our altar – and left it there till dust accumulated on it due to long disuse. Sometimes we may have memorized a few of its verses and happily quoted them as the official proof of our piety. If we stay stuck at this level of ignorant veneration of the Gita, we may get some religious merit but won't get much spiritual empowerment.

2. **Comprehension**: The Gita itself prods us towards comprehension by stating (18.70) that it is to be worshiped with one's intelligence. This implies that we use our intelligence in a prayerful and submissive way to analyse, appreciate and assimilate the Gita's message, thereby comprehending its verity, glory and relevancy. A sincere attempt at comprehension can empower even those of us who had no upbringing of cultural veneration for the Gita.

3. **Application**: The Gita is essentially a book for application. Comprehending it helps us to apply it, thus charting the most prudent and productive course of action for our life's trajectory. When we apply its message, we start experiencing for ourselves the higher spiritual realities it delineates.

4. **Transformation**: Application of the Gita is profoundly transformational; it redirects our love from matter to Krishna. Thereby it raises our consciousness beyond the temporary and miserable world of matter, eventually establishing us in our original life of eternal love in Krishna's supreme abode.

Thus does the Gita empower us to achieve life's ultimate success.

☙❧

And I declare that he who studies this sacred conversation of ours worships Me by his intelligence

The Gita is an intellectual adventure with an emotional climax

*W*e have two essential faculties: the head and the heart. The head is our intellectual center and the heart, our emotional center.

The Bhagavad-gita being a book of intellectual adventure with an emotional climax addresses both of our core faculties. Let's see how.

Intellectual Adventure: The Gita charts a clear pathway for us through the maze-like alternatives that the world presents. It first informs us that life's purpose and perfection is to connect with Krishna and then equips us with a conceptual framework to connect with him constantly. This knowledge empowers our intelligence to see beyond the veil of matter and perceive Krishna's reassuring presence. Using our intelligence to perceive Krishna's hand amidst life's ups and downs is life's greatest intellectual adventure.

Emotional climax: The Gita culminates in Krishna's unequivocal proclamations that he loves all of us intensely, that he desires our highest good, and that he stands ready to remove all obstacles from our path when we choose to return to him. The Gita's emotional climax is this disarming expression of Krishna's love. And wonderfully enough, the climax keeps climaxing for all of eternity because the more we love Krishna, the more we relish his love for us. This emotional climax enables our heart to see beyond life's crests and troughs and relish Krishna's empowering benevolence constantly.

Thus, Gita wisdom enables us to connect with Krishna with both our core faculties: to perceive his presence with our head and to relish his benevolence with our heart. By this dual divine connection, we become confident, like Arjuna (18.73), to do his will, thereby converting any challenge that life sends our way into an opportunity for spiritual growth.

ॐ

Arjuna said: My dear Krishna, O infallible one, my illusion is now gone. I have regained my memory by Your mercy. I am now firm and free from doubt and am prepared to act according to Your instructions

Ask not, "Is God with me?" Ask, "Am I with God?"

The Bhagavad-gita (18.73) expresses the summit of humanity's faith in divinity when Arjuna declares to Krishna, "I will do your will."

Our faith in God begins with the feeling that there exists a higher being who will help us if we petition him through prayer. At this level of faith, the question that defines our relationship with God is: "Is God with me?" Such a question indicates that we have faith in God's power, but not his wisdom. That's why we use our own wisdom to decide what we should do, ask for God's power to help us do it, and then wonder whether he will help us or not.

When we develop faith in God's wisdom, then we first let God decide what we should do and then seek his power for doing it. At this level of faith, the question that defines our relationship with God is: "Am I with God?" That is, we examine whether we are living in his presence by molding our life according to his guidelines given in the Gita. When we mold our life thus, we realize increasingly that God was always with us – the problem was that we were not with him, having strayed away from his remembrance because of infatuation with temporary worldly pleasures. We understand that even now, he is ready and competent to guide us out of our troubles if we just turn our heart to him.

If we study the message of the Gita submissively and seriously, as did Arjuna, then this study will broaden and deepen our faith in God. We will learn to trust not just his power but also his wisdom. Then we too will be able to declare, as did Arjuna, "Krishna, I am with you."

ॐ

Arjuna said: My dear Krishna, O infallible one, my illusion is now gone. I have regained my memory by Your mercy. I am now firm and free from doubt and am prepared to act according to Your instructions.

Treasure Krishna's message more than his miracles

Some of us may feel that our faith in Krishna would stabilize and increase if we could see his power through miracles: "If Krishna is truly supreme, then all he needs to do to solve my problems is just perform one miracle. Why doesn't he help me by doing that?"

Understanding the answer to this question takes us to the heart of Gita wisdom – its ascending trajectory from material religiosity to spiritual devotion.

At the level of material religiosity, we see Krishna primarily as a source of blessings; we approach him not for who he is, but for what he can give us. We expect him to miraculously solve our problems and satisfy our desires. Even if he does both, our relief will be short-lived because in material existence both problems and desires are endless.

At the level of spiritual devotion, we see Krishna essentially as the object of love; we approach him for who he is, not for what he can give us. Paradoxically, when we don't ask him for material blessings, we allow him to give us his greatest blessing: himself. By not being attached to our material desires we allow him to enter our heart and gradually conquer it by revealing his supreme attractiveness.

To get this ultimate blessing, we need to receive and live Krishna's message of love, as did Arjuna. After hearing the Gita, Arjuna didn't ask him to perform any miracles for removing obstacles. Instead, he firmly resolved to live Krishna's message by (18.73) doing his will.

When we, like Arjuna, treasure Krishna's message more than his miracles, he floods our heart with ever-increasing love and happiness. And that flood is his ultimate miracle.

ॐ

Arjuna said: My dear Krishna, O infallible one, my illusion is now gone. I have regained my memory by Your mercy. I am now firm and free from doubt and am prepared to act according to Your instructions

Don't let information overload make relevance irrelevant

*O*ur culture bombards us with irrelevant information. The attack on an embassy in Africa, a tennis tournament in America, an election in Europe – does such information change what we need to do today? Or even the day after? Not very frequently.

Never before in human history have people been fed so much information about which they can do nothing. Our society judges information not by its functional utility, but by its entertainment capacity. We have made relevance irrelevant.

Does this analysis suggest that we stay totally uninformed about worldly events? No, though we could substantially decrease the time we spend on getting information without losing much except the capacity to appear "informed" in pointless chit-chatting about irrelevant subjects.

The main purpose of this analysis is to help us realize that our culture has profoundly changed the way we look at information, a change that significantly alters our approach to scriptural information in two major ways:

1. **Superficiality in study:** Because we are so habituated, even addicted, to be entertained by new information, we look for similar new entertaining stuff while studying the Bhagavad-gita. On not being titillated, we dub the Gita "boring."

2. **Lethargy in application**: Because we habitually don't do anything about the information we acquire, we similarly don't apply the information we acquire from the Gita like, say, happiness is found not in material things, but in spiritual love for Krishna. Due to our lethargy in application, Gita reading doesn't benefit us much.

If Gita wisdom is to enrich us, we need to change the question that we ask while reading the Gita: not "What's new today?" but "What can I apply today?" The Gita itself points to this approach when it reports (18.73) that Arjuna was determined to apply what he had learnt.

☙❦❧

Arjuna said: My dear Krishna, O infallible one, my illusion is now gone. I have regained my memory by Your mercy. I am now firm and free from doubt and am prepared to act according to Your instructions

Relish the two wonders of Gita wisdom

Beholding the wonders of the world is often an anti-climactic experience. The splendor of the Taj Mahal is fascinating to see once, maybe twice, just maybe thrice. But then it becomes pale and stale. And we start wondering if there is anything else to see.

The much-touted wonders of the world usually disappoint us. Still, we long to behold or experience something that fills us with wonder.

Why? Because, Gita wisdom answers, the sense of wonder (*adbhuta*) is one of the aesthetic emotions (*rasa*) integral to our spiritual nature. Relishing the Bhagavad-gita can awaken this emotion in our heart, as Sanjaya testifies (18.76).

The word *wonder* has two connotations: experience of awe (e.g. I am struck by wonder on seeing the beauty of the rainbow) and absence of understanding (e.g. I wonder how a rainbow is formed in thin air during the rainy season).

Gita wisdom wakens both these senses of wonder in us. Let's see how:

1. **Experience of awe:** Gita wisdom answers life's toughest questions while delineating a majestic worldview that is both emotionally appealing and intellectually satisfying. The more we meditate on the Gita's verses, the more we become awe-struck at how its simple-seeming verses embody life's profoundest insights.

2. **Absence of understanding:** We can never fully understand Krishna's glory and beauty, yet every moment that we remember, serve and love him, our understanding deepens. Consequently, we become filled with a sense of wonder that is a celebration not of ignorance, but of the mystery of divine love. This mystery is increasingly, but never completely, unraveled at every moment for all of eternity.

Once our heart becomes awake to these twin wonders of the Gita, then life itself becomes an ongoing, unfolding wonder.

ॐ

O King, as I repeatedly recall this wondrous and holy dialogue between Krishna and Arjuna, I take pleasure, being thrilled at every moment.

CHOOSING INTELLIGENT HAPPINESS

Temptations in the consciousness are like dust in the carburetor

*W*hen dust enters into the carburetor of a finely tuned engine, the engine can no longer function optimally. Though the dust initially seems inconsequential, after some time the engine starts malfunctioning ; then we understand that the insignificant dust has caused significant trouble.

Just as dust particles are pervasive in our polluted environment, temptations, especially sensual temptations triggered by lust and greed, are pervasive in our materialistic culture. Therefore, it is almost natural and inevitable that temptations enter and stay in our consciousness – if not in the foreground, then at least in the background. As the temptations offer the prospect of imminent enjoyment, they seem not just harmless, but even pleasantly titillating.

However, what seems titillating initially soon becomes tormenting; the hope and the hankering for enjoyment distracts and drains us mentally. This mental tiredness makes us malfunction materially in our worldly responsibilities and especially spiritually in our devotional activities. When we try to fix our consciousness on Krishna while also entertaining temptations of material enjoyment, the Bhagavad-gita (2.44) indicates that we just can't get any devotional happiness.

Fortunately, this doesn't have to be our permanent despair. We can return to spiritual normalcy by forcing ourselves to think of Krishna. This remembrance acts as a cleanser for removing the dust of temptations. If we empower our intelligence with Gita wisdom, we will realize that fixing our consciousness diligently on him, even if it seems difficult initially, brings a double dividend:

1. It saves us from the far greater difficulty of dealing with the dust of temptations and

2. It supplies us with the ultimate spiritual fulfillment, thereby taking us beyond the reach of temptations.

രാജ

In the minds of those who are too attached to sense enjoyment and material opulence, and who are bewildered by such things, the resolute determination for devotional service to the Supreme Lord does not take place.

Titillating the senses ends in all pain, no gain

Our culture seems to offer us so much sensual pleasure for free. Alluring images in tantalizing poses invite us to enjoy them with our eyes for no apparent cost. Our mind prods us on: "Just titillate yourself with these images; it will relax you. I know that you are never going to enjoy these things in real-life because that will violate your devotional principles. But there's no harm in enjoying them mentally. You deserve happiness."

The mind is right: we do deserve happiness. However, it is dead wrong about how we can get that happiness. Far from providing happiness, sensual titillation strips us of happiness materially by increasing our torment and spiritually by increasing our tastelessness. Let's see how:

1. **Torment:** Titillation may provide a momentary sense of pleasure, but it also feeds our material desires, making them stronger. And the stronger these desires become, the more they torment us with demands to satisfy them. Struggling constantly to beat down these strengthened desires drains our energy. Moreover, their increased strength makes our inner battle tougher and riskier, and raises the chances that we may fall ruinously from our standards of integrity.

2. **Tastelessness:** Titillation quickens the senses and slackens the spirit. The more we become materially sensitized, the more we become spiritually desensitized. Consequently, we can't relish devotional stimuli like the delicious holy name or the gorgeous Deities. The more we find core devotional activities tasteless, the more the whole of devotional life becomes boring and burdensome.

Thus, by titillating ourselves, we end up losers both materially and spiritually: all pain, no gain. The Bhagavad-gita protects us from this double loss by urging us (02.58) to zealously avoid unnecessary contact of the senses with the sense objects.

ॐ

One who is able to withdraw his senses from sense objects, as the tortoise draws its limbs within the shell, is firmly fixed in perfect consciousness

Beware of the game that you can't win and can't quit

We may get the question: "Why do we need to give up material desires like lust and greed?"

Because of their two deadly characteristics: insatiability and irresistibility. To understand these characteristics, let's compare engaging with material desires to playing a game.

Insatiability: When we say yes to material desires, they don't become pacified, but instead become aggravated. They force us to repeatedly, even perpetually, keep saying yes to them. Analogically, trying to fulfill material desires is like trying to win the game. But, as these desires are insatiable, they just don't allow us to win.

Irresistibility: When we get fed up with the futile attempt to fulfill these desires and decide to say no to them, they charge into our consciousness regularly and relentlessly, and seem impossible to resist. Analogically, wanting to give up material desires is like wanting to quit the game. But as these desires are irresistible, they don't allow us to quit.

Thankfully, we have a third alternative: switch to playing a different game altogether.

All of us have an innate undeniable need for happiness. That's what makes us indulge in material desires. When we try to give up material desires, we try to deny our need for happiness. As this need is undeniable, material desires feel irresistible – but only as long as we don't know any happiness other than the material. The Bhagavad-gita (02.59) indicates that material desires become tolerable when we experience a higher, spiritual happiness. In practicing devotional service and relishing spiritual happiness therein, we metaphorically switch to a different game, thereby freeing ourselves from the doomed game.

CB80

The embodied soul may be restricted from sense enjoyment, though the taste for sense objects remains. But, ceasing such engagements by experiencing a higher taste, he is fixed in consciousness

Blunt the desire for enjoyment with engagement

The greatest obstacle on the spiritual path for most of us is the desire to enjoy material pleasures, especially anti-devotional material pleasures.

Because most of us have indulged wantonly in such pleasures during our pre-devotional life, the memories of those indulgences keep piercing us like pointed daggers. Additionally, our contemporary culture bombards us with provocative stimuli, thereby arousing and aggravating those memories. These stimuli not only prevent rust from forming on our dagger-like memories, but also sharpen the dagger so that it hurts more. Consequently, we often succumb not because indulgence is so pleasurable, but because resistance is so unbearable.

When we succumb repeatedly, we feel helplessly trapped: we can neither erase our past memories, nor evade the present stimuli. How, then, can we save ourselves from being pierced by dagger-like desires?

By constant engagement, declares Gita wisdom. The Bhagavad-gita (02.61) recommends that we stay constantly engaged in devotional service (*yukta asita mat-parah*). No desire can grow within us unless we give it time and thought. If we offer all our time and thought to Krishna, then the resulting divine absorption leaves no scope for worldly desires, which thereby become blunted.

Can aspiring devotees like us become so absorbed in Krishna? Yes, declares Gita wisdom, by purposeful planned endeavor. Purposefulness centers on contemplations such as these: "I don't have to take the stabs of these desires lying down; I can and will shield myself with remembrance of Krishna." Planning centers on arranging for both specific substantial services constantly and ready remedial resources whenever distraction makes us vulnerable. By thus endeavoring scrupulously to keep ourselves engaged, we can steadily blunt the dagger-like desires.

With practice, the absorption that is presently conscientious will become spontaneous. Then all material desires will become totally blunt – forever.

ॐॐ

One who restrains his senses, keeping them under full control, and fixes his consciousness upon Me, is known as a man of steady intelligence

Spiritual wisdom restores our freedom to choose our definition of happiness

The Bhagavad-gita (02.64) indicates that harmonizing our life with scriptural regulations is the way to happiness. Some of us may feel that regulating ourselves will take away our freedom to enjoy life. Gita wisdom responds by gently pointing out that we have already been deprived of a far more fundamental freedom: the freedom to choose our definition of enjoyment.

Our culture steals this freedom so stealthily and insidiously that most of us don't even realize that we have been robbed. The pressure of conforming to prevailing cultural norms is so overwhelming that we just accept that the materialistic, often hedonistic, pleasures popular today comprise the actual definition of enjoyment.

But is this definition of enjoyment correct? If it were, then why do we encounter contrary facts like the following?

1.   The champions of such enjoyment are themselves plagued with sufferings that range from depression to suicidal urges.

2.   Our own experiences of these enjoyments have always been an anti-climax: we have not got even a small fraction of the hyped pleasure.

Such calm contemplation will help us see the truth that the definition of happiness imposed on us is false.

By following the Gita's regulations, we reclaim our freedom to choose our own definition of enjoyment. More importantly, we also gain the willpower to choose the definition that is in harmony with the reality of who we are: spiritual beings meant to rejoice eternally by loving and serving Krishna. This factual definition places us on the highway to the supreme happiness of everlasting divine love.

ॐ

But a person free from all attachment and aversion and able to control his senses through regulative principles of freedom can obtain the complete mercy of the Lord.

To get happiness, get the happiness sequence right

All of us want to be happy. The world makes us believe that fulfilling our material desires will make us happy.

However, this makes us not happy but frustrated. Why? Because material desires are insatiable and innumerable.

1. **Insatiable:** The more we indulge in a desire, the more it blazes forth. Consequently, the brief satisfaction that comes from indulging in it becomes dwarfed by the prolonged dissatisfaction that comes from its increased magnitude.

2. **Innumerable:** Our unfulfilled desires far outnumber our fulfilled desires. So the torment arising from our unfulfilled desires far outweighs the joy arising from our fulfilled desires.

To become happy, we need to get the happiness sequence right. The Bhagavad-gita (2.66) gives this sequence through rhetorical negation: if we are not connected with Krishna, our intelligence can't be fixed; if our intelligence is not fixed, our mind can't be steady; if our mind is not steady, we can't be peaceful; if we aren't peaceful, how can we be happy?

Let's reverse this sequence to see how it leads to happiness:

1. We connect ourselves with Krishna through devotional service. This Krishna-connection fixes our intelligence in firm understanding of the natures of material happiness and spiritual happiness.

2. With this fixed intelligence, we steady our mind and don't let unwarranted material desires control it.

3. A steady mind helps us redirect our quest for happiness from the world to Krishna.

4. This redirected quest deepens our Krishna-connection thereby enabling us to relish lasting happiness.

So, next time when we feel dissatisfied due to worldly desires, let's get the happiness sequence right: start with enhancing our Krishna-connection, gradually experience spiritual happiness and finally get rid of both the dissatisfaction and the dissatisfaction-inducing desires.

ಠಠಠ

One who is not connected with the Supreme [in Krishna consciousness] can have neither transcendental intelligence nor a steady mind, without which there is no possibility of peace. And how can there be any happiness without peace?

Materialism shrinks our options for happiness

Cutting-edge technology prides itself for opening new avenues for enjoyment: so many TV channels, websites and video games, for example.

However, might the freedom offered by the opening of these multiple avenues be more delusional than substantial? This is the surprising and daring proposition of Gita wisdom. Let's try to understand its rationale.

We are spiritual beings encased in material bodies. Therefore, as the Bhagavad-gita (02.69) indicates metaphorically, we have two essential options for happiness: material and spiritual. The materialist option has many avenues that allure us with fantasies of endless enjoyment. However, as we explore these avenues for material happiness, we soon recognize a common pattern in all those avenues: the promise of material enjoyment rarely completes the journey from imagination to actualization. The enjoyment that we experience always turns out to be far lesser and poorer than our anticipation. The more we exhaust the avenues for material enjoyment, the more we understand by intelligence or experience or a combination of both that the materialist track to happiness is a dead-end.

This understanding pushes us to explore other options for happiness. If we are fortunate, we stumble on devotional service and relish authentic spiritual happiness thereof, which fulfills our heart far more than the best material enjoyment.

Unfortunately however, when the avenues promising material enjoyment are inexhaustible, as happens due to current technology, then we stay enamored by the vain hope that we will find material happiness in some avenue that we haven't yet explored: "I have just not browsed the right channel at the right time."

Thus our mind stays crowded with delusional hopes of material enjoyment, and we rarely, if ever, explore spiritual happiness.

Does this loss of the option for spiritual happiness deserve to be celebrated as an expansion of our freedom?

ॐ

What is night for all beings is the time of awakening for the self-controlled; and the time of awakening for all beings is night for the introspective sage

Sensual pleasures are easily visible, rarely relishable

Sensual pleasures tantalize us by their appearance and frustrate us by their experience. They last at the most for a few minutes; so the actual experience is never as relishable as the hyped appearance. After the enjoyment, the craving remains or even worsens. So we are left feeling dissatisfied.

Even after we experience such dissatisfaction, the worldly objects remains visually appealing, sometimes irresistibly seductive. We become deluded into believing that, even though the object we just experienced has disappointed us, the object now tempting us will surely deliver its promise. Thus we keep chasing a pleasure that remains ever visible, never relishable. The Bhagavad-gita highlights this misfortune by declaring (03.16) that those who live for such pleasures live in vain. Gita wisdom insightfully compares the enjoyment in a worldly object with the water in a mirage.

We don't have to stay trapped in such a vain pursuit. To break free, we can empower our intelligence through scriptural study. The philosophical wisdom thereof will enable us to see through the façade of sensual pleasures to their intrinsic, inescapable futility. The more we become convinced about this doomed nature of sensual pleasures, the more we can resolutely turn inward towards Krishna.

When we steadily and seriously cultivate his prayerful remembrance, we will discover the supreme happiness of Krishna consciousness – a happiness that is eminently achievable and eternally relishable.

ଔଯଔ

My dear Arjuna, one who in human life does not follow the prescribed cycle of sacrifice thus established by the Vedas certainly leads a life full of sin. Living only for the satisfaction of the senses, such a person lives in vain

Sex is extraordinarily ordinary

Nothing fascinates the human imagination as much as sex. Pictures, articles, TV programs, movies, novels, websites and almost all conceivable means of communication are frequently used to titillate people's sexual imagination. The sheer amount of time, energy and material dedicated to exploring sex makes it seem something extraordinarily special, rare and unique.

Factually however, sex is extraordinarily ordinary; it happens millions of times at every moment for every moment since the moment creation began. Moreover, it is available not just to humans but also to almost all species – many of whom can do it far more easily and freely than humans. Additionally, all of us have experienced it millions of times in the past, in all the countless lifetimes we have been in material existence.

Thus, in terms of all three – frequency, availability and familiarity – sex is totally pedestrian, completely commonplace, absolutely routine. Then, why does such a run-of-the-mill activity make us run off after it – mentally and even physically?

Gita wisdom indicates that it's due to the deluding power of lust.

The Bhagavad-gita (03.39) states that lust is the *nitya-vairi*, the eternal enemy of the soul. When lust controls our mind, it maliciously distorts our vision. Consequently, we see the activity that is extraordinarily ordinary to be extraordinarily special, even irresistible.

To protect ourselves from this pathetic perversion of our vision, we need to keep lust out of our mind by fixing our consciousness on Krishna. To the extent we keep cultivating Krishna consciousness, to that extent the ordinariness of sex will become obvious to us. Over time as we become seasoned in the art of remembering Krishna, we will no longer be fascinated and tormented by sex; instead, we will become increasingly fascinated and enlivened by the truly extraordinary glory of Krishna.

ॐ

Thus the wise living entity's pure consciousness becomes covered by his eternal enemy in the form of lust, which is never satisfied and which burns like fire.

When the heat hits, move away from the heat source, not towards it

When the environmental heat hits us, we naturally move away from the heat source.

Strangely however, we react in the opposite way to another kind of heat: sensual heat. This is the heat of intense craving that burns within us when we contemplate alluring sense objects. The Bhagavad-gita (03.39) insightfully refers to this acute craving as fire (*analena*).

When this sensual heat hits us, we instinctively move towards instead of away from the heat source. Why? Because we believe that the pleasure from the sense object will extinguish the inner fire. The falsity of this belief becomes evident in the end-result of indulgence: we get very little pleasure and instead get lot of misery in the form of escalated heat, that is, increased torturous craving. That's why the same Gita verse describes the fire of craving as insatiable (*dushpurena*). This describer underscores that indulgence is not a fire-extinguisher but a fire-fueller; it simply causes the fire to blaze bigger and longer.

We may protest, "It's undeniable that indulgence brings pleasure." Gita wisdom agrees, but helps us to see that this pleasure is not much more than a short-lived relief from an intense, intolerable craving. This relief is similar to the temporary decrease in the fire for the period when the fuel added to it has not yet ignited. Once the fuel starts burning, the fire blazes higher and stronger. Similarly, soon after the "pleasure" (read: relief) of indulgence ends, the inner fire becomes more intense and more intolerable.

That's why Gita wisdom recommends that when the sensual heat hits us, we move away from its source – if not physically, then at least psychologically. The Gita also shows us the way to get actual relief from the heat: by cultivating remembrance of Krishna, who is the supreme source of happiness. His remembrance acts as the ultimate coolant.

ॐ

Thus the wise living entity's pure consciousness becomes covered by his eternal enemy in the form of lust, which is never satisfied and which burns like fire.

Don't let your assumptions about happiness deprive you of happiness

"*I* want to go closer to Krishna, but it requires following so many rules that will restrict my happiness. How can I give up happiness?" This fear often checks many of us who are seekers on the devotional path.

Gita wisdom counters our fear by informing us that what we have to give up is not happiness, but our assumption about what constitutes happiness. We often assume that happiness means material happiness. However, Gita wisdom points out that this assumption is unquestioned and questionable. Let's see how:

Unquestioned: People around us in real life and especially in the media frequently glamorize and pursue material enjoyment. This propaganda is so overwhelmingly convincing that we rarely, if ever, question it.

Questionable: But the materialist propaganda is questionable because it depicts the reality selectively and deceptively. It never depicts that our bodily capacity to enjoy is limited inescapably. Material enjoyment being fleeting can never satisfy our longing for unending happiness, just as a drop of water can't satisfy a thirst-parched person in a desert.

Gita wisdom empowers us to question our assumptions about happiness in two ways:

1. By informing us that we as souls have a original and natural right to spiritual happiness, a happiness that is far superior to material enjoyment

2. By facilitating us to experience spiritual happiness through the practice of devotional service.

The Bhagavad-gita (05.21) assures us that if we turn our heart away from external material enjoyment to internal spiritual fulfillment, we will get unlimited happiness. Once we develop a taste for spiritual happiness, we will no longer fear that devotional life requires us to give up happiness. Instead, our only regret will be: why did I let my assumptions about happiness deprive me of real happiness for so long?

ॐ

Such a liberated person is not attracted to material sense pleasure but is always in trance, enjoying the pleasure within. In this way the self-realized person enjoys unlimited happiness, for he concentrates on the Supreme.

Seek the happiness that others don't have to pay for

When we enjoy materially, we often fail to notice that others have to pay for our enjoyment.

Here are a few examples:

1. When one team wins a sports championship, other teams are automatically deprived of that championship.

2. When we get or take a large helping of a delicacy, others have to settle for less of it.

3. When one person gets a particular attractive spouse, others don't.

Those deprived not only miss the pleasure, but also incur the psychological cost of frustration. Additionally, several material pleasures cause the innocent to pay costs other than psychological. Let's look at a few such examples:

1. When people smoke in public places, others have to inhale the toxic smoke and consequently pay in terms of spoiled health.

2. When car-drivers ride through crowded streets, those working, selling or living by the roadsides have to breathe the cars' toxic excrement and consequently pay medical and physiological costs.

3. When First World countries live luxuriously using technologies that cause climate change, Third World countries have to pay for the consequences.

Such an analysis raises the question: "Isn't there any way that we can be happy without causing others' misery?"

Gita wisdom answers that there is indeed: through spiritual devotion. When we learn to lovingly connect with Krishna through remembrance and service, we start experiencing an inner happiness that, far from costing others misery, radiates outwards to make them happy.

No wonder the Bhagavad-gita (05.21) urges us to turn away from outer material pleasures and delight in inner spiritual joys.

ॐ

Such a liberated person is not attracted to material sense pleasure but is always in trance, enjoying the pleasure within. In this way the self-realized person enjoys unlimited happiness, for he concentrates on the Supreme.

Happiness can't be got through a perpetual tickling machine

When children are tickled, they start laughing. Does their laughter indicate that they are happy? Not really. If happiness could be had just by tickling, then all of us could get a perpetual tickling machine for ourselves and become happy for the rest of our lives.

We dismiss the idea of a perpetual tickling machine as absurd because we know that the laughter produced by tickling is merely an automatic bodily reaction to a physical stimulus; it is superficial and peripheral to real happiness.

Gita wisdom urges us to recognize that all bodily pleasures are similarly superficial. When the fragrance of a delicacy enters our nose, the tongue starts salivating. Isn't this just a bodily response to a physical stimulus? And doesn't the same apply to the overhyped pleasure of sex? When the sight of a sexually appealing form enters our eyes, our body starts secreting certain chemicals that trigger a titillating sensation. Does such a sensation deserve to be the stuff of our fantasies? Is an adult's getting turned on due to a sexual stimulation essentially different from a child's laughter due to tickling?

Such serious unsentimental contemplation can make us indifferent to all superficial bodily sensations, as the Bhagavad-gita (05.21) indicates. This outer indifference enables us to focus on cultivating authentic inner happiness. Real happiness comes from the love that touches and transforms our innermost essence: love for Krishna. When we cultivate devotional remembrance of Krishna and render affectionate service to him, we feast on a happiness that goes far beyond bodily sensations. The more we experience this happiness, the more we can truly love everyone – not for the bodily sensations that they provide us, but for who they actually are: beloved parts of Krishna eternally related to us in his spiritual family.

⟨⟩

Such a liberated person is not attracted to material sense pleasure but is always in trance, enjoying the pleasure within. In this way the self-realized person enjoys unlimited happiness, for he concentrates on the Supreme.

Keep your intelligence FIT

The Bhagavad-gita (05.22) states that those who are intelligent don't delight in sense pleasures because they understand how such pleasures always end in misery.

This verse indicates that we need a functional or healthy intelligence to understand how sense pleasures end in misery. Just as regular physical exercise is essential to keep our body healthy, regular intellectual exercise is essential to keep our intelligence healthy.

What is the exercise for keeping our intelligence healthy?

It is unsentimental contemplation on the fate of sense pleasure.

A valuable contemplation tool for making our intelligence fit is the acronym FIT (Futility, Insubstantiality, Temporality) that encompasses the three possible fates of pursuing sense pleasure

Futility: Lust masquerading as love may induce within us the desire for a particular spouse. That person rejects us outright, thereby bursting the bubble of our fantasies in one go, with one unbearable prick.

Insubstantiality: That person accepts our proposal and formalizes the relationship, but then we discover that some essential and irreformable incompatibilities exist between us. We are left to watch in helpless dismay as the bubble of our dreams deflates and disappears.

Temporality: That person satisfies our heart to some extent, thereby inflating the bubble of our expectations, but then an untimely demise bursts heart-wrenchingly the giant bubble of our hopes.

As these three possibilities are exhaustive and as all of them end in frustration, we can safely infer that sense pleasure is an unavoidably doomed prospect. When we become firmly convinced of this inference, then we can seek unhesitatingly and savor undistractedly the supreme happiness that Gita wisdom offers: the happiness of loving Krishna.

ॐ

An intelligent person does not take part in the sources of misery, which are due to contact with the material senses. O son of Kunti, such pleasures have a beginning and an end, and so the wise man does not delight in them.

Materialism centers on gaining; spirituality centers on regaining

All of us have the drive to achieve, which we can direct either materially or spiritually. To aid us in choosing correctly, the Bhagavad-gita contrasts material enjoyment and spiritual fulfillment in its fifth chapter, exhorting exhorts us (05.24) to direct our drive to achieve in the spiritual direction. Let's understand why.

Materialism centers on gaining something that is external to us, something that has no intrinsic connection with our essence as souls. We do need basic material resources for survival. However, when we seek material achievements, we often pursue things that are not necessities but are desirables. Material things seem desirable not because they are innately related with us, but because they are culturally glamorized, making us crave for them. The hollowness of this glamorization is exposed when we achieve the glamorized objects and find that they don't offer any lasting satisfaction. They offer just a bit of fleeting titillation that is not worth the prolonged labor needed to attain them. Moreover, all material things are external to us. So, they will be taken away, sooner or later, by external upheavals.

In contrast, spirituality offers us a lasting reward because it centers not on gaining something external but on regaining something internal. Lying dormant within us is the latent potential to love Krishna and love all living beings as his children. As this love is intrinsic to us, it can never be taken away from us – unless, of course, we choose to neglect and forget it, as we have at present. Fortunately, all of us have the power to recollect our relationship with Krishna and regain the treasure of love for him.

Once we attain this ultimate spiritual achievement, it will never be lost again; the supreme fulfillment will be ours for the rest of eternity.

☙❧

One whose happiness is within, who is active and rejoices within, and whose aim is inward is actually the perfect mystic. He is liberated in the Supreme, and ultimately he attains the Supreme.

Seek the wealth that is unalienable

We often presume that to become happy, we need lots of wealth. However, the pursuit of wealth as a source of happiness inevitably frustrates us due to one of the three Us:

1. **Unattainable**: We may crave and strive to acquire lots of wealth, but due to external difficulties or internal deficiencies, we may not attain it despite lifelong endeavor.

2. **Unsustainable**: Even if we do attain it, we cannot sustain it for long. It will definitely be ripped away from us at the time of death – and possibly even before that by forces beyond our control.

3. **Unreliable**: Even while wealth stays by our side, it cannot be relied upon to protect us from sources of misery like relationship ruptures, incurable diseases, and death of loved ones. Even when these calamities don't befall us, wealth and the things it can buy rarely retain their charm for long. Their charm, which is almost irresistible as long as we don't have them, soon fades off after we get them and leaves us pining for more.

Wealth is thus unworthy of the fanatical reverence that we shower on it. The only source of happiness that is truly worthy of our efforts is one that is unalienable; once we get it, it should stay with us forever. That unalienable source is love for God, Krishna. Once we develop that divine love, nothing can stop us from connecting constantly with the one who is the treasurehouse of unlimited happiness.

No wonder the Gita (06.22) declares that those who have achieved love for Krishna no longer crave for anything else.

ॐ

Upon gaining this he thinks there is no greater gain. Being situated in such a position, one is never shaken, even in the midst of greatest difficulty.

The new life outside begins with the new life inside

We often feel dissatisfied with the same old things that keep repeating themselves in our life's routines. So, we try to acquire new things: delicacies, cars, jobs, houses or even spouses. Such new things excite us initially, but the sheen of their newness wears away soon, and the familiar old dissatisfaction returns to gnaw at our heart.

Why is our longing for a new life never satisfied?

Because, Gita wisdom answers, all material objects, no matter how new-looking, are always made of the same old substance: matter. And the emotions that we as living beings, souls, can experience by contacting dead matter are pathetically few. When we contact a new material object, we may initially experience some new pleasure as long as we are contacting the externals of the object, for that external is new. However, as soon as our contact with that object goes beyond its external appearance to its essential substance, we are forced to admit, "There's nothing new here."

If we truly wish to have a new life, Gita wisdom encourages us to redirect our search for newness from outside to inside, from matter to Krishna. He is the ever-fresh ocean of supreme beauty residing eternally within our own hearts. The Bhagavad-gita (6.28) proclaims the supreme happiness that results from this contact *sukhena brahma samsparsham atyantam sukham ashnute.* If we strive to increase our inner connection with Krishna, then we can constantly relish newer and newer aspects of his beauty and personality. Our deepening inner awareness makes us better attuned to detecting opportunities for remembering and serving him in the world around us. Tapping these opportunities brings constant freshness to our external life.

Thus does the new life within lead us to the new life without.

※

Thus the self-controlled yogi, constantly engaged in yoga practice, becomes free from all material contamination and achieves the highest stage of perfect happiness in transcendental loving service to the Lord.

Don't let needles determine your needs

All of us have so many desires to fulfill: desires for better dresses, gadgets, cars, homes, jobs. Even when we authentically need these things, the desires to get them in their trendiest forms usually stem not from those needs, but from outer needles.

The word 'needle' normally conjures the image of a pointed sewing tool. That image can also connote the pricking by which our materialistic culture prods and goads us, that is, needles us. Just as a needle can prick our skin sharply, the culture can prick our minds sharply.

Each time we see an ad promoting a product – and especially each time we see an acquaintance parading that same product – the acute jab of desire needles our mind. Just as the jab of a goad makes a load-bearing donkey run faster along a road, the jab of such desires makes us run faster along the road of materialism. No wonder the Bhagavad-gita (07.15) refers to those who live thus as donkeys (*mudhas*).

The more these desire-needles prick us, the more we feel the need to free ourselves from their pricks. Over time, we end mistaking the need for relief from the pricks to be our essential need. However, we are souls, spiritual beings, whose essential need is love: pure, undying love for the ultimate lover, Krishna. Only when we fulfill this innermost need for love can we relish lasting happiness. Unfortunately, we are so busy seeking relief from external needles that we have no time for fulfilling our authentic needs.

Gita wisdom shows us the way out of the misery: philosophically understand who we actually are, give our spiritual needs their due priority, cultivate prayerful remembrance of Krishna, and experience devotional fulfillment thereof. That fulfillment insulates us fully from the jab of outer needles.

⋆

Those miscreants who are grossly foolish, who are lowest among mankind, whose knowledge is stolen by illusion, and who partake of the atheistic nature of demons do not surrender unto Me.

Happiness is always a byproduct, never a product

*A*ll of us want to be happy. And the world is filled with activities that promise happiness – movies, music, video games, food, sex… Yet experience shows us that these activities offer a bit of initial titillation, but no real happiness. On occasions like long vacations when we make these happiness-promising activities our primary business, we soon find ourselves empty and bored. No matter how extravagant the ways in which we seek happiness, what we get is a temporary relief from emptiness and boredom, not any positive fulfillment.

Why is that?

The world's great wisdom-traditions tell us that happiness has a paradoxical nature. It forever eludes those who seek it as their explicit, exclusive goal. It comes as a byproduct to those who dedicate themselves to a cause greater than the attainment of happiness.

Gita wisdom echoes and expands this insight. It informs us that the greatest cause to which we can dedicate ourselves is love, love for Krishna. Why? Because Krishna is the all-attractive Supreme Person who has fully all the qualities whose fractional presence makes people lovable in our eyes. And most importantly, he already loves us and is waiting for us to revive our loving relationship with him. In loving him, our heart's longing to love and be loved is completely and eternally fulfilled. The Bhagavad-gita (10.09) indicates that those who engage in such pure devotional service relish as a natural byproduct immense sublime happiness (*tushyanti ca ramanti ca*).

However, this happiness will elude us if we let the goal of our devotional service shift from the pleasure of Krishna to our own happiness. The more we seek Krishna's pleasure, the more we will find our happiness-stock automatically filling and flooding.

☙❧

The thoughts of My pure devotees dwell in Me, their lives are fully devoted to My service, and they derive great satisfaction and bliss from always enlightening one another and conversing about Me.

The liberated life is far more than an eternity of daytime television

*A*s TV is popular nowadays, many people equate enjoyment with watching TV. Guzzling down hi-tech images of one's favorite TV program all daylong is their version of paradise.

When such people come across Gita wisdom and hear that the spiritual world is a place of eternal happiness, they expect life there to be something like an eternity of daytime television. Then they hear the specifics of the activities in the spiritual world: how Vrindavan is a pastoral paradise, how God as Krishna is a cowherd boy, and how everyone there is engaged lovingly in serving him. Due to their preconceptions about enjoyment, they question: "How can anyone be happy doing such simple things? Surely we need something more hi-tech."

This question originates in a misunderstanding about the nature of happiness. What brings satisfaction to the heart is not the technological sophistication of an activity, but the loving reciprocation underlying that activity. As there is no such loving reciprocation underlying TV watching, it provides no satisfaction – just a little fleeting titillation. To keep feeling titillated, people are driven constantly towards more hi-tech imagery.

The activities in the spiritual world may be simple, but as they comprise reciprocations of love with Krishna, they fully satisfy the heart. The Bhagavad-gita shows how love can make a simple activity like hearing supremely fulfilling when Arjuna expresses (10.18) his loving desire to hear Krishna's glories ceaselessly. Because all the residents of the spiritual world are filled with a similar love for Krishna, they are fully satisfied serving him by doing whatever pleases him.

Of course, Krishna can and does occasionally perform miracles that supersede TV's best special effects. But through the overall simple setting of his supreme abode, he graphically illustrates the simple truth: when we have love and service for him, we don't need anything else for happiness.

❦

O Janardana, again please describe in detail the mystic power of Your opulences. I am never satiated in hearing about You, for the more I hear the more I want to taste the nectar of Your words.

Our heart deserves more than a consolation prize

*O*ur heart is flooded with many desires for happiness. However, most of these desires are unfulfillable due to the limitations of time, financial resources, bodily capacity and other practical constraints.

Still, desires are our primary driving agents without which our lives would become insipid, even inert. So, we don't like to accept the reality that our desires are unfulfillable. We prefer to settle instead for fulfilling our desires partially. Among our many desires, we try to fulfill as many desires as possible; and within each desire, we try to fulfill it as much as possible. But such partial fulfillment never satisfies us; it is like a consolation prize for the heart, a prize that barely fills a small corner of the inner void.

Gita wisdom explains that we are souls, who are eternal parts of the all-attractive Supreme, Krishna. Being his parts, we are meant for something much better than a consolation prize; we are meant for the championship prize. The Bhagavad-gita (10.41) describes that any worldly object that evokes our desires gets its attractiveness from a spark of Krishna's supreme all-attractiveness. As the attractiveness of any such object is just a fragmental portion of Krishna's attractiveness, the fulfillment provided by even the best of such worldly objects is a fragmental portion of what he can provide us. Thus, all worldly objects are like consolation prizes for our heart, whereas he is like the championship prize.

All of us have the power to redirect our desires from worldly objects to Krishna. The process that best facilitates this redirection is devotional service. When we render devotional service to him, he mercifully makes himself fully and joyfully manifest to us in our hearts, thereby filling it with satisfaction. Thus does our heart attain the championship prize.

Why lose the championship prize for the sake of consolation prizes?

༺༻

Know that all opulent, beautiful and glorious creations spring from but a spark of My splendor.

Worldly beauty agitates, dissatisfies, pollutes; Krishna's beauty pacifies, satisfies, cleanses

Beauty ranks among the world's most fascinating – and frustrating – features. History is filled with stories of people who were captivated by beauty and ended up acting against their own best interests.

Can we not relish the fascination without the frustration?

Yes, we can, declares Gita wisdom, if we redirect our thirst for beauty from worldly objects to Krishna. The Bhagavad-gita (10.41) indicates that everything attractive – including worldly beauty – is a spark of Krishna's supreme all-attractiveness.

Attraction to the spark and attraction to the whole beget radically different results:

Worldly beauty agitates, Krishna's beauty pacifies: Worldly beauty is limited and temporary; only some people in the world are beautiful, and even they are beautiful for just some part of their life. That's why those attracted to worldly beauty sentence themselves to competition, agitation and tribulation. Krishna's beauty, however, is eternal and eternally available for each one of us. When we become attracted to his beauty, we become secure and peaceful, knowing that we have found an inalienable source of nectar.

Worldly beauty dissatisfies, Krishna's beauty satisfies: Even when worldly beauty is in its full bloom, it expresses at best only a spark of Krishna's beauty. Just as a spark doesn't illuminate adequately, worldly beauty leaves us dissatisfied. Just as the sun provides abundant illumination, Krishna's beauty provides us supreme satisfaction.

Worldly beauty pollutes, Krishna's beauty cleanses: When we are attracted to worldly beauty, our unsatisfied thirst goads us into immoral and perverse imaginations and actions – all of which pollute our consciousness. When we become attracted to Krishna's beauty, though we feel satisfied, we also long to relish more of his beauty. This longing gradually drives out all other longings from our heart, thereby cleansing us and elevating us to the spiritual level, where we can feast on his beauty eternally.

ॐ

Know that all opulent, beautiful and glorious creations spring from but a spark of My splendor.

Go beyond infinite longings and long for the infinite

Those new to the devotional path sometimes ask, "What is the practical difference between material desires and spiritual desires? Why do we need to give up material desires and cultivate spiritual desires?"

Because material desires make us perpetually dissatisfied, whereas spiritual desires make us perennially satisfied. Here's why.

We are finite, yet our longings for happiness are almost infinite; we crave for the innumerable worldly things that promise happiness. However, both our lifespan and our capacities are limited. So, our attempt to fulfill these unlimited longings is a lost cause right from the beginning. Still, because we don't know any better cause to live for, we struggle to serve this doomed cause as much as possible. We strain to offer our heart a consolation prize by trying to fulfill as many of its longings as are practical. But the consolation never truly satisfies us because, no matter how many worldly things we achieve, the very finitude of all worldly things makes our heart crave for more, thus entrapping it in perpetual dissatisfaction.

Gita wisdom shows us a way out of this predicament. It reveals to us an endearing and enchanting conception of the Infinite: Krishna. He is infinite and provides infinite fulfillment. And he manifests eternally in many human-like, non-material forms to reciprocate love with us for all of eternity. The Bhagavad-gita (12.14) indicates that devotees who focus their desires on him become satisfied (*santushtah*). When we make him the central longing of our heart, the resulting devotional remembrance of his glory suffuses and satisfies our heart completely and eternally.

Thus, material desires make us dissatisfied due to infinite longings, whereas spiritual desires make us satisfied in longing for the Infinite. That's why intelligent people free themselves from material desires and fill themselves with spiritual desires.

൦൭ൈඊ

One who is... always satisfied, self-controlled, and engaged in devotional service with determination, his mind and intelligence fixed on Me—such a devotee of Mine is very dear to Me.

Humiliation is false ego frustrated, humility is false ego rejected

The Bhagavad-gita (13.08) lists humility as the first of the twenty qualities that comprise wisdom. Significantly, the Gita mentions humility in a negative way to convey its subtlety: *amaanitvam*, absence of the craving for respect.

The craving for respect from others is the force that drives most people. This craving originates from their false ego, which misleads them foundationally into believing that their self-identity is their material body. Additionally, the false ego makes them imagine that their self-worth is the net worth of their talents and treasures, their positions and connections. It impels them to overtly and covertly display their assets before the world in the desperate hope of earning respect. When they don't get the respect that they think is their right, they feel humiliated. Humiliation, then, is nothing but false ego frustrated.

On the other hand, humility is an entirely different ball game, one that those shackled to false ego can scarcely comprehend. That's because the driving force of the lives of the humble is not the craving for respect, but the longing to serve: serve Krishna and serve all living beings as his children. The humble are confident about their self-identity as indestructible souls and are secure in their self-worth as the beloved children of Krishna. That's why they have no need for the pleasures that the false ego dangles before everyone. So, whenever the false ego tempts them, they are able to reject it determinedly and consistently. Having thus rejected the shackles of the false ego, they are free to act in the best interests of one and all. Therefore, they can always act honorably in ways that behoove their human dignity and spiritual sanctity, without being bothered about whether people honor them or not.

⚘

Humility; pridelessness; nonviolence; tolerance; simplicity; approaching a bona fide spiritual master; cleanliness; steadiness; self-control…—all these I declare to be knowledge, and besides this whatever there may be is ignorance.

Cut through delusion with the cutting edge of discrimination

The word "cutting edge" refers literally to the sharp cutting side of the blade of a knife. Figuratively, it has come to refer to the leading position in any field. While entering into an object, the cutting edge leads the rest of the knife. Similarly, while entering into the future, those at the cutting edge of a field lead everyone else in it.

To practice devotional life, we need to cut through appearances and see the spiritual underlying the material. The intellectual sharpness that enables us to cut through the surface of illusion and access the substance of reality is *viveka* or discrimination. By this metaphysical intelligence, we can see philosophical truths that lie hidden for those who have only worldly intelligence. Their intelligence is like a knife without any cutting edge. Their inability to perceive below the surface makes them mistake the surface of reality – matter – to be the whole of reality. Thus, they stay deluded.

Just as the knife follows its cutting edge, our consciousness follows the cutting edge of discrimination. If this cutting edge is blunt, then our spiritual life remains superficial. We need the cutting edge of discrimination especially to:

- Cut through the façade of enjoyment in material life and see the imminent misery
- Look beyond the initial austerity on the spiritual path and see the dormant joy.

Whereas the cutting edge of technology comes by *innovation*, the cutting edge of discrimination comes by *rejuvenation*. To be discriminating, we need to refresh and reinforce what we already know from scriptures. Our daily mantra meditation, regular scriptural study and other periodic devotional practices are all meant to sharpen the cutting edge of discrimination.

The Bhagavad-gita (13.35) indicates that those with such discrimination attain life's supreme success: eternal happiness in the spiritual realm.

CRRO

Those who see with eyes of knowledge the difference between the body and the knower of the body, and can also understand the process of liberation from bondage in material nature, attain to the supreme goal.

Desire the worthy, not the trendy

*O*ur capacity to desire is our most powerful resource, second only to our capacity to access Krishna's grace. Our desires shape our life's direction and destination; our past desires have molded us into what we presently are, and our present desires will mold us into what we will be in future.

Unfortunately, despite the defining role that desires play in our life, we often imprudently squander their power. The Bhagavad-gita (14.12) states that when we are predominated by the mode of passion, we become constantly inundated by desires to try out something new. We frequently let our desires be determined by *trendiness* rather than *worthiness*; we desire that which is praised in the current social mirror rather than that which is prized in the eternal scriptural mirror. Consequently, we end up desiring petty trinkets and paltry titillations that are entirely unworthy of our spiritual sanctity or even our human dignity. This colossal waste of desires cumulates into a tragic waste of an entire lifetime, when death forces us to leave behind all that we have desired and achieved.

Gita wisdom protects us from such a tragedy by revealing that which is truly worthy: our eternal loving relationship with Krishna. When we direct and focus our immense power of desire on loving and serving him, then the resulting devotional credits become our eternal and eternally increasing assets. Eventually, these credits elevate us, by divine grace, to the abode where our pure desires are perennially fulfilled – Krishna's world of eternal love.

When we thus desire the worthy instead of the trendy, our desires become not the cause of repeated disappointment but the way to perennial fulfillment.

CRεꙎ

O chief of the Bharatas, when there is an increase in the mode of passion the symptoms of great attachment, fruitive activity, intense endeavor, and uncontrollable desire and hankering develop.

The tried and the tired needs to be retired

All of us want to do something new. And our craving for newness seems ready to be fulfilled by all the new gadgets, new dresses and other new things glamorized in the materialistic culture.

Actually however, the glamor of new things hyper-activates our imagination and paralyzes our intelligence. As our fantasies carry us of our feet, we rarely ask the critical question: can these new-seeming things offer us anything really new?

Ultimately, all pleasures that the newest-looking material objects can provide boil down to the same old things: the pleasures of eating, sleeping, mating and defending. Thus, these pleasures offer nothing essentially new. That's why, though we may be initially excited by the external hype and the internal imagination, we end up disappointed. Repeatedly. Inevitably.

However, this disappointment doesn't make us tired of the tried because the apparent newness keeps goading our imagination.

Gita wisdom shows the way out of this perpetual re-enactment of the tried and the tired. Firstly, it gives us the philosophical vision to see the oldness, the sameness, the emptiness of all material pleasures. Secondly, and more importantly, it gives us the devotional process to experience a truly new happiness: the happiness of love for Krishna. He is a reservoir of unlimited, unending happiness. Every devotional contact with him bathes us in a new gush of happiness flowing out from that reservoir.

This double empowerment – philosophical grasp of the staleness of material pleasures, and devotional experience of the freshness of remembrance of Krishna – gives us the courage to retire from the tiresome chase after the tried and tired. The Bhagavad-gita (15.05) indicates that this state of realized retirement (vinivritta-kamah) is the takeoff point for launching into the ultimate happiness of endless love.

ॐ

Those who are free from false prestige, illusion and false association, who understand the eternal, who are done with material lust, who are freed from the dualities of happiness and distress, and who, unbewildered, know how to surrender unto the Supreme Person attain to that eternal kingdom.

Ignorance and obstinance push us to pursue pleasure in a prison of protoplasm

Our material body is a prison of protoplasm for us souls. Just as prison life inevitably involves sufferings like grueling work and unpleasant living conditions, the Bhagavad-gita (15.07) indicates that material life inevitably involves various sufferings like the threefold miseries. Just as a prison restricts the prisoners' freedom to move within its walls, the body restricts our freedom to enjoy within its extremely limited capacity to enjoy.

Despite the affliction and the restriction, we rarely long to get out of the bodily prison. Why? Because of ignorance and obstinance.

- **Ignorance**: We don't know that our real identity lies beyond the mass of flesh that we think is "me." We don't know of any pleasure better than that got by inducing sensations in protoplasm that does nothing more than process chemicals. We don't know that this superior pleasure is easily available through devotional service to Krishna.

- **Obstinance**: Even though we experience the shallowness and emptiness of bodily pleasures, we keep pursuing them obstinately without exploring any alternatives. Worse still, even when we experience the alternative devotional happiness to be much higher and richer, still we stubbornly crave for the lower bodily pleasures. Worst of all, even when the error of our ways is pointed out to us, we mulishly rationalize it: "This is just the way I am." Whom can we blame when over time the bodily prison imposes its inevitable sufferings on us with a smug retort: "This is just the way I am"?

Krishna provides Gita wisdom to help end our ignorance. But the responsibility to end our obstinance by using our free will intelligently is ours – and ours alone.

ॐ

The living entities in this conditioned world are My eternal fragmental parts. Due to conditioned life, they are struggling very hard with the six senses, which include the mind.

Material enjoyment falsifies materialism

*M*ost people are infatuated with material pleasures. Due to such infatuation, they consider matter to be the primary, if not the only, reality. Thus, they have a strong, even fanatical, faith in material pleasures and materialism, and so reject as false everything non-material like soul and God. The Bhagavad-gita (15.11) confirms that those who are obsessed with material pleasures just can't perceive anything non-material because their vision is locked in matter.

Ironically, the very material pleasures that they passionately enjoy falsify the materialism that they fervently believe. Let's see how.

The experience of pleasure requires the existence of a non-material experiencer; matter being dead and unconscious cannot experience anything at all, leave alone pleasure. Just as stones and corpses being non-living can't enjoy, nor can the material bodies of the materialists – both are made of the same insentient substance, matter. If they are able to enjoy now, that has to be due to something more than the matter that will be present in their corpses after death. That something more has to be non-material. Ergo materialism is false.

To evade this conclusion, some materialists claim that the pleasure is simply due to the firing of the brain cells. However, such firing is essentially nothing more than the flow of electric current. As the flow of current doesn't create feelings in a TV set, the claim that it creates feelings in the brain is just an article of unproven and unreasonable faith.

Of course, analyzing the fallacy of materialism theoretically is much easier than abstaining from its charms practically. Nonetheless, the same Gita verse (15.11) offers invaluable guidance. If we strive to live at the level of the soul by following the appropriate scriptural guidelines, we gradually experience the reality of spiritual peace and devotional bliss. Then material pleasures can seduce us no more.

ॐ

The endeavoring transcendentalists, who are situated in self-realization, can see all this clearly. But those whose minds are not developed and who are not situated in self-realization cannot see what is taking place, though they may try to.

Earning to become richer is like eating to become fatter

".*Is* the purpose of eating to get fatter?" Obviously not, we would unhesitatingly answer. We eat to get energy for pursuing worthwhile ends in life.

Gita wisdom urges us to apply this same reasoning to another fundamental human activity: earning money. Is the purpose of earning to get richer? Doesn't answering no to this question seem a bit harder? That's because our money-driven culture has made wealth a status symbol, an end in itself.

To grasp this point, let's analyze: are people who flaunt their financial bounty much different from people who flaunt their physical obesity? Granted that our culture may make money-flaunters feel euphoric and fat-flaunters feel embarrassed. But, from the perspective of our real identity as souls, neither can provide us any real happiness. No wonder then that the Bhagavad-gita (16.15) declares those who seek money as an end, as a mere status symbol, to be deluded by ignorance (*ajnana-vimohitah*).

Money can be valuable as a means to worthwhile ends, but not all people know or seek ends that are worthwhile. Many wealthy people abuse money for ends that harm others and even themselves, as in financial scams that fleece the innocent and land the perpetrators in jail.

Nonetheless, the Gita doesn't call upon us to reject money. Instead, it shows us the best use of money by revealing to us the best use of life itself. Life is not meant to seek some tottering and flickering worldly status, but to reclaim our original and eternal status as beloved parts of Krishna. If we make reviving our relationship with him the primary purpose of our life, and harmonize our pursuit of wealth with that purpose, then the wealth we earn and use for his service will enrich us emotionally and spiritually even in this life, what to speak of the next.

ᎧᏠᏂᎧ

The demoniac person thinks: "There is none so powerful and happy as I am. I shall perform sacrifices, I shall give some charity, and thus I shall rejoice." In this way, such persons are deluded by ignorance.

The secret to enlightened enjoyment is enlightenment about enjoyment

".*I* want enlightenment, but I can't give up enjoyment. What should I do?" This is the predicament of many of us as aspiring devotees who find ourselves caught in an inner tug of war between our spiritual aspirations and our material addictions.

Gita wisdom solves our predicament by exposing its false premise: the misconception that enlightenment is itself not enjoyable. The Gita reveals the secret that enlightenment offers us the supreme happiness in contrast with which even the best material enjoyment pales into insignificance.

The journey to enlightened enjoyment begins with the preliminary teaching of the Gita that we are not our material bodies but are spiritual souls. As souls, we have an eternal birthright to relish unlimited happiness by devotionally connecting with Krishna, who is the reservoir of all happiness.

To attain this happiness, we need to redirect our thoughts from the material to the spiritual, from worldly objects to the source of those objects: Krishna. Because our mind is habituated, even addicted, to contemplating worldly objects in the hope of getting some enjoyment, the prospect of giving up that worldly contemplation and subsequent enjoyment seems like poison.

Fortunately, we can tolerate the poison by gently but firmly fixing our mind on Krishna. To make meditation on him easier, he makes himself available to us in various accessible and relishable manifestations like his sweet holy names and his gorgeous Deities. When we consciously and lovingly contemplate such divine manifestations , that contemplation becomes our channel to transcendence. It gradually fills and eventually floods our consciousness with uninterrupted, unending fulfilment that is akin to a constant flow of nectar. The Bhagavad-gita (18.37) states this secret of enlightened enjoyment poetically: that which tastes like poison in the beginning will taste like nectar in the end.

ଓଛୀ

That which in the beginning may be just like poison but at the end is just like nectar and which awakens one to self-realization is said to be happiness in the mode of goodness.

Unregulated indulgence ends in material letdown and spiritual breakdown

"*What's* wrong with a bit of indulgence as long as one is not harming anyone?" This utilitarian-seeming rationale sometimes tempts us to transgress the moral boundaries given in the scriptures.

Gita wisdom gives the surprising response that our immoral indulgence harms at least one person for sure: ourselves. The Bhagavad-gita (18.38) states that passionate indulgences which seem initially like nectar turn out eventually to be like poison. What does this poison refer to? At one level, it refers to the karmic consequences that we will have to undergo in due course of time. But even without considering the eventual karmic consequences, we can understand this poison in terms of its two immediate consequences: material letdown and spiritual breakdown.

- **Material Letdown**: Material pleasures rarely, if ever, live up to the hype that our media and our mind accord them. Despite the dreaming and scheming that precede them for a duration extending from hours to years, the actual indulgence ends within moments, and we are left feeling disappointed at best and cheated at worst.

- **Spiritual Breakdown**: The passions and perversions that accompany immoral indulgences tend to dominate our minds, leaving us with little intelligence or inclination to cultivate loving remembrance of Krishna. This cuts off our access to devotional happiness and sabotages our determination to persevere on the path to transcendence, thereby accelerating our spiritual breakdown.

When we thus understand that the poison of consequence totally outweighs the nectar of indulgence, immoral pleasures stand exposed as brainlessly bad bargains whose rejection is an act of self-protection, not self-deprivation.

ॐ

That happiness which is derived from contact of the senses with their objects and which appears like nectar at first but poison at the end is said to be of the nature of passion.

Our fear of insignificance traps us in insignificance

"*If* I give up all my desires and just fulfill Krishna's desires, won't I be stripping myself of everything that makes me significant as a person?" Apprehensions like these may check us on the devotional path.

Surprisingly, Gita wisdom asserts that this fear of insignificance is what traps us in insignificance. Let's see how.

The Gita begins by explaining that we are souls who are presently misidentifying with our body due to the insidious influence of the false ego. Under the spell of the false ego, we mistake its desires to be our own desires. This misjudgment makes casting those desires aside seem like giving up something very significant.

However, if we unsentimentally contemplate the false ego's desires, we will realize that fulfilling them will yield insignificant results: we might at best get some fleeting pleasure that will keep us bound to material existence, chasing the same pleasures that countless other living entities are chasing. That's why as long as we stay wedded to those desires, we sentence ourselves to obscurity in material existence, thereby sealing our pact with insignificance.

To help us attain real significance, the Bhagavad-gita (18.58) urges us to harmonize our desires with Krishna's desires and to put aside all other desires, recognizing them to be what they are: the false ego's allurements. When we choose to apply this Gita injunction, we can endure the resulting temporary feelings of insignificance by philosophical conviction. Our bold choice and determined endurance will attract divine grace. That grace will empower us to pass over all obstacles and render significant devotional service, thereby facilitating many other souls in coming closer to Krishna. Most importantly, our committed devotional practices will deliver us to Krishna's own abode, where we will delight forever in a life of ultimate significance: the life of everlasting love.

ॐ

If you become conscious of Me, you will pass over all the obstacles of conditioned life by My grace. If, however, you do not work in such consciousness but act through false ego, not hearing Me, you will be lost.

Let your thoughts enrich you, not impoverish you

*F*ew things live as close to us as our thoughts; few things influence us as immediately as our thoughts; few things define us as much as our thoughts.

Yet we rarely examine the quality of our thoughts; we hardly endeavor to improve them; we scarcely recognize that they even need improvement.

Our thoughts usually dwell on enjoyable worldly objects. However, all our encounters with various worldly objects unavoidably meet one of these three fates:

1. Not attainable (e.g. the highest paying job in town) or

2. Attainable but not enjoyable (e.g. the job necessitates working with a tyrannical boss), or

3. Enjoyable but not retainable (e.g. the job ends with retrenchment or retirement).

When our thoughts are monopolized by worldly objects, we end up feeling restless, cheerless, helpless – in one word, impoverished.

That's why Gita wisdom cautions us against letting worldly objects dominate our thoughts. It recommends that we give worldly responsibilities the necessary thought and time. At the same time, it insistently and persistently urges us to stop evading the only responsibility that can make our thoughts enriching: our spiritual responsibility of practicing devotional service. This responsibility enables us to connect with Krishna, who is the reservoir of unending inner enrichment. When our devotion becomes steady and strong, our Krishna-connection gradually becomes attainable, enjoyable and retainable, eternally retainable. Then thinking about Krishna becomes increasingly habitual, natural and relishable; soon, our thoughts start enriching us constantly, as happened to Sanjay at the end of the Gita (18.76).

This inner enrichment not only makes us happy in the present but also offers two broad benefits: the side benefit of an enhanced ability to shoulder worldly responsibilities maturely, and the main benefit of an accelerated journey to the eternal abode of Krishna.

ॐ

O King, as I repeatedly recall this wondrous and holy dialogue between Krishna and Arjuna, I take pleasure, being thrilled at every moment.

Choose thoughts that lead to jubilation, not to frustration

*M*ost of our thoughts run along the default rails of eating, mating, sleeping and defending. These activities may be necessary bodily functions, but our thoughts about them – especially about eating and mating – consume far more of our mental energy than bodily functions require or deserve. We can engage physically in these activities for only a small part of our life, but we let thoughts about them possess us mentally for a large part of our life.

Their unwarranted possession of our mental energy causes us agitation and frustration. We become agitated by the thought: "When will I get it?" And we become frustrated by the thoughts: "Why didn't I get it? I got it, but why was it not good enough? Why did it have to end so soon?"

Instead of these impoverishing returns of agitation and frustration, our mental energy can get us the enriching returns of pacification and jubilation if we invest it in Krishna. Let's see how:

- **Pacification**: When we think about Krishna, we invoke his personal and powerful presence. His presence manifests as the mysterious peace that pervades our heart whenever we think of him steadily.

- **Jubilation**: When we gradually infuse our thoughts about Krishna with devotion, he reciprocates by revealing his glory and beauty, a revelation that surcharges our heart with joy. This jubilant state of heart was achieved by Sanjay (18.76) through hearing, repeating and especially contemplating the message of the Gita.

All of us can attain a similar inner life of jubilation if we guide our thoughts along the rails laid out by the Gita to the destination of Krishna.

೧೪೮౨

O King, as I repeatedly recall this wondrous and holy dialogue between Krishna and Arjuna, I take pleasure, being thrilled at every moment.

LEADING A PRINCIPLE-CENTERED LIFE

What we do reflects on what we do

" What we do" can refer to our specific behavior as well as to our general vocation. What we do in our specific behavior reflects on what we do in our general vocation. For example, if a doctor exploits a patient, that individual behavior reflects adversely on the whole medical profession.

This principle that our behavior reflects on our vocation is a consistent theme of the Gita. But as its message evolves, the Gita deepens our understanding of our actual vocation and also refines our reasons for harmonizing our behavior with that vocation.

At its start, the Gita recognizes that most of us conceive of our vocation materially, as determined by our social position. Further, we behave in ways that enhance, or at least preserve, our public image. Accordingly, it (02.03) urges its original student, the heroic warrior Arjuna, to avoid unbecoming cowardly behavior (*naitat tvayy upapadyate*).

At its summit, the Gita helps us recognize that we are all souls, who are by our spiritual nature devotees of Krishna. It also inspires us to behave in devotionally respectable ways by helping us understand that such behavior simultaneously enhances our own spiritual happiness internally and honors the dignity of all that we represent externally.

When we adopt the path of devotion, we become its representatives in the eyes of the world. Consequently, our behavior becomes the barometer by which people judge that path. Thus, their devotional prospects largely hinge on our behavior. If we accept this grave responsibility and behave properly, our inner life becomes rich because Krishna being pleased by our responsible conduct reveals himself more endearingly to us.

Thus do our externals and internals harmoniously fuel our swift return to Krishna.

ॐ

O son of Pritha, do not yield to this degrading impotence. It does not become you. Give up such petty weakness of heart and arise, O chastiser of the enemy.

Our values are our real valuables

*O*ur happiness depends not on our valuables, but on our values. Why? Because our values shape how we use our valuables, and that use actually determines our happiness.

If our values are materialistic, then we use our valuables to enjoy materially and to accumulate more material possessions. However, all our material gratifications and possessions can't address the deepest need of our heart: love. We long to love and be loved eternally. But our materialistic values impel us to direct our love at the material level. However, such love can be disrupted, even devastated, at any moment by worldly upheavals. The Bhagavad-gita (02.08) indicates that when our need for love is thwarted, no worldly attainment can relieve us of the resulting agony.

That's why Gita wisdom urges us to direct our love at the spiritual level towards Krishna. In other words, it urges us to change our values from material to spiritual. Spiritual values center on the diligent practice of devotional service and yield the supreme valuable: love for Krishna. This is the supreme valuable not just because it can give us the highest happiness, but also because it cannot be stolen by the worst worldly upheavals.

The different results of material and spiritual values are graphically illustrated in the seventh canto of Srimad-Bhagavatam. The demoniac monarch Hiranyakashipu, despite having more material valuables than anyone else in the universe, was perpetually dissatisfied because his materialistic values made him crave endlessly for whatever he didn't have. In contrast, the devotee-saint Prahlad, despite being stripped of all material valuables, was internally satisfied because his spiritual value of selfless devotion empowered him to constantly relish the remembrance of the Lord.

If we realize that our values are our valuables and treasure our spiritual values the way we treasure our material valuables, then we too can become, like Prahlada, supremely enriched with eternal love.

ༀ

I can find no means to drive away this grief which is drying up my senses. I will not be able to dispel it even if I win a prosperous, unrivaled kingdom on earth with sovereignty like the demigods in heaven.

We may be checked, but we won't be checkmated

Practicing spiritual life in the material world is challenging. This challenge exists at all times because materialism is inherent to this world. The challenge has increased during our times because materialism is dominant in this age.

Our materialistic environment may sometimes check our spiritual practices. For example, we may sometimes have to practice meditation secretly or study scriptures discreetly. When such situations are inescapably imposed on us, we may feel disheartened – all the more so when we see no checks on those indulging in blatantly materialistic activities.

At such times, we can take heart from the Gita verse (02.16) which states that the temporary has no endurance, and the eternal has no cessation. So all materialistic activities, even if unchecked presently, will ultimately at the time of death get not just checked, but also checkmated.

In joyful contrast, material circumstances can only check but never checkmate our spiritual life. All material conditions are, after all, temporary. Moreover, when our environment is unfavourable and checks our spiritual life, we can turn those checks to our spiritual advantage. We can utilize the external obstacles as internal tests for evaluating the sincerity and intensity of our devotional aspirations. Let's see how.

When our environment is supportive, we may sometimes engage in devotional practices just to create a positive impression on others. When our environment turns inimical and no one appreciates our devotional practices, that external superficial incentive is taken away. This forces us to engage in our devotional practices primarily, if not exclusively, for their original and pure purpose: the pleasure of Krishna and the resulting experience of love for him. The strengthening of this pure purpose is the surest guarantor of our authentic spiritual advancement.

Thus by purifying and intensifying our devotional intentions, we can convert the checks that slow us externally into spurs that speed us internally.

൰ඌ

Those who are seers of the truth have concluded that of the nonexistent [the material body] there is no endurance and of the eternal [the soul] there is no change. This they have concluded by studying the nature of both.

Value change, but don't change values

Our present existence is bi-dimensional: we are spiritual beings residing in material bodies. Harmonizing the material and the spiritual dimensions of our existence is a perennial challenge. If we wish to make spiritual advancement, our aspirations have to be primarily in the spiritual realm: developing selfless, spiritual love for Krishna. However, when we wish to express our love through practical service in this world, our actions have to be primarily in the material realm: taking care of our worldly responsibilities.

How do we balance acting principally in the material realm with aspiring principally in the spiritual realm? The Bhagavad-gita (02.16) offers a precious insight: the material never endures, the spiritual never ceases. Once we become rooted in this insight, worldly change may change our actions materially, but not our aspirations spiritually. Thus, we value change, knowing that it affects our actions, but don't overvalue it so much that it changes our values and aspirations. After all, even the most momentous material change can't change the twin realities that:

1. All pleasures and troubles from material changes are passing

2. Only the shelter and satisfaction from spiritual devotion is lasting.

When we internalize these facts by studying and applying Gita wisdom, we become expert in the art of valuing change without changing values.

౹౨

Those who are seers of the truth have concluded that of the nonexistent [the material body] there is no endurance and of the eternal [the soul] there is no change. This they have concluded by studying the nature of both.

Treat devotion as a business more serious than business

We take few things as seriously as business. Money usually makes the lazy busy; the frivolous serious; the nonconformists conformists.

In marked contrast to our zealous pursuit of money is our casual pursuit of devotion. Often when we don't stick to our devotional commitments, we give the reason: "I didn't feel like doing it". Would we use that reason for explaining why we didn't stick to our professional commitments? Rarely, if ever.

If we consider financial matters too important to be left to our mind's feelings, then why do we consider spiritual matters less important? Because of our spiritual shortsightedness; we are unable to see beyond our short-term this-life concerns to our long-term next-life concerns.

Gita wisdom helps cure our myopia by clearly explaining how we are not our bodies but are souls on a multi-life journey. We take money seriously because we often think that it is a matter of life or death. The Gita's multi-life perspective enables us to see why the pursuit of devotion is a business more serious than business: devotion is a matter of eternal life or repeated deaths. If we cultivate devotion seriously, we return to Krishna's eternal abode. If we don't, we continue in the cycle of birth and death for many, many lifetimes – till the time in some future lifetime we take devotion seriously.

Those with such philosophical far-sightedness cultivate devotion determinedly, as is conveyed by the word *vyavasaayatmika-buddhi* (determined intelligence) used in the Bhagavad-gita (02.41). The word *vyvasaaya* also means "business," especially in the vernacular languages that have emerged from Sanskrit. This meaning suggests that we need to invest our spiritual pursuits with a businesslike seriousness. If we thus become serious spiritual businesspersons, we will get life's supreme reward, far greater than that available to the best material businesspersons: eternal devotional enrichment.

ॐ

Those who are on this path are resolute in purpose, and their aim is one. O beloved child of the Kurus, the intelligence of those who are irresolute is many-branched.

Illusion makes the good seem better than the best

*W*hen we strive to practice devotional service, the power of illusion is ever-waiting to thwart our efforts. If we are casual about our practice, illusion straightforwardly drags us down to anti-devotional temptations. But if we are somewhat serious, then illusion attacks subtly by messing up our priorities, by making us mistake our worldly obligations to be more important than core-devotional activities. When we fall for this ruse, then our devotional determination gets starved. What began as a semi-devotional distraction over time ends as an anti-devotional destruction.

It's best to nip such misfortunes in the bud. Whenever the good starts seeming better than the best, we need to see this confusion as a reminder that our intelligence needs a reality check. We can conduct this reality check by comparing our thoughts with scriptural teachings. Pertinently the Bhagavad-gita (02.41) indicates that those on the spiritual path are resolute and one-pointed (*vyavasaayatmika-buddhi ekeha*). Being one-pointed doesn't mean that we abandon our familial, social and professional obligations, but that we intelligently integrate them with the devotional purpose of our life: learning to love Krishna.

This integration is not just a matter of sentiment but also a matter of clear prioritization. The first step towards such integration is to make time for regularly engaging in exclusively devotional activities: chanting the holy names, studying the scriptures and hearing about Krishna in the association of single-pointed devotees. These activities express the authenticity of our devotional intent to Krishna, and he reciprocates by granting us inspiring experiences of the reality of spiritual fulfillment. Thereby, we get the determination and the intelligence to harmonize all our activities with our ultimate purpose.

When we thus offer our best endeavors for the best goal, we get life's best result: eternal love.

⟨੪੭⟩

Those who are on this path are resolute in purpose, and their aim is one. O beloved child of the Kurus, the intelligence of those who are irresolute is many-branched.

Don't assume that your attachments are holding you – check if you are holding them

As aspiring devotees, we often find that our attachments abduct and drag our consciousness away from Krishna, as the Bhagavad-gita (02.44) outlines. Consequently, we may assume that our attachments are holding us in such a vicious grip that we can't do anything about it. This assumption may even make us rationalize our moral lapses.

Gita wisdom cautions us against assuming that our attachments are holding us; we might be holding them. How can we understand the difference between the two? Only if the tempting sense objects unexpectedly come our way without our desire to encounter them and trap us can we say that our attachments are holding us.

Usually, we are not so innocent. Although we externally say that we want to be detached, we internally hold on to the desire to enjoy the pleasure associated with that attachment. We secretly hope to somehow still enjoy that pleasure. We even plan to encounter those tempting sense objects. If any or all of these – desires, hopes and plans – precede our becoming trapped, then it is we who are holding on to our attachments.

Significantly, this recognition doesn't have to be guilt-inducing or depressing; it can be empowering and liberating. It can make us aware that we have the power to hold on to certain thoughts internally, irrespective of our external situation. If we just redirect this power devotionally, we will be able to hold on to Krishna internally by cultivating desires to love and serve him. Such devotional redirection of our desires will crowd all attachments out of our heart – both the attachments that we were holding and the attachments that were holding us. Additionally, our heart will become filled with joyous thoughts about Krishna, thereby making our journey towards him sweet and swift.

৩৮০

In the minds of those who are too attached to sense enjoyment and material opulence, and who are bewildered by such things, the resolute determination for devotional service to the Supreme Lord does not take place.

Endless nibbling at the tastes of this world dulls our taste for Krishna

All of us are innately pleasure-seeking. How we seek pleasure is largely shaped by our external culture. As our present culture constantly glamorizes material pleasures, we usually seek happiness materially. Although the actual experience of material enjoyment never lives up to the glamor, we keep seeking it because we don't know of any alternative.

When Gita wisdom enters our life, it introduces us to an alternative happiness: spiritual happiness. By connecting with Krishna through devotional service, we start relishing inner happiness. We also distance ourselves from immoral, anti-devotional pleasures, knowing that they will bring severe karmic consequences.

Although we re-orient our life spiritually, we still keep nibbling at many material pleasures, especially those material pleasures that are not explicitly immoral or anti-devotional: for example, gossip, TV, movies, status symbols and fast foods.

This endless nibbling keeps our consciousness locked at the material level, always seeking the next opportunity for worldly indulgence. The Bhagavad-gita (02.44) indicates that the more we are looking for material pleasures, the less we can find spiritual happiness, or even look for it properly. Consequently, we feel constantly dissatisfied even while practicing devotional service.

If we want substantial inner fulfillment, we need to concentrate our longings at the devotional level by spiritualizing our culture and association as much as possible. Of course, as we live in a materialistic culture, we may not be able to cut ourselves off entirely from all material pleasures. But we can and should cut ourselves off from the hope and the hype about those pleasures. By thus not getting materially overstimulated, we can preserve the devotional orientation of our consciousness, thereby preparing it to relish spiritual happiness.

ॐ

In the minds of those who are too attached to sense enjoyment and material opulence, and who are bewildered by such things, the resolute determination for devotional service to the Supreme Lord does not take place.

Attachment can steal our freedom of thought – and restore it too

The Bhagavad-gita (02.44) indicates that worldly attachments, especially attachments to sex and money, abduct our consciousness and sabotage our prospects for inner stability.

Whenever we indulge in gratifying our senses, a subtle invisible rope is formed between us and the corresponding sense object. This rope pulls us towards that object again and again. Each time we indulge in that pleasure, a new strand is added to that rope. As the rope thickens, its mental tug on us increases. Consequently, our thoughts get dragged to and imprisoned in that object, even when we are doing other things physically and want to focus on them mentally. Over time repeated indulgence makes the rope so thick that its tug becomes perpetual and irresistible. When this happens, the attachment transmogrifies into an addiction, which steals much of our freedom of thought.

Fortunately, our freedom of thought is never entirely or irrecoverably lost; we always have some mental freedom, some ability to choose what we think of, some time when we are not tormented by that attachment. We can use whatever freedom we still have to fix our thoughts on Krishna, who is the source of the highest pleasure. This connection with him will give us an experience of spiritual happiness. Due to that fulfilling experience, an invisible rope is formed between us and him – a rope that pulls us towards him. As we repeatedly practice fixing our mind on him, this rope of spiritual attachment strengthens. Over time, it pulls us so strongly towards him that we break free from the prison of our material attachment. Thus, we become free to delight forever in his devotional service.

ॐ

In the minds of those who are too attached to sense enjoyment and material opulence, and who are bewildered by such things, the resolute determination for devotional service to the Supreme Lord does not take place.

When spiritual life seems tasteless, our spiritual sensibility needs activation

As spiritual seekers, we sometimes go through dry phases when our devotional practices seem to give us no happiness.

More often than not, the cause of this tastelessness is misdirection of our consciousness. A person who has no aesthetic sensibility finds nothing to relish in a work of art, even when it is an artistic masterpiece. Similarly, those of us who have no spiritual sensibility find nothing to relish in the remembrance of Krishna, even though it is the sweetest and most satisfying experience in all of creation. Of course, all of us as spiritual beings do have an innate spiritual sensibility, but it is presently dormant. All our spiritual practices are meant to arouse and activate this dormant sensibility, thereby enabling us to relish the remembrance of Krishna.

However, when we let ourselves get carried away by prospects of material enjoyment, they sedate our spiritual sensibility. The Bhagavad-gita (02.44) states that when sensual indulgence and financial opulence infatuate our consciousness, they render us impotent to experience devotional happiness. Consequently, we become desensitized, even deadened, to spiritual experiences. Being bereft of higher spiritual joys, we inevitably get dragged down to materialistic fantasies and indulgences.

Fortunately, Gita wisdom can provide us discrimination and determination: discrimination to recognize the futility of these material allurements, and determination to dislodge them from our consciousness. Then we can redirect our heart to Krishna, regain our lost spiritual sensibility and relish the supreme joy of remembering him.

༺ঌঌ༻

In the minds of those who are too attached to sense enjoyment and material opulence, and who are bewildered by such things, the resolute determination for devotional service to the Supreme Lord does not take place.

Train yourself to avoid mental potholes

When we travel regularly along a pothole-filled road, we carefully avoid the potholes, thereby saving ourselves of unnecessary jolts.

By analogy, when the Bhagavad-gita (02.58) urges us to avoid unnecessary contact of our senses with the sense objects, it guides us to avoid mental potholes, the stimuli that jolt us mentally. For example, some billboards along our daily commute may incite lust or greed, thereby disrupting our mental balance. By planning and practice, we can train ourselves to avoid these mental potholes, thereby saving ourselves of unnecessary mental jolts.

Avoiding physical potholes comes naturally to us, but avoiding mental potholes requires conscious training. Why? Because we need to overcome three default attitudes that work against us.

1. **Inattention**: Though we usually notice things that cause us physical discomfort, we don't always notice things that cause us mental discomfort. By taking brief introspective breaks periodically, we can observe our mental state, thus identifying the stimuli that act as mental potholes for us.

2. **Illusion**: Physical potholes are obviously unpleasant, but mental potholes seem deceptively pleasant; they titillate us. To see through their deception, we need to remind ourselves that the titillation is only momentary and is followed by a much longer period of agitation.

3. **Impotence**: As we usually can't stop the contemporary culture from blatantly exhibiting provocative images, we may feel powerless. But we aren't; we can always do something, as we intelligently do when dealing with physical potholes. We usually can't remove them either; yet we don't resign ourselves to their jolts – we use our intelligence to avoid them. Similarly, we can use our intelligence and plan how to avoid mental potholes.

By thus training ourselves to protect ourselves from mental jolts, we can make our life-journey smoother.

ॐ

One who is able to withdraw his senses from sense objects, as the tortoise draws its limbs within the shell, is firmly fixed in perfect consciousness.

Let self-mastery be devotion's fruit, not determination's feat

Bending our impulses to our principles and thereby attaining self-mastery is vital for us to make tangible spiritual progress. At the same time, it is equally important that we choose the right means for achieving self-mastery.

There are two broad ways to self-mastery:

1. **As determination's feat**: We see self-mastery as a peak for our willpower to scale. As our focus is entirely on our own will, the only higher pleasure that we can get in our bid for self-mastery is the pleasure of the ego, the self-centered exultation of having conquered our desires. Self-mastery, if achieved in this way, often increases our ego, and makes us look down contemptuously or at least condescendingly at all those who cannot perform feats of determination like us. The self-centeredness, the infatuation of the ego and the condescension towards others – all these make our heart inhospitable for Krishna, thereby depriving us of any substantial devotional progress.

2. **As devotion's fruit**: When we long to offer our heart to Krishna, we see our worldly impulses as obstacles in offering our heart. To express our heart's longing for Krishna and to get rid of our passions, we busy ourselves in his service and absorb ourselves in his remembrance. Due to the resulting focus on Krishna, the Bhagavad-gita (02.59) indicates, we experience a higher happiness that enables us to automatically move beyond worldly passions. To remember and serve Krishna, we obviously need and use our determination, but we don't let determination dethrone devotion as our goal or our focus. So, self-mastery grows naturally and necessarily as an incidental fruit of our devotion to Krishna.

Self-mastery, when achieved as devotion's fruit, catapults us into an eternal life of love and service to Krishna.

ॐ

The embodied soul may be restricted from sense enjoyment, though the taste for sense objects remains. But, ceasing such engagements by experiencing a higher taste, he is fixed in consciousness.

The way to say no to temptation is to say yes to devotion

We may hesitate to adopt authentic scripture-based spirituality because of the fear that we will have to give up too many worldly pleasures. Such fears stem from an unduly negative focus in spiritual life. Let's see how.

In order to stay away from temptations, many of us use our moral conscience that tells us it is the *right* thing to do and our philosophical conviction that tells us it is the *beneficial* thing to do. This moral and philosophical discernment is necessary; without it, self-restraint often becomes an exercise in meaningless and purposeless self-torture. However, discernment is necessary, but not sufficient. With discernment, we recognize self-restraint to be right and beneficial, but don't experience it to be joyful.

That's why the Bhagavad-gita (02.61) urges us to complement discernment with engagement. When we engage ourselves in service to Krishna, then spiritual happiness becomes a concrete reality and a living experience. Service to him is not restricted to activities that are externally, directly connected to him. Even our worldly responsibilities can become a service to Krishna if we keep him in our hearts and strive to do those responsibilities as devotional offerings to him. When we start using our devotional creativity to discover in every situation, every event, every activity and every interaction the hidden opportunity to serve Krishna and then say "Yes" to that opportunity, the resulting devotional connection with him through internal remembrance and external service gives us profound spiritual fulfillment. Once we start tasting and valuing this fulfillment, then temptations become exposed as sources of distraction – not gratification. At that stage, saying "No" to them becomes not just right and beneficial, but also joyful.

Thus, the best way to say "No" to temptations is to say "Yes" to Krishna.

☙❧

One who restrains his senses, keeping them under full control, and fixes his consciousness upon Me, is known as a man of steady intelligence.

Guard against the tiny crack– it can end in mighty crash

A tiny crack in a dam is not a tiny thing. The massive pressure of all the dam water forces the crack to enlarge till one deadly day the whole dam crumbles with a mighty crash and results in a colossal disaster. It all began with a tiny reparable crack that could and should have been fixed.

The same principle applies to our spiritual lives. The spiritual philosophy and devotional culture of bhakti-yoga build in our consciousness a dam to check the water of our lower passions. This dam serves two purposes: it checks our passions from flowing imprudently or immorally, and it redirects those passions toward purifying and fulfilling devotional engagements.

For our steady spiritual journey, this dam is indispensable. But during our spiritual journey, it is not impenetrable. Cracks tend to form in it due to our past conditionings or our present circumstances or a combination of both. These cracks are our revived inclinations towards immoral pleasures that we ourselves had earlier dammed, that is, resolved to reject. Due to these revived inclinations, we contemplate those pleasures, thereby causing more of our passions to flow through the cracks. As the cracks enlarge due to this flow, still more passions start flowing, thereby unleashing a fatal cycle that terminates in a mighty crash. When the entire dam collapses, our passions propel us to immoral, even bestial, actions that can defile our devotional integrity, wreck our sacred relationships and ruin our entire life.

The Bhagavad-gita (02.62-63) outlines this scary spiral from the tiny crack of contemplation to the mighty crash of depravation. It all begins with a tiny reparable crack, a minor temptation that can and should be resisted.

If we can just convince ourselves that a tiny crack is not a tiny thing, we can save ourselves of tons of trouble.

ॐ

While contemplating the objects of the senses, a person develops attachment for them, and from such attachment lust develops, and from lust anger arises.

Be a leader of the mind, not its cheerleader

Daydreaming. It's so easy. Taking it easy in our thought-lives is one of life's most deluding distracters. We tend to think that nothing is wrong in wandering with the mind because neither we nor the people around us see anything untoward happening. When we are thus lulled into a false sense of complacency, we often let our mind indulge in fantasies that violate our moral and spiritual integrity. While the mind desecrates our inner sanctity, we stand by as passive onlookers – and sometimes even as active cheerleaders.

Occasionally, our conscience reproaches us for our perverse fantasies, but our mind silences it with the subterfuge: "All this is just in the imagination. You would never do this in real life. So why bother?"

Gita wisdom helps us understand why we need to bother. The Bhagavad-gita (02.62-63) indicates that the path from the mental to the physical is a slippery slope on which we can skid and fall at any moment. Our perverse fantasies can impel us, even against our better intentions, to reckless actions that may convert our lives into nightmares.

To preclude such nightmares, Gita wisdom urges us to stop our mind from indulging in immoral daydreams. Thankfully, this doesn't require us to still the mind – a task that is difficult, even impossible. Instead, Gita wisdom asks us to lead the mind's expeditions towards an alternative inner world: Krishna's world. By learning about the glory and the beauty of Krishna, we can engage our mind positively in Krishna – in exploring, experiencing and expanding our joyful devotional relationship with him.

Over time such mental engagement with Krishna entirely transforms our inner dynamics: instead of we being the mind's cheerleaders, we become its leader, and it becomes the cheerleader for Krishna and our service to him.

ॐ

From anger, complete delusion arises, and from delusion bewilderment of memory. When memory is bewildered, intelligence is lost, and when intelligence is lost one falls down again into the material pool.

Don't let the mind eat your head

*T*he mind sometimes makes us do self-defeating, short-sighted, stupid things. How? By making us headless.

The Bhagavad-gita (02.62) indicates that when the mind contemplates sense objects, it becomes infatuated by material desires. As its infatuation increases, it first tries to devour our memory and our intelligence – that is, our head.

Why is the head the mind's favorite delicacy, its first dietary choice? Because the head is the watchdog that prevents it from devouring anything else such as our dignity, our morality or our spirituality; the head checks it from forcing us into self-destructive actions. If the mind succeeds in consuming the head, the road to fulfilling all its dietary fantasies becomes clear. When the head falls, we fall (02.63: *buddhi naashaat pranashyati*).

That's why the infatuated mind becomes like a cannibalistic demon while attacking the head. At such times, it refuses to listen to any good advice; nothing can stop its marauding march. Nothing, that is, except Krishna. When we fervently chant his holy names and sincerely strive to remember him, we invoke his presence in our consciousness. Confronted with his omnipotence, the ravenous mind can do nothing except freeze in its predatory tracks. If we continue remembering Krishna steadily, the petrified mind is left with no alternative except to beat a timid retreat.

However, when the head is under threat, it may itself freeze and not think about calling out to Krishna for help. That's why in normal non-threatening situations we need to so regularly and diligently call out his names that it becomes our reflex habit which requires no conscious decision-making. Then we will be able to save our head, thereby saving ourselves.

That's why our daily chanting is not a casual ritual; it is survival training.

ॐ

From anger, complete delusion arises, and from delusion bewilderment of memory. When memory is bewildered, intelligence is lost, and when intelligence is lost one falls down again into the material pool.

Morning is the time for mooring our heart to Krishna

For us as aspiring devotees, worldly temptations pose formidable challenges to our spiritual integrity. The Bhagavad-gita (02.67) indicates that these temptations are like stormy winds that blow our boat-like heart towards alluring sense objects.

We may have noble intentions to preserve our spiritual integrity, but such intentions alone are not enough to weather the storms of temptations. By their sheer force, the storms can first blow away our noble intentions, and then blow us towards the sense objects. To resist these storms, we need to firmly moor our heart to Krishna. For this, we require a daily regimen of philosophical education and devotional experience.

Let's take a closer look at these two spiritual disciplines:

1. **Philosophical education**: When we immerse ourselves in scriptural wisdom, we get empowered by the conviction that a higher, better happiness awaits us in the near-future provided we don't let ourselves be blown away by petty material temptations.

2. **Devotional experience**: When we absorb ourselves in the remembrance of Krishna through mantra meditation, we experience the higher spiritual happiness that makes lower material pleasures unnecessary and unappealing.

Thus, these twin spiritual disciplines moor our heart to Krishna. The best time for such mooring is the morning because at that time distractions, both external and internal, are minimal.

When we thus moor our heart to Krishna, the resulting resolve and taste will enable us to fight off temptations more easily and efficaciously. This in turn will leave us with far greater mental energy for fulfilling our worldly obligations as well as achieving our devotional aspirations.

Cℜℰᴔ

As a boat on the water is swept away by a strong wind, even one of the roaming senses on which the mind focuses can carry away a man's intelligence

Use technology – don't be used by technology

In today's society, living without technology is almost impossible. As aspiring devotees living in a techno-centric society, we usually think of technology as a neutral tool that can be used for devotional purposes.

What we may not realize is that our relationship with technology is not one-way, but two-way. It is not we alone who use technology; technology also uses us.

How?

Technology is deeply, even inextricably, associated with certain uses. For example, television is so widely used for materialistic entertainment that its use for watching spiritual programs, though hypothetically possible, is practically rare. Even when we are using it spiritually, we may succumb to using it sensually at any moment. After all, the temptation is just one click away – always.

We are especially vulnerable to such temptations because the materialistic uses of technology are far more aggressively marketed than its spiritual uses. Additionally, to use technology, we often have to place ourselves in temptation zone, a cultural ambience that injects us with material desires. Due to these subtle but strong influences, we sometimes get carried away and waste our irreplaceable time on anti-devotional indulgences. Thus we end up being used by technology. That is, we end up exploited by those materialists who use technology to get to our time, heart and finally money.

To use technology safely, we need to adopt the self-protection measures outlined by Gita wisdom. Firstly we need to regularly connect ourselves with Krishna through exclusive devotional activities that remind us of the devotional purpose of everything, including technology. And secondly, whenever we are in a temptation zone, we need to conscientiously watch our mind and senses, as indicated in the Gita (02.68). Then and then alone will we be able to stop the materialistic influences associated with technology from sabotaging our devotional intentions.

ॐ

Therefore, O mighty-armed, one whose senses are restrained from their objects is certainly of steady intelligence.

Ever flowing, never flooding is the state of the serene consciousness

How can spiritual seekers stay peaceful amidst tempting circumstances? The Bhagavad-gita (2.70) shows the way with a metaphor from nature: just as rivers flow into an ocean without flooding it or causing it to overflow, desires flow into serious spiritualists without disturbing their inner calm.

Significantly, the metaphor talks about desires flowing inwards, not outwards. The absence of the outward flow of desires is also indicated by the words in the verse: *na kama-kami*, meaning not "a desirer of desires." This unidirectional flow of desires implies that though desires flow inwards from tempting objects toward them, this doesn't induce their desires to flow outwards towards those objects.

Why don't they desire the desires? Because they relish a far greater happiness than what those desires can offer. They are connected with the oceanic source of all happiness, Krishna, thereby experiencing happiness as vast as an ocean. Their self-satisfied undisturbed consciousness amidst the presence of temptations can be aptly described as the state of "ever flowing, never flooding."

Can we become undisturbed amidst temptations like them?

Surely, answers Gita wisdom. All we need to do is develop our divine connection by cultivating devotional remembrance of Krishna daily and diligently. When we start sensing and savoring the ocean within, the pleasures without will lose their charm and capacity to agitate us, and we too will experience unflappable peace.

ॐ

A person who is not disturbed by the incessant flow of desires—that enter like rivers into the ocean, which is ever being filled but is always still—can alone achieve peace, and not the man who strives to satisfy such desires.

Take exception to the hope for an exception

Our mind gets excited by any chance for material enjoyment. We have repeatedly experienced for ourselves that material enjoyment is at best an exasperating anti-climax, that it never lives up to the hype, that it is not worth getting excited about. Still, the mind never learns the lesson even after repeated experience. It may sometimes admit perfunctorily that our past attempts for enjoyment have failed, but it still believes that our future attempts will be successful. Thus, it claims that next time will be an exception to the general pattern of frustration.

In contrast with the mind's unreasonable claims about an imminent exception, Gita wisdom is far more reasonable in echoing our hard-nosed, real-life experience of the emptiness of material enjoyment. The Bhagavad-gita (03.16) states that the attempts for material enjoyment simply waste our life (*indriyaramo mogham partha sa jivati*). This resonance of scriptural testimony with our personal experience holds immense potential for empowering our intelligence.

Once we thus empower our intelligence, we can take exception to the mind's hope for an exception. We can challenge the mind: "Why should I believe your claim that material enjoyment brings happiness when my life's experiences have consistently and comprehensively disproved it?"

If we can summon the courage and conviction to take on the mind, we will soon see its baseless claim crumble under the pressure of sustained scrutiny. As the mind retreats, we will find the way clear for focusing undistractedly on cultivating remembrance of Krishna. The more we concentrate on tasting the beauty and the glory of Krishna, the more we will relish the ultimate inner fulfillment. Then we will have only one regret: why didn't I take exception to the mind's hope for an exception earlier?

Nonetheless, better late than never.

CRLSO

My dear Arjuna, one who in human life does not follow the prescribed cycle of sacrifice thus established by the Vedas certainly leads a life full of sin. Living only for the satisfaction of the senses, such a person lives in vain.

Do not make a virtue out of alienating people

When we adopt spiritual practices seriously, we soon gain a bit of self-mastery. This little self-mastery may make us feel morally superior to others: "I have renounced all those materialistic pleasures to which they are still addicted."

When people see such a condescending attitude in a devotee of God, it turns them away not only from that person but also from God. Seeing their alienation, we may be tempted to make a virtue out of it: "This only proves how degraded they are." Even if we are not condescending towards people, we may still alienate them by speaking spiritual principles too advanced for them.

To pre-empt such unnecessary alienation of people, the Bhagavad-gita (03.26) recommends that we not act or speak in ways that agitate the minds of people (*na buddhi-bhedam janayed*) who are spiritually uninformed (*ajnanam*) and materially attached (*karma-sanginam*).

To understand the rationale for this recommendation, let's recap the Gita's essential message. Most people in this world will be materialistic because this is, after all, the material world. Nonetheless, no one is essentially a materialist; everyone is actually a soul, a precious part of Krishna. Everyone is ultimately looking for Krishna because everyone is looking for happiness, and Krishna is the supreme source of all happiness. So, if people are not yet ready to connect with him directly, we can at the very least by our conduct and counsel convey a positive impression about *krishna-bhakti*. That positive impression (*ajnata-sukriti*) will slowly but surely prod them towards Krishna.

Thus, this recommendation brings realism and idealism together in an endearing balance, a balance that is the hallmark of Gita wisdom. Learning to achieve this balance in our own lives makes living the Gita a lifelong adventure.

☙❧

So as not to disrupt the minds of ignorant men attached to the fruitive results of prescribed duties, a learned person should not induce them to stop work. Rather, by working in the spirit of devotion, he should engage them in all sorts of activities [for the gradual development of Krishna consciousness].

Expecting the default to change by default is a dangerous fault

"Will these immoral thoughts ever go away?" Questions like these may trouble us devotee-seekers when temptations provoke us even after we have adopted purifying spiritual practices.

Surely, answers Gita wisdom reassuringly, provided we change our default thoughts from material to spiritual.

We have indulged in material and even immoral pleasures for a long time – in this life and in our previous lives. Consequently, our mind has developed a deep-rooted attachment to those pleasures. This attachment makes the dreams and schemes to achieve them our default contemplations.

These default contemplations don't change even when we adopt spiritual practices. Why? Because we tend to engage in spiritual practices mechanically and expect our internal default thoughts to change by default. This faulty expectation makes us lax about exerting to purify our thought-life. Due to our internal laxity, we experience neither substantial satisfaction, nor tangible transformation – and so continue being dangerously allured by material temptations.

The Bhagavad-gita (03.30) exhorts us to shed internal lethargy and fight (*yudhyasva vigata jvarah*) to make our default thoughts spiritual (*adhyatma-cetasah*). To spiritualize our default thoughts, we need to internalize our external spiritual practices by cherishing the devotional orientation that they bring to our thoughts. For example, after we gain an insight from Gita wisdom, we can internally preserve that insight and draw on it for triggering devotional contemplation when our thoughts return to their default material contemplation.

This internalization process may be deeply demanding but it is also richly rewarding. Over time, it makes our default thoughts devotional; the more we strive to think about Krishna, the more he becomes our default-thought. And as he is the reservoir of all fulfillment, default Krishna-thoughts means default fulfilling thoughts.

A ceaselessly fulfilling thought-life is life's richest reward. No effort is too much for it.

ॐ

Therefore, O Arjuna, surrendering all your works unto Me, with full knowledge of Me, without desires for profit, with no claims to proprietorship, and free from lethargy, fight.

Krishna is attained not by playing with the intellect but by striving with the will

*M*any people, especially intellectuals, use knowledge, even scriptural knowledge, as a play-toy for their intellect. Playing with the intellect involves memorizing, analyzing, synthesizing and verbalizing information. Often, such intellectual play is motivated by the vain (pun intended) desire to exhibit one's learning for the purpose of impressing others, thereby converting them to one's point of view. Such an intellectual performance based on scriptural knowledge may be dazzling for others, but it will be self-defeating if it inflames the very desire that scriptural knowledge is meant to extinguish: the desire to be an independent center of attraction as a competitor to Krishna.

The Bhagavad-gita (03.32) insightfully points out that even the knowledgeable fail to attain Krishna if their desires are misdirected towards imitating him instead of assisting him.

The purpose of acquiring knowledge about Krishna is to increase our attraction for him, not our competition with him. We become attracted to him not merely by *acquiring* scriptural knowledge, but by *applying* that knowledge. Only when we apply scriptural teachings can we transform our desires from selfishness to selflessness, from I-centeredness to Krishna-centeredness, from decoration of our ego to glorification of our Lord. To thus transform our desires, enormous exertion of our will is absolutely essential. We need to repeatedly and rigorously beat down the selfish desires and to boost up the selfless desires.

If we are game for this exertion of the will, we can attain a reward that is unattainable by the most brilliant intellectual game-play: the reward of love for Krishna that alone brings everlasting happiness.

૭૮૦

But those who, out of envy, do not regularly follow these teachings are to be considered bereft of all knowledge, befooled, and ruined in their endeavors for perfection.

Devotion protects our values from being held hostage by our impulses

*A*ll of us have experience of times when our impulses overpower our values and goad us into actions that we regret later. How do our impulses become so brutally strong?

This, in fact, is the question that Arjuna asks Krishna in the Bhagavad-gita(03.36). Gita wisdom points to the root cause of this conflict between impulses and values that characterizes our human condition. We are spiritual beings presently living in material bodies. As spiritual beings, we are naturally motivated by sublime values, with the supreme value being selfless love – love for God and all his children. However, our material bodies, geared as they are for self-preservation, make us prone to self-centered impulses, with the prominent selfish impulse being lust followed closely on the heels by greed and anger.

Thus the conflict between values and impulses in our heart originates in a conflict between the two dimensions of our present existence: the selfless spiritual core and the selfish material shell. Our contemporary culture, by its incessant glamorization of selfish materialism, fuels and fans our material side, thereby making our impulses far stronger than our values. That's why, if we wish to prevent our values from being held hostage, or worse still, being slaughtered, by our impulses, we need to connect with a culture that arouses, nourishes and reinforces our values. The Krishna-centered devotional culture with its focus on spiritual sound serves precisely this purpose. Seen in this light, participating in this devotional culture is not a mere religious obligation, as some people mistake. Actually, it is a profound and powerful tool for our vital self-development.

Of course, culture alone is not enough. We need inner purification and satisfaction that is found best through spiritual devotion. The more we connect with Krishna internally through the practice of bhakti-yoga, the more we find inner fulfilment, thereby enabling our values to rise above our impulses.

☙❧

Arjuna said: O descendant of Vrishni, by what is one impelled to sinful acts, even unwillingly, as if engaged by force?

Lust is a black hole – beware of its gravity pull

The Bhagavad-gita (03.37) states that lust is the all-devouring sinful enemy of the world. In its capacity to devour everything that comes within its reach, lust is like a black hole. Once lust catches us in its gravity pull, it can gobble everything that makes us human: our cherished spirituality, our social dignity, our foundational morality, our human decency and even our basic civility.

The invisible yet formidable gravity pull of lust acts primarily on the mind and through the mind. In fact, the Gita (03.40) says that lust is located in the mind of the person who is provoked by it. This implies that it is not located in the object that provokes it, as we often assume. By thus pinpointing the location of lust, Gita wisdom ensures that we don't blame externals for succumbing to it, thereby evading our responsibility to curb it.

Of course, an important part of our responsibility is to notice and avoid situations in which lust pulls us more forcefully. The mental pull of lust often increases when we are physically close to the objects that provoke lust. So the Gita (03.41) recommends that, as a beginning step, we regulate our senses, thereby maintaining a safe distance from provocative objects. As a more sustainable and comprehensive solution, the Gita (03.43) urges us to cultivate philosophical insight and situate ourselves in spiritual devotion. Devotion brings us within the spiritual pull of Krishna's supreme beauty. When we let ourselves be pulled by Krishna, the pull of lust gradually subsides and finally ceases. Thus, we become free.

⳾

The Supreme Personality of Godhead said: It is lust only, Arjuna, which is born of contact with the material mode of passion and later transformed into wrath, and which is the all-devouring sinful enemy of this world.

Let sleeping tigers sleep – don't pinch them

"*I* thought I had become free from that attachment. Why has it come back?" Questions like these often describe our inner trajectory as devotee-seekers. When we start practicing devotional service diligently, we are often pleasantly surprised to see how it frees us from attachments. But, over time, we find the old attachments returning.

What went wrong? We mistook hibernation to be termination.

Our past attachments are like tigers; just as tigers devour our body, attachments devour our consciousness. Deep-rooted attachments like those involving lust and greed get uprooted only after many years of consistent purification; they are tigers that don't die quickly. Nonetheless, diligent practice of sadhana-bhakti sedates them quite rapidly.

Those tigers remain dormant as long as we don't pinch them awake. Unfortunately, pinching sleeping tigers is what we metaphorically do when we carelessly or complacently expose ourselves to provocative stimuli. Sometimes the initial pinches may not wake the tiger, thereby making us over-confident about our self-mastery. But the next pinch may be one pinch too much.

So, the cause of our agitation is not the return of our old attachments, but their re-awakening. To curb the agitation, we need to carefully minimize our exposure to provocative stimuli, as the Bhagavad-gita (03.41) enjoins. Whatever provocations the normal course of life unavoidably brings our way, we have to determinedly subdue. But beyond that we don't have to deliberately expose ourselves to provocations for evaluating our purity. We just need to keep increasing our inner remembrance of Krishna and outer service to him till everything unconnected with him becomes increasingly unappealing.

If we can just focus on serving Krishna lifelong, the tiger will pass uneventfully from hibernation to termination, and we will progress undistractedly from the material world back to the spiritual world.

ॐ

Therefore, O Arjuna, best of the Bharatas, in the very beginning curb this great symbol of sin [lust] by regulating the senses, and slay this destroyer of knowledge and self-realization.

Watch what youwatch

Standard dictionaries give two meanings of the word *watch*: "follow with the eyes" and "be vigilant, be on the lookout or be careful." Interestingly, these two meanings correlate with the two steps for self-empowerment outlined in the Bhagavad-gita. Let's see how.

Our contemporary materialist culture diverts us from our values and purposes by constant visual distractions. Gaudy images seducing us with hedonistic pleasures assault our eyes on the streets through billboards and in our homes through TV commercials. Most of us know consciously that these advertisements are obvious exaggerations, if not outright lies. Yet many of us don't know their effect at the subconscious level. When we encounter an assertion repeatedly, our mind subconsciously moves that assertion from the category of the familiar to the category of the believable. This psychological tendency to subconsciously upgrade the status of repetitive impressions is exploited by ultra-visible, recurrent advertisements. If we expose ourselves unrestrictedly and uncritically to such materialist propaganda, it will subtly but surely erode our healthy skepticism, and we will be misled by unhealthy materialist infatuations.

That's why the Bhagavad-gita (03.41) states that our journey towards self-mastery begins with regulating our senses, or, in other words, watching what we watch. If we watch (carefully evaluate with our intelligence) the images that we watch (see with our eyes), then we will have two measures for psychological self-defense at our disposal:

1. Stop our eyes from seeing those images that are avoidable on our visual pathways

2. Stop our mind from naively believing those images that are unavoidable

By thus watching what we watch, we will be able to keep ourselves mentally focused on pursuing life's worthwhile purposes.

CRSO

Therefore, O Arjuna, best of the Bharatas, in the very beginning curb this great symbol of sin [lust] by regulating the senses, and slay this destroyer of knowledge and self-realization.

It's never too late –and it's already too late

Intelligence and experience help us see that material enjoyment is temporary and unsatisfying, and that spiritual fulfillment is eternal and supremely satisfying. This vision inspires us to redirect our attraction from matter to Krishna. Once we start this redirection project, two feelings threaten our progress: we may become either disheartened or complacent.

To help us overcome these two obstructing emotions, Gita wisdom offers twin insights:

1. **It's never too late**: We may become disheartened on seeing that our conditionings seem deep-rooted, endless and irreformable. But Gita wisdom assures us that no matter how great the power of our conditionings, it is no match to the power of Krishna. As long as we are fighting a solitary battle, overcoming our conditionings is nearly impossible. But when we are sheltered and strengthened by Krishna through the process of bhakti-yoga, overcoming our conditionings is entirely possible.

2. **It's already too late**: At the same time, Krishna's omnipotence shouldn't become the cause of our complacence. Even with his power, the onus for redirecting our desires is on us. And bringing about this redirection is usually a lifetime project that is best started in childhood. So from that standpoint, we are probably quite a bit behind time – by several years, if not decades. Fortunately, the process of bhakti-yoga can place us on the fast-track to spiritual advancement and help us make up for lost time. Yet again, it is we who need to press the bhakti accelerator by hiking the intensity of our practices.

Through analyses like these, we can gain the impetus to apply the exhortation of the Bhagavad-gita (03.41: *adau*) to start serious spiritual practices confidently and immediately.

ক৪৮৩

Therefore, O Arjuna, best of the Bharatas, in the very beginning curb this great symbol of sin [lust] by regulating the senses, and slay this destroyer of knowledge and self-realization.

Let temptation trigger an alarm bell, not a welcome tune

The Bhagavad-gita (03.41) urges us to recognize carnal temptation as a symbol of sin (*papamanam*) and to curb it as soon as it rears its ugly head in our consciousness.

This ability to see the true colors of temptation is a prime barometer of our intellectual health. When we are intellectually sick, the arrival of a carnal temptation sets off a welcome tune in our consciousness; our unhealthy intelligence has no strength or spunk to unmask the treacherous façade of temptation. Consequently, we get helplessly, even eagerly, carried away by the doomed hope that indulging in the temptation will make us happy.

But when we are intellectually healthy, the same stimulus triggers an alarm bell in our consciousness. Our robust intelligence recognizes that the temptation is a forerunner of emotional distraction which can over time snowball into spiritual destruction. Consequently, we gird ourselves determinedly for an inner battle. If we seek shelter and strength in the remembrance of Krishna, then we can slowly but surely win the battle.

Sometimes, it may appear that the arrival of temptation leads to no response: neither a welcome tune, nor an alarm bell. That is, we feel neither materially agitated, nor spiritually activated. Does this absence of response indicate that we have transcended temptation?

Unlikely. The absence of material agitation just indicates that due to our past devotional practices, we have become a little more immune to temptations than earlier. However, temptations remain a threat always, and prolonged exposure to them will inevitably agitate us. And the absence of spiritual activation indicates that our intelligence has fallen asleep due to a complacency that can be suicidal. Therefore, the absence of alarm should itself trigger alarm, or at least concern. It should galvanize us to arouse our intelligence, ward off the temptation and protect our spiritual integrity.

৵৪৪৹

Therefore, O Arjuna, best of the Bharatas, in the very beginning curb this great symbol of sin [lust] by regulating the senses, and slay this destroyer of knowledge and self-realization.

The mind traps us materially and trips us spiritually

We like our job one day and detest it the next day; we feel excited about our devotional activities sometimes and bored at other times. Why does our mind oscillate like this? Because it has learnt from experience that the charm of worldly objects doesn't last for long.

This lesson can help us realize that no material object can ever offer us lasting satisfaction. However, the mind evades this realization by imagining that the past worldly objects were not enjoyable because something was wrong in the practical details. For example, "I don't like my job because my boss is lousy." Due to this blunder of judgment, the mind keeps us entrapped at the material level with the futile hope that we will become happy if we just get the next worldly object alluring us from round the corner.

More damagingly, the mind doesn't let us stay fixed when we do contact the one object that can offer lasting satisfaction: Krishna. He is eternal and eternally enchanting. Yet due to its default oscillatory habit, the mind imagines that the charm of Krishna will also not last long. So it starts looking for something externally new in devotional service without going deep into the remembrance of Krishna while doing that activity. The mind thus causes us to look here and there and everywhere –except straight towards Krishna. No wonder we frequently trip on our devotional path, thereby suffering unnecessary slips and falls.

If we strengthen our intelligence by deep deliberation on our true identity as souls, who exist beyond the mind with its fickle desires, the Bhagavad-gita (03.43) indicates that we will conquer our inner enemies.

☙❧

Thus knowing oneself to be transcendental to the material senses, mind and intelligence, O mighty-armed Arjuna, one should steady the mind by deliberate spiritual intelligence [Krishna consciousness] and thus—by spiritual strength—conquer this insatiable enemy known as lust.

Conviction is the fuel for our resolutions to fly from take-off to landing

We often make resolutions to conquer our lower passions such as selfishness, ego, greed, lust or anger. Most such resolutions for self-improvement often have a high mortality rate in the flight from conception to implementation. Why?

Often, the cause lies not in the flight, but in the takeoff. We frequently try to externalize our resolutions without internalizing them adequately. This means that we start attempting to do a thing externally without doing enough to convince ourselves internally why we should do it.

Usually, we start our internal journey for self-improvement because of an external stimulus: for example, hearing an electrifying talk, reading a stirring scriptural passage or having a moving interaction with a saint. Such an external stimulus may be enough to initiate our self-improvement journey. But to sustain the journey, we need the fuel of internal conviction. Unfortunately, while starting off, we neglect boosting our conviction adequately; we are too eager to take off. This unwarranted haste causes our resolution to run out of fuel in mid-air and crash to a premature death.

To prevent this, we need to adopt the inside-out approach to self-improvement recommended by Gita wisdom. The Bhagavad-gita (03.43) indicates that intellectual conviction developed by conscious deliberation is critical for self-conquest. When an external stimulus inspires us to make a resolution, before takeoff we can seriously contemplate and systematically note the rationale for the resolution: we are not material bodies but souls; material passions block us from relishing spiritual happiness; no one else can overcome those passions for us; if we have to conquer them sometime, then why delay?

Thereafter, whenever our conviction-fuel meter starts showing a low, we can replenish it by meditating on those contemplations. By such replenishment, our flight will safely reach the destination of self-mastery.

ೞ൏

Thus knowing oneself to be transcendental to the material senses, mind and intelligence, O mighty-armed Arjuna, one should steady the mind by deliberate spiritual intelligence [Krishna consciousness] and thus—by spiritual strength—conquer this insatiable enemy known as lust.

The material is not spiritual, but it is spiritualizable

"Everything that devotees do is spiritual, so even their material life is spiritual," we may hear statements like these in devotee circles. Naturally, we may wonder: are they correct?

Gita wisdom indicates that they are correct in principle, but not always in practice – especially for aspiring devotees. To understand why, let's first clarify basic terms: "spiritual" refers to that which is made of *sat-cit-anand*, whereas "spiritualized" refers to that which is made of material elements but is used for a spiritual purpose. Our material life cannot become spiritual, but can become spiritualized. The Bhagavad-gita (04.24) indicates that everything material becomes spiritualized for those who work in a spirit of selfless sacrifice (*yajna*) for the Absolute Truth, Krishna. How much we have internalized this spirit can be known only by Krishna – and occasionally and partially by us when we are in a clear-thinking, introspective mode.

As aspiring devotees we aspire to offer our full heart to Krishna; so, we strive to offer even our material activities to him by doing them in a devotional consciousness. Still, material activities tend to trigger worldly desires in our heart. Such desires can overwhelm us if we have gone off guard due to assuming to be spiritual the activities that trigger those desires. That's why it's safer to err on the side of caution and see those activities as material, as needing spiritualization by our devotional consciousness. To keep our consciousness devotional, we need to engage in explicitly devotional activities like sadhana and seva. The more we do these activities in a mood of selfless service, the more that mood will carry over in our consciousness to our material activities and spiritualize them too.

Thus, infusing a steady devotional mood into our consciousness is the art of spiritualizing our material life.

೫೮೧

A person who is fully absorbed in Krishna consciousness is sure to attain the spiritual kingdom because of his full contribution to spiritual activities, in which the consummation is absolute and that which is offered is of the same spiritual nature.

Don't blame gravity for the sinking of the boat

"*I* succumbed to immoral indulgences because my material desires were too strong." Sometimes we may thus rationalize our fall from principles of spiritual integrity. This justification is fallacious, like blaming gravity for the sinking of a boat.

When we start practicing devotional service, we metaphorically board a boat for going to Krishna's eternal abode. Just as gravity is ubiquitous, so are material desires. Just as physical boats are designed to float in spite of gravity, so the boat of devotional service is designed to float in spite of the gravity force of material desires.

Some of us may have deep-rooted material conditionings; so, we may feel strongly dragged down by material desires. But the Bhagavad-gita (04.36) assures that, whatever be our past conditionings, the boat of spiritual knowledge can take us across the ocean of material existence.

A normal boat may sink because of either the boatperson's mistakes or factors beyond human control like stormy waves. When we board the special boat of devotional service, Krishna can take care of all factors beyond our control. But we alone have to protect ourselves from our mistakes. If we fall from our principles, the cause is not the gravity force of material desires but our own carelessness. Fortunately, the boat of devotional service is transcendental and indestructible; we can always re-board it and re-commence our spiritual journey.

When we understand these philosophical truths, we will no longer resort to fallacious rationalizations. Instead, we will become confident and cautious: confident about the capability of the boat and the competence of Krishna's protection; and cautious about avoiding our own errors. This combination of confidence and caution will take us safely to Krishna.

༺༻

Even if you are considered to be the most sinful of all sinners, when you are situated in the boat of transcendental knowledge you will be able to cross over the ocean of miseries.

Patience is humility, not apathy

Our culture infatuates us with instant things: instant tea, instant food, instant messaging, to name a few. This infatuation often makes us impatient about things that work at their own pace. Such impatience can be detrimental, even lethal, for our spiritual life, which centers on redirecting our love from matter to Krishna. As we have misdirected our love for many lifetimes, its redirection is unlikely to happen overnight.

That's why the Bhagavad-gita (04.38) declares *kalenatmani vindati*: in due course of time, we will relish inner happiness. As an illustration, the expansion of our love from matter to Krishna is often compared to the blossoming of a flower.

Just as a bud is constricted in size, our love is presently constricted to the limited arena of matter. Just as the bud blossoms gradually and actualizes its potential beauty, our love gradually expands by devotional service till it reaches and embraces Krishna, and thereby actualizes our potential spiritual beauty. Just as we can't accelerate the blossoming of a flower beyond the rate decided by nature, we can't accelerate the expansion of our love beyond the rate decided by Krishna. That's why patience is indispensable on the spiritual path.

At the same time, being patient doesn't mean being apathetic about our spiritual practices. It essentially means being humble and not expecting instant spiritual happiness prematurely or unrealistically. We can surely desire to love Krishna purely and fully. But instead of presumptuously demanding that love and its concomitant ecstasy, we can modestly express that desire through our diligence in devotional service. The more we render expectation-free service, the more we relish satisfaction in that service itself. And we advance towards a love and happiness that exceeds all our expectations.

CREO

In this world, there is nothing so sublime and pure as transcendental knowledge. Such knowledge is the mature fruit of all mysticism. And one who has become accomplished in the practice of devotional service enjoys this knowledge within himself in due course of time.

Don't let the sword sleep in the hand

*S*uppose medieval warriors with their hands on the swords by their side were surrounded by marauders, who were attacking innocent civilians and charging to strike the warriors themselves. If their hands on the swords stayed motionless, the question would naturally arise: "Why is the sword sleeping in the hand?"

The realized teachers of Gita wisdom similarly arouse us with a call to intellectual arms. The Bhagavad-gita (04.42) compares its spiritual knowledge to a sword (*jnana-asina*) that can cut to pieces all worldly illusions and doubts. When we study the Gita, we acquire this sword to counter the onslaughts of illusions and doubts. These onslaughts come in our times through the contemporary culture that aggressively spins fantasies about material pleasures, and relegates God to irrelevance, if not non-existence.

All of us have the power to fight these onslaughts; we just need to use the sword of Gita wisdom in two ways:

1. **Rigor in application**: To the extent we are lazy in applying Gita wisdom in our own lives, to that extent we are like the warriors under attack who let the sword sleep. When we apply the knowledge rigorously to cultivate sustained devotional remembrance of Krishna, we use the sword to unmask and repel the deceptive worldly propaganda.

2. **Vigor in outreach**: To the extent we are lethargic in sharing Gita wisdom with others, to that extent we are like the warriors who let their swords sleep while watching civilians being attacked. When we share the knowledge vigorously, we use the sword to protect our fellow humans from being misled by illusions and doubts.

When we can do so much good for ourselves and for the world, why should we let the sword sleep any longer?

ಌ

Therefore the doubts which have arisen in your heart out of ignorance should be slashed by the weapon of knowledge. Armed with yoga, O Bharata, stand and fight.

Self-denial is meant not for self-torture but for self-fulfillment

People sometimes ask, "Why do we need to torture ourselves with acts of self-denial such as fasting?"

Whenever Gita wisdom recommends such acts, the purpose is not self-torture, but self-fulfillment. Fulfilling our bodily requirements is necessary for survival, but not sufficient for satisfaction. Satisfaction comes only by the fulfillment of our spiritual necessity of a loving connection with the reservoir of all satisfaction, Krishna. However, as long as we are caught up in catering to bodily demands – as we usually are – we neglect our spiritual necessity and miss the lasting fulfillment available thereof.

The Gita recommends acts of self-denial to gently compel us to relish what we have been unnecessarily missing. Self-denial stops our bodily preoccupation and forces us to look at the spiritual level for fulfillment. If we look by the right process under the right guidance, then we get so much spiritual fulfillment that we don't even miss the bodily needs that we normally consider indispensable. The Bhagavad-gita (05.21) indicates that those who detach themselves from external pleasures and concentrate on seeking inner joys relish inexhaustible fulfillment.

The quickest, easiest and safest way to experience self-fulfillment is by practicing devotional service centered on remembrance of Krishna. This is evident in Shrimad-Bhagavatam (10.1.13), wherein the emperor Parikshit, despite fasting for a prolonged period, declares that he is not missing food or water because he is relishing the nectar of remembrance of Krishna.

ॐ

Such a liberated person is not attracted to material sense pleasure but is always in trance, enjoying the pleasure within. In this way the self-realized person enjoys unlimited happiness, for he concentrates on the Supreme.

To give up the ocean for a drop is a rank bad bargain

"*I* would like to make spiritual advancement, but giving up worldly pleasures is too much of a price to pay for it." Such thoughts may dissuade us from following the regulative principles that urge us to eschew the anti-scriptural worldly pleasures of meat-eating, gambling, intoxication and illicit sex.

However, Gita wisdom overturns our paradigms about what costs too much; it states that giving up spiritual happiness for the sake of these worldly pleasures is too much of a price to pay. The Bhagavad-gita (05.21) emphasizes that by becoming indifferent to external allurements we can concentrate better on the divine within, thereby relishing unlimited happiness.

With Gita wisdom, we become freed from illusion, and see reality as it is. Material enjoyment, being inescapably limited by our body's tiny capacity for enjoyment, can never be more than a drop. And as Krishna is an unlimited ocean of happiness, spiritual fulfillment coming from connection with him is oceanic – it is capable of filling and flooding us with happiness forever and ever.

Without Gita wisdom, we come under the spell of illusion – we mistake the drop-like material enjoyment to be oceanic, and the oceanic spiritual fulfillment to be drop-like. Just as giving up the vast ocean for a tiny drop of water is a rank bad bargain for a fish, giving up lasting spiritual fulfillment for fleeting material enjoyment is a rank bad bargain for us as spiritual beings.

When we understand Gita wisdom, we can no longer be deceived by such a bad bargain. And when we apply Gita wisdom, we start relishing regularly, if not constantly, the fruits of a far better bargain: giving up the drop and gaining the ocean.

CR80

Such a liberated person is not attracted to material sense pleasure but is always in trance, enjoying the pleasure within. In this way the self-realized person enjoys unlimited happiness, for he concentrates on the Supreme.

Go down the consequence lane of memory to go up the devotion lane of life

*O*ur mind loves to go down the pleasure lane of memory, especially when those pleasures are materialistic. It not only glues itself to those memories but also replays them repeatedly, thereby inciting us to indulge in those pleasures again. Thus, the pleasure lane is the most traveled lane in the city of our memory.

The mind also frequently travels back on the misery lane, especially when the blame for that misery can be laid on someone else. Whenever we meet or even think of that person, the mind rushes down that lane and hyperactively re-enacts its blame game.

But what if the misery was caused by our own misdeeds, especially our reckless attempts for material enjoyment? Then the mind becomes curiously lethargic, even paralytic, to go down that lane. We can call this lane the consequence lane of memory because it contains memories that demonstrate the miserable consequences of material indulgences. The mind rarely recollects any such memory – unless it can somehow use the recollection to perversely incite us towards the same indulgence.

When we strive to move towards Krishna on the lane of devotion, worldly pleasures act as the most prominent roadblocks. The Bhagavad-gita (05.22) functions as a roadblock-remover by declaring that material pleasures are the wombs of misery. Initially, this verse may seem to be a mere theory for us. It may even appear to be a counter-factual theory when temptations promise us material pleasure. However, we just need to push ourselves down the consequence lane of memory. Then we will realize that the Gita is precisely stating a reality that we ourselves have repeatedly experienced.

Thus, by going down regularly on the consequence lane of memory, we will get the impetus to go up undistractedly on the devotion lane of life.

ॐ

An intelligent person does not take part in the sources of misery, which are due to contact with the material senses. O son of Kunti, such pleasures have a beginning and an end, and so the wise man does not delight in them.

Tolerance is the stopper between temptation and transgression

"I have been striving for selflessness and purity, yet I feel repeatedly tempted by selfish and impure pleasures. Will I never make spiritual advancement?" As aspiring devotees we may become disheartened by such thoughts when we find anti-devotional desires rising in our consciousness.

At such times, we can take heart from the encouraging insight offered in the Bhagavad-gita (05.23). This verse indicates that as long as we are situated in a material body, our bodily situation makes us naturally prone to material temptations. To make spiritual advancement in such a situation, we don't have to be temptation-free; we have to be transgression-free.

Temptations involve impure desires, whereas transgressions involve impure actions. The stopper that prevents temptations from growing into transgressions is tolerance. This Gita verse assures that as long as we determinedly tolerate temptations, we are well-situated and connected (*yuktah*) on the spiritual path.

How can we increase our capacity to tolerate temptations? By cultivating knowledge and devotion.

When we assimilate scriptural knowledge about how material pleasures are short-lived and counter-productive, the resulting intellectual conviction boosts our capacity to tolerate impure temptations. When we increase our spiritual devotion for Krishna, we find it easier to redirect our thoughts from temptations to him. Whereas temptations are sources of fleeting titillation, Krishna is the source of lasting fulfillment. So, thinking about him gives us profound inner satisfaction, thereby enabling us to tolerate and eliminate temptations.

Thus, by the combination of knowledge and devotion, tolerance becomes not just possible but also relishable.

⊂੧੪⊃

Before giving up this present body, if one is able to tolerate the urges of the material senses and check the force of desire and anger, he is well situated and is happy in this world.

Don't fall for the mind's "no time" trick

"*You* don't have any time." This is how the mind often summarily rejects our plans for devotional activities like mantra meditation.

We may indeed have a lot of things to do. But doing one thing after another drains and stresses us. At such times, the mind gleefully whispers, "Watch TV to get some stress-relief."

Whatever happened to "no time"? That was just the mind's trick to keep us away from Krishna and keep us tightly in its clutches.

TV rarely relives our stress. Many programs leave us bored and set us off on a titillating-but-unfulfilling channel surfing spree. When we become fed up with TV, the mind takes another tack for making our life miserable. It first shames us, "You are a fool; you wasted so much time." Then it scares us, "There's so little time and so much to do. You will never be able to do it." Finally it sentences us, "You are a goner."

TV watching is just one of the many ways in which the mind deceives us. Basically, it wastes our precious time and aggravates our stress with frustration and discouragement. No wonder the Bhagavad-gita (06.05) urges us to treat the mind like an enemy.

To protect ourselves from this inner enemy, we need to see through and reject its "no time" deception. By making time for devotional meditation, we connect ourselves with Krishna, who being the source of all energy replenishes our inner energy. This energization not only frees us from stress, but also enables us to manage our obligations efficiently and effectively.

Moreover, rejuvenation is just the incidental reward of connecting with Krishna. The real reward is the revival of our dormant devotion, for that ultimately catapults us beyond the mind's tricks to the world of eternal love.

☙❧

One must deliver himself with the help of his mind, and not degrade himself. The mind is the friend of the conditioned soul, and his enemy as well.

You can change your mind, but don't let your mind change you

The Bhagavad-gita (06.05) enjoins that we elevate ourselves with our mind and not degrade ourselves with it. This intriguing verse indicates the volatile nature of our relationship with our mind. When we control our mind, our actions tend to be elevating. But when our mind controls us, our actions tend to be degrading.

How can we understand who is in charge: we or our mind?

One way is by introspectively examining our explanations of our actions. Sometimes, we may act in ways that are not in harmony with our words. When asked about the difference, we may explain, "I changed my mind." This usage may represent our flexibility in the face of life's changing situations, and flexibility does have a valid and valuable place in a principle-centered life. If our introspective examination reveals that our response was due to our flexibility, then we can infer that we were in charge of our mind.

However, sometimes after resolving to act according to scriptural principles, we act impulsively in the face of tempting or provoking situations. If our introspective examination reveals that our response was motivated by the desire for selfish pleasure or the desire to avoid personal inconvenience, then we can infer that our mind was in charge. On such occasions "I changed my mind" is a cover-up for the reality "My mind changed me."

How can we make our control of our mind steady and strong? By strengthening ourselves spiritually through a deep connection with the supreme source of all strength, Krishna. This spiritual strength will gradually enable us to silence and subordinate our obstinate mind, and make it act in harmony with our long-term spiritual interests. Then the mind will no longer be able to change us, for we will have changed it permanently.

ॐ

One must deliver himself with the help of his mind, and not degrade himself. The mind is the friend of the conditioned soul, and his enemy as well.

The mind can impel, but not compel

The Bhagavad-gita (06.06) points out the two opposite roles that the mind can play in shaping our destiny: if controlled, it can be our friend; if uncontrolled, it can be our enemy.

This verse implies that we can control the mind if we decide to. This may seem impossible, especially when it wildly and repeatedly disrupts our normal functioning. However, it will become entirely possible if we empower ourselves with a critical guiding insight: the mind can never take the steering wheel from us. The body is like a car and the soul, the driver. In our bodily car, we are always in the driver's seat.

But we have a default traveling partner sitting permanently next to us: our mind. It constantly proposes dangerous ideas of where we should travel, and fabricates crazy images of the pleasures that we will get there. By its propositions and fabrications, it prompts, prods, pushes, pinches and punches us to fulfill its wanderlust. However, as we are in the driver's seat, it can only impel us, never compel us.

Nonetheless, resisting the mind's deceptive and persuasive incitation is not easy. To be able to resist it consistently, we need another traveling partner who gives us good counsel. That additional partner is Krishna. He is already present in our heart as the Supersoul, but we need to attune ourselves to his presence and voice by practicing devotional service. When we hear and follow his voice, he helps us see the folly of the mind's schemes and the falsity of its promises. By hearing Krishna and neglecting the mind, we can steer our life-journey safely so that we can do our best materially during our journey and attain the best destination spiritually at the end: Krishna's eternal abode.

✿

For him who has conquered the mind, the mind is the best of friends; but for one who has failed to do so, his mind will remain the greatest enemy.

The mind is predictably dangerous and dangerously unpredictable

"*I*know that work is important, but I just can't make myself do it; I am not in the right mood." "Stop; don't irritate me further, otherwise I will explode. I am in a bad mood today." Sentiments like these come up periodically during our everyday routines. Because they are common, we often don't think seriously about them. If we did, we would be chilled by what they betray: the mind through its moods dominates us and acts as our worst enemy, as stated in the Bhagavad-gita (06.06).

The mind acts inimically in two broad ways:

1. **Predictably dangerous:** Based on our past experiences, we can predict reasonably the times when the mind will vex, nag, worry, seduce, disorient or discourage us.

2. **Dangerously unpredictable:** The mind sometimes ambushes us. At the least expected time, we find ourselves overwhelmed by an attack of undesirable emotions. During such ambushes, the intensity of the emotion and the unpredictability of its onset together can overwhelm us and provoke us to self-defeating kneejerk reactions.

Through these two modus operandi, the mind can jeopardize our career, our relationships, our integrity, our spirituality, and even our sanity.

How can we counter the mind? By a combination of willpower and divine power.

Our willpower alone can rarely stop the marauding mind. That's why we need to use our willpower to gain access to divine power. For accessing divine power, we need to connect ourselves with Krishna by contemplating his message and chanting his holy names.

When we thus empower ourselves, we can not only stand firm amidst the mind's predictable and unpredictable attacks but also march through them towards life's ultimate destination: the spiritual world, where the messy material mind can no longer harass us.

☙❧

For him who has conquered the mind, the mind is the best of friends; but for one who has failed to do so, his mind will remain the greatest enemy.

Study makes us steady and sturdy

*W*hen we strive to live with spiritual and moral integrity, we often find our mind tormenting us. It tantalizes us with dreams and schemes of immoral and unspiritual pleasures. Over a period of time, we may find that resisting these allurements becomes a tiresome torture. We may even start losing our will to fight.

Times like these are ideal for us to experience the transformative power of scriptural study. This scriptural power comes to us in two installments:

1. **Steadiness**: At the seeker's level, the most important reason to study scripture is to convince and re-convince ourselves about where we will find real happiness: in Krishna. When we don't study scriptures regularly and seriously, then we keep taking perpetual u-turns in our quest for happiness, sometimes seeking material enjoyment and sometimes seeking spiritual fulfillment. Scriptural study strengthens our philosophical conviction that the mind's proposals for material enjoyment are all misleading and degrading; we will get real fulfillment only by purifying ourselves, and absorbing ourselves in inner remembrance of Krishna and outer service to him. This philosophical conviction enables us to neglect the disturbing mind and stay steady on the spiritual path.

2. **Sturdiness**: The more we habituate ourselves to scriptural study, the more we become internally empowered. This power enables us to take the next step after neglecting the mind: silencing it. As we become increasingly convinced of the folly of material enjoyment and the glory of spiritual fulfillment, we become sturdy enough to nail the wild mind into submission. When we thus tame the mind, it torments us no more. We soon relish undistracted, undiluted fulfillment.

The Bhagavad-gita invites us to this sublime state of consciousness when it declares (06.08: *jnana-vijnana triptatma*) that scriptural knowledge and realization make us fully satisfied.

ॐ

A person is said to be established in self-realization and is called a yogi [or mystic] when he is fully satisfied by virtue of acquired knowledge and realization. Such a person is situated in transcendence and is self-controlled. He sees everything—whether it be pebbles, stones or gold—as the same.

When attention seems like detention, we need education

Attention is crucial for enjoying anything. When a reputed sports player is in action, fans enjoy by attentively watching all the action and even the replays.

We need attention to relish devotional life too. While performing spiritual activities, we experience devotional happiness only when we become internally attentive to the presence of Krishna.

Otherwise, if we are inattentive in, say, our daily meditation, we soon find the meditation sessions uninspiring and uninteresting. At such times, attention feels like detention. The Gita injunction to be attentive seems like a deprivation of our mental freedom to think of more enjoyable things.

But the same Bhagavad-gita (06.21: *sukham atyantikam*) declares that the spiritual platform offers the ultimate happiness. Why don't we experience this happiness? Because of misdirection of desires caused by deficient conviction.

Krishna, being the all-attractive Supreme Person, is the reservoir of all happiness. When we concentrate on him, we relish spiritual happiness far greater and deeper than any material pleasure. But we are not yet convinced that he is the source of the supreme happiness. Instead, we believe that worldly objects are the sources of real happiness. So, even while doing devotional activities externally, we internally desire worldly objects instead of Krishna. Our situation becomes like that of sports fans forced to watch one sport when they desire to watch another sport on a different TV channel. Just as they would feel detained, so do we.

Our feelings of boredom are signs that we need to restrengthen our intellectual convictions. Contemplative scriptural study is a potent conviction-booster. By such educational study, we will feel inspired to redirect our desires to Krishna. Once we become desirous of him, we will see attention not as detention but as the gateway to supreme satisfaction.

♋

In that joyous state, one is situated in boundless transcendental happiness, realized through transcendental senses. Established thus, one never departs from the truth

Determination comes from the conviction that the prize is greater than the price

"*Yet* again I failed to keep my resolution! I will never be able to achieve self-mastery." The mind may dishearten us with haunting thoughts like these when we repeatedly fail in our inner struggles.

Such a discouraging mind can be silenced, the Bhagavad-gita (06.25) indicates, by the conviction of our intelligence (*buddhya dhriti-grihitaya*). How can we develop this intellectual conviction? By calmly contemplating the Gita's central message that we are souls who can attain real happiness only by curbing our material desires and striving to lovingly serve Krishna. Self-mastery essentially means redirecting our heart from the material level to the spiritual level. Thus, self-mastery demands a price – giving up material enjoyment – and delivers a prize: gaining spiritual happiness.

Contemplation on Gita wisdom grants us general conviction in the goal of self-mastery. However, when we make specific resolutions for achieving that self-mastery, we start wavering. Why? Because the mind starts whispering, "The price is too much for the prize."

At such times, we need to prayerfully seek answers to probing questions such as the following:

1. What is the prize that I will get by sticking to this resolution? Eternal, fulfilling happiness.
2. What is the price that I will have to pay for it? Temporary, unsatisfying enjoyment.
3. Is the prize greater than the price? Definitely, massively, infinitely.

These unequivocal answers will boost our intellectual conviction, which will silence the mind with irrefutable rejoinders when it starts whispering its lies.

By thus cultivating intellectual conviction, we will ensure that our resolutions not only survive, but also thrive. Thereafter, as our determination becomes increasingly firm, self-mastery doesn't remain a distant dream, but becomes a living reality.

ॐ

Gradually, step by step, one should become situated in trance by means of intelligence sustained by full conviction, and thus the mind should be fixed on the self alone and should think of nothing else.

Change of values is more significant than change of desires

When we as spiritual seekers find ourselves becoming repeatedly afflicted by greed, anger or lust, we may become discouraged, thinking, "Despite my practice of devotional service, why is my inner life not changing?

The fact, though, may pleasantly surprise us: our inner life has already changed. That change is evident in our questioning the presence of anti-devotional desires in our heart. This questioning itself indicates a fundamental change in our values.

Before we started practicing devotional service, we probably valued material desires, and looked forward to them as sources of pleasure and symbols of success. But now we are valuing freedom from material desires and are looking forward to the time when we will relish the peace that the cessation of material desires brings. More importantly, we now cherish the resulting capacity for undistracted remembrance of Krishna, and utilize that capacity to serve and please him, thereby savoring the supreme happiness of pure love.

This change in our values – from looking forward to material desires to looking forward to freedom from material desires – is irrefutable evidence of our inner change. The Bhagavad-gita (06.26) acknowledges that the conditioned mind has the nature to wander (manash canchalam asthiram). Based on its past experiences, the mind by default wanders towards material pleasures.

Gita wisdom urges us to not be disheartened by this default movement but to expect it and to plan for countering it. If we preparedly and determinedly keep resisting its default movement and keep looking beyond material desires, gradually these desires will wane and fade. To persevere till we attain that state, we need to overlook the unreliable barometer of inner life, our desires, and focus on the reliable barometer, our values.

ॐ

From wherever the mind wanders due to its flickering and unsteady nature, one must certainly withdraw it and bring it back under the control of the self.

The mind may stray away; let it not stay away

"Yet again the mind has gone astray. How many times can I keep struggling against it?" This is our common reaction when we try to fix the mind on Krishna, but it strays off to thoughts of immoral pleasures and offensive actions. When the slippery mind keeps thwarting our efforts repeatedly, we may get discouraged, feeling that we will never be able to devote ourselves internally to Krishna.

Significantly, Gita wisdom anticipates and addresses our concern. One of the most stimulating features of Gita wisdom is its adeptness, even proactiveness, in catering to our spiritual concerns at our level. The Bhagavad-gita (06.26) encourages us by stating that, no matter how often the mind strays away from Krishna, we have the power to not let it stay away. This verse contains the word *yato* twice (*yato yato nishchalati*). This double occurrence hints at the two circumstances in which the mind may wander off: at various times and in different places. Whenever (*yato*) or wherever (*yato*) the mind strays off, the Gita encourages us to bring it back to Krishna.

If we abide by this guideline, we will be pleasantly surprised at how the mind will slowly but surely start mending its ways. The more we persevere in bringing the mind back to Krishna, the more we – and even our mind – will realize that thinking about him is much better than thinking about anything else. Worldly thoughts seem alluring, but they soon become agitating, exasperating and agonizing. In delightful contrast, Krishna-thoughts are pacifying, energizing and enlivening.

When this realization sinks into our heart, then the mind will no longer want to stray away from Krishna. From that time onwards, our life will become constantly and increasingly joyful.

ॐ

From wherever the mind wanders due to its flickering and unsteady nature, one must certainly withdraw it and bring it back under the control of the self.

Physical location doesn't have to limit spiritual meditation

We often compartmentalize our lives into the material side and the spiritual side. Such compartmentalization is initially helpful in ensuring that we allocate adequate time for our spiritual growth. Eventually, however, we need to go beyond such compartmentalization. Authentic devotion calls for a complete spiritualization of consciousness that permeates even the material side of our life.

Given the contemporary social, cultural and financial reality, most of us will have to spend much of our life in non-devotional, if not anti-devotional, environments. Consequently, if our life is compartmentalized into the material and the spiritual side, we will have to frequently postpone our spiritual growth: "I will think of Krishna later when my environment is more conducive." Such procrastination may keep us bereaved of deep Krishna consciousness for our entire lifetime, or God forbid, multiple lifetimes.

Therefore, we need to chart for ourselves a more proactive course by making the firm resolution: "No matter what my location, I will make Krishna my meditation." This resolution will motivate us to intensely absorb our consciousness in remembrance of Krishna when our externals are devotionally congenial, and to sustain that consciousness even when our externals are devotionally uncongenial.

By such diligent practice of devotional service, over time we will be able to see all of reality in new devotional light. We will view:

1. Our entire life as the arena for our loving service to Krishna

2. Worldly events as teachers demonstrating his message in real-time

3. The whole world as a potential offering of love to him

Once we gain such a holistic, devotional vision, the Bhagavad-gita (06.30) declares that we will never be lost to Krishna, nor Krishna to us.

৩৯০

For one who sees Me everywhere and sees everything in Me, I am never lost, nor is he ever lost to Me.

Conquer provocative mind with evocative mantra

We may sometimes doubt: "The mind is so wild. Will I ever be able to conquer it?" Surely we can, reassures the Bhagavad-gita (06.36), provided we strive by appropriate means.

The mind provokes us by fantasizing about worldly pleasures. However, these fantasies of the mind are just that: fantasies. No matter how real and rapturous the fantasized pleasure appears, the real pleasure in all worldly indulgences is meager and measly.

As we cannot live without pleasure, the only way we can sustainably save ourselves from the provocative mind is by experiencing a higher happiness. The easiest way to experience this higher happiness is by chanting mantras comprising the holy names of Krishna. Among various such mantras, the Hare Krishna mahamantra is the most recommended mantra for the current cosmic age.

Chanting this mantra evokes the higher happiness in two ways, through remembrance and service:

1. **Remembrance**: All of us have an innate, inalienable relationship of love with Krishna. Just as the remembrance of a loved one warms our heart with joy, the remembrance of the supreme beloved Krishna warms our heart with the supreme joy.

2. **Service**: Love is expressed and intensified through service. As the Hare Krishna mahamantra is a manifestation of Krishna in sound, it offers us the opportunity to serve him by attentive hearing. By thus serving him, the resulting love intensifies and heightens our experience of the higher happiness, thereby silencing the noisy mind.

Thus, we can counter the power of the provocative mind to tempt us toward lower pleasures by the power of the evocative mantra to channel higher happiness.

ॐ

For one whose mind is unbridled, self-realization is difficult work. But he whose mind is controlled and who strives by appropriate means is assured of success. That is My opinion.

Our days of cowering to the mind are over

"*I* will never be able to manage my mind." We may feel thus disheartened, especially when we observe how the mind suddenly and vehemently disrupts our plans for managing it.

Arjuna felt the same way. The Bhagavad-gita (06.33-34) narrates how Arjuna felt that disciplining the mind is impossible. Krishna responded (06.35-36) by confirming that mind management is indeed impossible – but only as long as we don't strive by the right means. The Gita assures that when we strive by the right means, what had seemed utterly impossible earlier becomes entirely possible.

The right means is to take help from a power greater than the power of the mind: the power of Krishna. The best way to get his help is by remembering him, especially by chanting his holy names. Such remembrance equips us to not only tolerate the mind, but also retaliate against it. Let's see how.

The mind is like a big bully. In the past, whenever we have tried to fight back against this bully, we have often ended up getting beaten badly. Consequently, we may have concluded subconsciously that we will suffer less if we just cower to the mind.

But remembrance of Krishna is the ultimate game-changer. When we regularly insulate our consciousness in his remembrance, we realize gradually that such remembrance serves as both a shield and a mace: a shield against the blows of the mind, and a mace to pound the mind. This realization is thrilling. After all, what can be more joyful than paying the bully back in his own coin?

Few moments are as life-transforming as the moment when we get the conviction: our days of cowering to the mind are over.

ॐ

For one whose mind is unbridled, self-realization is difficult work. But he whose mind is controlled and who strives by appropriate means is assured of success. That is My opinion.

We can't avoid being haunted, but we can choose who haunts us

As aspiring devotees, our devotional determination may waver when we are confronted with temptations of material pleasures.

Often these temptations haunt us like ghosts; they keep popping up again and again, possessing our mind and pushing us to act in distressing or even disgusting ways.

If due to this repeated pushing we give up our devotional principles and indulge in those pleasures, we will find them strangely insipid. Even if we seek those pleasures in grosser forms and with greater frenzy, still the same tastelessness will dog us relentlessly.

Such tastelessness, Gita wisdom informs, is a sign that we are haunted by another ghost: the ghost of devotional happiness. The great Vaishnava commentator Vishvanatha Chakravarti Thakura uses the ghost metaphor to convey the unforgettability of spiritual happiness. Unlike the ghost of material happiness that torments us at the conscious level, the ghost of devotional happiness usually acts at a subconscious level. There, it exposes the emptiness and hollowness of all material pleasures by contrasting them subliminally with devotional joys.

Due to this double possession during our transition from material pleasure to devotional happiness: we will be inevitably dissatisfied – either by the conscious craving for material pleasure or the subconscious longing for devotional happiness. Giving in to the material craving will never make us happy because we have already tasted the far greater devotional happiness. Even if our inner conditioning and outer culture don't let us realize the superiority of devotional happiness, the Bhagavad-gita (06.44: *hriyate hy avasho pi sah*) indicates that this higher taste will drag us back to devotional practices – sooner if we cooperate, later if we resist.

Therefore, knowing that the pursuit of material pleasures is now a lost cause, let us gird ourselves to fight the material craving, thereby ensuring that we get the ultimate happiness sooner rather than later.

☙❧

By virtue of the divine consciousness of his previous life, he automatically becomes attracted to the yogic principles—even without seeking them. Such an inquisitive transcendentalist stands always above the ritualistic principles of the scriptures.

Our vulnerability points to our opportunity

*W*hen we succumb to temptations repeatedly, we may get the question, "Why do we get tempted and deluded so easily? Why are we so vulnerable?"

Gita wisdom answers that our vulnerability to temptation and delusion originates internally in our own immoral inclinations. More importantly, this vulnerability points compellingly towards a vital spiritual opportunity. Let's understand how.

All of us as souls are destined to rejoice eternally in a loving relationship with the all-attractive Lord, Sri Krishna. But our destiny depends on our desires. Only when we choose to love Krishna can we relish our eternal destiny. When we choose anything else, that desire misdirects our consciousness from spirit to matter, thereby depriving us of our glorious destiny. For impelling us to reclaim what we have lost, Krishna kindly entrusts us to a coach: Maya. She is his external energy, as the Bhagavad-gita (07.14) indicates.

Maya coaches us in the school of hard knocks. She incites us towards wrong choices and inflicts upon us their inevitable consequences. With her meticulous microscope, she zeroes in on our ungodly desires. By exposing us to the corresponding temptations, she magnifies those desires till they delude us. When we indulge in those desires and experience firsthand their futility, gradually with the help of Gita wisdom we realize the doomed nature of all material desires. This realization inspires us to leave no material desire in our heart to be found by Maya's microscope. To do this effectively, we need to offer all our heart's desires to Krishna by surrendering to him, as the same Gita verse exhorts. Over time this focused devotion enables us to regain our destined eternal ecstasy in loving Krishna.

Thus our vulnerability to temptation compels us to tap the opportunity to practice devotional service and thereby reclaim eternal happiness.

☙❧

This divine energy of Mine, consisting of the three modes of material nature, is difficult to overcome. But those who have surrendered unto Me can easily cross beyond it.

By living for animal pleasures, we violate our human rights

The Bhagavad-gita (07.15) uses the word *mudhas*, meaning asses, to refer to those unfortunate people who violate their own human rights.

Our society exalts as *human* rights those claims that nature automatically and adequately endows to animals: bodily protection and maintenance. Gita wisdom prods us to rethink whether we might have got our definition of human rights wrong. True, our mismanagement of nature's gifts has made these natural endowments rare for a large number of our fellow humans.

Nonetheless, our essential *human* right – the feature that differentiates us from animals and defines us as humans– is our faculty for philosophical thought: our ability to contemplate the meaning and purpose of our existence; and our capacity to enquire about our actual identity and final destiny. Our essential human right is the right to spiritual enlightenment.

If we let our lives be motivated and directed by the animal pleasures of food, sex, sleep and show of strength, then we cheat ourselves of the opportunity for enlightenment that our human body offers us. Thus, we end up violating our own human rights. Not only that, our unbridled pursuit of bodily pleasures causes us to consume disproportionate quantities of material resources. As our planet provides these resources in a finite capacity, our unnecessary consumption inevitably encroaches upon others' necessary quota of material resources. So, when we violate our human right in the spiritual sense of the word, we also collude in violating others' human rights in the material sense of the word.

Therefore, if we wish to contribute in stopping the violation of others' human rights, we can begin right now by checking ourselves from violating our own human right to enlightenment.

ॐ

Those miscreants who are grossly foolish, who are lowest among mankind, whose knowledge is stolen by illusion, and who partake of the atheistic nature of demons do not surrender unto Me.

Let devotion be your steering wheel, not your spare wheel

The demands and desires of our material life frequently press on us so insistently that our devotional life gets pushed to the background of our consciousness. We subconsciously treat our Krishna-connection like a spare wheel for the drive of life: "It's important; I need to give it time – but not right now. If things don't work out in my material life, then my Krishna consciousness is my backup plan."

We will benefit by connecting with Krishna at any level. Still, to realize our life's full potential, we need to give our Krishna-connection its due priority. We need to elevate it from the position of a spare wheel to that of a steering wheel. This essentially means that we make our Krishna-connection the central pivot of our life, the foremost focus around which we harmonize all our life's decisions. The Bhagavad-gita points to this when it (08.07) urges us to first fix our minds on Krishna and then shoulder our necessary worldly responsibilities.

We may doubt: "Won't this distract me from my worldly obligations and aspirations?" No, it will enable us to do them better.

Gita wisdom allays our doubts by pointing out that the Krishna-connection is life's best steering wheel. When we don't have this steering wheel, we inevitably use our default steering wheel: our own mind. And the mind being short-sighted and misguided is an extremely dangerous steering wheel. With it as our decision-maker, we end up at best underutilizing our talents and at worst ruining our entire life.

On the other hand, if we make our Krishna-connection our steering wheel, we will be able to curb our depraved mind, use our talents tangibly and contribute effectively in this world – and also travel smoothly and swiftly towards life's ultimate destination.

ॐ

Therefore, Arjuna, you should always think of Me in the form of Krishna and at the same time carry out your prescribed duty of fighting. With your activities dedicated to Me and your mind and intelligence fixed on Me, you will attain Me without doubt.

Be not scared of the sacred

We may be held back in our spiritual quest by the subconscious apprehension that the advanced, sacred states of spiritual realization may be too difficult to attain or sustain. We may fear that the constant devotional remembrance of Krishna, as recommended repeatedly in the Bhagavad-gita, may be too impractical to attain or sustain: it might make us too other-worldly, thereby damaging our worldly prospects. Thus, we may be scared of the sacred.

Our fear originates in the misconception that the sacred states of consciousness require a permanent withdrawal from the world. The Gita recommends that the sacred vision permeate and motivate our action in the world when it (08.07) urges us to both remember Krishna and do our prescribed duties.

According to the Gita, the sacred is to be found not just in the silent sanctuary of our inner heart, but also in the thick of action in the outer world through devotional service to Krishna. If we have an enlightened service attitude, then we can see the material-seeming ups and downs of life as demonstrations of spiritual truths and as expressions of Krishna's love in action.

Of course, for us to preserve this devotional service attitude amidst the passions and pressures of worldly engagement, we need to balance our periods of external service with periods of withdrawal for focused remembrance of Krishna. Once we achieve this balance of outer service and inner remembrance, the excitement and fulfillment of life in the consciousness of the sacred starts enriching our heart.

When our heart is thus enriched, then we will realize that our past fears were entirely unfounded: the sacred is not something to be *scared* about, but is something to be *cared* about.

ॐ

Therefore, Arjuna, you should always think of Me in the form of Krishna and at the same time carry out your prescribed duty of fighting. With your activities dedicated to Me and your mind and intelligence fixed on Me, you will attain Me without doubt.

Devotion enables us to strike a deal between the extraordinary and the ordinary

As spiritual seekers living in a material body and a materialist culture, our lives have two sides: the spiritual and the material. Given that materialism is the common or ordinary way of living in our culture, our material side becomes our ordinary side, and our spiritual side becomes our extraordinary side.

Both these sides require our time. For effectively catering to both, we need to strike a deal between them in our own heart. To help us strike this deal, the Bhagavad-gita (08.07) offers us a broad recommendation: think of Krishna while doing our prescribed duties.

How can we think of Krishna while doing our worldly obligations that are usually not explicitly connected with him? By ensuring that our hearts are implicitly connected with him.

We can progressively connect ourselves with Krishna by reserving some time each day for exclusive and intensive attention to him through sadhana. Let's understand the rationale for this daily allocation.

We can't practically offer all our time to him directly as our material obligations need much of our time. Still, we can't, in the name of being practical, let these obligations encroach upon all of our time. To check their encroachment, we can remind ourselves that our spiritual side is extraordinary because it alone can grant us the supremely extraordinary result: eternal happiness. The material side, no matter how urgent it seems, can at best offer us only an ordinary result: a little bit material happiness followed by continued suffering in the cycle of birth and death. With this realistic understanding, we can arrive at our internal deal.

Once we commit to offer a certain amount of time regularly to Krishna, come what may, we will pleasantly discover that our clear intelligence and Krishna's grace will combine to make whatever comes much easier to manage.

❦

Therefore, Arjuna, you should always think of Me in the form of Krishna and at the same time carry out your prescribed duty of fighting. With your activities dedicated to Me and your mind and intelligence fixed on Me, you will attain Me without doubt.

Fasting is an opportunity for feasting

Some people think of fasting as a means of achieving mastery over their body. They fast to increase their willpower by refusing to let bodily appetites control them.

As spiritual seekers, if this self-centered motive seduces us, then we miss the devotional benefits of fasting, irrespective of whether our fast fails or succeeds. If we fail to fast due to not having enough willpower, then fasting becomes the cause of self-torture. If we succeed in fasting due to having enough willpower, then fasting becomes the medium for expressing and expanding our false ego.

To avoid this lose-lose dilemma, we need to shift our focus from self-centeredness to Krishna-centeredness. The Bhagavad-gita (09.14) points to this divine focus when it asserts that the great souls complement their resolve for strict vows with constant glorification of Krishna. Concentration on Krishna changes our vision of fasting: instead of seeing it as an opportunity to demonstrate our willpower, we see it as an opportunity to experience the power of the non-material nourishment latent in his remembrance. Actually, Krishna consciousness can satisfy us far more than the best food –at any time and at all times. However, we don't usually experience this satisfaction. Why? Because to get this satisfaction, we need to pay the price of focusing our consciousness on Krishna. We have little impetus to pay this price when multiple alternative sources of satisfaction are available for us – as happens on normal days.

Fasting cuts us off from most other sources of satisfaction, thereby making remembrance of Krishna not an optional choice, but a vital necessity. When this necessity causes us to fill our consciousness with him, then we discover to our delight that we are experiencing not the agony of fasting from food, but the joy of feasting on his divine remembrance.

☙❧

Always chanting My glories, endeavoring with great determination, bowing down before Me, these great souls perpetually worship Me with devotion.

When the immediate encroaches repeatedly on the ultimate, we need an immediate reality check

We often get caught in the exigencies and emergencies that keep coming up in our lives. Despite knowing the importance of developing our relationship with Krishna, we are just not able to allocate time for it. When this unfortunate pattern becomes repetitive, it is a sure sign that the immediate is becoming the enemy of the ultimate. In other words, the urgent this-worldly to-dos are encroaching on the time meant for the important other-worldly must-dos.

No doubt, emergencies do crop up occasionally; at such times, our worldly obligations cannot and should not be avoided or postponed. But if emergencies crop up daily, then probably we need the emergency treatment more than the situations. It is we who by our unbalanced priorities are breeding emergencies.

To give ourselves an emergency treatment, we need to subject our priorities to an unsentimental reality check. We may feel that we are giving priority only to things that are unavoidable. If we give in to such feelings, then we will rarely be able to prioritize our relationship with Krishna.

To counter such feelings, we need to firmly remind ourselves that nothing is more unavoidable than death. At that fateful moment, our immediate worldly to-dos will no longer count, because the ultimate will have become the immediate. But by then it will be too late to do much about the ultimate.

We can allay our doubts about how we will be able to shoulder the immediate if we prioritize the ultimate by meditating on Krishna's assurance in the Bhagavad-gita (9.22) that he will personally take care of our needs.

That's why we need to voluntarily make the ultimate the immediate by allocating adequate time for it in our schedule. This will ensure that we don't leave the ultimate at the mercy of the immediate, thereby squandering the eternal for the sake of the temporary. Instead, we will maturely balance both for our holistic well-being.

※

For those who worship me with exclusive devotion, to them I carry what they lack and I preserve what they have.

Seek not a problem-free life – seek a purpose-filled life

The endless problems of life may wear us out and make us long for a problem-free life. Such a longing, however, is unrealistic and unfulfilling. Let's see how.

1. **Unrealistic**: The Bhagavad-gita (09.33) declares that the entire material existence is an intrinsically temporary and troublesome arena. Just as swimmers can never be dry in an ocean, we can never be problem-free in material existence.

2. **Unfulfilling**: We may dislike problems, but what we actually dread is purposeless problems. For example, patriots willingly, even eagerly, embrace the problem of a risk to their life for protecting their country. They don't dread becoming martyrs on a battlefield, but they dread becoming casualties in an accident before they reach the battlefield. The first is purposeful, fulfilling and even glorious, whereas the second is purposeless, unfulfilling and even ignominious.

Gita wisdom helps us discover that purpose is innate to life, even in its seemingly meaningless incidents and pointless accidents. Krishna is orchestrating all the events in the world and in our life to further our devotional growth, which is the ultimate purpose of existence.

Most of us conceive of material advancement as the natural purpose of our life, but this purpose can – and will – be frustrated irreparably by the very nature of the world. However, if we embrace spiritual advancement as our life's foremost purpose, then we will uncover within every situation the opportunity to enrich our devotion.

That's why the same Gita verse (09.33) that communicates such a gloomy assessment of material existence also conveys one of the most upbeat and uplifting messages of the Gita: the power of devotion can transport one and all to an eternal ecstatic life with Krishna.

ॐ

How much more this is so of the righteous brahmanas, the devotees, and the saintly kings. Therefore, having come to this temporary, miserable world, engage in loving service unto Me.

The loose ends never end

*M*any of us delay taking up spiritual life because of the pressures to improve our material life: our finances, fitness and family's prospects, for example. We tell ourselves, "I know I have to focus on spiritual life. But first I have to fix a few loose ends."

However, the process of fixing loose ends has no end. By the time we finish fixing our present set of loose ends, a set of earlier-fixed ends become loose and a whole new set of loose ends comes up. The Bhagavad-gita (09.33) acknowledges this permanently problematic nature of the world (*anityam asukham lokam*) and so urges us to practice devotional service (*imam prapya bhajasva mam*). Here, the Gita recommends not material pessimism, but intelligent optimism.

To appreciate the Gita's reasoning, we need to look at ourselves from a multi-life perspective. We have spent all our previous lives struggling to fix loose ends – and what has that struggle given us? This life's struggle to fix loose ends. And what will this struggle give us? Future lifetime(s) of struggles to fix loose ends.

This way, the loose ends will never end. That's why letting our material obligations monopolize our time is tragically self-defeating.

We need to balance our material obligations and our spiritual opportunities by allocating time for both according to a thoughtful plan. Within the time allocated for our material obligations, we act as diligently and competently as possible. But irrespective of whether these efforts are successful or not, we uncompromisingly offer a basic minimum time to Krishna through exclusive engagement in devotional service. That offering – and that offering alone – will end our struggle to fix loose ends by taking us to a place where there are no loose ends to fix, a place free from all material anxiety: Vaikuntha.

ॐ

How much more this is so of the righteous brahmanas, the devotees, and the saintly kings. Therefore, having come to this temporary, miserable world, engage in loving service unto Me.

Find the balance between fidelity and flexibility by sincerity

When we try to live according to traditional devotional culture in our contemporary material surroundings, we face a constant challenge: "How much do I stick to the tradition and how much do I adapt to my surroundings?"

To meet this challenge, we need to tread the fine line that balances fidelity and flexibility. We connect with the tradition through fidelity, our faithfulness to its essential and inviolable principles. We connect with our surroundings through our flexibility, our readiness to adapt to the exigencies and opportunities of our surroundings.

Treading the fine line that balances fidelity and flexibility may seem like walking on a tightrope, a tense and ticklish endeavor at best. Fortunately, we have the example of advanced spiritual preceptors who walk across the tightrope with ease and grace.

How do they discover with such felicity the balance between fidelity and flexibility? By their sincerity.

They realize that the essence of devotion lies not just in fidelity and flexibility, but in the inner connection with Krishna. They refine their Krishna-connection by fidelity to the principles provided by the tradition. But they know that this Krishna-connection is to be lived not just in the memory of the past, but also in the dynamics of the present. So they see their surroundings as an opportunity to live in the light of that inner connection, and to also share that light with the world. By their inner connection with Krishna, they receive his guidance, as is promised in the Gita (10.10), about how best to integrate flexibility into their devotional repertoire.

By learning from their example and cultivating sincerity, we can also, by Krishna's guidance, learn to balance fidelity and flexibility.

CR80

To those who are constantly devoted to serving Me with love, I give the understanding by which they can come to Me.

Time is irrecoverable and unstorable

The great diplomat Chanakya Pandita pointed out that one moment of time is more valuable than wealth equivalent to millions of gold coins. Why? Because lost wealth can be regained, whereas lost time can never be regained. It is irrecoverably gone.

Time is not only irrecoverable, but also unstorable. We can choose whether to spend our wealth or not; but we cannot choose whether to spend our time; with the passing of each moment, it is automatically, unavoidably spent. All that we can choose about time is how to spend it.

The Bhagavad-gita points to this inexorable nature of time. It states (10.30) that time is the greatest of all subduers and is, in fact, a manifestation of Krishna in the realm of subduers.

To avoid being subdued by time, we need to utilize our time for rendering devotional service to Krishna. Then we will be able to gradually realize our spiritual nature as souls and revive our pure love for Krishna. Eventually, we will be able to return to the spiritual world that is forever beyond the destructive power of time.

Still, as long as we are in the material world, time always remains irrecoverable and unstorable. That's why we need to be extremely meticulous in investing our time properly. And our greatest time-waster is our own mind.

When the mind prompts us to take up any activity, one way to ensure a wise choice is to ask this self-probing question: "If someone would ask me to spend money on this, would I be persuaded to do so? If not, then should I be persuaded by my mind to spend something even more valuable than money on this activity?"

By thus guarding and investing our time, we can safely attain life's supreme destination in the least possible time.

❈❦❈

Among the Daitya demons I am the devoted Prahlada, among subduers I am time, among beasts I am the lion, and among birds I am Garuda.

Pride demands and blames, humility begs and waits

"Why am I not advancing fast enough?" This question sometimes troubles our heart and makes us feel dissatisfied with our spiritual lives.

This dissatisfaction can lead us to unwittingly playing the blame game in which we try to find a scapegoat for our slow spiritual advancement. Generally this mental blame game finds one or more of the following three targets:

1. Krishna: "He is not compassionate enough or not helpful enough."

2. Bhakti: "This process doesn't work or it's not strong enough."

3. Ourselves: "I am too fallen; I will never make spiritual advancement."

However, this blame game never works, because it is played out on a platform of error. None of the above three charges leveled by the mind are true. Krishna is super-eager for us to attain him; bhakti is the supremely potent of all processes for spiritual advancement; and we are never so fallen as to be spiritually irreformable. The platform of error in this blame game is our wrong presumption: we presume that we deserve spiritual advancement and our blame game is an indirect demand for that advancement. But demands proceed from the platform of pride, whereas bhakti is founded on the platform of humility – of accepting that we don't deserve spiritual advancement.

When we are humble, we beg for the divine grace that rewards even the undeserving. We are ready to wait for that grace to be bestowed according to Krishna's sweet will. Such a humble attitude is poignantly exemplified by Arjuna in the Bhagavad-gita (11.04) while seeking a special favor from Krishna, "If you feel i am qualified, kindly bestow your grace on me."

ॐ

If You think that I am able to behold Your cosmic form, O my Lord, O master of all mystic power, then kindly show me that unlimited universal Self.

Don't let the ticking of the clock become tricking by the clock

*O*urs is a clock-driven society. We have so many things to do and so little time to do it in that we frequently feel pressured to beat the clock – or to at least meet the clock. The clock controls our life much more than we do.

Our clock-controlled condition demonstrates a fundamental spiritual truth: we cannot get away from the control of Krishna. The Bhagavad-gita (11.32) states that time is a manifestation of Krishna. When we don't submit willingly to him, then we have to submit unwillingly to his *kala-rupa* (form as time).

Due to our unwillingness to submit to Krishna, our awareness of reality becomes trickily distorted. We become acutely conscious of the ticking of the clock – the passing of minutes and hours. But we remain abjectly unconscious of the ticking of time – the passing of years and decades. We become obsessed with our short-term and medium-term interests of succeeding materially in the world, but stay oblivious to our long-term interest of developing a relationship with Krishna. If we don't correct our perception disorder before our time runs out, we may sadly discover that the ticking of time has become the tricking by time.

Fortunately, correcting our perception disorder is not difficult. We begin by reminding ourselves regularly that time is a manifestation of Krishna. We proceed by cultivating the awareness that our time is not ours; it is Krishna appearing to gift us an opportunity for attaining eternal happiness by remembering and serving him. This sacred vision of time empowers us to stop material exigencies from stealing away the time meant for our spiritual enrichment. When we thus offer Krishna as time to Krishna as the Lord of our heart, then we can be assured that time by its ticking is taking us towards existence's ultimate treasure: Krishna.

લ80

Time I am, the great destroyer of the worlds.

Krishna is not an optional filler in our life – he is its central purpose

*O*ur time is among our most wanted resources. Our fast-paced culture places so many demands on us that fitting all the items on our to-do list into a twenty-four-hour day is something like fitting a roomful of objects into a suitcase. It *seems* impossible because it is impossible.

The only way ahead is to shortlist. Even in our abbreviated list, the sequence of filling is important. If we put the big objects in the suitcase first, then we can fit in the smaller objects in between. However, if we put the small objects first, then we just can't fit in the big objects later. Similarly, if we allot time for our big to-dos, those things that require substantial and quality time, then we can fit the smaller to-dos in between. However, if we allot time to the smaller to-dos first, then we will have no time left for the big to-dos.

As aspiring devotees, we consciously know that our devotional activities like chanting and studying scripture are big to-dos. Yet while allotting time, we tend to subconsciously place these activities last by thinking: "I will do these whenever I get time." This thought implies that we are treating Krishna as a filler in between our other more-important priorities. Moreover, as 'whenever' includes the possibility of 'never', we end up treating him as an optional filler.

The Bhagavad-gita (11.55) urges us to make Krishna our supreme goal and our foremost priority (*mat-parah*). This may seem impractical initially. But if we just try to start by taking a modest leap of faith, Krishna will reciprocate in many unexpected ways by giving us the intelligence and the ability to adjust and accelerate other things. That divine reciprocation, indeed, is the magical dynamism of Krishna consciousness.

ᙜᙝ

My dear Arjuna, he who engages in My pure devotional service, free from the contaminations of fruitive activities and mental speculation, he who works for Me, who makes Me the supreme goal of his life, and who is friendly to every living being—he certainly comes to Me.

When we do what we can, Krishna helps us to do what we can't

Spiritual life sometimes presents us with standards that seem impossible to follow. For example, we may feel that thinking of Krishna constantly is impractical.

Certainly, many spiritual standards are too lofty to be reached by our solitary efforts. But our efforts don't have to be solitary. We can have assistance, the best assistance, Krishna's personal assistance. Because he is omnipotent, he can enable us to do that which we could never have done otherwise.

Krishna wants to help us, but he doesn't want to infringe on our free will. That's why he doesn't force his help on us. He waits till we show him unambiguously that we want his help.

How can we show that to him? By trying our best to do the very activity for doing which we need his help. We may not be able to think of Krishna *always*, but we can surely think of him *sometimes*. We may not be able to chant all our rounds attentively, but we can surely chant some mantras attentively. At the very least, we can definitely avoid consciously seeking distractions during our mantra meditation.

By thus taking baby steps towards Krishna, we show him our desire to come closer to him. And when he sees the sincerity and the intensity of our desire, he not only empowers us to take giant leaps towards him, but also comes personally to carry us to him. This is the proclamation of the Bhagavad-gita (12.06-07), wherein Krishna declares that he becomes the swift deliverer of those who strive to fix their minds on him.

Meditating on this promise of Krishna can give us undying, unfading hope.

※

But those who worship Me, giving up all their activities unto Me and being devoted to Me without deviation, engaged in devotional service and always meditating upon Me, having fixed their minds upon Me, O son of Pritha—for them I am the swift deliverer from the ocean of birth and death.

Humility means to accept but not expect respect

We may sometimes wonder, "How can I stay humble amidst the devotional culture of respectfulness? If nobody would notice me, it would be easier to be humble. But when others address me with respectful honorifics like 'Prabhu' or 'Mataji', offer obeisances and sometimes even glorify me, how can I possibly stay humble?"

By accepting, but not expecting, respect, answers Gita wisdom. This attitude is indicated in the precise word for humility used by the Bhagavad-gita (13.08: *amaanitvam*), which Srila Prabhupada insightfully explains as to "not be anxious to have the satisfaction of being honored by others."

To free us from anxiety for respect, bhakti wisdom helps us see all living beings as the beloved children of Krishna. We see all devotees as his especially beloved children, for they have voluntarily chosen to live according to his will. This vision underlies the devotional culture of respectfulness.

With this vision in mind, when others offer us respect, we can accept it with the understanding that they are seeing us as connected with Krishna and so are offering respects to us and through us to him. This understanding will reinforce our internal Krishna consciousness, thereby increasing our humility; the more we become aware of Krishna and his greatness, the more we become aware of our own smallness.

Moreover, just as others see our connection with Krishna, we can see their connection with him, and offer them our respects, good wishes and prayers, as appropriate. This too will boost our devotional consciousness and consequently our humility. However, if we expect respect from others, we will stay respect-conscious and won't be able to become Krishna conscious.

Thus by seeing the devotional culture of respectfulness as a facility to share Krishna consciousness, we can not only safeguard but even strengthen our humility.

ॐ

Humility; pridelessness; nonviolence; tolerance; simplicity; approaching a bona fide spiritual master; cleanliness; steadiness; self-control…—all these I declare to be knowledge, and besides this whatever there may be is ignorance.

Information is not enough in formation of character

We may have seen normal, sensible people suddenly act abnormally and insensibly. They knew well the harms of what they were doing – or at least they knew it before and after their deed. Yet they did it anyway. Why?

Gita wisdom helps us understand that our actions are determined not just by the information we carry in our head, but also by the character we cultivate in our heart. The Bhagavad-gita (13.08-12) describes knowledge in telling terms: not as the degrees that comprise our information base, but as the qualities that comprise our character base.

How can we develop this character-centered knowledge?

Gita wisdom aids us in forming and reforming our character by showing us the fastest expressway to developing virtuous qualities: bhakti-yoga. By our own individual, determined efforts, we may be able to develop some virtues. But we will get quicker and better results if we complement those efforts with a parallel effort to connect with Krishna, who possesses all qualities in their fullest and best manifestation.

The easiest way to connect with Krishna is through mantra meditation. Far from being a mere ritual utterance of some sound, mantra meditation is a subtle and sophisticated science that uses sacred sound as a bridge to link us with Krishna. When we focus our consciousness on his holy names, we pave the way for him to manifest in our heart. His manifestation in our heart dissipates all negative, self-destructive traits, just as the sun's rising dissipates darkness. This devotional illumination not only protects us from our self-defeating impulses, but also empowers us to become channels for Krishna to share the same illumination and protection with others.

Being able to help ourselves and help others in the best way – isn't that the essence of character?

ॐ

The importance of self-realization; and philosophical search for the Absolute Truth—all these I declare to be knowledge, and besides this whatever there may be is ignorance

Give your prime time to the highest bidder, not the loudest bidder

Television channels charge phenomenally for their prime time. Knowing that maximum TV audience is available during this time, they allocate those slots to the highest bidder: the programs that provide maximum returns.

For us spiritual seekers, the early morning hours are our spiritual prime time. The Bhagavad-gita (14.06) indicates that, among the three modes of material nature, the mode of goodness is most conducive for cultivating spirituality. Gita wisdom recognizes that the mode of goodness naturally prevails in the atmosphere during the early morning hours.

Moreover, as we have not yet entered the thick of action of the day, we can offer the maximum attention and best reception to Krishna in the morning. That's why, if we try to engage in devotional activities like mantra meditation and scriptural study during this time, these activities become easier to do and relish. Additionally, they bear quicker and greater results in terms of increasing our sagacity and purity. Therefore, devotional activities are by far the highest bidder for our prime time.

Sadly however, we often give our prime time not to the *highest* bidder, but the *loudest* bidder, which, usually, is the mind. If it starts yelling, "Sleep," we give in. If it starts screaming, "Read the news," we acquiesce. The mind thus promotes innumerable alternatives to Krishna. Almost never do these deserve our prime time. And some of them don't deserve any time at all.

To reject the mind's coercive techniques, we can learn from TV channels. Just as they would never allocate their prime time based on the decibel level of the bidders, neither should we. By recollecting our priorities, we can say a firm no to the mind: "Nothing doing. My prime time is not so cheap. It is precious and is meant for my supreme priority, Krishna."

ॐ

O sinless one, the mode of goodness, being purer than the others, is illuminating, and it frees one from all sinful reactions. Those situated in that mode become conditioned by a sense of happiness and knowledge.

The body, mind and soul are all best geared for meditation in the morning

Some people ask: "Krishna resides in our heart and is available at all times. Then why emphasize morning for connecting with him?"

Because we are best available in the morning, answers Gita wisdom.

Though Krishna is always available in our hearts, we can connect with him only by turning inwards. Doing that is not easy, given the fact that our lives are so externally, materially directed. That's why we need to choose the time when the difficulty level is the least. That time is morning because then all three levels of our being – physical, mental and spiritual – are best tuned for inner exploration. We are:

1. **Uncluttered physically**: As the world has not yet started off on its daily round of passionate activities, one thing after another is not rushing at us uncontrollably.

2. **Fresh mentally**: As we haven't yet had to deal with daily life's routine stresses, we don't feel irritated or exhausted; our mental energy is still intact.

3. **Receptive spiritually**: The natural vibrations in the morning are in the mode of goodness, which, the Bhagavad-gita (14.06) indicates, is the most illuminating and purifying of all the modes of material nature. Moreover, the early morning hours, called *brahma-muhurta*, are surcharged with spiritually potent vibrations. Both these supportive factors make us most spiritually receptive in the morning.

When we tap these three aids and connect substantially with Krishna in the morning, we experience his presence in the foreground of our consciousness. That experience helps us during the rest of the day, making it easier for us to be conscious of him, at least as a background presence. Thus, we get tangible realization of his round-the-clock availability. Without such realization, we may say that Krishna is available at all times but we will not experience him at any time.

CRSO

O sinless one, the mode of goodness, being purer than the others, is illuminating, and it frees one from all sinful reactions. Those situated in that mode become conditioned by a sense of happiness and knowledge.

Our feelings are not always our feelings

*T*he Bhagavad-gita (14.22) points to a fascinating thought-exercise that involves taking on the role of an observer towards our feelings. Let's understand the whys and hows of such a thought-exercise.

Sometimes our mind gets flooded by negative feelings like anger towards an irritating colleague or hopelessness over an unsolvable problem. When such feelings arise, we often identify with them, get carried away and act in ways that we regret later. Or when faced with such feelings repeatedly, we start fretting: "Why do I get such feelings? Why do I have to fight them so often? Why can't I win the fight against them once and for all?" Such negative feelings imprison us in an under-performing, self-pitying mode of functioning.

Gita wisdom frees us from such under-performance by targeting its root: our misidentification with our feelings. We can challenge and counter this misidentification by taking on, as this Gita verse recommends, the role of an observer towards those feelings. When we observe them dispassionately and intelligently, we will discover that they are usually not expressions of our authentic values and deep concerns – expressions that need to be carefully addressed. We will realize that most of them are merely projections of changing social fads and individual moods – projections that can and should be firmly neglected.

Observing our material feelings will be difficult as long as we depend on them for gratification. That's why the less we delight in material enjoyment and the more we relish spiritual fulfilment, the more easily we will be able to observe our material feelings.

When we thus recognize that many of our feelings are not actually our feelings, huge amounts of our inner energy will be released for serving Krishna, enabling us to do tangible good for others and pave the way to our lasting spiritual happiness.

ॐ

The Supreme Personality of Godhead said: O son of Pandu, he who does not hate illumination, attachment and delusion when they are present or long for them when they disappear…—such a person is said to have transcended the modes of nature.

Navigate the troughs of consciousness by focusing on the peak

As aspiring devotees, we may find the state of our consciousness oscillating up and down like a sine wave. We may feel sometimes attracted and sometimes averse to Krishna. The feelings of attraction and aversion correspond respectively to the peaks and the troughs of the sine wave of our consciousness.

We enjoy the peaks. During these positive phases, we find ourselves cheerful and purposeful. We feel cheerful because our attraction to Krishna gives us inner satisfaction. And we feel purposeful because our satisfaction convinces us that we are on the right path and inspires us to press on enthusiastically.

Conversely, we dread the troughs. During these negative phases, we find ourselves cheerless and purposeless. We feel cheerless because our aversion to Krishna drains away all our inner satisfaction. And we feel purposeless because our inner dryness makes us doubt whether we are on the right path and whether we might be better off taking an about-turn.

Gita wisdom allays our doubts by identifying the cause of our oscillatory feelings. They arise from the three modes, which influence all living beings in the material world, even aspiring devotees. The Bhagavad-gita (14.23) urges us to take the role of observers while dealing with the natural and predictable effects of the modes. This role helps us understand that what we consider as our inner feelings of aversion, the troughs, are actually outer influences of the modes. More importantly, we recognize that the feelings of attraction, the crests, are our original feelings. Our present experiences of those feelings are the precursors of what awaits us eternally if we just persevere in devotional service, thereby transcending the modes.

By such philosophical contemplation and devotional perseverance we can navigate through the troughs and advance steadily towards a perennial peak of constant attraction for Krishna.

৵৶

He who ...is unwavering and undisturbed through all these reactions of the material qualities, remaining neutral and transcendental, knowing that the modes alone are active...—such a person is said to have transcended the modes of nature.

If we wait for inspiration, we are waiters, not worshipers

*M*any of us wait for external inspiration to intensify our devotional practices like chanting. When we don't get such inspiration, we let our moods determine the quality of our devotional practices. However, the caliber of our devotional practices will determine our eternal destiny, and our destiny is too important to be left to something as fickle as our moods.

If we wait for external inspiration, we may be kept waiting for a long time; we will be waiters for who knows how long. Our destiny deserves something much better than such passivity. We need to become proactive worshipers who worship Krishna without becoming distracted by moods. The Bhagavad-gita (14.26) assures us that if we don't let our devotional service be interrupted by the modes and their resultant moods, then we will gradually go beyond the reach of the modes.

To ensure that our devotional practices don't become interrupted when inspiration is unavailable externally, we need to mine it internally through two sources:

1. **Convictions:** Patients who are convinced that a medicine is potent take it even when it doesn't taste good because they know it will do good. By scriptural study and personal contemplation, we can strengthen our conviction that our devotional practices will heal us spiritually, and can thereby stick to them even if they don't feel good.

2. **Commitments:** Devotional life is centered on relationships. Just as our family and office relationships depend on our keeping our commitments, so does our relationship with Krishna and his devotees. By contemplating the importance of our devotional relationships, we can inspire ourselves to honor their associated commitments.

When we base our devotional practices on our inner convictions and commitments, we will discover that we have struck a rich vein of unfading inspiration.

ॐ

One who engages in full devotional service, unfailing in all circumstances, at once transcends the modes of material nature and thus comes to the level of Brahman.

Lust is our longest and worst life-partner– divorce it

Lust is our longest life-partner – from the first hints of adolescence to the last gasps of old age, even to the death-bed; from the moment of waking to the moment of sleeping and, of course, into the sleep.

Lust is also our worst life-partner: no one else promises so much and delivers so little. It paints its pleasures in the most glowing colors, yet the actual enjoyment is pathetically paltry, no matter how much we crave and scheme to increase it.

If any other normal life-partner had betrayed us so many times, we would have divorced that person long ago. But not lust. Nothing breaks our trust in lust. Sometimes, when its deceptions land us in excessive trouble, we profess to banish it. But we still leave a secret place for it at the back of our mind; we still believe that somehow, someday it will keep its promises.

Why do we trust lust so naively? Because we don't know any other source of happiness.

The Bhagavad-gita presents us that alternative: Krishna. Gita wisdom explains that lust is a perversion of our original love for Krishna, and outlines the process of devotional service that provides experiences of richer, deeper happiness.

If we want those experiences to last, we need to divorce lust, as the Bhagavad-gita (15.5: *vinivrtta kamah*) indicates. Why? Because lust is a material emotion. It drags our thoughts away from Krishna, who resides at the spiritual level.

Initially divorcing lust may seem impossible. But it becomes possible when we focus not on disconnecting from lust but on connecting with Krishna. If we offer Krishna just a fraction of the trust that we have offered lust, we will soon discover that he will be a far better life-partner, in fact, the best life-partner – and an eternal life-partner at that.

ଓଃ୫ଠ

Those who are free from false prestige, illusion and false association, who understand the eternal, who are done with material lust, who are freed from the dualities of happiness and distress, and who, unbewildered, know how to surrender unto the Supreme Person attain to that eternal kingdom.

Don't assume that faultfinding is an obligation – it may well be a temptation

The Bhagavad-gita (16.02) mentions that the godly are averse to faultfinding. Gita wisdom explains the rationale. All of us have a godly side and a godless side. The godly side begets virtues and the godless side, faults. When we delight in finding others' faults, that delight symptomizes our ungodly mentality which sees only the godless faulty side of others and not their godly virtuous side. Such an ungodly fault-finding mentality makes us not god-conscious, but godlessness-conscious – as do all temptations. Therefore, such faultfinding is nothing but a temptation, hence the need to be averse to it.

Of course, in some real-life situations, faultfinding may not be a temptation; it may well be an obligation. The Gita hints at such situations by enjoining not a ban on faultfinding, but an aversion. Sometimes the faults of others may harm them or those connected with them. So, to help them, we may have to tell them their faults. Or if they are incorrigible, we may have to tell their faults to those who may be otherwise harmed. In intent, this is essentially education, though in content, it may be fault-finding.

Even in such situations, we shouldn't assume that we are finding faults as an obligation – it may well be a temptation if we delight in it. Moreover, our attitude will inevitably reflect in our words, gestures and expressions. When others detect or even suspect that we are sadistically motivated, they will neglect or reject our attempts to help them and may even become hostile to us.

That's why we need to pray to Krishna to give us the right words to express the faults of others sensitively, not judgmentally; and to give them the open-mindedness to understand and the willpower to reform. Such a careful and prayerful attitude will increase the likelihood that our faultfinding is not unproductive or counter-productive but productive.

ೞಕೋ

...Nonviolence; truthfulness; freedom from anger; renunciation; tranquility; aversion to faultfinding; compassion for all living entities; freedom from covetousness; gentleness; modesty; steady determination...—these transcendental qualities, O son of Bharata, belong to godly men endowed with divine nature.

Pride (P + Ride) takes us on a Perilous Ride

The Bhagavad-gita (16.04) states that pride is a characteristic of the ungodly. Pride originates in the misconception that we permanently own the things that we only temporarily possess: talents and abilities, positions and possessions. Intoxicating us with our temporary possessions, pride sends us off on a dangerous ego trip, being propelled by the imagination that we are superior to others and independent of Krishna.

The ride that pride takes us on is perilous from the beginning to the end. From the moment we become proud, we sentence ourselves to loneliness and insecurity. We feel lonely because our very desire for superiority alienates us from those around us, as well as from Krishna. We feel insecure because of the fear that our sources of pride may be taken away from us at any moment. Hoping to get rid of the insecurity, we bury our fears by increasing our external bluff and bravado. Tragically, this only increases our loneliness, which in turn makes us more insecure, thereby activating a vicious cycle.

The ride of pride is even more perilous in the end. Why? Because when pride unceremoniously dumps us off, that is, when we lose our sources of pride, we wake up to the horrifying reality that we have hugely alienated ourselves from all those who loved us – including especially Krishna.

That's why it's best to never climb aboard the ride of pride – or to get off as soon as we realize what we have got into. Gita wisdom makes this easier by offering us a far better ride: the ride back to Krishna in the plane of devotional service. Once we experience the intimacy and the security of his presence in our heart, pride will no longer allure us.

ॐ

Pride, arrogance, conceit, anger, harshness and ignorance—these qualities belong to those of demoniac nature, O son of Pritha.

Let our words be like windows, not walls

*W*ords are indispensable tools for communicating our ideas and feelings with others. These verbal tools have become increasingly critical in our hi-tech age of phones and emails that don't allow the non-verbal forms of communication possible in direct, personal conversations.

Our words can act as windows or as walls. As windows, they give others a clear view of our thoughts and feelings, and facilitate understanding. As walls, they block others' vision of our perspective, and breed misunderstandings.

How can we ensure that our words act as windows not walls? By applying the guidelines of the Bhagavad-gita (17.15) for tapping the power of words: speak words that are non-agitating, truthful, pleasing, beneficial and scripturally-based.

Let's focus on the first guideline. When we speak in ways that agitate others, their emotions arise as instinctive reflexes for self-defense. This relegates their rational faculty to the background, leaving us with little or no facility for having an intelligent discussion. Soon the conversation degenerates into a shouting match or a name-calling competition. Over time, our words end as bricks in the Chinese wall that separates us.

To avoid such confrontations, do we have to suppress genuine facts or authentic concerns? No, because the same Gita verse also urges us to speak truthfully. The recommendation that we speak gently is meant to ensure that the form of our message doesn't unnecessarily alienate others from its content.

How do we balance sensitiveness and truthfulness? By patience and prayerfulness. Before starting a high-stakes conversation, we can pause to gather our spiritual bearings; remind ourselves that this situation, like all situations, is ultimately an arrangement of Krishna to deepen our wisdom and devotion; and pray for his guidance. This devotional reorientation will empower us to use words that break walls and build windows.

☙❧

Austerity of speech consists in speaking words that are truthful, pleasing, beneficial, and not agitating to others, and also in regularly reciting Vedic literature.

Careless words can cause cureless wounds

The Bhagavad-gita (17.15) explains that speaking the truth in a way that is beneficial, pleasing and non-agitating is the discipline of speech. Neglecting this verbal discipline can have grave consequences, as most of us will have witnessed or even experienced. Harsh words can break hearts and wreck relationships. Even when the effects are not so devastating, still careless words can intensely scar the hearts of those to whom they are directed. These scars are often severe and sometimes incurable – especially if the inconsiderate words come from loved ones.

It is not that we don't know about these dire consequences of inconsiderate words. Being aware, we often resolve to avoid uttering such words. Yet, when we feel provoked, we frequently find ourselves, to our dismay, lashing out with the very kind of words that we had resolved to avoid.

How can we check ourselves during the heat of the moment? The same Gita verse also mentions regular recitation of scriptures as the last discipline of speech. This verbal discipline reveals the secret that can empower us to follow the preceding disciplines. When we regularly recite scriptures and also the holy names that are the consistent and conclusive gist of scriptures, we become connected with the almighty power of Krishna. This power enables us to take charge of ourselves when our lower self incites us to speak insensitively.

We can use whatever willpower we presently have to cultivate this critical discipline of recitation of divine sounds– both on a regular basis and especially when we feel provoked. This discipline will empower us to speak sensitively so as to address problems without attacking people.

☙❧

Austerity of speech consists in speaking words that are truthful, pleasing, beneficial, and not agitating to others, and also in regularly reciting Vedic literature.

Conviction and purification take us from the poison to the nectar

As devotees who wish to rise from the material level to the spiritual level, we often face the question, "How do I sustain myself during the long transitional phase when I have to abstain from material enjoyment but can't yet experience spiritual fulfillment?"

The Bhagavad-gita (18.37) acknowledges that this initial phase is like poison but reassures us that we will relish nectar permanently on reaching the spiritual level. To tolerate the poison and penetrate till the nectar, we need conviction and purification.

1. **Conviction**: Intellectual conviction helps us understand that material enjoyment being temporary is undesirable, whereas spiritual fulfillment being eternal is eminently desirable. By thus facilitating us to see beyond appearances to consequences, conviction enables us to stay away from anti-devotional material indulgences. Being convinced that far greater than the material enjoyment we have given up is the spiritual happiness awaiting us ahead, we persevere optimistically on the spiritual path. To deepen our conviction, we need to study scriptures scrutinizingly and ponder their teachings introspectively.

2. **Purification**: As souls, spiritual fulfillment is natural for us, whereas material enjoyment is unnatural. But when we are covered by impurities such as lust, anger and greed, our tastes become perverted, and we seek happiness in sensual indulgences, although they don't give us any actual happiness. The more we become purified, the more our original taste gets restored. We start finding spiritual fulfillment to be familiar and natural, and material enjoyment to be alien and artificial. To become purified, we need to seriously cultivate remembrance of Krishna, who is supremely pure and supremely purifying.

Thus, by conviction and purification, we can move from the initial poison to the eventual, perennial nectar.

೫೯೦

That which in the beginning may be just like poison but at the end is just like nectar and which awakens one to self-realization is said to be happiness in the mode of goodness.

Go beyond denial and dismissal to determination

"I fell from the scriptural standards yet again. What should I do now?" We often respond to such predicaments by either denial or dismissal. In denial, we hide our failures from others and even ourselves. In dismissal, we reject the scriptural standards as impractical or irrelevant. Either way, we pretend as if nothing is wrong.

However, our concealed shortcoming is like a festering wound hidden under good-looking clothes. Somebody finds out, or over time as the wound worsens, the pain becomes intolerable. Similarly, when we conceal our moral lapses, we are either discovered or we find the pretense unbearable due to guilt or tastelessness.

Fortunately, Gita wisdom offers us a better way: change the way we see moral lapses. We usually take them personally as deficiencies in our very self, so we don't consult anyone as we fear the resulting disgrace. However, we wouldn't be so fearful if we were re-educated to see our moral lapses as signs of an external infection, not as blemishes of our core self. The Bhagavad-gita (18.40) re-educates us to understand that everyone in material existence is impelled by material nature through its three modes. We act immorally when the infection of the modes becomes excessive. Nonetheless, we always remain at our core untainted souls with the potential for purity.

When we thus understand the problem rationally, we neither waste time in denial or dismissal, nor dissipate emotional energy in concealment or embarrassment. Instead, we become determined to remove the infection by all necessary means – including consulting a mature spiritual guide. Our determination enables us to cultivate systematic, sustained, sober remembrance of Krishna. This gives us a higher happiness that makes immoral pleasures unappealing and distasteful, thereby uprooting moral lapses.

ॐ

There is no being existing, either here or among the demigods in the higher planetary systems, which is freed from these three modes born of material nature.

If we can't shun senselessness, we can at least shun the senseless mind

*P*racticing devotional life means embarking on an inward devotional journey to connect with Krishna. On this journey, the mind poses the primary roadblock by constantly craving for external pleasures.

For removing this roadblock, we can derive a two-pronged strategy from the Bhagavad-gita (18.42):

1. *Shama* **(Peacefulness)**: This is the strategy for converting the mind. We draw on the strength of our intellectual convictions to show the mind the true nature of material pleasures: despite all their promises, they disappoint us at best and devastate us at worst. Then we contemplate the taste of our devotional experiences to show the mind their superiority as alternative sources of happiness. Thus, we let the mind see for itself the emptiness of material pleasures and the richness of spiritual pleasures. When confronted with this undeniable contrast, the mind shuns worldly cravings as senseless and becomes peaceful.

2. *Dama* **(Sense Control)**: This is the strategy for controlling the mind if it refuses to get converted. Sometimes despite all our logical presentations, the mind remains illogically addicted to material pleasures. When we are blocked by such a senseless mind, we need to respond in kind by blocking its sources of nourishment. The mind derives its food from the images provided by the senses. If we resolve rigidly to never indulge sensually in the pleasures that the mind is craving for, then it eventually runs out of food and shuts up. During the transitional period when the mind is still adamant, we can neglect it by keeping ourselves fully engaged in devotionally purposeful activities.

By this dual strategy for converting or at least controlling the mind, we can remove the mental roadblocks on our devotional journey.

❄

Peacefulness, self-control, austerity, purity, tolerance, honesty, knowledge, wisdom and religiousness—these are the natural qualities by which the brahmanas work.

Don't waste time on the mind's futile pastime: comparison

As soon as people enter our familiarity perimeter, our mind starts comparing us with them. Comparison is its favorite pastime.

However, unlike Krishna's pastimes that lead to purification, inspiration and liberation, the comparison pastime leads only to contamination, depression and detention. Let's see how:

1. **Contamination**: If comparison makes us feel inferior to others, then we get victimized by an inferiority complex. If comparison makes us feel superior to others, then we get seduced by a superiority complex. Both these complexes contaminate our heart with self-centeredness.

2. **Depression**: The media exploits our mind's addiction to comparison by holding aloft the best specimens within any comparison category: individuals with the best bodily contours, the best IQ scores, the best luxury products, and the best life-partners. Regular comparison with such ideal or idealized specimens makes us depressed, no matter how much we have.

3. **Detention**: Comparison may sometimes goad us to perform better, but that goading detains us at best in insecurity and at worst in futility. Even if we succeed in out-performing others, we remain insecure that someone may at any time out-perform us. And if we fail to out-perform others, then we feel that all our efforts have been futile.

The Bhagavad-gita (18.54) indicates that when we focus on our spiritual identity, "I am a soul whose happiness lies in loving and serving Krishna," then we realize that nothing material matters for our ultimate destiny. That realization enables us to see the futility of comparison, and empowers us to see all living beings equally, as parts of Krishna. This equal vision frees us to relish wholeheartedly remembrance of Krishna and his pastimes.

ॐ

One who is thus transcendentally situated at once realizes the Supreme Brahman and becomes fully joyful. He never laments or desires to have anything. He is equally disposed toward every living entity. In that state he attains pure devotional service unto Me.

Those who don't spare time for meditation squander time infrustration

"*I* just don't have time." This is how we often respond to suggestions that we commit ourselves to devotional practices such as mantra meditation.

No doubt, we all have a lot of things to do. Still, while coping with the burden of all this work, what takes our time is not just the work but also its burden. How does the burden take our time? By making us spend time on activities for relieving the burden. These activities may be watching TV, playing video-games, surfing the net, gossiping, overeating and oversleeping.

Such activities may offer us a break, but they don't internally rejuvenate us. Sometimes, they leave us frustrated, thereby making us more mentally unequipped to do our work. For example, our TV watching often ends with frustration: "I wasted so much time. I have so much to do. How will I manage?").

Thus, by saying no to meditation and then seeking relief in activities that only worsen our mental state, we end up saying yes to frustration. Such frustration, the Gita (18.58) outlines, is the inevitable effect of Krishna unconsciousness. The same verse also states that Krishna consciousness frees us from frustration. Let's see how this works out.

Gita wisdom offers us a far more effective way of dealing with life's burdens: meditation. When we invest time in devotional meditation, it replenishes our inner energy by connecting us with the source of all energy: Krishna. This energy not only frees us from the sense of burden, but also enables us to manage our obligations intelligently, responsibly and competently.

And this mental refreshment is just the fringe benefit of connecting with Krishna. The real benefit is inner enrichment of our devotion, an enrichment that ultimately catapults us to the supreme realm of eternal happiness.

☙❧

If you become conscious of Me, you will pass over all the obstacles of conditioned life by My grace. If, however, you do not work in such consciousness but act through false ego, not hearing Me, you will be lost.

Krishna walks with us, but not for us

*W*hen we strive to live spiritually, we often find ourselves succumbing to materialism, despite our prayers to Krishna for protection. At such times, we may start doubting whether he actually helps us.

Such doubts arise when we don't understand the nature of the help that Krishna offers on the spiritual journey. He has gifted all of us with the precious gift of free will, and he never takes back what he has given; he never forces his will upon us.

The Bhagavad-gita demonstrates this in its concluding section. There, Krishna tells Arjuna (18.63) to deliberate and decide for himself what he wishes to do. This principle applies for all of us too. Krishna has done his part by outlining clearly through Gita wisdom the destinations of the various paths that beckon us from the crossroads where we stand. Now he expects us to do our part: to walk along the right path – the path of pure devotional service to him. This implies that the onus for rejecting materialist allurements is on us; Krishna will not reject them for us, for that would infringe on our free will.

Lest this make us feel lonely or insecure, we need only look to the Mahabharata to see how, once Arjuna started off on the right walk, Krishna as his charioteer was walking with him constantly, encouraging, cautioning and counseling him to make the right moves. Similarly, once we resolve to walk the good walk on the path of pure devotional service, Krishna will be constantly right next to us, gifting us ideas, insights and inspirations for honoring our resolution.

Why should we blame Krishna for not doing what is our part: making the resolution? And why should we burden ourselves with worries about his part: providing the strength to honor that resolution?

Let's be done with both the blame and the burden.

☙❧

Thus I have explained to you knowledge still more confidential. Deliberate on this fully, and then do what you wish to do.

Surrender is not about giving up, but about going up

The Bhagavad-gita (18.66) concludes by calling upon us to surrender to Krishna. To some of us, the word "surrender" may conjure images of a defeated military general reluctantly and resentfully giving up a lost fight. The Gita's understanding of surrender is totally different: it connotes a voluntary offering of our heart's love to Krishna expressed by harmonizing our human will with his divine will.

How do we surrender to Krishna during the course of our daily life when we fight our many battles? Do we quit those battles or do we keep fighting?

The essence of surrender is to do Krishna's will. That may sometimes require persevering in a battle and sometimes require putting aside a battle. What we do specifically is not as important as the consciousness in which we do it. When we surrender to him, we hand our will to him and ask him to use us as he sees fit. The resulting divine connection helps us see the situation from a higher perspective. With that raised consciousness, we discover in life's battles hidden opportunities to experience his love for us and to express our love for him. Tapping those opportunities is the heart of surrender.

Thus, surrender is not about giving up: abandoning a battle unwillingly. It is about going up: raising our consciousness willingly to connect with Krishna and become an instrument of his will. By going up, we naturally grow up in our relationship with him, which is far more consequential than engagement in or withdrawal from our daily battles. By surrendering, we win the far greater battle within us and march towards life's ultimate victory: attainment of love for Krishna and return to his eternal abode.

CRSO

Abandon all varieties of religion and just surrender unto Me. I shall deliver you from all sinful reactions. Do not fear.

LEARNING TO LOVE KRISHNA

Determination is the first thing, the main thing, the only thing

Nothing glorious can be achieved without single-pointed, sustained determination. The Bhagavad-gita (02.41) indicates that determination (*drdha-vratah*) is essential for the most glorious achievement of life: reviving our love for Krishna and thereby relishing eternal happiness. In fact, for attaining love for Krishna, our determination is the first thing, the main thing and the only thing:

The first thing: Our spiritual journey begins with our determination. Devotees can come in our life and invite us, even prod us, but our journey actually starts only when we desire determinedly to go closer to Krishna.

The main thing: When we start practicing devotional service regularly, the external performance of spiritual activities does not automatically lead to our advancement; it adds to our spiritual credits, thereby setting a platform for eventual devotional take off. We actually take off only when our external engagement is accompanied, even motivated, by our internal desire to love and serve Krishna – which is a function of our determination.

The only thing: On the devotional path, our advancement ultimately depends on Krishna's mercy. But this doesn't imply that nothing is in our hands – and it certainly doesn't justify our laziness in fighting our conditionings. We sometimes passively cave in to our conditionings and lackadaisically wait for Krishna's mercy to empower us in the future through some inner flash of lightning-like illumination. However, Krishna usually gives us his mercy by offering us opportunities to practice devotional service. We need to become determined to utilize those opportunities. If we don't become determined, even Krishna can't help us, for he doesn't infringe on our free will.

Therefore, Krishna's mercy is never missing; what is missing is our determination to benefit from it. Once we muster our determination, we will find Krishna's mercy empowering us in our journey to eternal love and joy.

ॐ

Those who are on this path are resolute in purpose, and their aim is one. O beloved child of the Kurus, the intelligence of those who are irresolute is many-branched.

See rituals as opportunities to spend quality time with Krishna

The various rituals that are a part of spiritual life – chanting, praying, worshipping and meditating – are opportunities for us to spend time with Krishna. If we forget or neglect this core purpose of the rituals, then they become hollow shells; their performance becomes a boredom and a burden that brings little spiritual purification or enlivenment. Worse still, the Bhagavad-gita (03.06) warns that they can degenerate into exercises not only in futility, but also in hypocrisy – especially when the external engagement in spirituality is belied by an internal obsession with non-spiritual or even anti-spiritual indulgences.

But if we infuse our performance of spiritual activities with the quality of devotion, with the sincere intention to love and serve Krishna, then they become precious opportunities to bask in his sublime presence, to let our troubled minds be reassured and pacified by the healing stillness of his presence, to let our hearts be illumined and kindled by the resplendent power of his presence. When we start experiencing that potent presence, then the time that we spend with Krishna becomes the most eagerly awaited period of our schedule, the most cherished part of our day, the foremost divine passion of our life.

ରଙ୍ଗ

One who restrains the senses of action but whose mind dwells on sense objects certainly deludes himself and is called a pretender.

04.09 Give yourself permission to love Krishna by suspending disbelief

*W*hen we are practicing devotional service externally, internally we may be checked by the doubt: "How can I love Krishna when I am not sure that he even exists?"

Actually, many people love characters like spiderman, batman, superman that they know for sure don't exist. How? By suspending disbelief.

If they can suspend their disbelief for loving a character that is definitely false, can't we suspend our disbelief for loving a person who is at least possibly real?

If we choose to, we have several additional reasons to boost us:

1. **Quality of lovers**: Fictional heroes attract for a few years some fans, who are mostly not deep thinkers and who rarely ponder the reality or unreality of their hero. In contrast, Krishna has attracted for thousands of years millions of people whose ranks have included many of the world's greatest thinkers who have explained systematically how Krishna is not just a reality, but is the supreme reality.

2. **Explanation of life**: Fictional heroes don't provide any philosophy or logic to explain real life; all that is on offer is a call to stop thinking for the sake of enjoying. In contrast, Krishna provides coherent philosophical and cogent logical answers to life's fundamental questions. What is on offer is rigorous thinking about a higher kind of enjoyment that continues eternally.

3. **Entry into a higher world**: Fictional heroes don't offer any process by which their fans can enter into their world simply because there is no such world. In contrast, Krishna offers an extensively delineated process of purification by which we can enter into his delightful world, as indicated in the Bhagavad-gita (04.09). If we give that process an honest try, we can experience the resulting purification even in this world and also sense the reality of Krishna's world.

Therefore, why not suspend our disbelief and give ourselves permission to love Krishna?

ॐ

One who knows the transcendental nature of My appearance and activities does not, upon leaving the body, take his birth again in this material world, but attains My eternal abode, O Arjuna.

Krishna's pastimes are not just amusing – they are amazing

The Bhagavad-gita (04.09) makes the remarkable claim that when we understand Krishna's appearance and activities in truth, we will attain liberation. Central to understanding this claim is the key word in this verse: *tattvatah*, in truth.

Many people who know about Krishna through their culture or tradition consider him amusing – especially due to his childhood pranks like stealing butter. However, the *tattvatah* understanding, the philosophical vision given in the Gita, helps us see Krishna in truth, as what he actually is: as God himself. Unmindful of his godhood, God chooses to take on the role of a sweet and naughty child just to reciprocate love with those who love him.

Isn't it amazing that God who is the ultimate father of all becomes a tender child for the sake of love? Isn't it even more amazing that God renounces that which everyone in this world longs to have – the majesty of godhood – just to relish the intimacy of love? And isn't it most amazing that God, though he has the love of billions and billions of his devotees, considers our love for him as so invaluable and irreplaceable and indispensable that he personally descends to this world to invite us with his love-call?

Indeed, how can we not love the Lord who is so given to love? And when we choose to love him, how can he stop himself from fulfilling his heart's longing to take us back to him and reinstate us his world of love?

Thus, Gita wisdom helps us cross the bridge from amusing to amazing in our understanding of Krishna's pastimes. And when we thereby fall in love with him, he helps us cross the far greater bridge from the material world to the spiritual world.

ॐ

One who knows the transcendental nature of My appearance and activities does not, upon leaving the body, take his birth again in this material world, but attains My eternal abode, O Arjuna.

Krishna ends the misdirection and frustration of our love

Loving anyone is a challenge. The poets frequently sing about the thrill of falling in love at first sight, but they rarely sing about the thrill of living in love after many sights. That's because the thrill of love is agonizingly short-lived. At best, it gradually fizzles out when our object of love repeatedly fails to live up to our expectations. At worst, it transmogrifies into a chill when our object of love abruptly leaves us.

Is our longing for love meant to be always frustrated?

Only as long as it is misdirected, answers Gita wisdom. It explains that we as souls are meant to love the all-attractive, all-loving Supreme Person, Krishna, and delight eternally in that loving relationship.

When we don't direct our longing for love towards Krishna, the Bhagavad-gita (04.10) indicates three broad ways in which we become frustrated:

1. **Raga (Attachment)**: We search for some worldly object to love and end up frustrated, as explained earlier.

2. **Bhaya (Aversion due to fear)**: We feel that our longing for love is the cause of our suffering, so we try to repress and extinguish it.

3. **Krodha (Anger due to indecision)**: We can't decide whether to express or repress our longing for love, so we lead lives of angry indecision.

Gita wisdom guides us to redirect our love towards Krishna through the process of devotional service. When we learn the art of loving him, we discover that his glory and beauty is ever-fresh and that his remembrance brings fresher and deeper joy.

Once our longing for love is thus satisfied, we become instruments of divine love in the world and form Krishna-centered loving relationships that uplift us and others towards the world of endless love. Loving others still remains a challenge, but the devotional intention makes it a fulfilling challenge.

℘

Being freed from attachment, fear and anger, being fully absorbed in Me and taking refuge in Me, many, many persons in the past became purified by knowledge of Me—and thus they all attained transcendental love for Me.

Loving the unlovable is the characteristic of God – and the character of the godly

*M*ost of us know someone who annoys, irritates or enrages us. We may even feel that if only that person would be out of our life, everything would be so much better.

On this vexing issue, Gita wisdom offers us a refreshing and empowering insight. It informs us that the world is like a university meant to teach us lessons in love. These lessons expand our love till it reaches its full potential of loving Krishna and through him all of his creation and creatures.

Loving God is an essentially transformative process that requires us to become godly, to learn to love like God loves. An essential characteristic of Krishna is that he loves even those who are unlovable, as is evident in an example that is uncomfortably nearby: we ourselves.

Krishna offered us his love even when we were unlovable, at a time when we had sold our souls to selfish indulgences. Leave alone the past, even at present, if we look within, we will probably find much there that is unlovable for Krishna. Yet he looks beyond these unlovable accretions to our real self, our pure soul, and helps us in getting rid of those accretions.

The Bhagavad-gita (04.35) indicates that the fruit of wisdom is this vision of love, this ability to see, as Krishna sees, the lovable divine spark within everyone. Even the unwise can love the lovable; it takes the wise to love the unlovable. It takes wisdom to see beyond the unlovable periphery of others to their lovable core, and to help them act according to their core, not their periphery.

The presence of the unlovable in our lives is an opportunity to grow in our character. They force us to do what we actually want to do: become godly, thereby coming closer to God.

ॐ॰॰

Having obtained real knowledge from a self-realized soul, you will never fall again into such illusion, for by this knowledge you will see that all living beings are but part of the Supreme, or, in other words, that they are Mine.

Bhakti is not just about believing in God – it is about belonging to God

The Bhagavad-gita (04.35) explains that when we become illumined by spiritual knowledge, we understand that we are Krishna's, that is, we belong to him.

Many people may believe generally in God or even specifically in Krishna as God. This Gita verse indicates that its spiritual wisdom can take us far beyond *believing* in Krishna to *belonging* to him. When we believe in Krishna, we often tend to think of him as our facilitator and expect him to make things work for us. When we belong to Krishna, we recognize that he is our Lord and master, and realize that we are expected to make things work for him; we are to lovingly offer him our very selves and thereby become instruments of his will. Believing in Krishna can give us a sense of security, "He will protect me." But belonging to Krishna gives us a sense of purpose: "He loves and values us so much that he believes I can be a part of his plan."

In life we need not just security but purpose. Our heart longs not just to live, but to love. And integral to love is the understanding that we belong to our beloved. That's why, we find lasting fulfillment not just by believing in Krishna, but by belonging to him.

ଔଓ

Having obtained real knowledge from a self-realized soul, you will never fall again into such illusion, for by this knowledge you will see that all living beings are but part of the Supreme, or, in other words, that they are Mine.

Stop running away from Krishna – run down the mind instead

The Bhagavad-gita (06.44) indicates that those who have tasted the sweetness of Krishna, even if they subsequently get deviated from the path to him, are attracted back to him helplessly.

As aspiring devotees, we have probably relished Krishna in one or other of his various manifestations: his holy name, his beautiful deity or, if nothing else, his delicious prasad. Despite having relished this sublime sweetness, our mind being addicted to materialism keeps impelling us toward mundane pleasures. Thus, our consciousness becomes the battleground for two opposing forces: consciously our mind goads us toward sensual pleasures, whereas subconsciously we long to taste again the joy of remembering Krishna.

Often, our mind deceives us into returning to the same wanton enjoyment that we had earlier rejected because of its emptiness and pointlessness. As long as we let ourselves be deluded by the mind, we stay infatuated by worldly pleasures and keep running away from Krishna. But our flight from him is inescapably doomed because our subconscious never lets us forget what we are missing. Even more significantly, Krishna doesn't want us to continue in material existence, wherein miseries are concomitant with pleasures. So, he personally arranges to repeatedly remind us of the sweetness of loving him and the tastelessness of loving anything else.

Consequently, by trying to run away from Krishna, we get no happiness. Instead, we simply prolong and increase our suffering. Therefore, rather than futilely trying to *run away* from Krishna, why not expend the same energy to *run down* the mind? If we can combat and conquer the mind's addiction to worldly pleasures, we will become free to relish the nectar of loving Krishna forever.

༒

By virtue of the divine consciousness of his previous life, he automatically becomes attracted to the yogic principles—even without seeking them. Such an inquisitive transcendentalist stands always above the ritualistic principles of the scriptures.

Bhakti is characterized by simple-heartedness, not simple-mindedness

Some people think that the path of bhakti is too simplistic and so is meant for sentimental non-intellectual people. However, the simplicity characteristic of bhakti is not simple-mindedness – it is simple-heartedness. Let's understand the difference between the two:

1. **Simple-mindedness:** In much contemporary intellectual discourse, the word "mind" is used to refer to the intellectual faculty, as when a thinker is honored as "one of the greatest minds of the century." With this usage, simple-mindedness refers to intellectual naiveté, the inability to reason critically and coherently. Is bhakti for the simple-minded? No; only the most historically ignorant people can claim that bhakti is only for the simple-minded. The leading exponents of bhakti like Ramanuja, Vyasatirtha and Jiva Goswami rank among the best minds that the world has ever seen, as even a cursory perusal of their intellectual works will reveal. Of course, bhakti, being a matter of the heart, can be practiced even by the non-intellectual. But that is evidence of its inclusiveness, not its simple-mindedness.

2. **Simple-heartedness:** The simplicity characteristic of bhakti is simple-heartedness: the simple faith in the heart's intuitive truths. These include the following. Love, the deepest longing of our heart, is not to be rejected, but redirected to life's highest spiritual level. We can invoke the ultimate power in existence, Krishna's grace, by our sincere calls of humble devotion. His omnipotent grace can compensate for all our limitations and faults. His holy name is the best expressway to his grace. And life's greatest attainment is pure love for him, culminating in attaining his eternal abode.

This simple-hearted faith is often the rich, refined climax of the most sophisticated intellectual deliberation, as is indicated in the Bhagavad-gita (07.19): when intellectuals reach their zenith, they surrender to Krishna and embrace the path of bhakti.

ॐ

After many births and deaths, he who is actually in knowledge surrenders unto Me, knowing Me to be the cause of all causes and all that is. Such a great soul is very rare.

Go beyond naughty desires and knotty doubts

*W*hen we embark on our inward spiritual journey towards Krishna, our mind blocks us with naughty desires and our intelligence, with knotty doubts.

Bhakti removes both these roadblocks, as indicated in the Bhagavad-gita (08.07): those who offer their mind and intelligence to Krishna positively attain him. Let's see how bhakti removes these inner obstacles:

1. **Naughty desires**: The mind is like a naughty child that is readily allured by anything that seems new or pleasurable. Certainly, the mind can do much more harm than a naughty child. Still, we cannot execute or exile it; we have to live with it lifelong. And we can't silence or shackle it lifelong; we need to provide it a safe playing arena. Bhakti offers it just that: freedom to explore and enjoy within the perimeter of service to Krishna.

2. **Knotty doubts**: The intelligence shackles us with doubts about knotty philosophical paradoxes that we just can't comprehend at our present level of consciousness. A common such knotty doubt is: how did we fall from the spiritual world? The spiritual world is beyond the arena of time as we know it. There, causality – the system of connection between cause and effect – is radically different from causality here, within the arena of time. Consequently, we are as likely to resolve this doubt as a monkey is likely to understand quantum physics. Bhakti frees our intelligence from such futile endeavors by providing it a far more relishable and profitable engagement: comprehending Krishna's glories, thereby boosting our conviction about the reality of his love. That conviction empowers us to neglect irresolvable doubts as irrelevant, and march confidently and joyfully towards him.

ॐ

Therefore, Arjuna, you should always think of Me in the form of Krishna and at the same time carry out your prescribed duty of fighting. With your activities dedicated to Me and your mind and intelligence fixed on Me, you will attain Me without doubt.

Bhakti purifies, sanctifies and amplifies our emotions

Emotions differentiate us conscious beings from unconscious things. As matter doesn't have the capacity to experience emotions, the presence of that capacity in us suggests that there is more to our identity than matter – it points to our spiritual essence.

Yet it is a sad irony that the very emotions which suggest our spiritual identity also often obfuscate that identity. Our emotions generally tend to get activated primarily by matter in its various colors and shapes, thereby binding us to material existence.

So, some people equate becoming spiritual with becoming unemotional. As bhakti is centered on emotions, these people often look down upon bhakti as low-level spirituality. If they are to understand the glory of bhakti, they need to "please see again" or PSA, an acronym that indicates the three broad parts in the remarkable redirection of emotions that bhakti brings about: Purify, Sanctify, Amplify. Let's look at this threefold redirection:

1. **Purify**: Bhakti connects us with the supremely pure being, Krishna, thereby purifying us of entangling material emotions.

2. **Sanctify**: Bhakti directs our emotions towards the supremely sacred being, Krishna, thereby sanctifying those emotions.

3. **Amplify**: Bhakti reveals to us how Krishna is far more attractive than anything of the material world. This revelation gradually makes our emotions for him stronger and deeper than our past emotions for anything material. Thus our life acquires an emotional amplitude that we never knew was possible.

Thus, bhakti utilizes our natural emotionality to fuel our spiritual journey. And such transcendental emotions connect us strongly with Krishna, the reservoir of all pleasure. This connectedness makes our spiritual journey a joyful journey, as the Bhagavad-gita (09.02) confirms.

৺

This knowledge is the king of education, the most secret of all secrets. It is the purest knowledge, and because it gives direct perception of the self by realization, it is the perfection of religion. It is everlasting, and it is joyfully performed.

Fasting is an opportunity to sacrifice the good for the best

As spiritual seekers, we recognize that immoral sinful pleasures are obstacles on the spiritual pathway. What we may not recognize is that even innocent pious pleasures are obstacles. Let's see how.

Whatever gives us pleasure occupies a place in our heart. When we seek pleasure in sins, we exile Krishna from our heart and enthrone the sin-inducing objects there. When we seek innocent pleasures, we don't exile Krishna from our heart, but we force him to share our heart with the pleasure-providing objects. This mixed devotion falls far below the standard of pure devotion, of making Krishna the only master of the heart, as indicated in the Bhagavad-gita (09.13: *bhajanty ananya manaso*).

Being aspiring devotees, we know that such pure devotion is our ideal. Special holy days beckon us as opportunities to make the ideal the actual. Fasting on these holy days is a time-honored way to leave ourselves with no source of nourishment and fulfillment except the remembrance of Krishna.

Some of us may wonder, "Food sanctified by offering to Krishna is non-different from him. Why do we need to fast from a manifestation of Krishna to progress in Krishna consciousness?"

Because we usually see sanctified food, *krishna-prasad*, more as food – an object for our gratification – and less as Krishna, the object for our devotion. Due to this lop-sided vision, even prasad can distract us from our Krishna consciousness. Therefore, fasting from prasad paves the way for us to sacrifice even the good – prasad – for the best: Krishna.

Fasting thus enables us to offer our heart fully to Krishna with the meditation: "Nothing and no one is the owner of my heart except you, O Krishna. You and you alone!"

☙❦❧

O son of Pritha, those who are not deluded, the great souls, are under the protection of the divine nature. They are fully engaged in devotional service because they know Me as the Supreme Personality of Godhead, original and inexhaustible.

Transform your heart into a blossoming garden

*L*ove is not just a feeling, but also a doing; not just an emotion, but also an action. In fact, love as a feeling is the root that grows and blossoms into the flower of love as an action. And, paradoxically, love as an action acts as the root that grows and blossoms into the flower of love as a feeling. Thus, when we cultivate simultaneously the feelings and the actions of love, they nourish each other mutually, and our heart transforms into a beautiful garden filled with blossoming flowers of love.

The love in our heart may blossom temporarily in the presence of a person who seems attractive, but the blossom soon dries and dies when that person disappoints or departs. Our heart's love blossoms completely and permanently only in the presence of the all-attractive supreme person, Krishna, because:

1. He is the perennial reservoir of all endearing qualities, so he never disappoints us

2. He is eternally committed to loving us, so he never departs from our hearts.

No wonder the Bhagavad-gita (09.13-14) indicates that those who are connoisseurs of love are one-pointed and undistracted in focusing their love on Krishna (*bhajanty ananya manaso*); they are convinced that by loving Krishna they will get everything that they might get by loving anyone else, for he is the imperishable source of everything (*jnatava bhutadim avyayam*). Significantly, these two verses also reflect the feeling and acting aspects of love: the first verse describes their feelings, and the second, their actions.

By following in their footsteps and cultivating both the feelings and the actions that express love, we too can transform our heart into a garden blossoming with the flowers of love.

☙❧

O son of Pritha, those who are not deluded, the great souls, are under the protection of the divine nature. They are fully engaged in devotional service because they know Me as the Supreme Personality of Godhead, original and inexhaustible.

Love is in the SOUND

The Bhagavad-gita (09.14) states that advanced devotees engage constantly and determinedly in speaking and singing about Krishna. The fact that they focus so much on divine sound points to its defining role in their devotional advancement. In fact, sacred sound is one of the most important ways to express and experience devotion.

Among all sacred sounds, the sound of the holy name is the most potent. Its characteristics can be expressed as the acronym SOUND:

S: Satisfying: Unlike material sounds that leave us bored if we repeat them too many times, the sound of the holy name makes us increasingly satisfied when we repeat it more and more.

O: Omnipotent: Krishna has invested all his supreme power in his holy name, so it has the power to break what the most powerful nuclear bomb can't break: the shell of ignorance and selfishness that obstructs the unfolding of our spiritual potential.

U: Universal: The sound of the holy name can attract and transform the hearts of all people everywhere because it acts at the level of the soul, a level that transcends all sectarian barriers of language, culture, nationality and even religion.

N: Non-material: The holy name is itself spiritual, and chanting it invokes the transcendental grace of Krishna.

D: Direct: As Krishna and his holy name are non-different, we directly contact him through the sound of his holy name. That's why the more we tune ourselves devotionally to that divine sound , the more we realize and relish his direct presence and love.

CRSO

Always chanting My glories, endeavoring with great determination, bowing down before Me, these great souls perpetually worship Me with devotion.

Krishna is a coach, not a critic

The Bhagavad-gita (09.18) states that Krishna is present in the hearts of all of us as the witness. Fortunately for us, he is present there not to catch us doing wrong, but to coach us in doing right. He does indeed witness all our deeds – many of which, sadly, happen to be misdeeds. Naturally then, the knowledge of Krishna's indwelling presence may make some of us apprehensive. However, this knowledge can also reassure us when we understand that Krishna witnesses our deeds with the desire to help, not the tendency to find faults.

If while walking on a dark street we come to know that a policeperson is witnessing us, that knowledge will make us fearful only if we had intended to break the law. But if we had no such intention, that same knowledge will reassure us of our safety. Additionally, if a habitual law-breaker had been tempting or threatening us into breaking the law, knowledge of the policeperson's presence will empower us to resist the law-breaker.

Similarly, while walking in the darkness of material existence, the knowledge that Krishna is witnessing us will make us fearful only if we intend to violate his injunctions. But if we intend to honor his injunctions, then the knowledge of his presence will make us feel reassured. Additionally, it will make us feel empowered to fight the habitually godless mind that is always tempting or threatening us into violating Krishna's guidelines.

Krishna is present in our heart not to blame us whenever we succumb to the mind, but to bolster us whenever we resolve to fight it. He is not a critic for whom we are an object of cold analysis. He is a coach for whom we are all objects of his warm affection. After all, he loves us.

ॐ

I am the goal, the sustainer, the master, the witness, the abode, the refuge and the most dear friend. I am the creation and the annihilation, the basis of everything, the resting place and the eternal seed.

If we have the capacity to worry, we have the capacity to meditate

Many people avoid meditating because they feel that meditation requires some extraordinary ability to concentrate that they don't possess. However, the fact is that all of us have the ability required for meditation, as is evident whenever we get lost in a common activity: worry. When we worry, thoughts often leave our immediate circumstances and go towards some problem, be it real or imagined. And letting our thoughts take us away from our circumstances is the essential ability required for meditation. Thus, all of us have the ability to meditate; we just need to redirect the focus of our thoughts from a temporary worldly situation to an eternal other-worldly reality, Krishna.

Of course, this redirection may initially seem difficult due to the default momentum of the mind to gravitate towards worldly situations. We can, however, muster the determination to counter the default motion by contemplating the contrasting effects of worrying and meditating:

1. Worrying agitates us, whereas meditating pacifies us

2. Worrying confuses us, whereas meditating illuminates us

3. Worrying exhausts us, whereas meditating energizes us.

Lest we fear that things will go wrong if we don't worry about them, we can take heart from Krishna's assurance in the Bhagavad-gita (09.22) that for those who meditate on him, he takes care of their worries about protecting what they have and providing what they lack.

CRSO

But those who always worship Me with exclusive devotion, meditating on My transcendental form—to them I carry what they lack, and I preserve what they have.

Devotion is Krishna's appetizer

*S*ome people ask, "God is complete and doesn't need anything. As he never feels hungry, what is the need to offer him food?"

This question is understandable because God is often depicted as a self-satisfied Supreme Being. Gita wisdom acknowledges this depiction, but also reveals a much higher conception of God: as an all-attractive person Krishna who delights in loving reciprocations with his devotees. At this level of revelation, God as Krishna delights in loving reciprocations so much that he hungers for them. His hunger, however, is not like our hunger that is driven by bodily necessity. His hunger is completely transcendental, motivated only by the profound dynamics of pure spiritual love.

So, while it is true that Krishna doesn't feel materially hungry, a higher truth is that the devotion in his devotee's heart acts as his appetizer. When a devotee offers him food with devotion, he feels so acutely hungry that he becomes ready, even eager, for the simplest of foods. That's why he says in the Bhagavad-gita (09.26) that he accepts even a leaf, a flower, a fruit or just a little bit of water when any of these is offered with devotion.

Krishna's transcendental hunger, when understood properly, becomes a merciful opportunity for us aspiring devotees to enter deeper into a personal relationship with him. By offering him food with whatever devotion we presently have, we can feel a sense of connection with him. Over time, when we keep rendering the practical service of offering food to him, he mercifully enriches our heart with pure spiritual bliss.

Thus, by carefully understanding the transcendental nature of Krishna's hunger, we can render him affectionate service that will end our heart's hunger for eternal love.

CRISO

If one offers Me with love and devotion a leaf, a flower, fruit or water, I will accept it.

Let Krishna permeate, pervade and possess our heart

*D*evotional advancement essentially means letting Krishna enter and rule our heart. This may happen in the following three progressive stages:

1. **Permeation**: Just as water from the clouds permeates into a field through the top soil, Krishna through his manifestations such as the holy names, Deities and scriptures permeates into our heart through our senses. Just as the field primarily contains earth but allows water to permeate, our heart at this stage primarily contains other attachments but allows Krishna to permeate. We can equate this stage with the Bhagavad-gita (09.27) where the devotees offer whatever they do to Krishna. The erudite Gita commentator Vishvanatha Chakravarti Thakura underscores that at this level prescribed action precedes the devotional offering, so it is not a very advanced level.

2. **Pervasion**: By gradual permeation Krishna spreads his presence all over our heart till he becomes the primary consideration, and the prescribed duty becomes secondary. We can correlate this stage with the Bhagavad-gita (08.05) where the devotees offer their mind and intelligence to Krishna, indicating thereby his pervasion of their being. Naturally therefore, they first remember him and then perform their prescribed duty. As Krishna comes first in the devotees' thought-process, Vishvanatha Chakravarti Thakura deems this level higher.

3. **Possession**: At this summit stage, Krishna becomes the devotees' be-all and end-all. They care only for him, and they do whatever he instructs, irrespective of whether it harmonizes with their prescribed duties or not. The Gita (18.73) culminates with this level of devotion: *karisyhe vacanam tava* "I will do your will." Herein, devotees don't just gracefully submit to the will of God, as in the famous "Let thy will be done," but go further and dynamically become instruments for executing that will.

☙❧

Whatever you do, whatever you eat, whatever you offer or give away, and whatever austerities you perform—do that, O son of Kunti, as an offering to Me.

Krishna's love is unconditional yet conditional

The Bhagavad-gita (09.30) urges us to recognize as saintly a devotee who, though guilty of grievous misconduct, is still determined to serve Krishna. The next verse (09.31) first assures that such a devotee will soon get reformed and then proclaims that Krishna due to his unfailing love will forever protect that devotee.

The first verse offers a glimpse of the unconditional nature of Krishna's love: there is nothing that we can ever do, no matter how terrible, that can stop Krishna from loving us. He forever acts as our well-wisher and benefactor, just as the sun forever gives illumination.

At the same time, though love can be unilateral, a loving relationship cannot be unilateral; it always has to be bilateral. If we neglect or reject Krishna's love by filling our heart with non-devotional or anti-devotional desires, then we paralyze our capacity to experience his love, just as closing our eyes disables our capacity to see sunlight. So, Krishna's love is conditional in the limited sense that we need to cultivate a certain condition of the heart to experience his love.

Knowing this, we shouldn't misuse Krishna's proclamation in Gita (09.30) to rationalize our own moral lapses. We can see the verse primarily as an exhortation to continue respecting other devotees who have succumbed to immoral temptations: "If Krishna considers them saintly, so should I."

If we ourselves commit any misdeed, we need to fervently regret it. And, in the spirit of the next verse (09.31), we can return to morality so as to make our heart receptive for experiencing Krishna's love. This verse assures us that return to moral and spiritual integrity is definitely possible, even inevitable and imminent (*kshipram bhavati dharmatma*). Then, knowing that an inner battle is necessary for attaining that state, the verse inspires us to fight by declaring that Krishna with all his omnipotence will protect us (*na me bhaktah pranashyati*).

☙❧

Even if one commits the most abominable action, if he is engaged in devotional service he is to be considered saintly because he is properly situated in his determination.

Place Krishna at the center of your secret life

All of us have a public life where we interact with the world and a personal life where we interact with our loved ones. Additionally, we also have a secret life where we live and relive our fondest dreams. This secret life underlies and shapes our public and personal lives. We may be addressing a thousand people or talking to a family member, but in both cases we may be in our secret life if our thoughts are dwelling on that which we hold dearest.

One way to understand what resides in our secret life is to evaluate what thoughts occupy us when we have nothing to do; or when we seek relief amidst boredom or distress; or when we contemplate our greatest joys. To make spiritual advancement, we need to place Krishna at the center of our secret lives by making him the stuff of our dreams. This doesn't imply that we equate him with a character of our night dreams or that we fantasize him performing intimate pastimes with us. It essentially implies that we make the desire to serve him the deepest, most intense and most cherished longing of our heart. Our dreams will then naturally revolve around him as the planets revolve around the sun.

The Bhagavad-gita (10.09) characterizes exalted devotees using the phrase *mac-cittah*. This phrase conveys not just that they always think about Krishna, but also that their consciousness becomes offered to and absorbed in him. In other words, he reigns supreme in their secret life.

To emulate their example, we need to consciously desire Krishna at all times and especially at the times when we are exposed to devotional stimuli. This will gradually ensure that he permeates, pervades and possesses our secret life, thereby enriching us with the highest happiness.

☙❧

The thoughts of My pure devotees dwell in Me, their lives are fully devoted to My service, and they derive great satisfaction and bliss from always enlightening one another and conversing about Me.

Buddhi-yoga comprises both the eyes and the wings for our spiritual flight

To advance on the devotional path, we need both eyes and wings. The eyes help us see the spiritual world of love that is invisible to our material eyes. And the wings enable us to rise to the lofty level of selfless love for Krishna.

The Bhagavad-gita offers us eyes through its philosophical wisdom, and wings through its devotional practices. How both these gifts bless us is conveyed in the Gita (10.10) through a meaning-packed compound word: *buddhi-yoga* (the yoga of wisdom). To grasp the dynamics of these two gifts, let's unpack this word in two ways:

1. **The yoga that awards buddhi**: When we serve Krishna by engaging in devotional service or the yoga of love (yoga), he grants us the wisdom and the vision (buddhi) to see beyond the material reality that usually occupies our eyes and minds. This philosophical vision helps us focus our attention on the eternal spiritual reality, a world of endless love. Within this world, the Gita reveals the highest reality to be the all-attractive, all-loving Supreme Being, Krishna.

2. **The buddhi that awards yoga**: When we use this philosophical vision to serve Krishna and fulfill his benevolent purposes in this world, he purifies us and awakens within us the selfless spiritual love necessary for entering his world. Devotional practices thus act like wings that, by Krishna's mercy, enable us to rise to the thrilling heights of the world of eternal love. There, we are forever united with him in an ecstatic relationship of love – a love that is the culmination of all yoga.

Thus, the Gita's philosophical wisdom gifts us the eyes to see Krishna's world of love and its devotional practices grant us the wings to fly to that world.

༄

To those who are constantly devoted to serving Me with love, I give the understanding by which they can come to Me.

Let adversity pave the way to the discovery of real prosperity

*W*hen we practice devotional service, we often expect that we will automatically get protection from worldly adversity. So we become baffled on discovering that devotees are not exempt from material adversities. We naturally get the question: Why?

Many millennia ago, this same question was asked by the virtuous king Yudhishthira to Krishna. The gist of Krishna's answer in Srimad-Bhagavatam (10.88.8) is that material adversities pave the way for devotees' spiritual prosperity. Let's see how.

The eternal, unchangeable reality is that our relationship with Krishna is our only real prosperity. Everything in this world is material and temporary, whereas we as souls are spiritual and eternal. So nothing of this world can give us actual happiness; none of it is our real wealth. Still, we sometimes get allured by worldly things, imagining that they will make us prosperous. Such imagination can divert us from Krishna or even drag us away from him.

That's why Krishna occasionally allows adversities to take away our pseudo-prosperities so that we are left with no alternative except to turn to him for shelter – and thereby realize how our relationship with him constitutes our only true prosperity. Of course, what causes those adversities is our own past karma, not Krisna. But he orchestrates those adversities so that they become opportunities for us to realize our actual prosperity.

When material adversities strike us, if we prayerfully seek shelter of Krishna, he will give us the intelligence, as the Bhagavad-gita (10.10) promises, to understand and utilize those adversities as opportunities for realizing that our relationship with him is our supreme treasure – connectedness with him comprises real prosperity. Being reassured by the presence of that inner treasure, we can with restored fortitude find the best way to deal with the outer adversity.

CRSO

To those who are constantly devoted to serving Me with love, I give the understanding by which they can come to Me.

Don't miss the feast of the heart because of the lethargy of the mind

*L*ove has its own life, and it needs its own food to survive and thrive. The food that love feasts on is the glory, the beauty and, in fact, every attractive quality of the beloved.

This universal principle underlying all love is the basis of the primary activities of devotional service: hearing, chanting and remembering centered on Krishna. The more we hear, speak and think about him, the more we feed our tender love for him. And the more we nourish that love , the more it assumes its own life and speed of growth. It grows – and grows fast – thereby making us even more eager to hear about him.

Increased contemplation on Krishna and enhanced love for him mutually enrich each other in a joyous and glorious cycle that fills our heart with divine ecstasy. Though such ecstasy may be presently inaccessible to us, we can glimpse it by hearing the words of advanced devotees who are relishing it. The Bhagavad-gita (10.18) shares with us one such first-person account when Arjuna expresses his intense and immense longing to hear Krishna's glories ceaselessly.

Such ecstasy beckons us, but our mental inertia shackles us. This inertia refers to our mind's tendency to become lethargic in thinking about and connecting with Krishna. Under the spell of inertia, we miss the feast of relishable devotional activities.

Meditating on verses like these reminds us of the feast that awaits us, thereby stimulating our devotional hunger. By such stimulation, we can overcome the inertia and engage in devotional service enthusiastically. Earnest engagement in devotional activities prepares our heart to gradually relish the ultimate feast: ongoing, absorbing and fulfilling remembrance of Krishna.

ॐ

O Janardana, again please describe in detail the mystic power of Your opulences. I am never satiated in hearing about You, for the more I hear the more I want to taste the nectar of Your words.

"So much, O Krishna, do I long for you"

*L*ove is characterized by desire: strong, sustained, single-pointed desire. As spiritual seekers, we aspire to awaken our love for Krishna. In the ultimate sense, that love is a gift bestowed from without; when Krishna reveals his supreme all-attractiveness to us, then we cannot but fall completely in love with him. Additionally, in an immediate sense, that love is a choice exercised by us from within; we show him our desire for that love by choosing him over the things of the world.

Normally, our desires get splayed and split over a wide variety of worldly things. Consequently, our desire for Krishna remains mere background music, a noble but feeble aspiration that we hope to act upon sometime in the future. To aid us in intensifying and accelerating our desire for him, Krishna gives us the holy days that periodically adorn the calendar.

These holy days provide us precious opportunities to concentrate the full power of our desires on Krishna. Abstaining from food and similar innocent pleasures of life frees our desires so that we can focus them on Krishna. Whenever our mind reminds us of food or any such innocent worldly object, we can remind ourselves of the proclamation of the Bhagavad-gita (10.41) that the beauty of everything stems from a spark of Krishna's beauty.

The corollary to this proclamation is important and inspiring: whatever satisfaction any worldly object could have offered us, Krishna can offer us all of that – and much, much more. To help him in providing us that satisfaction, we just need to open our heart to him. Fasting helps us open our heart by showing him: "So much, O Krishna, do I long for you – as much as I long for food and more."

CR80

Know that all opulent, beautiful and glorious creations spring from but a spark of My splendor.

Krishna's ladder of love helps us rise from wherever we presently are

*L*ove for Krishna may sometimes seem a distant, abstract concept. But Gita wisdom offers a systematic pathway by which we can slowly but surely attain that love. The Bhagavad-gita (12.08-10) outlines a ladder of love that extends down from the highest level:

1. Offer the mind and intelligence to Krishna entirely, thereby living in him (12.08)

2. Practice sadhana-bhakti to fix the mind on Krishna and thereby increase our desire for him (12.09)

3. Work for Krishna (12.10). This level includes two implicit sub-levels:

    3.1 - Direct: Do his work, that is, render service to him

    3.2 - Indirect: Offer him the fruits of our work

In principle, these levels may be discrete. But in practice we as aspiring devotees will function at different levels at different times. When we do sadhana, we may be at level 2; when we do seva, we may be at level 3.1; when we work and earn with the intention of donating for devotional purposes, we may be at level 3.2.

The higher the level of our practice, the closer we are to Krishna. Still, whatever our present level, by diligent practice, we can gradually attain him. Even if our present level is way below these levels, still the Gita (18.56) indicates that we can begin practicing devotion from wherever we presently are and we will rise to higher levels.

Levels like these are expanded and elaborated in the Bhakti Rasamrita Sindhu, a sixteenth century devotional classic. By studying such levels, we can recognize where we are and where we are going. This understanding will bring clear direction and tangible ambition to our devotional practices, thereby inspiring us to enthusiastically rise towards Krishna.

☙❧

Just fix your mind upon Me, the Supreme Personality of Godhead, and engage all your intelligence in Me. Thus you will live in Me always, without a doubt.

Feeling is a springboard for chanting, but chanting is also a gateway to feeling

*S*ome people doubt the benefit of daily mantra meditation: "What is the use of repeating the names of God mechanically and unfeelingly? Better to wait till we get the feeling of devotion and then chant whole-heartedly."

This doubt originates because they mistake the causal relationship between feeling and chanting to be one-way instead of two-way. That is, feeling can inspire chanting, but chanting can engender feeling too. Let's take a closer look at these two scenarios:

Feeling as a springboard for chanting: This applies primarily for two categories of people. For advanced devotees, the feeling of devotion is a constant inner reality that expresses itself as constant chanting. For those who are devotionally inclined but are not practitioners, an intense devotional stimulus or an unsolvable problem may sometimes induce the feeling of devotion and impel them to chant.

Chanting as a gateway to feeling: This applies primarily for the spiritual practitioners who lie between the spiritually advanced and the spiritually inclined. Unlike the spiritually inclined who are satisfied with occasional and short-lived feelings of devotion, practitioners long for feelings that are sustained, substantial and transformational. They want to redirect their love from matter to Krishna in a real and tangible way. For bringing about this redirection, they apply the guideline of the Bhagavad-gita (12.09) that the practice of regularly remembering Krishna increases one's attraction for him. This guideline implies that the feeling of being attracted to him is a result of remembering him, not a pre-condition for remembering him.

Of course, practitioners do experience devotional feelings periodically. But knowing that at the practitioner's level feelings can be fickle and fallible, they don't make feelings the fuel for their devotional journey, for they don't want their journey to be sporadic and erratic. They replace feeling with commitment as their fuel, thereby ensuring that their journey towards Krishna is steady, smooth and swift.

ભ∞

My dear Arjuna, O winner of wealth, if you cannot fix your mind upon Me without deviation, then follow the regulative principles of bhakti-yoga. In this way develop a desire to attain Me.

Let your love break free of all limitations

Our love constantly longs to rush forth beyond all limitations. But as long as we love anyone at the material level, the flow of our love remains constrained by two often-subconscious fears:

1. We limit the love that we offer to others due to the fear that it may be at worst rejected insensitively or at best reciprocated inadequately.

2. We also fear that focusing our love on one person may limit our capacity to love others.

However, when we consciously and consistently offer our love to Krishna, we gradually discover that it breaks free from both these limitations. Here's why:

1. Krishna notices attentively every drop of love that we offer him and reciprocates perfectly by flooding our heart with fulfilling waves of love. When we experience his magnificent reciprocation, we feel inspired to offer him all the love of our heart and more still.

2. Krishna being the source of everything encompasses all of existence; all living beings are his beloved children. So, the love we offer him doesn't stay stuck with him, but returns through him to embrace as many living beings as our heart desires. That's why, when we focus our love on Krishna, we become increasingly capable of loving more and more people. The Bhagavad-gita points to this majestic expansion of our capacity to love when it states (12.13) that devotees who love Krishna become the benefactors of all living beings.

Thus, by loving Krishna, we let our love break free from its limitations and flow freely, bringing the supreme happiness in our own lives and the lives of many others.

ᘓᘔᘖ

One who is not envious but is a kind friend to all living entities, who does not think himself a proprietor and is free from false ego, who is equal in both happiness and distress, who is tolerant…—such a devotee of Mine is very dear to Me.

Love not just ideal people, but also real people

We often long for an ideal person to love. Gita wisdom introduces us to that ideal person: Krishna. It also shows us how Krishna's pure devotees are ideal people in their exemplary love for Krishna. By offering our love to them, we develop the inspiration and aspiration to become ideal like them, thereby learning to love Krishna as they do.

While we traverse the path to become ideal, we have to live in a world where ideal people are few, even among devotees striving to become ideal. So, we will inevitably find ourselves in a social circle comprising many *real* people, those who have a blend of virtue and vice – as do we. If we decide to reserve our love for a social circle of only ideal people, then we will stay waiting for the rest of eternity; such a circle doesn't exist in the material world. If somehow somewhere we could find such a circle, we ourselves wouldn't gain entry into it because, whether we admit it or not, we are not ideal.

That's why we need to learn to love non-ideal people. To get inspiration for this, we need to look no further than our own ideal. Krishna himself doesn't reserve his love for ideal people alone. He loves everyone, including non-ideal people, so much that he always acts as their well-wisher, as the Bhagavad-gita (05.29) indicates. Like Krishna, his pure devotees also love everyone, as the Gita (12.13) indicates. They express that love by helping everyone learn to love Krishna.

By learning how to intelligently love non-ideal people, we will be able to assist Krishna and his devotees and gain their mercy, thereby accelerating our journey to the world of eternal love.

৹৪৮৹

One who is not envious but is a kind friend to all living entities, who does not think himself a proprietor and is free from false ego, who is equal in both happiness and distress, who is tolerant…—such a devotee of Mine is very dear to Me.

Be adept to adopt and adapt

*M*any of us may have suspected that the Bhagavad-gita being an ancient book might not be practical in our times. Some of us may have been surprised to discover its practicality on encountering advanced devotees who had molded their lives according to it.

Such seasoned devotees can bring about this paradigm shift in us because they are adept (*daksha*), as mentioned in the Gita itself (12.16). While this adeptness can have many aspects, its one essential aspect is the mature ability to apply the Gita according to time-place-circumstance. The Gita adept knows what to adopt and what to adapt in its message and in the spiritual tradition that it has engendered. This tradition has a central core and a circumferential periphery. The adept knows how to hold on to the core and to adapt the periphery according to the context.

These devotional adepts grasp the core of the Gita: the heart of Krishna, a heart longing to love us and be loved by us. Due to their inner harmony with Krishna, they know how to make that sublime love accessible and relishable to the emotional and intellectual ethos of their times. Thus, they become receivers and radiators of divine love, with their radiations emanating at the frequency of vibration of their contemporary generation.

By observing, serving and learning from such an adept, we too can gradually become adept and develop a spiritual intuition to know what to adopt and what to adapt. The resulting devotional dynamism will make living the Gita an exciting, enlightening experience.

ॐ

My devotee who is not dependent on the ordinary course of activities, who is pure, expert, without cares, free from all pains, and not striving for some result, is very dear to Me.

Devotion kindles an inner drive that is beyond jeers and cheers

*O*ur drives determine our destiny. Gita wisdom reveals our ultimate destiny: eternal, ecstatic love for Krishna. For realizing this destiny, we need to have a strong drive to practice devotional service.

To sustain this drive, we need to transcend the world's opinions. Why? Because they originate in a fallible conception of life that rarely accords Krishna significance or even existence. No wonder the Bhagavad-gita (12.18) asserts that serious devotees transcend the world's jeers and cheers (*manaapamanayoh*). Let's see how they transcend the world's views:

Jeers: The world may scorn devotees, but they march on undaunted. They know that these jeers are simply ways by which Krishna is exhausting their past negative karmic reactions so that they can attain him faster. Of course, devotees are humble and alert enough to check and correct themselves if they are alienating anyone unnecessarily. But they don't let the fear of alienating others impede them in their necessary devotional practices.

Cheers: The world may sometimes cheer devotees, especially when they achieve something materially significant. Devotees know that these material achievements are important to the extent they contribute to their devotional aspirations. Otherwise, they see these achievements as mere fringe benefits on the path of devotion. So they don't let the cheers of the world distract them from their central goal of reviving their love for Krishna.

We can take inspiration from the consciousness and commitment of such serious devotees, thereby learning to transcend the world's jeers and cheers for Krishna's sake. The more we let our drive center singularly on Krishna, the more he enriches our heart by revealing his presence and love there. That epiphany is life's ultimate fulfillment.

CRROD

One who is equal to friends and enemies, who is equipoised in honor and dishonor, heat and cold, happiness and distress, fame and infamy…—such a person is very dear to Me.

Hubris is the recipe for debris

Debris usually doesn't need a recipe. It results from a violent force that reduces an attractive structure to an unattractive mess. A recipe, on the other hand, is a step-by-step guideline meant to convert raw items into delicious food.

The process of bhakti-yoga is a recipe for refining our consciousness so as to make it attractive for Krishna. Central to this metaphorical cooking of our consciousness is the careful cultivation of humility, a virtue that the Bhagavad-gita (13.08) lists first among the virtues that comprise knowledge.

The polar opposite of humility is hubris. This overbearing pride originates from obsessive self-absorption and terminates in obnoxious megalomania. Such self-absorption is noxious for our capacity to absorb ourselves in Krishna. Hubris makes us full of ourselves: our abilities, our achievements, our aspirations. Even if these are within the perimeter of devotional service, still they can become the enemies of our devotion if they inflate our ego. Hubris prevents us from calling the names of Krishna fervently, leave alone enthroning him as the Lord of our heart.

Worse still, hubris makes us imagine that, just because we may be more materially talented than others, we are better than them, even when they may actually be more spiritually advanced than us. This distorted imagination impels us to disrespect, even offend, great souls, thereby releasing destructive forces that reduce our devotional attainments to debris. Of course, our devotional assets are indestructible, but offenses can make them inaccessible to us till we make amends. And during that period the external forms of those assets may factually be reduced to debris.

Thus, hubris is indeed a recipe for debris. By contemplating regularly on its inbuilt destructiveness, we can vigilantly keep hubris out of our heart.

ॐ

Humility; pridelessness; nonviolence; tolerance; simplicity; approaching a bona fide spiritual master; cleanliness; steadiness; self-control…—all these I declare to be knowledge, and besides this whatever there may be is ignorance.

Humility opens the door to wisdom

The Bhagavad-gita (13.08) mentions humility as the first among the twenty virtues that comprise wisdom. This indicates that humility is the doorway that enables us to enter the house of wisdom. Humility activates our awareness that no matter how much we know, there is so much more to know. Such humble awareness makes us gradually acknowledge that just by our own speculative efforts, we can never figure out the world or our place and purpose in it. To gain reliable knowledge on this critical subject, we need to receive it from the maker of the world, Krishna, who alone knows it completely. We can connect with Krishna through his words, as given in scriptures like the Bhagavad-gita and explained by his erudite devotees.

When we assimilate and apply Gita wisdom, we see creation in new light: as demonstration of Krishna's creative glory and beauty. This vision catalyzes within us an untiring willingness, even eagerness, to learn more about Krishna, which in turn makes us receptive to hear his inner voice. That divine voice guides our sights and thoughts so that our daily experiences serve to confirm the wisdom that we have learnt in the revealed scriptures. As our wisdom deepens by such realizations, we feel increasingly inspired to devote ourselves to Krishna. When we fall completely in love with him, we return back to his eternal abode, which has been the supreme aspiration of the wisest seers throughout history.

Thus, humility transforms our life into a dynamic educational experience that reinforces our wisdom, enriches our devotion and finally catapults us to life's greatest attainment.

C320

Humility; pridelessness; nonviolence; tolerance; simplicity; approaching a bona fide spiritual master; cleanliness; steadiness; self-control…—all these I declare to be knowledge, and besides this whatever there may be is ignorance.

When Krishna seems far away, it is we who have strayed away

The Bhagavad-gita (13.16) states that Krishna is situated far away from us – and is simultaneously very close to us. Paradoxical scriptural statements like this point to the inconceivable attributes of Krishna. At the same time, they can also refer to our changing, conflicting feelings while trying to approach him.

During our spiritual practices like praying, chanting or meditating, we may sometimes sense Krishna's presence distinctly, almost tangibly, thereby feeling that he is very close to us. More often, we may go through our spiritual practices sensing Krishna's presence weakly or not at all, thereby feeling that he is very far away from us. This may dishearten us and may even trigger second thoughts about continuing our spiritual practices.

At such times, we need to urgently reverse the discouraging train of thoughts set in motion by the dubious second thoughts. For bringing about this reversal, we can trigger spiritually encouraging thoughts by faithfully contemplating on the Gita's declaration (15.15) of Krishna's proximity, indeed his indwelling presence. He is personally, constantly, lovingly present with us in our own hearts, closer than anyone else can ever be.

Remembering such scriptural declarations of Krishna's proximity will give us the strength to persevere in our spiritual practices, which will soon restore our devotional disposition. This disposition will enable us to re-experience Krishna's presence in the form of divine solace and sublime warmth. Then we will recognize that he had never gone far away... it was we who had temporarily strayed away.

ॐ

The Supreme Truth exists outside and inside of all living beings, the moving and the nonmoving. Because He is subtle, He is beyond the power of the material senses to see or to know. Although far, far away, He is also near to all.

Long to belong where we eternally belong

*F*ew things define us as much as our longings. They occupy our thoughts, shape our words and determine our actions. Sadly however, most of our longings remain unfulfilled.

Why? Because that is the typical fate of most material longings. As our culture is largely materialistic, most of our longings tend to be material. Moreover, our longings are infinite, whereas the material resources of the world are finite. So, most material longings are bound to be frustrated. As the Bhagavad-gita (15.07) aptly states, material existence is characterized by our vain struggle to fulfill the longings of our mind and senses.

The same verse also hints how we can become truly happy when it states our original position as eternal fragmental parts of Krishna. As souls, we are meant to delight eternally in a loving relationship with him. All our material longings are misdirected expressions of our original longing for him. By the process of devotional service, we can redirect our longing back to him and thereby revive our love for him.

However, our love for Krishna stays superficial if it centers only on longing for him. Love comprises not just longing but also belonging: the feeling that we are committed to our beloved through service and sacrifice. We can cultivate a sense of belonging to Krishna by rendering unflinching service to him. By so doing, our love deepens till we get the life-transforming realization that, after lifetimes of searching, we have finally found the person we have been searching. Krishna is the person who loves us, values us, accepts us, elevates us, liberates us. We get the sweet conviction: "To Krishna do I belong – eternally."

Thus, by longing to belong to Krishna, we cultivate the selfless love that takes us to life's supreme destination: his ecstatic eternal abode.

☙❧

The living entities in this conditioned world are My eternal fragmental parts. Due to conditioned life, they are struggling very hard with the six senses, which include the mind.

Krishna is ever-waiting, ever-willing and ever-working

The Bhagavad-gita (15.15) states that Krishna personally resides in the hearts of all of us so as to guide us to our ultimate good. From this strategic vantage point, he observes our misadventures in material existence and strives to bring them to an adventurous, auspicious ending. Let's see how:

Krishna is ever-waiting: In a friendship, if one friend neglects the other for a long time, it's natural and reasonable for the neglected friend to give up the neglecting friend. But Krishna's love for us far exceeds the bounds of the natural and the reasonable; although we have neglected him for so many lifetimes, he neglects our neglect and waits patiently for us to renew our friendship with him.

Krishna is ever-willing: If one friend not only neglects but also displeases or offends the other friend, the second friend is entirely justified to be unwilling to resume the friendship. But Krishna's friendship is so unfailing and unflinching that, despite our many sins and offenses through which we have repeatedly displeased him, he remains ever-willing to resume our relationship with him.

Krishna is ever-working: Krishna being God is perfect and complete. He has no work to do and has nothing to gain from his relationship with us. Yet due to his selfless and tireless love for us, he voluntarily and constantly works to help us return to him and thereby realize fully our potential for happiness. The Srimad Bhagavatam (8.3.17) states that Krishna is tireless (*alayaaya*) in his endeavors to help us.

When we understand how much Krishna loves us and to what lengths he is ready to go in his love for us, how can we not reciprocate?

CRŁSD

I am seated in everyone's heart, and from Me come remembrance, knowledge and forgetfulness. By all the Vedas, I am to be known. Indeed, I am the compiler of Vedanta, and I am the knower of the Vedas.

Memorizing scripture doesn't burden the head – it unburdens the heart

The Bhagavad-gita (17.15) recommends regular recitation of scriptures as a means to discipline our power of speech. Such regular recitation becomes easy when scripture is readily accessible to us. And the most accessible place for keeping scripture is our own memory.

If we find the prospect of memorizing scripture burdensome, that is probably because we have not experienced the blessings available through timely recitation of memorized scriptural verses.

Let's look at some of those blessings. Humble recollection and prayerful recitation of verses can:

1. Calm our stressed minds by giving us a feel of the steady eternal underlying the shaky ephemeral

2. Empower us to resist temptations by stimulating our intelligence with wisdom and our heart with devotion

3. Help us base our decisions on time-tested insights, not spur-of-the-moment impulses

4. Usher us into the presence of Krishna as *shabda-brahma* (sacred sound), thus boosting our confidence and courage

5. Bring authority and sanctity to our efforts to share our faith with others.

If we take shelter of scriptural verses regularly, they will gradually move from our brain into our heart, thereby becoming our ever-ready counselors. Whenever our heart feels burdened by life's inevitable perplexities, we will be able to turn to them for relief and get not just relief but also rejuvenation and wisdom. Then we will realize that the same scripture memorization that we had feared would burden our head has actually unburdened our heart.

৩৪৪০

Austerity of speech consists in speaking words that are truthful, pleasing, beneficial, and not agitating to others, and also in regularly reciting Vedic literature.

Choose to be holy now – don't wait for a holy cloud to form around your head

"Surely, but not now." This is often our default response when saintly people urge us to make our relationship with Krishna a priority. We rationalize: "At present I don't always feel happy while serving Krishna; people around me don't appreciate what I am doing. Let me wait till things improve – internally and externally."

We can call this expectation "waiting for a holy cloud to form around our heads." We have probably seen pictures of smiling seers with a halo, giving discourses to respectful masses; their radiant smile reflects their inner joy, and their reverent audience reflects their outer influence.

Might we be procrastinating because we are expecting grace to bestow a similar inner joy and outer influence in our spiritual life? If yes, then we are overlooking the fact that spiritual advancement is a matter of not just divine grace, but also human choice. The Bhagavad-gita (18.58) outlines the process of spiritual advancement succinctly: when we become conscious of Krishna, he mercifully removes all obstacles. Let's analyze this verse into three stages:

Stage 1 Grace: Krishna gives us the opportunity to practice devotional service.

Stage 2 Choice: We accept the opportunity gratefully and practice devotional service wholeheartedly.

Stage 3 Grace: Krishna removes our inner and outer obstacles, and we start relishing constant inner happiness.

If we expect stage 3 to precede stage 2, aren't we shirking our responsibility in our relationship with Krishna? Waiting for the beloved to do everything in the relationship and not doing anything oneself – is that love?

Only when we persevere in devotional service amidst internal and external obstacles do we tangibly show Krishna our love for him. Therefore, the time to make our relationship with Krishna reciprocal and substantial is *now*.

☙❧

If you become conscious of Me, you will pass over all the obstacles of conditioned life by My grace. If, however, you do not work in such consciousness but act through false ego, not hearing Me, you will be lost.

Devotion takes us beyond being hunted and haunted

We sometimes face problems that seem to hunt us externally and passions that seem to haunt us internally.

Hunted: We may feel attacked by problems due to misunderstandings with others (*adhibhautika klesha*) and environmental misery ranging from unpleasant weather to natural disasters (*adhidaivika klesha*).

Haunted: The passions of the mind like lust, anger and greed may possess us and push us towards self-defeating acts (a major part of *adhyatmika klesha*).

When we thus feel hunted and haunted, Gita wisdom shows us how we can transcend them.

Transcended: Being beloved children of Krishna, we are meant to delight eternally in a transcendental life of love that lies beyond the body and the mind. Krishna aids us in tasting transcendence by providing facilities and impetuses. He provides facilities in the form of spiritual manifestations like the holy names, Deities and scriptures. Unfortunately, we don't avail of these facilities due to our material preoccupations. So, he provides us impetuses in the form of the threefold miseries.

Of course, Krishna doesn't cause those miseries; our own past bad karma does. But he arranges those miseries so that they also act as impetuses for us to seek his shelter. When we thus become conscious of him, he empowers us to transcend misery, as the Bhagavad-gita (18.58) declares. By experiencing solace and strength in remembering him, we become convinced that transcendence is for real. This realization enables us to deal with the miseries without undue disturbance. More importantly, it also inspires us to accelerate our journey back to Krishna's abode, where we transcend all miseries forever.

ଓଡ଼ିଆ

If you become conscious of Me, you will pass over all the obstacles of conditioned life by My grace. If, however, you do not work in such consciousness but act through false ego, not hearing Me, you will be lost.

Love for Krishna is a love that doesn't appoint to DIS-appoint

*W*henever we love anyone, we hope fondly that the relationship will make us happy; we fix an appointment with fulfilment. Sadly however, worldly love promises much but delivers little; it appoints to dis-appoint. But Krishna's love never disappoints. To understand why, let's use an acronym DIS (the difference between *appoint* and *disappoint*):

1. **Durable**: Love for Krishna is durable, in fact, eternal. Why? Firstly, because Krishna himself is eternal. Secondly, because that love is based on the platform of our eternal spiritual identity. In contrast, all worldly love being based on the platform of our temporary material identity is inevitably perishable.

2. **Integral**: Love for Krishna is not something external to us that we have to develop. It is something innate that we simply have to revive through loving remembrance. On the other hand, all worldly love is external and superficial to our core identity as souls.

3. **Supra-real**: Worldly love may appear real to us at present, but it will be washed away by the waves of time. However, this reality of time, which is the supreme reality in the material world, can do nothing to destroy or even deteriorate our love for Krishna. That's how our love for Krishna is supremely real or supra-real.

The Bhagavad-gita (18.64) reveals the intensity of Krishna's love for his devotees: "You are dearly loved by me." Then it invites us to love Krishna: "Becoming My devotee, offer your mind and heart to Me." By striving to practice pure devotional service, we can set the stage for our appointment with him. In fact, by remembering him sincerely, we can relish his presence here and now. And in due course of time, we can meet him in person in his eternal world of love.

ॐ

Because you are My very dear friend, I am speaking to you My supreme instruction, the most confidential knowledge of all. Hear this from Me, for it is for your benefit.

Meditation is not a dulling duty – it is a thrilling opportunity

As devotee-seekers, we often begin mantra meditation with enthusiasm and anticipation. However, our mind soon starts coming in the way of our meditation with increasing frequency and ferocity. Why does this happen? What can we do about it?

The mind due to its past memories of material indulgences is by default externally, materially directed. So even during meditation it frequently keeps our consciousness in the external, material realm, thereby interrupting our inner remembrance of Krishna. This remembrance is central to the experiential joy of meditation; without it, meditation becomes an empty ritual. If we don't strive to remember Krishna, meditation starts appearing like a dulling duty that takes our time away from the interesting and important business of life.

To improve our meditation, we can seek inspiration from scriptural descriptions of its sweetness. The Bhagavad-gita (18.77) gives us a glimpse of that sweetness when it declares that the remembrance of Krishna and his message brings thrills at every moment. These verses, coming as they do towards the end of the Gita, indicate that comprehending its message empowers us to practice and relish meditation. The Gita gives us a sound philosophical understanding of the glory and the beauty of Krishna. This understanding serves as our intellectual firepower for blowing away the roadblocks created by the mind in the way of our meditation on Krishna. Of course, the understanding alone cannot give us the experience of Krishna. But it can help us become determined to fight off anything that blocks us from that experience.

Once we start connecting with Krishna through loving remembrance, then we will find that remembrance to be fulfilling and empowering. Thereafter, we will experience meditation as what it actually is: a thrilling opportunity to relish the joy supreme.

ॐ

O King, as I remember the wonderful form of Lord Krishna, I am struck with wonder more and more, and I rejoice again and again.

Acknowledgements

My first thanks to my foremost spiritual mentors, His Grace Radheshyam Prabhu, His Holiness Bhakti Rasamrita Maharaj, His Holiness Jayadvaita Maharaj and His Holiness Radhanath Maharaj – their blessings are the engine for my writing service.

My next thanks to my diligent editors. Avatari Chaitanya P's consistency and clarity, Hari Parayana P's logical acuity, Muralidhar P's focus on flow, Revati Vallabha P's overall sharpness and Manish Vithalani P's candor all contribute to making my writing better.

Vaishnava Seva P provided an excellent place for undistracted writing.

Varun Sharma designed the cover image and gave many helpful inputs.

Janardan Salkar P made the sketches for the various articles when they were published in BTG.

Arjuna Sarthi P, Rohan Ahirwar P, Mahesh Jadhav P did the appealing layout. Trivikrama P helped with proofreading. Many others helped in various ways.

My heartfelt thanks to them all.

- **Chaitanya Charan**

Books Published by VOICE

Books Published by the author

The Spiritual Scientist series:
- The Spiritual Scientist Vol I (Selected Newspaper articles)
- The Spiritual Scientist Vol II
- Science and Spirituality (The Spiritual Scientist Vol III)

QA books:
- Frequently Un-Answered Questions
- Idol Worship or Ideal Worship? (Questions & Answers)
- Oh My God! (Re-answering the Questions)
- My Little Bhakti Companion (Questions & Answers)
- 10 Leadership Sutras from Bhagavad-gita

Spiritual Observer Books
- OMG – Re-answering the Questions
- GK for PK
- Timeless Insights on Today's Issues

Gita-daily Series
- The Gita for Daily Enrichment
- The Eye to See the I
- Belong

Pocket Books
- E.N.E.R.G.Y- Your sutra for Positive Thinking
- Recession- Adversity or Opportunity?
- Why do we need a T.E.M.P.L.E?

Other books
- From Me to We: Reflections on Ramayana

***

To read the author's daily meditations on the Bhagavad-gita, *Gita-daily*, and his weekly articles, you can register for daily feeds on his site www.thespiritualscientist.com. You can also ask him questions on his site

Other books published by VOICE

Essence of Bhagavad-gita (EBG) series:
- EBG Course-1: 'Spiritual Scientist'
- EBG Course-2: 'Positive Thinker'
- EBG Course-3: 'Self Manager'
- EBG Course-4: 'Proactive Leader'
- EBG Course-5: 'Personality Development'
- EBG Vol -1 of 2 (Marathi)
- EBG Vol -1 of 2 (Hindi)

Spirituality for the Modern Youth series
- Discover Yourself
- Your Best Friend
- Your Secret Journey
- Victory Over Death
- Yoga of Love

Pocket Books
- How to Harness Mind Power?
- Practical Tips to Mind Control
- Can I Live Forever?
- Do We Live More Than Once?
- Misdirected Love

Other Books
- Youth Preaching Manual
- Bhagavad-gita 7 Day Course
- Values

Children's Books:
- My First Krishna Book
- Getting to Know Krishna
- More About Krishna
- Devotees of Krishna
- Wonderful Krishna
- Krishna's Childhood Pastimes
- Janmashtami
- Krishna Colors

Bring out the LEADER in you series

These books will be suitable for college students as well as corporates. The first book in this series has been published and the remaining will be released in the near future.

1. Stress Management
2. Time Management
3. Art of Self Management
4. Power of Habits
5. Secret of Concentration
6. Mind Your Mind
7. Positive Mental Attitude
8. Team Playing & Winning Trust of Others
9. Overcoming Inferiority Complex
10. Constructive Criticism – How to Give It or Take It?
11. Fate and Free Will
12. Karma – The Law of Infallible Justice
13. Key to Real Happiness
14. Conflict Resolution
15. Eight Qualities of an Effective Leader
16. Managing Our Anger
17. Self Development
18. Personality Development and Character Buildup
19. Proactive Leadership
20. Art of Living and Leaving

About the Author

Chaitanya Charan is a monk and spiritual author. He has done his Electronics & Telecommunications Engineering from the Government College of Engineering, Pune. He secured 2350 out of 2400 in the GRE exam, bagging the top rank in Maharashtra.

He is a member of ISKCON's topmost intellectual body, the Shastric Advisory Council, and is the associate-editor of ISKCON's global magazine, Back to Godhead.

He travels all over the world giving talks on spiritual subjects.

He is the author of the world's only Gita-daily feature, wherein he writes daily a 300-word inspirational reflection on a verse from the Bhagavad-Gita. Till now he has written over 1200 Gita meditations that are posted on www. gitadaily.com and are read through daily feeds by thousands from all over the world.

His articles have been published in many national newspapers including Indian Express, Economic Times and Times of India in the Speaking Tree column. His writings in English have been translated into several foreign languages including German, Chinese and Romanian and several Indian languages including Kannada, Telgu, Bengali, Hindi and Marathi.

He is the author of eighteen books: *ENERGY – Your Sutra for Positive Thinking; Science and Spirituality; The Spiritual Scientist series, volumes 1 and 2; Recession – Adversity or Opportunity?;Why do we need a temple?; Frequently Unanswered Questions; Idol Worship or Ideal Worship?; The Gita for Daily Enrichment; Oh My God! Re-answering the Questions; My Little Bhakti Companion; Timeless Insights on Today's Issues; 10 Leadership Sutras from Bhagavad-gita, GK for PK!. Prabhupada: The Moments that Made the Movement, The Eye to See the I, Belong and From Me to We: Reflections on Ramayana.*

Printed in Great Britain
by Amazon